BEFORE THE WILDERNESS

To Sing of Balance Between Heaven and Earth

"A flicker feather band, fragrant bay leaves, clam shell beads, the tan and brown hues of basketry plants--all represented in multiples of the sacred four--express an integration of the spiritual and physical aspects of life. To live in spiritual and physical balance in the same small area for thousands of years without feeling the need to go somewhere else, as my people did, requires restraint, respect, and knowledge of the ways of each animal and plant. As my mother taught me, and she, in turn, was taught, the plants, animals, birds--everything on this earth--they are our relatives, and we had better know how to act around them, or they'll get after us."

Kathleen Rose Smith, Mihilakawna Pomo/Olemitcha Miwok

BEFORE THE WILDERNESS

Environmental Management
by
Native Californians

Compiled and Edited
by
Thomas C. Blackburn and Kat Anderson

A Ballena Press Publication

General Editors: Sylvia Brakke Vane
                   Lowell John Bean

Volume Directors: Karla Young
                   Pauline Sanchez

Ballena Press Anthropological Papers Editors:
                   Thomas C. Blackburn
                   Sylvia Brakke Vane
                   Lowell John Bean

Library of Congress Cataloging-in-Publication Data

Before the wilderness : environmental management by native
  Californians / compiled and edited by Thomas C. Blackburn and Kat
  Anderson.
     p. cm. -- (Ballena Press anthropological papers : no. 40)
  Includes bibliographical references and index.
  ISBN 0-87919-127-9 : $41.50. -- ISBN 0-87919-126-0 (pbk.) : $31.50
  1. Indians of North America--California--Economic conditions.
  2. Human ecology--California. 3. Environmental protection--
  California. 4. Indians of North America--California--Agriculture.
  I. Blackburn, Thomas C. II. Anderson, Kat. III. Series.
  E78.C15B45   1993
  304.2'8'089970794--dc20   93-6936
                                                                 CIP

Copyright © 1993 by Ballena Press
              823 Valparaiso Avenue
              Menlo Park, CA 94025

Printed in the United States of America.

CONTENTS

6

TABLES

FIGURES

12

14

INTRODUCTION: MANAGING THE DOMESTICATED ENVIRONMENT

Thomas Blackburn and Kat Anderson

> We did not think of the great open plains, the beautiful rolling hills and the winding streams with tangled growth as 'wild.' Only to the white man was nature a 'wilderness' and...the land 'infested' with 'wild' animals and 'savage' people [Standing Bear, Ogalala Sioux, quoted in Nash 1982].

> I have no difficulty in accepting certain spiritual entities in the landscape as domesticated, for the purpose of understanding human action. In the Cape York Peninsula such entities and forces lose their domesticatory qualities when humans are removed from the landscape, and interaction ceases. It is only then that the entire landscape in all its empirical and non-empirical diversity is considered by Aboriginal people to have 'come wild' and, thus, to have become potentially dangerous for humans who have lost the practical knowledge for 'correct' (i.e., authorized) interaction [Chase 1989:47-8].

During the last two decades, a quiet but nonetheless significant transformation has been occurring in the study of past and present human subsistence systems, and consequently in our understanding of such related (and possibly interrelated) issues as changes in demographic factors, the evolution of complex social and political forms, and the origins and spread of specialized agroecosystems dependent upon domesticated species of plants and animals. A new appreciation for the diversity and potential complexity of nonagricultural economies, in conjunction with a better understanding of the often sophisticated systems of traditional knowledge upon which they are based, has led to a growing recognition that the rigid and rather monolithic conceptual dichotomy traditionally drawn between the seemingly passive 'food procurement' lifestyle of 'hunter-gatherers' and the apparently more active 'food production' adaptation of 'agriculturalists' is inadequate, overly simplistic, and dangerously misleading. Instead, human adaptive systems increasingly are being seen as occurring along a complex gradient and/or continuum, involving more and more intensive interaction between people and their environment, progressively greater inputs of

16

human energy per area of land, and an expanding capacity to modify or transform natural ecosystems (e.g., Harris 1989). All human societies, it might even be suggested, have therefore been involved over many millennia in an ongoing process of *domesticating* the environment, cumulatively employing one or more of a wide array of progressively more effective techniques--ranging from the simple pruning of vegetation to the use of genetically-altered and human-dependent species of plants or animals--to gain a greater or lesser degree of control over the world around them.

One of the more surprising aspects of the paradigmatic transformation mentioned above is that it has occurred largely without reference to California. Native California societies, for example, are barely mentioned in a recent compendium of papers on the emergence of cultural complexity among hunter-gatherers (Price and Brown 1985), while an important conference report stemming from an international symposium on the evolution of plant exploitation (Harris and Hillman 1989) contains only a single paper (Shipek 1989) devoted to the subject. For several reasons, this seeming neglect of such a significant ethnographic region is unfortunate and, to some extent at least, ironic. First, California's various rich, diverse, and *carefully managed* habitats supported (through the medium of an exceptionally effective extractive and storage technology) the highest population densities, as well as some of the largest population concentrations, in all of North America; in fact, it now appears that the population levels present in California prior to European contact possibly may have been the highest to have ever characterized societies without a well-developed and relatively intensive agricultural subsistence base. Second, these sedentary population concentrations provided a necessary (if certainly not a sufficient) condition for the development of a variety of surprisingly complex social, economic, political, and religious cultural patterns; certainly some of the most complex 'hunting and gathering' societies that have ever been described ethnographically existed in California, and some of the social patterns that developed here appear to have been unique among nonagricultural peoples. Third, the archaeological, ethnohistoric, and ethnographic database that now exists for Native California societies is extensive, easily accessible, and remarkably detailed; consequently, California would seem to be an obvious social laboratory for testing a wide range of anthropological theories on the nature of 'hunter-gatherers,' environmental 'intensification,' or the evolution of cultural complexity. Finally, California scholars (as a number of the papers that are reprinted here will attest) were often among the first to raise certain of the issues or point out the implications of some of the conceptual distinctions involving 'hunting and gathering' vis-à-vis 'agriculture' that are increasingly engaging the attention of anthropologists elsewhere; certainly a predilection for employing ecological models in various ways in anthropological research has a long and distinguished history here.

Before The Wilderness will, we hope, partially redress the current theoretical imbalance alluded to above by (1) consolidating and republishing some of the more noteworthy papers on environmental management in Native California that have appeared sporadically over the last two decades; (2) combining these with previously unpublished studies that accurately reflect the present status of research on the topic and suggest future avenues for exploration; and (3) making this important corpus of information readily available in a convenient form to as wide and diverse an audience (e.g., resource managers, ecologists, environmentalists, Native Americans, historians, and anthropologists in other regions) as possible. Nearly half of the essays in this volume had their inception in papers that were initially presented at the Seventh Annual California Indian Conference in October, 1991, in conjunction with a symposium devoted to the past and present resource management practices of Native Californians. The interest generated by the symposium, as well as the uniformly high quality of the papers that resulted from it, encouraged us to subsequently invite the various scholars involved to revise and expand their papers for publication here. All but two of the remaining essays originally appeared in the *Journal of California Anthropology* or the succeeding *Journal of California and Great Basin Anthropology*; each was chosen because it is either an important contribution to, or an immediate intellectual antecedent of, current research in the field. The final two papers (by Bean and Lawton, and by Lewis) form a complementary set, and were first published jointly in 1973 as the initial monograph in the *Ballena Press Anthropological Papers* series; they are of particular significance, since they can be viewed as either the inspiration for or the precursor to almost all subsequent research on environmental management in California. Because of their critical role in the development of interest in this topic, and because Lewis' seminal essay has been out of print for many years and therefore has not been readily accessible, their inclusion in the present anthology seemed singularly apposite and worthwhile.

Each of the essays presented here contributes in some degree to our better (though still very incomplete) understanding of the subtle, complex, and efficient manner in which native people managed, maintained, and *effectively transformed* various habitats and their constituent resources. Some papers focus rather narrowly on particular techniques of resource utilization or on the micromanagement of individual species, while others discuss the broad management of entire plant communities, resource groups, or populations. Although the evidence that is adduced by the various authors is occasionally fragmentary, and too often more suggestive than decisive, the cumulative effect is compelling, and the final conclusion that emerges seems inescapable and unequivocal: the extremely rich, diverse, and apparently 'wild' landscape that so impressed Europeans at the time of contact--and which traditionally has been viewed as a 'natural, untrammeled wilderness' ever since--was to some extent actually a product of (and more importantly dependent upon) deliberate human intervention. In other words, particular habitats--in a number of important respects-- had been *domesticated*.

Although the term domestication has usually been rather narrowly applied in the past to the gradual process in which the reproductive systems of particular species--as well as their genetic and/or phenotypic characteristics--become so modified by human intervention that continued intervention is necessary for their survival, its application to entire habitats (e.g., Chase 1989, Yen 1989) seems to us to be both useful and felicitous, particularly in the present context. As Ucko has recently pointed out with regard to Australia,

> ...the fact that Australian Aborigines did not adopt agriculture (in the strict sense) does not in any way imply a lack of understanding of, or a capacity to modify, the ecology of the plants around them. Indeed, the hunting and gathering Australian Aborigines 'domesticated' the environment, *including plants, not* by practicing agriculture but by developing a complex system of mental categorizations which gave them control over their plants (and animals) [Ucko 1989:xii-xiii].

However, we believe that it is important to emphasize the fact that the level of environmental management that was achieved in California--in contrast to that present in Australia--was such that native peoples did not simply exercise a certain degree of 'control' over specific resources or 'modify the ecology' of particular biological communities. Instead, the domesticatory process here seems to have reached the point where important features of major ecosystems had developed as a result of human intervention, and many habitats (e.g., coastal prairies, black oak savannas, and dry montane meadows) were deliberately maintained by, and essentially dependent upon, ongoing human activities of various kinds. In fact, the various essays in this volume strongly suggest that the vertical structure, spatial extent, and species composition of the various plant communities that early European visitors to California found so remarkably fecund were largely maintained and *regenerated* over time as a result of constant, purposive human intervention. When that intervention ceased, a process of environmental change began that led to a gradual decline in the number, range, and diversity of many of the native species and habitat types that once flourished here. When elders today are asked why the rich resource base and fertile landscape that they remember as having existed in the past has changed so drastically, they are apt to respond by saying simply, "No one is gathering anymore." The idea that human use *ensures* an abundance of plant and animal life appears to have been an ancient one in the minds of native peoples.

The most powerful, effective, and widely employed tool in the native repertoire for directly manipulating the environment was undoubtedly fire. Indigenous groups used fire for a variety of purposes, including stimulating new plant growth and inducing early stages of succession; creating and sustaining vegetational mosaics with numerous ecotones beneficial to animal life; controlling plant diseases and insect infestations; increasing the frequency and range of useful plant species; eliciting desirable plant growth characteristics; minimizing the severity and number of uncontrolled wildfires; and facilitating hunting by the reduction of undergrowth. However, several other techniques capable of significantly modifying the habitat also appear to have been employed by various Native California societies. These included (but were not necessarily limited to) the following activities: the sowing or broadcasting of seeds; the transplantation of shrubs or small trees to new locations; the construction of ditches and the diversion of water for irrigation purposes; the pruning and coppicing of plants to encourage particular patterns of growth; the weeding and tillage of specific plant communities; and the construction of water diversion structures for erosion control. We believe that additional management techniques involving direct environmental interaction almost certainly will be identified through future research.

Several of the papers in this volume also emphasize the more indirect but nonetheless significant role that harvesting strategies and techniques played in environmental management in Native California, and underline the fact that harvesting was controlled by a complex web of social, political, and ideological regulatory mechanisms that ensured native groups of a sustained, reliable yield generation after generation. Specific gathering sites or resource locations were exploited in accordance with strict rules--sanctioned by myth and custom, and mediated by a variety of political and ritual specialists--that took into consideration such factors as rights of ownership; the frequency and extent of harvests; the maturity or condition of particular resources; potentially significant weather conditions and seasonal variations; the importance of utilizing the appropriate tool or technique; and the knowledge of which plant parts or specific individuals should be taken and which should be left behind to ensure regeneration and replacement. Among the Pomo, for example, "hunters commonly knew every deer in the territory and maintained a balance between the herds and the available vegetation to keep the animals from straying outside Pomo territory" (Aginsky 1970:210). Today, native peoples still retain a deep respect for the natural world, and retell stories that remind them of the absolute necessity for judicious harvesting. Elders are quick to tell younger gatherers, "Do not take all--and leave the small ones behind." Such an approach to resource exploitation inevitably had measurable consequences in terms of the productivity of ecosystems and their ability to sustain large, sedentary human populations over long periods of time.

One intriguing question concerning harvesting technology that is raised here involves the possible effect that some of the techniques employed may have had on the productivity of certain resources within the context of indigenous habitat management practices. Many plants, for example, store nutrients in underground vegetative reproductive parts that comprised an important element in the native diet. The selective harvesting of larger bulbs, corms, and tubers for food may have had the practical effect of 'thinning' the resource; the digging stick that was employed aerated the soil, separated and dispersed the smaller bulbs or corms, and activated their growth, thus essentially increasing the size of the tract and its potential productivity. (In addition, it is possible that the range of the particular species involved may have been gradually expanded as well--future research might profitably examine the relative distribution and genetic characteristics of such species in relationship to their consumptive popularity.) It is highly likely that a very similar mechanism was operating with regard to shellfish as well. Baker (1992), for example, has recently described the tragic decline of the formerly rich clambeds of Tomales Bay that occurred after passage of strict regulations that severely limited shellfish harvests. It is interesting that Mirschitzka (1992:10) has cited data indicating that both clams and the California mussel (*Mytilus californianus*) were "semicultivated" along the Northwest Coast, and incidentally has suggested that salmon may have been transplanted from one location to another; there is every reason to suspect that a comparable situation existed in California.

As might be expected, most of the papers in *Before the Wilderness* are concerned with the technological means by which Native Californians managed and maintained the important botanical resources which they exploited for food, medicinal substances, and construction materials. However, a few authors touch upon other topics which richly deserve more study than they have received thus far. King, for example, raises the previously neglected subject of fuel use, and points out that supplying the large quantities of wood necessary for sustained cooking and heating in a typical settlement would have required careful management, and might very well have had measurable environmental and technological effects over time. Swezey and Heizer discuss the management and harvesting of salmonid fish resources in Northern California, and emphasize the significant role that ritual systems played in controlling the entire process. Shipek briefly describes the way in which Kumeyaay ritual specialists carefully kept track of, and controlled, populations of various mammals within their territory, and suggests the complexity of both the system of traditional ecological knowledge and the network of social, political, and ceremonial relationships within which these individuals operated. Finally, Lawton et al. and Shipek examine water management, flood control, and erosion control practices in eastern and southern California that appear to predate European contact, and present data that raise significant questions regarding the validity of certain models of cultural development that have been frequently cited in the past. Hopefully, future research will greatly expand our understanding of these and many of the other important issues that are touched upon in this volume.

Like other scholarly compendia of its kind, *Before The Wilderness* should be viewed less as an integrated overview of a mature field of investigation than as a prolegomenon to future research, and one moreover that raises as many questions as it answers. Clearly, our ultimate goal-- the full understanding and explication of the remarkable array of means by which Native California societies managed particular habitats--will only be achieved through the sustained and cooperative efforts of scholars in a variety of disciplines, and through the development of a better rapprochement between the social, historical, and biological sciences than presently exists. Unfortunately, many contemporary botanists and plant ecologists still distrust or discount the kind of anecdotal information contained in ethnographic and historical accounts (and which is utilized so extensively in the present volume), and tend to be rather skeptical toward the suggestion that nonagricultural native societies could have played anything but a negligible role in local ecosystems, or had either the knowledge or the ability to effectively alter natural landscapes to any significant extent. Consequently, future research efforts should perhaps initially be directed at compiling a valid body of the type of experimental or quantitative data that could then be utilized to objectively document both the existence and the efficacy of native environmental management practices in a manner acceptable to scholars in any discipline. We should like to conclude this introduction by suggesting several lines of investigation that might provide just such data.

First, detailed longitudinal reconstructions of specific California habitats should be carried out, using currently available analytic methods, in order to document any significant modifications that may have occurred historically to local ecosystems as a direct consequence of the post-European suppression of precontact management practices. Susan Bicknell (Professor of Forest Ecology at Humboldt State University, Arcata), for example, has recently been involved in a series of studies of particular locales along the Northern California coast, and has utilized opal phytoliths (in conjunction with other evidence) to demonstrate that a majority of the coastal prairie habitat was anthropogenic in nature and quickly reverted to woody vegetation after Euro-American settlement of the area (Bicknell 1992). There is clearly an urgent need for similar research to be conducted in other areas and on other habitats in the State.

Second, experiments need to be designed to empirically test potentially significant hypotheses, such as the suggestion (outlined above) that native harvesting techniques had a measurable impact upon the quality, productivity, distribution, and biological characteristics of important resources. A study of the productivity of wild plant management systems, for example, could lead to the development of working hypotheses and ecological field experiments that could eventually influence theoretical advances in the study of disturbance ecology and patch dynamics. Such research could also provide a basis for the design of guidelines for optimal plant production and management systems that simultaneously met native cultural needs and conserved the soil and biota for such other purposes as wildlife habitat, wilderness conservation, and outdoor recreation. Particular areas could then be set aside as 'cultural use zones' and appropriately managed for specific purposes. Anderson (n.d.) is currently conducting a series of experiments to empirically test the effects of various management and harvesting techniques (specifically tillage, coppicing, and burning) on the growth and production of three important native plants: wild hyacinth (*Dichelostemma pulchellum*), redbud (*Cercis occidentalis*), and deergrass (*Muhlenbergia rigens*). Hopefully, this study will serve as a model for similar experiments on other culturally significant species.

Third, quantitative models--based upon the detailed study of museum specimens, as well as careful experimentation and replication-- need to be developed to better understand the sustained resource needs of a typical community in precontact California, and test the hypothesis that only careful and effective management could have supplied the phenomenal quantities of raw materials required to support such a community over long periods of time. The following figures, drawn from a variety of sources, suggest the magnitude of the supply problem faced by many groups in the State. Approximately 65% of the material culture items utilized by the Chumash were manufactured entirely or primarily from plant materials (Hudson and Blackburn 1982-1987). Among the Sierra Miwok, Western Mono, Foothill Yokuts, Southern Maidu, Washo, and Paiute, over 75% of such plant-based items were made from epicormic branches or adventitious shoots from several different species; this special type of material was required for making ten different categories of objects: baskets, cordage, clothing, tools, weapons, structures, games, musical instruments, snares and traps, and ceremonial items (Anderson 1992:49). Making a single cradleboard would have required 500 to 675 straight sourberry sticks from six separate patches that had been burned or pruned prior to being harvested (Lorrie Planas, personal communication 1991; Norma Turner, personal communication 1992); similarly, a medium-sized cooking basket would have required 3750 deergrass stalks harvested from at least 75 healthy plants that also had been previously burned or pruned (Norma Turner, personal communication 1991; Anderson 1992). Craig Bates of the Yosemite Museum has estimated that approximately five stalks of Indian hemp (*Apocynum* spp.) or milkweed (*Asclepias* spp.) would have been required to manufacture one foot of cordage (Craig Bates, personal communication 1992); a Sierra Miwok feather skirt or cape contained about 100 feet of cordage made from approximately 500 plant stalks, while a deer net 40 feet in length (Barrett and Gifford 1933:178) contained some 7000 feet of cordage, which would have required the harvesting of a staggering 35,000 plant stalks (Anderson 1992:164-165). If one considers the fact that an "average" tribelet in Central California probably consisted of some 850 people almost totally dependent upon a territory of approximately 150 mi^2 (Kunkel 1962), the large quantities of food, fuel, and raw materials that were necessary to maintain such a group over an extended period of time can begin to be appreciated. Further quantitative research is needed to provide a firm basis for more accurate estimates of human subsistence and sustainable resource requirements in precontact California; such estimates would then make it possible to develop more accurate models of the kinds of management systems that would have had to exist in the past to meet those requirements, and test some of the hypotheses that are proposed in this volume.

Finally, an intensive program needs to be initiated to study floristic anomalies that might be the result of former indigenous land management practices or that might be significantly associated with past habitation or activity areas. In the Sierra Nevada, for example, two plants that were important food resources for local groups--mule ears (*Wyethia mollis*) and Bolander's pea (*Astragalus bolanderi*)--occur in extensive patches or areas that comprise distinct habitats within red fir forests; they are floristic anomalies in the middle to higher elevations because they are located on the same slope, aspect, and soil type as the adjacent red fir forest. In the past, such areas were burned frequently to keep the forest from encroaching, as it is presently doing. Another Sierra Nevada habitat which may to some extent be anthropogenic involves black oaks and ponderosa pines, which comprise a common subtype within the mixed conifer forest in this region. Black oaks flourish on nutrient-poor dry outcrops, but can not compete successfully with the more shade-tolerant conifers in locations with richer soils without frequent fires; nevertheless, they occur in large belts on rich sites throughout the region, possibly as a floristic anomaly. Such anthropogenic plant communities are usually in transition at present, and there is an urgent need to document and study them before they disappear forever. In addition, archaeologists should be made cognizant of the fact that there may be an important botanical dimension to site location or identification that might prove to be of considerable significance for the elucidation of past human activities.

A volume such as this can only materialize as a result of the dedication, cooperation, and enduring efforts of many people, and we should like to take this opportunity to acknowledge their invaluable assistance and express our sincere appreciation for their varied contributions. We owe a particular debt of gratitude, of course, to the various friends and colleagues who originally participated in the 1991 symposium on environmental management at the Seventh Annual California Indian Conference, for without their interest, scholarship, and willingness to undertake the sometimes arduous task of revising their papers for publication, this book would not exist. We should also like to thank Philip Wilke and the Editorial Board of Malki Museum Press for permission to reprint several papers that originally appeared in either the *Journal of California Anthropology* or the *Journal of California and Great Basin Anthropology*; Dr. Wilke was also kind enough to provide us with copies of many of the original figures, which would otherwise have been costly to duplicate. The expert staffs of the Graphic Communication Services and the Instructional Technology Center at California State Polytechnic University, Pomona, provided us with a great deal of technical support in the form of word processing and photographic duplication, for which we are most grateful; we also wish to thank Jon Corbridge for exercising his cartographic skills on our behalf and recasting an almost incomprehensible map into one considerably easier to read. As always, Sylvia Vane and her staff at Ballena Press have quietly performed their usual fine job of putting many disparate pieces together to create a recognizable whole, and we should like to take this opportunity to thank them for their important contribution. Finally, we should like to express our profound gratitude--and acknowledge our immense debt--to the many indigenous peoples who have fought to preserve an ancient and incalculably valuable body of traditional ecological knowledge that might still have much to teach us all. We are beginning to listen.

SOME EXPLANATIONS FOR THE RISE OF CULTURAL COMPLEXITY IN NATIVE CALIFORNIA WITH COMMENTS ON PROTO-AGRICULTURE AND AGRICULTURE[1]

Lowell John Bean and Harry W. Lawton

INTRODUCTION

Current anthropological interest in hunter-gatherer ecology and research findings on hunters and gatherers in marginal-subsistence environments of Australia, South Africa, and the Great Basin of the United States have brought renewed attention to the California Indians. Anthropologists are finally coming to a realization that cultural development in California was extraordinarily rich and complex despite what would appear to have been the limitations of the native economic system.

Henry Lewis's paper (1973, and this volume) on burning patterns in northern California represents an extremely important new contribution to our knowledge of California's hunting and gathering economy. Lewis has employed a systems approach to present the first geographically broad and ecologically oriented demonstration of a primary means of environmental manipulation used by northern California Indian groups to increase plant and animal resources. In fact, it seems probable in view of Lewis's findings that burning was the most significant environmental manipulation employed by California Indians. A new understanding of the role of native burning, coupled with our knowledge of other aspects of hunting and gathering in California, makes it now possible we believe to provide a more adequate explanation than previously presented for the failure of agriculture to spread across the state prior to European contact.

Until the twentieth century, the problem of why agriculture did not become established in California was never really dealt with except in terms of aboriginal lassitude or deficient intelligence. Any survey of

---

[1] This paper was originally published in **Ballena Press Anthropological Papers 1**, 1973. It is reprinted here with only minor corrections.

historical accounts by Spanish missionaries and explorers reveals for the most part an abysmal lack of curiosity about the culture of California Indians. As Harrington (1934:1) pointed out, nothing worthy of being called an ethnological treatise survived the Spanish occupation of California except Father Geronimo Boscana's *Chinigchinich*, written in 1821, late in the mission period. The primitive state of the native economy was characterized for Father Boscana (Harrington 1934:55) by the fact that "...in no part of the province was to be found aught but the common, spontaneous productions of the earth." If agriculture was a hallmark of civilization to the Spanish, so it was with the later nineteenth century American historians, products of an agrarian society, who viewed farming as the evolutionary goal of human civilization. The romantic myth of the mission fathers tutoring culturally retrograde Indians in crop-growing achieved such popularity in this period that the native cultures of California had little appeal for scholars. Even to Bancroft (1883:I, 324), it was axiomatic that along the shores of the Pacific man had "sunk almost to the darkness of the brute."

Despite views of some early anthropologists to the contrary (Barrows 1900; Gifford 1931), pioneer researchers in California generally accepted the historical dogma that the westward extension of southwestern agriculture halted among the Yuman peoples of the Colorado River. Any data suggesting agricultural knowledge existed among some California groups was attributed to being the result of mission influence. Hooper (1920:328), for example, first noted the presence of characteristic plants of southwestern agriculture in Cahuilla myth, but left unexplored Kroeber's (1908b:41) assertion that the Cahuilla were not farmers. Only recently have anthropologists begun to investigate the extent to which crop-growing may have penetrated California and why it was not extensive.

In another recent paper, Henry T. Lewis (1972:217) pointed out one of the main barriers to a more profound understanding of the cultures of native California and the means by which these predominantly hunting and gathering peoples exploited their environment:

> Ecologically, we must ignore the evolutionary assumptions that the development of agriculture was somehow natural and desirable. Instead of viewing agriculture as an imminent goal of human evolution, we should rather ask the question: Why should hunters and gatherers become agriculturists? While this suggestion may be at variance with our most cherished ideas of 'progress' and 'human

development,' we can more effectively pose ecologically
pertinent questions if we are not overburdened by a mass
of unexamined folk assumptions which cannot be tested.

Lewis (1973) has suggested such ecosystem analyses as his own
may assist anthropologists in posing new questions as to the role which
men, using certain technological strategies, played in a given system of
environmental relationships. Indeed, his paper is rich in suggestive
material deserving study by anthropologists. We shall concern ourselves,
however, with the light which his paper may throw on the problem of why
agriculture failed to spread in California. First, we will briefly review the
literature concerned with this problem. Then, we will summarize some
additional data compiled by Lewis and ourselves indicating that burning
was also a significant form of environmental manipulation among Indians
in the southern part of California. Although Aschmann (1959) presented
evidence that fires set by Indians in southern California were a factor in
the persistence of the wild landscape, he provided no data from Spanish
sources showing the practice was aboriginal and little data on burning
among specific Indian groups. Finally, we shall discuss Heizer's thesis that
California was in a Preformative stage that can be termed "semi-agricultural" at the time of the Spanish conquest, and seek to apply this idea in
terms of Lewis's findings.

THE PROBLEM OF ABORIGINAL AGRICULTURE
IN CALIFORNIA

Although his hypothesis in recent years has been credited to
others, H.J. Spinden (1917) appears to have been the first to suggest that
the acorn economy of California prevented dispersal of agriculture
westward from the Colorado River, where it was practiced in the pre-
hispanic era. In discussing those intermediate types of environment most
favorable to agriculture but where it failed to become established, Spinden
(1917:Z70), wrote:

The abundant harvests of wild acorns in California, of
wokas in southern Oregon, of wappato along the Columbia, of camas and kous in the pleasant uplands of Idaho,
and of wild rice in the lake regions of Minnesota and
southern Canada were effectual barriers against the

intervention or spread of agriculture among the tribes inhabiting these regions.

While Spinden's views on the origin and distribution of agriculture in the Americas were immensely influential in their time, his hypothesis concerning California remained almost forgotten until it was revived independently by other researchers in the 1950's.

As early as 1908, A.L. Kroeber explained the presence of a gourd rattle obtained from the Desert Cahuilla as a trade item from the Colorado River. Kroeber (1908b:62) asserted: "If the Cahuilla of aboriginal times used such rattles they must have obtained them by trade, as they did not practice agriculture or raise gourds." Two decades later, Kroeber formulated the first major hypothesis to receive any considerable attention for the lack of agriculture in California. His hypothesis was primarily cultural, and considerably more sophisticated than the cultural explanations of earlier historians. Kroeber (1925:41) wrote as follows:

> Agriculture had touched only the periphery of the state, the Colorado River bottom, although the seed-using and fairly sedentary habits of virtually all the other tribes would have made possible the taking over of the art with relatively little change of mode of life. Evidently, planting is a more fundamental innovation to people used to depending on nature than it seems to those who have once acquired the habit. Moreover, in most of California, the food supply, largely through its variety, was reasonably adequate, in spite of a rather heavy population--probably not far from one person to the square mile on the average. In most parts of the State there was little mention of famine.

Six years later, admittedly influenced by the views of his colleague, Carl Sauer, the cultural geographer, Kroeber abandoned his cultural explanation for an environmental one, which he set forth in his book *Cultural and Natural Areas of Native North America*. Although first written in 1931, this work was not published until eight years later, but presumably represented Kroeber's final evaluation of the problem. At the same time, it must be noted that Kroeber was always open to new ideas, and he is known to have entertained other explanations in his classrooms.

Heizer (1958:25) recalled Kroeber discussing the possibility that the efficient acorn economy was a chief barrier to agriculture as early as 1935 in his classrooms.

Kroeber's (1939:211) environmental hypothesis asserted that native agriculture failed to develop in California, "because of its dry summer, for which so far as maize was concerned no amount of winter precipitation could compensate." This same argument was presented first in print by Sauer (1936:295) as follows:

> Lack of contact with agricultural peoples can hardly account for the absence of agriculture on the Pacific Coast of the United States. The Indians of southern California were in communication with agricultural peoples along the Colorado. It is not likely that California Indians refrained from experimenting with the crops grown on the Colorado River. The resistance to the westward diffusion of agriculture was probably environmental rather than cultural. The crops which were available had little prospect of success in winter-rain lands. Maize and squash especially were ruled out by the rain regime, but the conditions also are predominantly unfavorable for beans. The Pacific Coast of the United States as a land of Mediterranean climate, had to wait on the introduction of crops from the European Mediterranean.

Although Heizer (1958:25) has stated that since 1946 he has accepted the concept that the acorn economy of California constituted the chief obstacle to acceptance of agriculture, the environmental position advanced by Kroeber and Sauer has dominated much of the literature on the subject for the past two decades. Driver (1961:55) summed up the climatic-environmental position in his textbook, *Indians of North America*, where he noted that rainfall west of the Colorado River averages only a few inches annually, and that where there is sufficient quantity of rainfall "it comes at the wrong season for maize." More recently, Underhill (1965:252) wrote:

> West of the Colorado the Desert continues with plenty of seed grasses and berries and with small game; but there is no summer rain for corn growing.... Among these

southern California Shoshoneans, there were no planters
in ancient days and no planting ceremonies.

While it is true that there is a very direct relationship between
rainfall and yield of maize and that the so-called "corn belt" of the United
States appears to possess the best combination of temperature, rain,
sunshine, soil, and topography for high-yield production, few anthropological writers on the subject have really understood the matter fully in
agricultural terms. Most frequently they have confused the pertinent issue
of amount and spacing of rainfall with the idea of a "wrong" rainfall
regime for corn in California. However, there is no need to engage in a
long technical discussion of optimum conditions for corn-growing since the
historical record indicates this problem is beside the point.

Forbes (1963:1) first attacked the notion that a summer rainfall
regime was essential to corn-growing in California. In spite of dry
summers, he pointed out that California's subsistence was largely based
upon maize from 1769 until the 1850's, and California Indians were
principal growers of those crops. Actually, despite repeated statements in
anthropological literature that California has never been a notably corn-
producing state, corn production reached its peak in 1890 when more than
two million bushels were harvested in the state (Hardy 1929:221).
Nevertheless, Forbes neglected to consider whether corn-growing became
possible only with introduction of irrigation by the Spanish. Concerning
this problem, a wealth of data indicates California agriculture in the post-
contact period was not always irrigation dependent.

A few examples will suffice: Lt. E.0. Ord (1848:123) reported
Indians in the San Dieguito Valley near San Diego gathering from twenty
to forty *fanegas* of maize on unirrigated lands. Hayes (1929:92) noted in
1853 that an American settlement near Los Angeles "raised every species
of vegetable and corn, without irrigation, such is the humidity of the soil."
Indian Superintendent Thomas J. Henley reported in 1854 that corn yields
that year were far below average on Tejon Reservation because crops
were not irrigated and a drought had occurred (Caughey 1953:138).
Brockett (1882:592) stated that corn planted in April and May in California matured without rain in areas where soil moisture was abundant.
Finally, although a summer rain regime may be desirable for high yields
of corn, it should be noted that the Spanish explorer Lt. José Estudillo
(Bean and Mason 1962:36) observed Cahuilla Indians near Thermal on the
Colorado Desert planting corn, pumpkins, melons, and watermelons in the
month of December, 1824.

In recent years, various researchers have pointed out flaws in the environmental argument (Weatherwax 1954; Jennings 1956; Heizer 1958; Meighan 1959; Forbes 1963; Bean 1968; and Lawton and Bean 1968). Jennings (1956) suggested that the dry southern California desert played a role in impeding the advance of agriculture from the Colorado River to the coast, but felt climate could not be accepted as the sole explanation. One major cultural reason he offered for the failure of agriculture to become established among coastal Californians was the specialization to a marine environment which these people had adopted. The cultural efficiency attained by Indian groups along the coast in exploiting the sea, he hypothesized, permitted them a reasonably abundant living. Meighan (1959) pointed out that the Archaic stage was not necessarily inferior in subsistence techniques to simple agricultural communities. Where the environment is favorable, as it was in all of California except the desert regions, Meighan suggested, the people may work out such an efficient ecological adaptation that they are actually better off than developmental agricultural peoples. He viewed the fact that California supported the greatest density population in the United States without agriculture as of the greatest significance to discussion of this problem.[2] Walton Bean (1968) also emphasized the general abundance of a natural food supply in California, hypothesizing that agriculture failed to spread into California because the native population was in a "Malthusian equilibrium."

Only a few researchers have challenged the prevailing view of anthropologists that California Indians were non-agricultural by arguing that pre-contact agriculture may have actually existed in certain parts of California (Barrows 1900; Gifford 1931; Treganza 1946; Bean and Mason 1962; Forbes 1963; Lawton 1968; Lawton and Bean 1968; Shipek 1971; Bean 1972; Bean and Saubel 1972; and Wilke and Fain 1972). Although Patch (1951) reported on the presence of irrigation ditches in east central California, which he believed might be aboriginal, he did not concern himself with whether crops were grown or the ditches employed solely to carry water to stands of native plants. Presumably, Patch assumed that the irrigation ditches of Eureka Valley were used in the same manner as

---

[2] Current conservative estimates of California's aboriginal population place it at 250,000 persons (Heizer and Whipple 1971:66). Villages of 1,000 or more persons have been estimated for some California groups (Kunkel 1962).

ditches constructed by the Owens Valley Paiutes to irrigate natural plots (Steward 1930).[3]

The earliest of these arguments for aboriginal agriculture in California was presented by David Prescott Barrows (1900), who was the first anthropologist to work with the Cahuilla. Unfortunately, Barrows so fully accepted his own premise that agriculture was aboriginal that he failed to solicit data on the question at a time when it might have been solved ethnographically. Barrows (1900:71) summarized his position as follows:

> It is easier to imagine that knowledge of agriculture with seed of corn, squash, and bean came to them (the Cahuilla) long ago across the desert, than that they learned of these things only in this century.

Gifford (1931) reported that the Kamia of the New River and Jacumba areas were planters, but Castetter and Bell (1951:36) found his data inconclusive, since it covered only the historic period. Treganza (1946) argued the feasibility of agriculture among the Kamia and Southern Diegueño, although he noted his archaeological evidence was based on caches of crop seeds from the Jacumba area stored in the historic era. Bean and Mason (1962:36, 104) urged consideration of pre-contact agriculture among the Cahuilla, observing the Romero expedition of 1823-24 found Indians planting crops near present-day Thermal.

Forbes (1963) presented an area-by-area sequence of historical data relating to agriculture among Indians west and northwest of the Colorado River. The data presented on native agriculture, even for the Cahuilla, were only semi-persuasive in arguing a case for aboriginal agriculture in California. Forbes, however, did present highly convincing data for pre-contact agriculture in northern Baja. His work had the virtue

---

[3] The possibility that the Owens Valley irrigation ditches were aboriginal, as Steward (1929) originally believed, was subsequently weakened with the discovery that these Indians could have learned ditch irrigation from Anglo settlers moving into the area in the 1850's. Recently, however, the authors have found a new source (Guinn 1917) tending to support Steward's initial opinion that the ditches were aboriginal. As early as 1859, an expedition under Lt. Col. Edward F. Beale of Fort Tejon discovered extensive irrigation ditches, miles in length, being used by Owens Valley Paiute to irrigate grass seeds and tuberous roots (Guinn 1917). Proto-agriculture in Owens Valley thus deserves renewed investigation. [Eds. note: See Lawton et al. elsewhere in this volume.]

of being a pioneer study suggestive of the merits of applying an ethnohistorical approach to the problem.

Lawton (1968)[4] surveyed myths of both missionized and non-missionized California Indian groups for agricultural motifs or elements (such as mention of crop plants). He found no crop plants mentioned in more than 200 myths of missionized coastal groups and some of the non-missionized northern California groups. Agricultural motifs or elements were present in the myths of the non-missionized Cahuilla, Kamia, and Southern Diegueño. All three groups also had corn or crop origin myths. Lawton also noted that native words for corn, beans, and watermelon were present among the Cahuilla. Although the same held true for the Southern Diegueño and Kamia, their languages are Yuman and therefore crop words are Yuman-derived. Crop words among coastal missionized groups were all of Spanish derivation in word lists from the historic period.[5]

Lawton and Bean (1968) reported the presence of proto-agricultural techniques among the Cahuilla and argued the agricultural technology of the Cahuilla in the early post-contact period conformed more closely to that of the native Colorado River Agricultural Complex than to that of the Spanish missions. They suggested agriculture diffused in the pre-hispanic period to a number of Indian groups in desert areas west of the Colorado River, forming what they termed the Western Frontier Agricultural Complex. In subsequent unpublished research, they have concluded this complex was mostly confined to certain ecological niches of the Colorado Desert capable of supporting agriculture, both in northern Baja California and California. Among groups they believe engaged in limited agriculture, mostly of the "kitchen garden" type, are the Cahuilla, Kamia, Southern Diegueño, Chemehuevi, certain Paiute groups, and possibly the Serrano, Paipai, and Kiliwa. (Note: many researchers now prefer the native word Kumeyaay for all Diegueño.)

Shipek (1971) presented ethnographic data on wild plant cultivation and environmental manipulation among the Diegueño and Luiseño and

---

[4] Eds. note: See also Lawton 1974.

[5] Corn may have occasionally reached the coast through trade in the pre-contact period. The Cabrillo log reported the Chumash as being familiar with maize in 1542, which they said was grown three days journey into the interior (Bolton 1967:26). The word Oep was recorded as the Chumash word for maize, but it appears in no subsequent vocabulary lists.

some historical data on agriculture. Wilke and Fain (1972) reported discovery of a cultivated gourd in a rock shelter near Cahuilla fields known to have been farmed in the 1850's. Wilke is engaged in seeking archaeological evidence for aboriginal agriculture on the Colorado Desert.

In summary, the case for aboriginal agriculture in northern Baja California appears established, although how widespread it was remains unknown. Corn, beans, pumpkins, and watermelons were being grown in 1788 by *gentiles* near Mission San Vicente (about 135 miles south of San Diego) with seeds obtained from Colorado River Indians (Forbes 1963: 8-9).[6] Mission diffusion is unlikely, since crop-growing was not yet established at this mission. For California, during the past year Lawton, Bean, and Wilke have turned up several sources (Heintzelman 1857; LeConte 1855; and Veatch 1858) indicating farming was practiced as early as the first decade of the nineteenth century by Indians along the New River and at Alamo Mocho, who principally carried out flood-water farming. Crop-growing was not well established at Mission San Diego until 1777, and the first successful crops were grown at Mission San Gabriel in 1773. Thus, unless new ethnohistorical evidence to the contrary can be found, there remains only a gap of a quarter century or more in which it would have been possible for agriculture to diffuse from the missions to non-missionized Indian groups of California on the Colorado Desert. This quarter century should be weighed in considering the problem against hundreds of years in which agriculture had the opportunity to spread from the Colorado River tribes to the New River. Nevertheless, despite the increasingly strong circumstantial case for agriculture in the California portion of the Colorado Desert, the problem is unlikely to be resolved without archaeological proof. Current research on aboriginal agriculture in the desert interior, however, does not challenge the general view that agriculture was neither adaptive nor necessary for an attractive existence for most California Indian groups. It does suggest that the desert was no barrier to diffusion of agriculture from the Colorado River to

---

[6] On April 13, 1785, Second Lt. José Velásquez, four days out of San Diego and probably about 20 to 40 miles south of Jacumba in northern Baja, climbed a hill to survey the desert plain. He noted smoke at the base of the mountains, and was told by his Indian guide that this was a rancheria where wheat was planted. (See C-A 3, Bancroft Library, p. 195; we are grateful to William Mason for calling this report to our attention.) Wheat, a European introduction, reached the Colorado River about three-quarters of a century before the Spanish conquest in California.

coastal areas.[7] Probably the less extensive food resources of the desert were a stimulus to adoption of agriculture. The San Bernardino and San Jacinto mountain ranges appear to have been the boundaries of the farthest westward extension of native agriculture.

PATTERNS OF BURNING IN SOUTHERN CALIFORNIA

Downs (1966b) summarized data demonstrating that environmental manipulation played a significant role in the subsistence of Great Basin hunting and gathering groups, and discussed the much abused concept of "incipience" as it relates to a period before fully developed agriculture appears in a culture. Reviewing Downs' findings, Riddell (1966:256) suggested a closer look at California groups might reveal more evidence of environmental manipulation than previously suspected and show that aboriginal subsistence patterns were more complex than usually imagined. A review of ethnohistoric and ethnographic sources conducted by the authors over the past two years on southern California Indian groups supports Riddell's assertion. In this essay, however, we shall confine ourselves chiefly to providing examples of burning from the literature which indicate Lewis's (1973) findings for northern California also are applicable to the southern part of the state.

Lewis contends that burning by northern California groups was a means of enhancing both plant and animal resources. Aschmann (1959) was first to suggest in detail that native burning in southern California had such an influence. "The wild landscapes are products of plants and animals adjusting to reasonably stable physical environments and each other," Aschmann (1959:34) observed. At the same time, he argued, deliberate extensive burning by the native population had been a continuing feature

---

[7] Cabrillo's log indicates that the coastal Indians were familiar with corn, which may have occasionally reached the coast through trade. Two intriguing references to maize occur in the diaries of members of the Portolá expedition. Father Crespi reported that north of Pismo an Indian brought the Spaniards liberal quantities of "pinole, atole, and some very good tamales which seemed to be made of corn" (Bolton 1927:271). Miguel Costansó also noted that the tamales "appeared to have been made of corn" (Costansó 1911:145). That both men, accustomed to Indian foods, were impelled to record similar comments suggests the problem was discussed with some perplexity by the Spanish around their evening campfire.

of those environments, not only for hunting, but to maintain desirable plant associations (Aschmann 1959:48):

> Above all, the Indians would burn the landscape to promote the growth of desired grasses and herbs in the following season. Modern authorities are still uncertain of the long-range effects of repeated burning in specific situations. Did it cause the degradation of a complex chaparral to the less useful chamise or coastal sage association or did it expand the oak-grassland parks? Most likely shifts in both directions occurred in different climatic and ecologic situations. In any event, the wild landscape the European explorers found was a product of millennia of such disturbances.

Aschmann concluded that disturbances such as burning produced an extremely favorable environment in southern California for plants which invested much of their vital energy in storing concentrated food in their reproductive parts. Such plants made it possible to maintain a rich flora and were crucial factors in the human population density of southern California, one of the most concentrated districts in the continent north of Central Mexico (Aschmann 1959:56).

Evidence burning was practiced for various purposes prior to the establishment of the Spanish missions can be found in a number of sources contemporary with European contact. The earliest mention of fire being used by Indians in southern California is in the log of the Cabrillo expedition, which reported "many smokes" were seen in early October along the San Diego coast northward (Bolton 1967:24, 33). These fires may have been only signalling activity or hearth fires, but they were so ubiquitous around one region of the mainland that the Spaniards gave the name Bahía de los Fumos (Bay of Smokes) to Santa Monica Bay.

In 1602, Vizcaino reported that between Coronado Islands and San Diego the Indians "made so many columns of smoke on the mainland that at night it looked like a procession and in the daytime the sky was overcast" (Bolton 1967:80). On that same voyage, Father Ascensión also commented on the numerous smoke columns from the mainland, which he attributed to efforts by Indians to signal the Spanish offshore (Bolton 1967:116). Johnston (1962:87-88) argued that such spectacular blazes would not be a product of ordinary domestic activities. She suggested that the fires were beacons to guide Indian fishermen in from the sea at night, although she provided no firm evidence for nighttime maritime activity among the coastal groups.

The extensiveness of the blazes, however, and the fact that they seemed so impressive both by day and night far out at sea suggests they may not have been simple signal fires. Both Cabrillo and Vizcaino sailed up the coast in September-October. Some of the blazes may have been natural, since these periods coincide with the peak of the southern California brushfire season. At the same time, however, burning during this period when all grass seeds had already been harvested would conform to Lewis's findings of a summer and late fall burning pattern in northern California.

Significantly, evidence that southern California Indians practiced burning as a means of environmental manipulation is supplied in the 1792 journal of the naturalist José Longinos Martínez (Simpson 1938). Longinos Martínez makes it clear that the practice was widespread from the middle of Baja California at Fronteras (Mission San Borja) upward into Alta California (Simpson 1938:51):

> In all of New California from Fronteras northward the gentiles have the custom of burning the brush, for two purposes; one, for hunting rabbits and hares (because they burn the brush for hunting); second, so that with the first light rain or dew the shoots will come up which they call *pelillo* (little hair) and upon which they feed like cattle when the weather does not permit them to seek other food.

During the Portolá expedition march of 1769-1770 from San Diego to San Francisco, Father Crespi repeatedly observed burned-over grasslands. His first report of burning was south of San Onofre, where the expedition "crossed some mesas covered with dry grass, in parts burned by the heathen for the purpose of hunting hares and rabbits" (Bolton 1927:132). Seven other examples of burned grassland were also reported by Crespi (Bolton 1927:143, 197, 199, 201, 214, 222, 225). Near Chualar, Crespi stated that a valley was "short of pasture on account of fires set by heathen" (Bolton 1927:201). On Soquel Creek, he reported that good pasture was found "although it has just been burned by the heathen who do not permit themselves to be seen" (Bolton 1927:214). The fires may well have been a product of rabbit hunting, but it should be noted that Crespi at no time actually witnessed a rabbit drive in progress. In all likelihood, he was extrapolating the purpose from practices observed among Indians elsewhere. The time of the burnings reported were from July to October.

One entry in Crespi's journal merits close attention. On the fourth day of the Portolá march, north of Carlsbad in the valley where Mission San Luis Rey was later founded, Crespi (Bolton 1927:129) reported that the expedition "descended to a large and beautiful valley, so green that it seemed to us that it had been planted." Crespi was an attentive traveler, who routinely made detailed comments on the abundance of native grasses and intermixed plant cover. Significantly, two Indian villages lay at opposite extremities of the valley plain. Agricultural specialists to whom we showed this passage suggested that the effect described would most likely be produced if the natives of the village had burned the adjacent plain. Such burning would have encouraged growth of annual grasses at the expense of perennial plants and given an appearance of cultivation.

Father Serra noted a similar valley in his march up the Baja peninsula. Two weeks journey south of San Diego in June of 1796, Serra (Tibesar 1955:I, 101) reported entering a valley "more than a league in width, and in parts so green that, if I did not know in what country I was, I would have taken it, without any hesitation, for land under cultivation." Here again signs of Indian occupance were found, although the natives had fled.

Among the Yuman Indians of the Colorado River agricultural plots were cleared prior to planting by burning (Castetter and Bell 1951:140). Despite Longinos Martínez's early observation that burning to encourage wild plant production was widespread, however, only a few examples of this practice can be found in anthropological and other modern literature on southern California Indians. This probably reflects the extreme disruption of the native economic system which occurred in the south as compared with the greater stability in the post-contact period of many of the northern California groups covered in Lewis's (1973) essay.

Bean (1972:47) reported that grasses were periodically fired by the Cahuilla to improve production. Chia was also fired by the Cahuilla (Bean and Saubel 1972:115). Drucker (1937:9) reported chia was burned for plant improvement by the Cupeño, Mountain Cahuilla, Northern Diegueño, and Southern Diegueño. Katherine Luomala (personal communication) reports that grasslands were fired by the Diegueño to improve seed yields. Shipek (1971:10, 11) said coastal Diegueño informants reported their ancestors burned to encourage grasses and flowering annuals, which provided supplementary foods as well as browse to keep deer, antelope, and rabbit populations at a high level. Basket grass, she reported, was burned every three years to maintain quality. Ground was also kept clear beneath oaks and pines by burning. Lee (1937:48) wrote that burning of basket grass by the Southern Diegueño encouraged taller plants with thicker stalks. Lee (1937:52-53) also stated hillsides were fired to encourage growth of desirable food plants. Shipek (1971:11) reported that diaries of San Diego settlers and local newspaper accounts indicated Indians of the area were still burning extensively as late as 1870. According to Shipek (personal communication) these latter sources indicate most burning took place in the late summer through late fall.

Evans (1873:208), traveling through the Coachella Valley in 1863, reported that the Cahuilla were burning their mesquite groves and smoke columns could be seen throughout the valley. He was told that burning destroyed mistletoe which afflicted the mesquite. Informants have told us that burning also encouraged new growth in mesquite and thinned stands. Native palm stands of *Washingtonia filifera* were regularly fired by Cahuilla shamans to kill pests and diseases causing damage to trees and decreased crops (Patencio 1943:69). This technique was rediscovered in the 1930's by the U.S. Department of Agriculture as an effective means of killing parlatoria date scale and red spider mites in palm oases (Stickney, Barnes, and Simmons 1950:8). Vogl (1968:86) stated such burning of native palms kills off outer vascular bundles, making more of the limited water supply in an oases available for palm reproduction or for a larger palm population. It may also expose enriched, moist mineral soils beneath palm fronds and other heavy litter, favoring new palm growth and germination.

Data obtained by anthropologists from informants on the use of fire in hunting in southern California is much less detailed than information on the northern part of the state. No information has been recorded for some of the coastal mission groups, whose populations were already decimated by disease early in the mission period. However, there is sufficient data to suggest use of fire in hunting was probably widespread in southern California. A cursory survey of the literature provides the following examples.

Harrington (1942:6) recorded use of fire in rabbit drives by the Fernandeño and in driving antelopes into enclosures by the Emigdiano Chumash and Kitanemuk Serrano. Sparkman (1908:198) reported firing of wood rat nests and use of fire to drive squirrels from burrows among the Luiseño. Drucker (1937:7) listed communal animal drives (game not stated) with fire among the Mountain Cahuilla, Southern Diegueño, Chemehuevi, and Yuman Indians. Hooper (1920:368) recorded a Desert

Cahuilla myth in which rabbits were driven from brush by fire. Bean (1972:65) reported fire was generally used among the Cahuilla to flush game. Castetter and Bell (1951:217) noted that the Cocopa and Mohave fired tule areas to flush rabbits, and the Cocopa set fire to rats' nests. The Yumans built circles of brush fire to concentrate prey, especially rabbits (Castetter and Bell 1951:214-15). Brush along river sloughs was fired by the Kamia in rabbit hunts (Gifford 1931:26). Spier (1923:337) reported that the Southern Diegueño used fire to drive rabbits from brush.

Among more northerly groups in the southern part of the state not covered in Lewis's (1973) paper on burning, Steward (1933:253, 254; 1934: 434; 1934:39, 184) listed rabbit drives with fire by the Mono Lake Paiute, use of fire in deer drives by the Owens Valley Paiute, and use of fire in communal antelope and rabbit drives by the Ash Valley Paiute.

THE PREFORMATIVE STAGE IN CALIFORNIA

Heizer (1958:23) urged that the nature of the economy and density and stability of population achieved in late prehistoric times in Central California and western southern California was such that these areas should be classified as Preformative in the historical development classification of archaeological cultures developed by Willey and Phillips (1955). The Preformative Stage, which follows the Archaic, is signalized by the introduction of agriculture, which is dependent upon marked population increase and large stable villages. Heizer defined Preformative as "semi-agricultural" and argued that this status had been achieved in California through an abundant and assured food supply primarily provided by the acorn.

In attempting to verify Heizer's contention that gathering in California was fully equivalent to the manner of life of other aboriginal peoples who practiced primitive forms of farming, Ziegler (1968) employed the term "quasi-agricultural" as descriptive of the acorn-salmon economies of north-central California. He concluded that these quasi-agricultural economies were reasonably equivalent to proto- or semi-agricultural societies elsewhere. Such economies allowed manifestations of leisure time and diversity of labor not only in "non-vital" occupations, but also in an apparent over-elaboration of assignments even in "vital" professions (Ziegler 1968:64).

Quasi-agriculture seems to us an appropriate term to apply to the acorn-salmon industry, but not to the over-all pattern of native economies in California. Here, for reasons we shall indicate in our discussion later, Heizer's term "semi-agricultural" seems most satisfactory for an all-encompassing term for the native California economy. California's native economy, we suggest, should be viewed holistically rather than by tribelet or cultural region to be seen in broad ecological perspective. To distinguish some regions as "semi agricultural" only on the basis of greater food abundance or superior gathering management is to fail to recognize that quasi-agricultural or semi-agricultural processes overlap into every cultural region in California. Indeed, California's native economy was far more complex in terms of energy extraction processes than can be apprehended by a primary focus upon such features as the acorn-salmon industries with the assumption that all other hunting and collecting activities were supplementary.

Without challenging the idea that the acorn economy, where wild oaks were harvested like horticultural tree crops, was indeed a "quasi-agricultural" gathering activity, we should like to emphasize that it was not the only feature of native plant gathering which suggests that California was in a pre-agricultural stage. Lewis's (1973) paper, as we shall see, provides new insight into another possibly equally important aspect of the hunting and gathering economy.

Even for the marginal-subsistence environment of the Great Basin, Downs (1966b:41) demonstrated that variations on the primary hunting and gathering theme and environmental manipulations had considerable significance. They were probably even a more significant part of gathering activities in California, because there was a far greater range of plant resources to be exploited, requiring a continuum of plant knowledge which had to be applied in the context of a rich variety of specific plant associations. Without denying the importance of the acorn as a primary staple, we question the over-emphasis on the acorn economy in the literature, which has tended to make researchers neglect other features of the gathering pattern deserving scrutiny. The "quasi-agricultural" pattern postulated by Ziegler for the acorn harvest also may be said to be applicable to methods of harvesting mesquite, pine-nut, and agave. In addition, one also finds present among some California groups--possibly most of them if sufficient information were available--evidence for both incipient agriculture and proto-agricultural manipulations. In support of the latter statement, we shall briefly summarize some of the available data on proto-agriculture in California.

Wild tobacco was planted and grown by the Diegueño (Luomala unpublished), Cahuilla (Bean and Saubel 1972:92), Wintu, Maidu, Miwok,

Yokuts, Panamint, Hupa, Yurok, and Karok (Kroeber 1941:14-15). No evidence for tobacco planting exists among most of the missionized coastal groups, which led Kroeber (1941:14) to hypothesize that tobacco planting was confined to a long, irregular area stretching southeastward from the Oregon coast to south-central California. The recent addition of the Cahuilla and Diegueño as tobacco planters, however, suggests that a preference for Spanish tobacco grown at the missions may have resulted in abandonment of native plantings, if they existed, and a subsequent lack of ethnographic knowledge of the practice by most missionized southern California groups.[8]

The Diegueño sometimes planted seeds from wild plants or transplanted wild plants to areas where they could be better tended (Luomala unpublished). According to Luomala's informants knowledge of the care of wild plants was handed down from generation to generation. Among plants they recalled as being transplanted were the wild onion (*kamashuk*) and tuberous roots called *mishwi* and *ptokolp*. Shipek (1971:10) reported her Diegueño and Luiseño informants "knew exactly which of the native plants could be propagated by cuttings, which could be transplanted, and which could not." Cuero (1968:32), a Diegueño woman, reported her people always cleared a small spot near their dwelling to plant "some of the greens and seeds and roots that they liked, just the things that grow wild." The Cahuilla replanted smaller corms of the wild hyacinth to ensure crops the following year (Bean and Saubel 1972:47), as well as various other tubers (Lawton and Bean 1968:23). J.P. Harrington (field notes, 1925) recorded a Cahuilla myth on the planting of agave. Cahuilla medicine men cultivated their own special plots of medicinal herbs and tobacco (Lawton and Bean 1968:23). Patencio (1943:91-95, 99-102) stated native palms were planted at some of the desert oases by Cahuilla.

Semicultivation of several wild seed plants, a practice that was aboriginal and first observed by Alarcón in 1540, is reported for the Mohave, Yuma, Cocopa, and Maricopa among the Colorado River Indians, who were also agricultural (Castetter and Bell 1951: 167-168). Among such plants cultivated were panic grass, foxtail millet, crowfoot grass, and curly dock. Planting of sunflower seed may also have been aboriginal with

---

[8] Father Junípero Serra set aside a section of the garden at Mission Carmel in 1774 for tobacco planting (Tibesar 1957:11, 147). Serra's decision to plant tobacco at the missions was prompted by the fact that from San Diego to Monterey the natives invariably begged him for Spanish tobacco.

the Mohave (Castetter and Bell 1951:196). Steward (1933) reported that the Owens Valley Paiute increased the natural yield of several species of wild plants by irrigation (see note 2). Patch (1951) reported the possibility of aboriginal irrigation, presumably of wild plants, for the Eureka Valley.

The proximity of the Great Basin to California also makes it worth noting that fifteen of nineteen groups covered by Steward (1941:281) and seven of fourteen groups reported by Stewart (1941:376) burned vegetation to encourage growth of wild plants. In addition, Steward (1941:281) reported that seven of his nineteen groups engaged in collective sowing of wild seeds, most frequently lamb's quarters. Sowing occurred after burning.

The Cahuilla regularly pruned mesquite by breaking and cutting branches to improve growth patterns and provide easier access to beans in their mesquite groves (Patencio 1943:59). In the historic period, the Cahuilla are known to have conducted an irrigation ditch to mesquite stands near Thermal and flooded them. Irrigation of mesquite traces back as early as the 1850's (Wilke and Lawton unpublished). McMillan (1956:29) reported that Lily Baker, a Maidu informant, stated her people cleaned around elderberry bushes and removed dead portions for better growth of this natural food. Some tending may have occurred with the wild grape among California Indians. Father Crespi (Bolton 1927:4) reported in 1769 that the plain near the port of San Diego was dotted with wild grapevines "which look as if they had been planted...." Again, in the valley where Mission San Luis Rey was later founded, Crespi (Bolton 1927:131) reported that in the vicinity of two native villages there were many wild grapes and "one sees some spots that resemble vineyards." Fallowing was a regular practice among the Cahuilla with certain plants not gathered in some years "to let the ground have more seeds for another year" (Patencio 1943:69). Similar practices are reported for the Diegueño and Luiseño (Shipek personal communication). Pedro Fages reported fires were set at the foot of the *teczuma* plant, a flower he described as similar to the rose of Castile, to make the buttons eject an oily seed (Priestley 1937:79).

The proto-agricultural activities summarized here for California groups testify to considerable sophistication in knowledge about practices needed to improve harvests for specific plants and plants in general. We are still in need of a full inventory of proto-agricultural practices throughout California, but this cursory review indicates that incipient agriculture existed among some California groups.

THE IMPLICATIONS OF LEWIS'S PAPER ON NATIVE BURNIN

In projecting ethnographic reports onto models of ecosystem relations, Lewis (1973) has demonstrated that fire was a major factor in a system of aboriginal environmental relationships and functioned in a number of ways to increase both animal and plant resources in California. His paper opens up many avenues deserving investigation, but we shall concentrate on problems raised specifically by his discussion of burning of the Woodlands-Grass environments. The ideas offered here should be considered primarily as hypotheses deserving of more intensive research.

Lewis has shown that burning of the woodlands grass belts increased grasses and forbs and would have improved browse for deer, antelope, and other game. The extraordinary abundance of game in California, particularly in woodlands-grass areas of the coastal valleys, is testified to by all of the Spanish explorers of the contact period. La Pérouse (1968:I, 441) during his 1785-88 voyage, expressed his astonishment at the wealth of game, saying "No country is more abundant in fish and game of every sort." Partridges alone in the grassland plains, he noted, were found in coveys of three or four hundred. Father Serra, who commented repeatedly on the plentifulness of game, was struck by the lack of timidity of rabbits in grassland valleys, "which frisk playfully and plentifully around" (Tibesar 1955:107). Other comments on the abundance of deer, antelope, elk, rabbit, and other game by Spanish writers may be found in Smith and Teggart (1909:19, 259), Costansó (1910:67), Tibesar (1955:87), Bolton (1967:74-75, 80), Priestley (1937:12, 35, 60, 77), Bolton (1911:149, 153), Bolton (1927:34, 127), not to mention many other sources.

Burning the woodlands grass belt, particularly in areas near villages, would have concentrated game in specific locations for ready accessibility in hunting, since browse in burned-over areas would have been richer. Thus, we suggest burning may have constituted a form of game management or incipient herding. Data on hunting technology of California Indian groups is sparse in most ethnographies and chiefly concerned with describing weapons and other tools employed. Few researchers have investigated hunting concepts, including the extent to which taboos may have served to abet game management. McMillan (1956:29) did report an example of the Maidu cutting grass during the fall months and piling it near water so that waterfowl would concentrate near this food supply during winter.

Dimbleby (1967:81-82) suggested that the opening up of woodlands to grasses, through some form of human activity such as herding, provided a shock stimulus for grasses to gain a foothold, subsequently resulting in man's exploitation of cereal grains through agriculture. Hunting drives by California Indians over many generations could well have provided such a shock stimulus in the Woodlands-Grass belt, leading to an eventual ecological understanding that fire was also a tool for increasing grass seed plants and should be regularly employed in the California environment. Although Burcham (1959), Clar (1959), and Heady (1972), as Lewis points out, are skeptical that the California Indians had sufficient numbers and technological skills to have any significant impact on the environment, such an impact need not have been massively widespread to have substantially improved the subsistence level of native populations in the coastal valleys. The primary effect of burning would be to greatly increase both plant and animal resources near villages, where hunting and gathering could be better organized and more efficiently concentrated over a smaller area, thus resulting in increased leisure for other pursuits.

One of Lewis's most stimulating ideas concerning native burning appears in another paper (Lewis 1972:213). When California shrublands are burned in late autumn, he notes, the seasonal pattern of succession begins with grasses which sprout earlier and more readily because of the nutrients provided and the clearing of surface cover), followed by legumes and other forbs through winter, spring, and early summer. The pattern of succession lasts several years, until individual species of grass become rare and absent, succeeded by other taxonomic groups until a chaparral stage is reached. With reburning, this succession is repeated. In view of these facts, Lewis (1972) suggests:

> ...By taking advantage of the internal dynamics of the secondary succession induced by fire man would without any introduction of seed on his part, create a series of successions of resources essentially no different (except that cultivation, planting, and weeding would not take place) from the harvesting pattern of some swidden farmers who exploit successive but often different crops following a first-year burn.

The analogy with swidden farming strikes us as particularly apt. We would like to hypothesize, however, that the plant succession was probably of less interest to California Indians than the first stage in that succession--the native grasses. Almost nothing is known about the native grasses of California at the time of contact. The European wild grasses

48

rapidly invaded California ranges after Spanish contact and gained the dominant foothold. By the middle of the nineteenth century, wild oats, wild mustards, wild radishes, and other Mediterranean cover had spread over most of the California rangeland. Native grasses may still be found, but as Anderson (1956:763) observed it takes a well-informed botanist going over the vegetation item by item to show how small a percentage of the range is made up of California indigenous plants.

Regular burning by the Indians of the coastal valleys may have exercised a selective influence on the genotypic strains of native grasses. Literature from Spanish sources indicates that some of the wild grains were impressive even to Europeans. The Cabrillo log (Bolton 1967:30) speaks of a seed "the size of maize" which was white and used in making tamales by the natives. Vizcaino (Bolton 1967:85) reported the Californians had a "grain like the *gofio* of the Canary Islands." Father Garcés stated that the San Jacinto plain was thickly grown with grasses, one species of which bore a seed much like rye. Garcés (Bolton 1930:II, 346) added: "I have no doubt this is the grain which the Gileños call wheat, for they told me that near the sea there was wheat which they harvested without planting it...." Coastal Diegueño insist that the white seeds of a grain which is no longer part of the native flora was harvested by their ancestors and even up into the early twentieth century (Shipek 1971:18). They described this grain as larger than the native grasses, but only about half as large as wheat. Grass seeds in archaeological sites in California are rarely given close scrutiny beyond a routine botanical identification. More intensive study might determine if there were grains with the unusual characteristics mentioned in Spanish accounts.

The Spanish literature of the contact period is full of extravagant praise for the verdant grass meadowlands of the coastal valleys, where population concentration was heaviest. Frequently, references are made to Indians harvesting their "fields" near villages. There is considerable testimony to the effect that these "fields" had circumscribed boundaries and were considered property by the Indians.[9] Father Jayme (Geiger 1970:39-

---

[9] In 1943, Heizer and Beardsley (1943) first described seven fired clay human figurines found in California. Since then other figurines, making a total of 28, and two hollow body effigies, have been described from central California to northern San Diego County (Heizer and Beardsley 1943; Heizer and Pendergast 1955; True 1957; Wallace 1957; Davis 1959; and Hedges 1973). The figurines are believed to have been used in ceremonial or ritual contexts, although the exact nature of their functions remains undetermined (Hedges 1973). Elsewhere in the southwest, effigies have been known to have been placed in the

40) in a letter of October 17, 1772 complained that the Spanish soldiers had turned their animals into the "fields" of the Indians at a village near Mission San Diego and "they ate up their crops (*semillas*)." Three other villages about a league or so from the mission, he reported, had made similar periodic complaints. Clearly, these "fields" were richer than other pasturage, leading to disputes between the Spanish and Indians.

Spanish accounts also make frequent mention of harvesting activities by the natives, but fail to describe these operations in specific detail. Often seedbeating is mentioned, but rarely in the context of any specific plant being gathered. In 1790, Captain James Colnett reported seeing the Indians near Bodega Bay using seedbeaters to gather "grass or wild wheat seed" (Howay, 1940). The anthropological literature customarily assumes seedbeaters were used throughout the state on grasses as well as other plants. Drucker (1939:9) reported that almost all of his southern California informants said grass was gathered with a seedbeater. One third of these informants, however, also said grass was cut. What we do not know is whether some grass species, possibly taller ones, were cut in southern California, whereas the seedbeater may have been employed with others.

The most intriguing reference to harvesting wild plants by California Indians in the Spanish literature appears in an official 1772 report on the establishment of Mission San Diego. Father Francisco Palóu (Pourade 1969:II, 17) states in this report:

> The savages subsist on seeds of the *zacate* (wild grass)
> which they harvest in the season. From these they make
> sheaves as is the custom to do with wheat....

---

fields by some agricultural groups to protect crops. True (1957) noted that association of figurines and increase rites in many agricultural societies has been well documented, but that lacking direct archaeological evidence or ethnological information the use of figurines in increase rites locally was unlikely. True (1957:296) added: "However, ownership of hunting grounds, oak groves, and other seed sources by individuals, families, and village complexes, suggests a grove management situation that was conceivably not far removed from early agricultural economies in other areas. Ceremonies to increase the acorn crop are said to have been performed in the old days." We should like to call attention to a historical reference which suggests effigies were used in California to protect wild plant crops. In his description of the Chumash, Pedro Fages (Priestley 1937:32-33) wrote: "They are idolaters like the rest. Their idols are placed near the village, with some here and there about the fields, to protect, they say, the seeds and crops. These idols are nothing but sticks, or stone figurines painted with colors and surmounted with plumage...."

Bundling of grain into sheaves has always been considered an innovation introduced by the missions. Yet here we find the Diegueño harvesting grass in sheaves at the close of the aboriginal period. How extensive this harvesting method may have been and whether it was employed by other coastal groups we don't know. The implications of such a technique are highly significant, however. Although we have found no other reference to sheaving in the Spanish literature for California, Shimkin and Reed (1970:!73-174) assumed that sheaving was aboriginal with the Shoshoneans of the Carson River Basin, Nevada.

Sheaving of grasses by the Diegueño, however, does suggest that they probably also engaged in sowing and that these grasses may have been "semi-domesticated" or on the way to becoming semi-domesticated when the Spanish arrived in California. Harvesting methods have a direct influence on the strain of a species if the process is repeated over a number of generations. If the method of harvesting demands that the inflorescence remain intact, then only seeds which do not disperse themselves readily will be collected (Helbaek 1960; Wilke, Bettinger, King, and O'Connell 1972:205). As a result, collected seeds can be expected to have a high frequency of genes responsible for sturdy, non-shattering inflorescences and a concomitant low frequency of genes responsible for a fragile, easily shattered inflorescence (Zohary 1969:60). When harvested seed is planted and the process repeated over a number of generations, a relatively pure strain of species ultimately results. On the other hand, if the method of harvesting utilizes the natural ability of the plant to disperse seeds, such as occurs in seedbeating when seeds are simply knocked from plants, then harvested seeds have gene dispersal frequencies comparable to the vast majority of wild plants (Wilke, Bettinger, King, and O'Connell 1972:205).

Unless sowing were carried out by the Diegueño, sheaving alone would have tended to remove superior strains of grass from the fields eventually, since seed dispersal would have been predominantly from the inferior plants missed during cutting. We therefore should like to hypothesize that the Diegueño in all probability engaged in sowing of native grasses. Burning, sheaving, and sowing would have been selective factors resulting in superior and possibly even semi-domesticated strains of grasses among the Diegueño.[10] The only mention of sowing in the literature for southern California is among the Diegueño. Shipek (1971:17) reported that elderly Diegueño informants told her that wild grass in aboriginal times was cultivated first by burning the land and then by broadcasting seed. While scholars generally have reservations concerning statements made by informants about aboriginal times, Palóu's account would appear to provide reinforcement for the practice of sowing.

How important were the native grasses in the California Indian diet? Anthropological emphasis has usually been on the acorn as the primary staple for much of California. As Kroeber (1971:297) pointed out, however, the oak is absent from many areas and did not grow in the higher mountains, in the desert, and on most of the immediate coast. Food resources were bountiful, however, with hundreds of available foods to fall back upon. A review of the Spanish literature indicates to us that grass seeds were an extremely significant staple. Both Palóu (Pourade 1969:II, 17) and Longinos Martínez (Simpson 1938:51) stressed grasses as a significant element in the coastal diet. During the march of the Portolá expedition of 1772, acorns and pine-nuts were occasionally given to the Spanish by the Indians of the coastal valleys, but pinole and atole made from the native grasses were available in large surplus and brought forth and given to the Spanish in large trays and baskets at almost every village (i.e., Bolton 1927:44-45).

THE RISE OF CULTURAL COMPLEXITY IN CALIFORNIA

Lewis's paper (1973) on native burning has forced us to reevaluate the food-subsistence patterns of California Indians, particularly the significant role of grasses in their economy. This reevaluation has led us to the conclusion that no single factor, neither the acorn complex nor marine technology, was primary in militating against the spread of

---

[10] Michael Kearney (personal communication) suggests burning and harvesting practices of California Indians may have resulted in semi-domesticated grasses less able to resist the invasion into California of wild European species. After 1769, when the coastal Indians had been rounded up by the missions, normal native practices related to burning and harvesting of native grasses would have been disrupted. Spanish cattle over the next fifty years probably weakened stands of native grass, creating numerous ecological niches for invasion by Mediterranean grasses well adapted to grazing. This may explain the rapidity with which European grasses took over.

agriculture in California. We conclude that Heizer was correct in hypothesizing that California was in a "semi-agricultural" stage at Spanish contact. This can be seen reflected in the existence of proto-agricultural techniques, in the quasi-agricultural patterns of harvesting acorn, yucca, mesquite, and pine-nuts, and in the application of burning to enhancing plant and animal resources. In short, agriculture was an unnecessary alternative for the California Indian because of an efficient, interlocking series of energy extraction processes, some of which were semi-agricultural.

Until Lewis's (1973) paper, the significance of the burning process in the large inventory of techniques of environmental manipulation used by California Indians was not demonstrated and considered by most authorities to be conjectural at best. Lewis has shown that burning was an important part of the rich technological inventory of energy extraction processes and tools used by California Indians, which included invention of leaching for acorn and buckeye, grinding implements for hard seeds, canoes for acquiring marine mammals and fish, complex fishing and trapping gear, granaries for storing large supplies of food, hermetically sealed containers, artificial water-utilization methods such as digging wells and building reservoirs on the desert, and a variety of proto-agricultural techniques.

The technological processes and complex social organizations of California's hunters and gatherers were integrated with value systems which encouraged increased productivity and the acquisition of surpluses. The abundance of plant and animal resources and the development of storage techniques and other truly skilled applications of human ingenuity allowed these people to develop beyond the normal parameters of hunting and gathering, particularly in the sociological, philosophical, and religious realms. The social structures of native communities, autonomous corporate groups called tribelets by Kroeber, were characterized by extra tribal alliances and political confederations sometimes achieving the level of nationhood. Within communities, populations were administered by very powerful hereditary chiefs and a bureaucratic elite whose principal functions appear to have been control and management of production and distribution (Strong 1929; White 1963; Bean 1972; King 1973). Between groups, intra-group adaptive mechanisms existed which included such institutions as ritual and kinship reciprocity and the trade fairs which encouraged and routinized controlled production and redistribution of foodstuffs and manufactured goods. In many instances, native groups had reached the level of an incipient class system, which recognized hereditary ruling elites, bureaucrats and artisans, ordinary persons, poor or lower classes, and sometimes slave or outlaw groups. Elites intermarried with elites among other groups, speaking and behaving in ways that affirmed and maintained their status (Bean 1973).

There is considerable evidence now that after the Europeans arrived and imposed their status concepts and economic system upon native California, traditional social hierarchies were generally obscured from view, weakened, or destroyed. Chester King (1973) has suggested that Spanish colonization resulted in (1) imposition of the new dominant hierarchy headed by a Spanish king; (2) a reduction in the importance of local native hierarchies with a loss in the significance of food storage and other facilities controlled by these hierarchies; and (3) introduction of new agricultural and pastoral technologies with a reduction in native population from disease which made possible opportunities for attaining wealth and power on the part of those of low birth. This view is counter to Gifford (1934) and others who have argued that the extraordinary cross-tribelet leadership roles in the nineteenth century of such leaders as Juan Antonio and Antonio Garra were a product of European contact. Instead, ethnographic reconstructions now indicate these historic roles were more consistent with native traditions and that the Spanish built on the foundation of the aboriginal hierarchies by appointing "generals" among Indian groups who were also traditional leaders of local political units.

Within the aboriginal social-religious institutions, which had probably been established for several thousand years, smoothly articulated intergroup relationships were regulated by ritual institutions of ritual congregations and secret societies or cults, confirming and demonstrating who had economic and political privileges, always supported in a ritual and cosmological referent of some sort. These institutions were responsible for distributing energy within the various subsystems, so that temporal or spatially related inequities in food and other economic goods could both be alleviated or maintained, depending on the particular needs of a corporate group. Such institutions provided a buffer against extremes in energy potential among different groups, which sometimes were a cause of conflict or wars. They also significantly increased the productive capacity of any single group beyond that permitted by environmental and technological limitations.[11]

---

[11] Much new material and current views on California social organization will appear in an anthology of essays edited by Lowell John Bean and Thomas King entitled 'Antap: **California Indian Political and Economic Organization**, scheduled for future publication by Ballena Press. [Eds. note: Subsequently published--see Bean and King 1974.]

Alliances and trade fairs also increased the energy input for any single group. Trade routes appear to have reached the logical parameters of natural barriers and ecological needs. For example, in southern California, where there were few barriers to intercultural communications, trade alliances associated with military commitments extended from the west coast across the state into Arizona. Several such alliances provided routinized trade routes allowing a considerable exchange of goods across several ecological zones and directed that flow along ecological lines rather than cultural or linguistic ones. Agricultural products also must have occasionally passed along these trade routes in addition to shell beads, obsidian, and other goods, and undoubtedly knowledge of agricultural practices along the Colorado River. The abundance of California's food resources and highly developed techniques of energy extraction, however, made it unnecessary to adapt an agricultural mode, except in some of the marginally productive desert areas.

The style of cultures represented in California now appear to provide the model sought by cultural evolutionists who pursue knowledge about the upper limits of sociocultural integration possible without an agricultural base. California stands out as perhaps exemplary of many hunting and gathering regions which were later occupied or transformed by agricultural systems. Frequently, anthropologists have concluded that hunting and gathering peoples were forced into marginal environments by people adopting agriculture or that those hunters and gatherers who achieved maximal sociopolitical development proceeded to adopt agriculture and thus have been lost for analytical purposes. A reexamination of California from a fresh viewpoint--the idea that hunting and gathering societies there may have been analogous to many primitive agriculture societies elsewhere--should provide new perspectives on ideas suggested by cultural evolutionists and ecologists. It should help in answering many questions about the upper or maximal levels of sociocultural integration that hunting and gathering groups can achieve. From such knowledge will come a better understanding of the complex processes by which man thrusts forward toward the logical potential of his environmental and technological growth.

PATTERNS OF INDIAN BURNING
IN CALIFORNIA:
ECOLOGY AND ETHNOHISTORY[1]

Henry T. Lewis

It would be difficult to find a reason why the Indians (of California) should care one way or another if the forest burned. It is quite something else again to contend that the Indians used fire systematically to "improve" the forest. Improve it for what purpose?.... Yet this fantastic idea has been and still is put forth time and again... [C.R. Clar, California Government and Forestry 1959:7].

There seems little question that Indians across the United States used fire as a land-management tool.... The California Indians probably molded the Sierra landscape with fire for more than 3,000 years [V.R. Johnston, The Ecology of Fire 1970a:81, 85].

Our kind of people never used the plow.... All they used to do was burn the brush at various places, so that some good things will grow up.... they do not set fire for nothing, it is for something that they set fire for [quotation from an Indian informant in J.P. Harrington, Tobacco Among the Karok Indians of California 1932:63].

INTRODUCTION

Indigenous uses of fire and the consequent effects upon the environments of California have been discussed in terms which, at one extreme, see the Indian as a noble, primitive conservationist and, at the other, as a careless or indifferent incendiary. Unfortunately, the varied ethnographic references to aboriginal burning often note little more than that Indians did in fact set fire to California's grass, chaparral, and forest lands. Consequently, the evidence supports either position depending upon

---

[1]This paper was first published in 1973 as **Ballena Press Anthropological Papers** 1. It is reprinted here with minimal revisions and corrections, and with the original acknowledgements deleted.

56

one's predisposition for finding an aboriginal fire ecologist or a primitive pyromaniac.

The three comments quoted above represent different perspectives on the significance and aims of aboriginal burning in California. Regrettably, there are very few which even mention the third view presented, that of the native participants. Largely as a consequence of this, the arguments presented here purposefully avoid the question of whether or not California Indians were ecologically aware or environmentally indifferent as to the impact of fire on local habitats. Because California Indians no longer burn tracts of forest, brush, and grassland such questions are probably impossible to answer. In any event, it is not the motivations, whatever they may have been, that I am concerned with but, rather, what can be reconstructed regarding effects of aboriginal burning on some of the environments of historic and prehistoric California. At the same time, is it possible to formulate the broad outline of ecological relationships that must have been involved?

The most fundamental assumption which underlies the following argument is simply that hunter-gatherers are necessarily responsive to local environmental fluctuations and perturbations, whether natural or man-made. Like men everywhere, hunter-gatherers cannot long ignore disruptions which adversely effect their day-to-day subsistence. However, because their subsistence strategies are more directly and immediately linked to environmental imperatives, they must soon make accommodations or else become one more evolutionary failure. We do not have to drag forth Rousseauean assumptions that hunter-gatherers do (or in the past did) live in "primeval harmony" with nature, or that they possess mystic insights about the workings of natural phenomena. The argument simply assumes that men must sooner or later, with varying degrees of effectiveness, adjust to their surroundings. The various strategies of hunting and gathering--whether adapted to dry deserts, the subarctic, or tropical forests--require that it be sooner rather than later. How part of such an adaptation obtained, involving the use of fire in the woodland-grass, chaparral, and forest lands of California, is the subject of this paper.

ETHNOHISTORY AND ECOLOGY

In recent years increasing numbers of ethnohistorical studies in anthropology have employed methods which combine anthropological and biological data to develop generalizations about the ecology of man. A region widely covered from a combined ethnohistorical-ecological perspective is the Great Plains (Eggan 1966; Ewers 1988; Fisher 1968; Levy 1971; Murphy, R. and Y. Murphy 1960; Secoy 1953), the most comprehensive single work being Oliver's *Ecology and Cultural Continuity as Contributing Factors In the Social Organization of the Plains Indians* (1962). Elsewhere, Geertz's (1963) study of swidden farming and wet rice agriculture in Indonesia involved a comprehensive ecological interpretation of ethnographic and historical source materials. Studies by Barth (1956, 1962), Downs (1966a, 1972), Downs and Ekvall (1965), Hickerson (1965), Knight (1965), Leeds (1965), Piddocke (1965), Suttles (1968), Sweet (1965a, 1965b), Vayda (1961), and others have all made use of ethnographic and historical source materials for making ecological interpretations. Each of these studies have examined various systems and subsystems within the total complex of man-environmental relationships. Most often the researchers have employed, though not always explicitly, the idea of ecological niche in the sense that the studies delineate various factors which concern the role of populations in their environments. More traditional anthropological studies often did little more than describe the "places" in which societies live; cultural-ecological studies have been specifically concerned with "what-is-going-on" between society and place.

For the majority of anthropological studies the concepts and techniques involved in ecosystems analysis, laboratory simulation, food chains, energy transfers, biogeochemical circulation, secondary succession, etc., are either precluded--given the nature of the available data--or else fall outside the scope and competence of the cultural ecologist. Standard definitions of the concept of ecosystem include the interactions of biotic and abiotic materials along with the transfer and circulation of energy and matter within a multivariate system.

While such a concept has an attraction for the anthropologist, little if any anthropology has involved the formal application of ecosystems analysis--though this has not inhibited the wide, often inappropriate, use of such terminology. Elsewhere I have used an ecosystems approach in prehistoric studies in order to examine the role that fire may have played in the emergence of plant and animal domestication in western Iran (Lewis 1972). Cumberland (1962, 1965), a geographer, has studied the prehistoric impact of fire use by early moa hunters in New Zealand. Rappaport's (1971) outline study of energy transfers within a system of swidden agriculture is another such exception. However, short of becoming a biologist, what utility does a concept like ecosystem have for anthropological studies?

The major significance that ecology has for anthropology is that it provides new perspectives and insights for recognizing and solving anthropological problems. Whereas the natural sciences have a great deal to say about the ecology of man, the anthropologist concerned with problems of human adaptation need not forsake his discipline to become a biological ecologist any more than an anthropologist interested in matters economic needs become an economist. As Shepard has noted, "Ecological thinking...requires a kind of vision across boundaries" (1967:2). Thus, ecology offers the potential for broadening anthropology, not abandoning it.

Ecology can influence anthropology in essentially two ways. First, there are general perspectives and theories which are applicable to understanding man's role in natural environments (Odum 1969; Margalef 1968). Secondly, there are particular studies within specific environments which the cultural ecologist may use for developing generalizations regarding the behavior of either past or extant populations in a given area. Using the example of California Indians, the approach employed here makes use of both general ecological theory and specific environmental field studies to reconstruct certain patterns of aboriginal behavior in selected habitats. As outlined below, the approach was developed in order to "fit" unrelated ethnographic-historical statements concerning Indian uses of fire into a system of relationships based on what is now known about the ecology of fire on some of the grass, chaparral, and forest lands of California. At the same time, an approach to the solution of related problems in prehistory and ethnohistory is suggested.

Omer C. Stewart has maintained that he has "definite evidence that almost every tribe in the Mountain and Pacific Coast States deliberately set the vegetation on fire" (1955c:5). Unfortunately, such a compilation of references tells us little that is ecological since we learn virtually nothing concerning any of the various systems of relationships that existed between California Indians and particular environments. To simply note that all Indians used fire to modify their environments is no more an ecological generalization than to note that all farmers use plows. Instead, to be ecological it must be shown how the aboriginal use of fire was a factor within a system of environmental relationships and that it functioned in a number of ways. However, our thinking about fire, as is so often the case with other environmental phenomena, tends towards simple cause-effect interpretations and we do not view fire as a dynamic physical component with a multivariate system of environmental relationships.

FIRE AND NATURAL ENVIRONMENTS

The anthropologist is probably as well indoctrinated in the fire myths of his own society as any other layman and knows that wilderness fires are bad. Popular American folk beliefs strongly support the public and, in most cases, governmental beliefs that forest, brush, and grassland fires are bad *per se* and that the elimination of fire is fundamental to preserving our natural environments. Obviously, it is argued, the continuous destruction, year after year, of thousands upon thousands of acres of timber is self-evident proof of the dangers of fire to the balance of nature itself. Despite the fact that repeated studies have for many years shown the significance of natural fires and the dangers of total fire exclusion, the general public is all but totally ignorant of these facts. Consequently, when research on the ecology of fire concludes that the solution to the ever-increasing problem of wildfire is the application of more fire, it is not surprising that until recently such work has received little public attention or, from the standpoint of most professional firefighters, is viewed with some alarm.

However, as any casual observer of natural phenomena will have noticed in watching electrical storms, it is simply not the case that "Only You Can Prevent Fire!" In fact, contrary to popular belief, man does not set most forest fires; lightning is, in fact, the single greatest cause of forest fires. On the other hand, man does start some of the worst forest fires; even more significantly, man permits (in fact requires) the buildup of dangerous fuel conditions which result in the most disastrous of forest fires--this a direct consequence of his fire exclusion policies.

When one concedes that lightning does cause an enormous number of fires (the U.S. Forest Service lists over 16,000 in California alone between 1910 and 1968 [Komerak 1968]), then the logical question is: What prevented all the trees in all the mountains from being totally destroyed prior to the twentieth-century practices of fire exclusion? What kept California green when there were no firefighters to dispatch on each lightning fire or to extinguish conflagrations set by Indians? From the point of view of ecology the answer is that fires were an important, dynamic factor in both the evolution and maintenance of natural environments and that attempts by modern man to exclude fire have created a number of new problems. Again, one of the most serious of these has been the very real destruction wrought by wildfires, in large part a consequence of the unnatural accumulations of fuel which, when eventually ignited, create fires of holocaust proportions.

The importance of natural fires in California (and elsewhere, of course) has been recognized for some considerable time, and arguments by a few scholars and laymen were made in opposition to policies of total fire suppression. However, as existing public practices and popular beliefs clearly show, the arguments for fire exclusion and suppression came to dominate and, except for small amounts of controlled burning (mostly on grasslands), a concerted and increasingly massive effort to eliminate fire from the natural environment was and is maintained. Yet, even the advocates of controlled burning did not normally view fire as an integral part of nature but rather as a tool for the direct management and control of natural habitats. The role that "primitive" Indians might have played in the restructuring of natural environments was seen to be of little interest or significance:

> If we find controlled burning valuable we are not required to look to the Indians for precedent to justify its use--it will stand or fall on its own merits. It must be applied by us in the light of findings of modern research, and through understanding of ecological processes, not on the basis of traditions that stand in the dim past. Range men and foresters of today are much more capable of appraising the worth of planned burning as a management practice--in our times and under our conditions--than were the California Indians [Burcham 1959:181].

In recent years research in the ecology of fire has received both the interest and support of those agencies most concerned with the effects of fire. A great deal of this research, as well as reports on its applications, has been published since 1962 in the *Proceedings of the Annual Tall Timbers Fire Ecology Conference* (Tallahassee). As a consequence of these studies and the recognition that a policy of total fire suppression does not prevent wildfires--that in fact it makes conditions worse--both state and national agencies became involved in programs and research which emphasize the dynamic role of fire in natural environments.

The natural history of fire in the various vegetational zones of California was early pointed out in the studies of W.S. Cooper (1922), Jepson (1921), Kotok (1931), Show and Kotok (1921), and Storer (1932). In the past twenty years, ever-increasing amounts of field research on the ecology of fire have been carried out on grass, brush and forest lands. As detailed below, some of these studies offer conclusions which make it possible to understand the broader ecological features of Indian burning practices.

To restate the proposition made earlier, this understanding is arrived at by "projecting" the available evidence on aboriginal burning against the findings of recent ecosystems studies on the ecology of fire in California. The approach used involves the collection and examination of the few desultory ethnographic and historic statements about Indian burning and then attempts to fit these into the findings and recommendations of contemporary ecological research.

At the same time, the strategy employed for the solution of this problem involves an approach which may be applicable to the solution of other problems in ethnohistory and prehistory. As mentioned above, the more usual approach in ecologically-focused studies in anthropology involves a reconstruction of the systems of relations which obtain between societies and their environments, the emphasis being upon those variables which constitute the ecological niche of a given group. The method employed here makes use of the wider ecosystemic relationships, in which men are viewed as but representatives of one species in the cycling of energy and matter between animals, plants, and inorganic matter in a multivariate system.

The first step in the analysis which follows entails an outlining of the general pattern of relationships that are found within the cycles of secondary succession in woodland-grass, chaparral, and coniferous forest vegetation belts.

CALIFORNIA INDIANS

In this paper, the California Indians considered are those which were found within the San Joaquin and Sacramento valleys, throughout the foothills and western slopes of the Sierra Nevadas, and over virtually all of coastal and interior northern California. In large measure the inclusion of particular tribal groups is determined by the availability of ethnographic data applicable to the selected vegetational zones. For instance, the major tribal groups within the woodland-grass and chaparral belts of the central and southern coastal range--mainly the Costanoan, Salinan, and Chumash --are not included due to the absence of ethnographic data. The general distribution of tribal groups for central and northern California is shown in Fig. 3.1; the vegetation zones and land forms are illustrated in Fig. 3.2.

Acorns provided the main subsistence resource for all Indian groups within the areas examined, with other plants, along with hunting and fishing, being of variable significance in different regions. On the major rivers of the northwest coast salmon fishing was of particular significance, as it was also on the San Joaquin and Sacramento rivers. Baumhoff (1963) describes the Indians of the northwest coast as "river and coastal fishermen" and those from the Central Valley as "gatherers-huntersfishermen." Throughout the remainder of the region considered the subsistence type is classified as "gatherers-hunters." The more general definition of hunter-gatherers used by Lee and Devore (1968) is that they are people who subsist primarily on resources other than meat [wild plants and fish) and who live in small groups while moving about a great deal. This broad definition includes within it all tribal groups considered in California's woodland-grass, chaparral, and coniferous forest zones.

Most California Indians depended on more than two major vegetational zones for subsistence, and all made use of a variety of vegetational sub-types and microhabitats found in any one of the zones. For those groups living along the foothill margins of the Sierra Nevadas, all three major vegetational zones were exploited, the Indians taking advantage of the progression of plants and animals found with the seasonal migration of populations from lower to higher altitudes and back again.

Most of the ethnographic literature cited below provides descriptions of the subsistence patterns followed by California Indians. A general study of the relationships between the abundance of resources within particular areas, and the estimated population densities which these resources were able to support, has been elaborated by Baumhoff (1963). For the State of California as a whole it has been estimated that the aboriginal population was about 275,000 (Cook 1964). Baumhoff's analysis of the population for most of the vegetational zones considered here are proportionally as high: 111,667 (1963:231). The relatively heavy concentration of aboriginal inhabitants can perhaps be further explored when considered in terms of how fire effected the production of plants and animals in the primitive wildlands of California.

Indian tribes

Figure 3.1. Major tribes of central and northern California.

VEGETATIONAL ZONES

Woodland-Grass Belt

The lower portions of the California foothills are composed of irregular stands of trees and brush interspersed by larger areas of grass cover, the dominance or extent of one or the other being dependent upon a number of specific factors; e.g., altitude, rainfall, soils, exposure, grazing, fire, etc. West of the Sierras this vegetation type covers 7.5 million acres. In the lower margins the woodland-grass type grades off into the grass vegetation type, the two being similar in many respects except for the upper zone's landscape of many more shrubs and trees.

The tree vegetation is dominated by blue oak (*Quercus douglasii*), liveoak (*Q. wislizenii*), and digger pine (*Pinus sabiniana*) while willows (genus *Salix*) and sycamores (*Platanus racemosa*) are found in streamside associations. Also, various amounts of brush vegetation are found scattered (though in the absence of fire, brush can become dominant) throughout the woodland-grass area, especially large amounts of buckbrush (genus *Ceanothus*, esp. *C. cuneatus*) and manzanita (genus *Arctostaphylos*).

Within the woodland-grass and grass areas, fire reduces brush cover to favor a parkland of grasses, trees, and intermittent stands of brush. The effect is to lessen the hazards of wildfire, increase plant and animal productivity, and improve the flow of springs by maintaining a sub-climax condition. This maintenance of a youthful stage of succession provides a favorable environment for deer. The winter range for deer is described in the northern California foothills as follows:

> Browse (buck brush, mountain mahogany, manzanita, scrub oak, silktassel, and many deciduous browses) appear to constitute the staple item of diet throughout the winter. The leafage and acorns of the deciduous oaks contribute heavily to the early fall diet, and as the foothills "green up" with the advent of fall rains, the deer graze heavily on the annual grasses and forbs. This annual forage production reaches its height in March, when it contributes most to the diet of the deer. Early in April the browse plants begin to leaf out with new growth and the deer appear to switch entirely to browse diet [Leach and Hiehle 1957: 177-178].

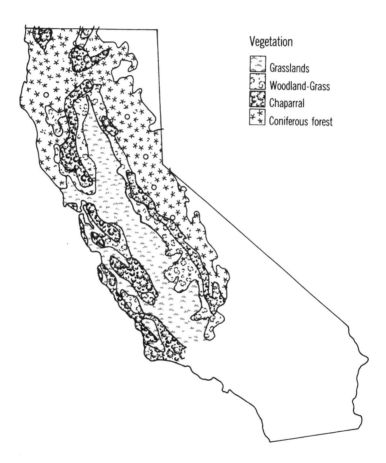

Vegetation

Grasslands
Woodland-Grass
Chaparral
Coniferous forest

Figure 3.2. Vegetational zones in central and northern California.

66

Recommendations for the management of rangeland have commonly emphasized the significance of prescribed burning to increase the grazing potential for domestic animals (Humphrey 1962). At the same time and in conjunction with an improved habitat for livestock, prescribed burning has been advocated so as to improve the conditions for deer and game birds as well. In fact, most applications of controlled fire have taken place in woodland-grass and grass vegetation cover.

In these areas, as it is elsewhere, the time of burning is important: "Prescribed burning in woodland-grass vegetation is usually done in the summer when the grasses are dry and will carry fire from one brush area to another" (Biswell 1967:82).

In the absence of fire, trees and shrubs have increased, particularly in the upper margins of the woodland-grass belt. Much of the brush cover within the woodland-grass vegetation is composed of nonsprouting species, and burning during the summer months is most effective in reducing such species, with the result that grasses and forbs are increased. At the same time, if regular grass fires are maintained mature blue oaks are not adversely affected; in fact the production of both acorns and leafs is increased as a result of the reduced competition from the thinned understory of brush.

Chaparral Belt

Vast areas of hills and mountains of California are occupied by a unique vegetation called chaparral which corresponds in gross form but not in detail to the vegetation of similar mild Mediterranean climates in Australia, Chile, South Africa, and the Mediterranean Region. The California chaparral is a dense, shrubby, sclerophyllous cover characterized by exceptionally deep-rooted species. Multitudinous aspects are formed depending upon topography, substratum, and depth of soil accumulation. Recurrent fire is a conspicuous and important factor in the dynamics of this vegetation and one to which it is highly adapted. Such adaptations include postfire seedling establishment and rapid regeneration from surviving subterranean parts [Muller, et al. 1968:225].

Chaparral lands are designated in terms of the broad-leafed shrubs which dominate coastal and inland foothill regions of California as thick, often impenetrable covers of woody plants. However, pure chaparral stands constitute only the mature, or "climax" stage of secondary succession which is reinitiated, most commonly following a fire, with a cover of herbaceous plants followed by a regeneration of shrub cover in five, six, or more years. One kind of mature chaparral cover is composed of almost solid stands of chamise, or "greasewood" (*Adenostoma fasciculatum*), with some admixtures of wedgeleaf ceanothus (*Ceanothus cuneatus*), yerba santa (*Eriodictyon californicum*), poison oak (*Rhus diversiloba*), and others.

Figure 3.3. One year following a fire in a coastal, or "soft" chaparral stand shows a dramatic growth of early succession species of grasses and forbs, along with the rapid regrowth of sprouts from many species of chaparral. New sprouts provide food for browsing animals and a renewed life cycle for plants.

Figure 3.4. In the southern Sierra Nevada this solid stand of chamise chaparral in the foreground, cut only by a road-break, and the mixed chaparral cover in the distance are serious fire hazards. Frequently burned and/or opened areas of brush reduce fire hazards and support a greater abundance of game.

This chamise dominated chaparral is characteristic of south-facing slopes, whereas north-facing slopes are characterized by mixed chaparral stands. On these north exposures, slopes are vegetated by live oak (*Quercus wizlizenii*), scrub oak (*Q. dumosa*), eastwood manzanita (*Arctostaphylos glandulosa*), California laurel (*Umbellularis californica*), toyon (*Photinia arbutifolia*), birchleaf mahogany (*Cercocarpus betuloides*), deerbush (*Ceanothus integerrimus*), chamise, and others. In wetter areas, along ridge tops or on variant soil types, other species may predominate or become more important.

In the chaparral regions of California fires are frequent and periodically reburn the same areas. Many species of plants and numerous individuals not previously evident "suddenly" appear following fire.... Many such herbaceous plants are so characteristic of burned areas in the chaparral that they are often referred to as "burn" species. Some species occur in abundance only the first season following fires and are rarely encountered in abundance on open sites adjacent to the burns. Other species have been observed to persist in varying numbers and for

varying numbers and for varying periods of time on older
burns.... [Sweeney, 1956:143].

    Perhaps the most remarkable feature of chaparral succession is the pronounced change in herbaceous growth which takes place in the first few years following the reintroduction of fire. Whereas the aerial portions of shrub species are destroyed, sprouting varieties of brush rapidly return with new, highly nutritious growth attractive to browsing animals. Coupled with this, the species of grasses and forbs which appear following fire, as well as those which continue into subsequent years, make up a new, highly productive, if only transitory community. The recurrent appearance and florescence of particular genera and species is directly dependent upon and has evolved within the fire cycling of California chaparral. The repeated sequence and structure of serial stages demonstrates the ordered, systemic features of chaparral succession.

    The secondary succession initiated by fire results in an overall increase in the production of both shrubs and herbaceous plants, with both direct and indirect benefits for hunting and gathering. In the mature stages of succession plant growth involves little more than maintenance of the plant community, mostly in shrub growth. It is where production far exceeds respiration that conditions are favorable to primary, secondary, and tertiary consumers (Odum 1969). It is this general feature of fire succession that benefits man the hunter-gatherer.

    Odum (1969) has emphasized the importance of "community control" which exists within the pattern of ecosystem development. These controls, both synergetic and antagonistic, affect the internal structure at any one stage of development as well as the sequential pattern in the development of stages over time. Thus, any level of secondary succession is determined by both those levels which precede and those levels which follow, the total ecosystem being the recurrent and regenerative pattern of youth and maturity. A dynamic balance is achieved through the periodic reestablishment of secondary succession initiated by fire. If chaparral becomes fixed at maturity then it is effectively unbalanced and both increasingly and dangerously unstable. As with many other natural environments, it is the unnaturally protected, statically maintained forest, brush, or grassland climax environment that is nonhomeostatic. Consequently, fire is a crucial and dynamic part of the chaparral succession that is necessary for the perpetuation of chaparral ecosystems as they exist in the context of cyclical change. Chaparral is more than simply adapted to fire; fire is part of the overall adaptation of California's brushlands.

An important factor in chaparral succession concerns the role of toxins, chemical inhibitors, produced with the regeneration of shrub stands. The studies of Muller (1966, 1969), Muller and Muller (1964), and Muller, et al. (1968) have shown the significance of the various woody sclerophyllous species in producing water soluble compounds, volatile terpenes, which effectively inhibit the germination and growth of herbs. As a result of rain wash onto leaves and a ground cover of leaf litter, toxins are exuded and the chemical composition of the soil altered, with the result that herbaceous seed germination and growth are quite effectively inhibited. Fire, by removing litter, changing the chemical components within the soil, and stimulating germination, initiates secondary succession:

> The chaparral fire cycle thus emerges as a sequence of events consequent to the destruction of toxins and their shrub sources by fire. This is followed by the germination of seeds no longer inhibited by shrub toxins. The germinating species include many highly adapted annual herbs whose seeds exhibit impressive longevity. Shrub regeneration is largely dependent upon sprouting from underground rhizomes and burls, a form of adaptation particularly prominent in chaparral. Thus the potential for toxin production again increases and is accompanied by gradual suppression of seed germination and resulting elimination of annual species. The seeds of most species remain viable until after the next fire and in this manner the cycle is reinitiated [Muller, et al., 1968:231].

Following the reintroduction of fire, a large number of annual and some biennial grasses and forbs appear, arising from the seed supply that has lain dormant since the last fire, in some cases for ten or more years. The majority of grasses and forbs persist for no more than one season. Numerous species of lily, such as common brodiaea (*Brodiaea capitata* or *pulchella*), soap plant (*Chlorogalum pomeridianum*), camus (*Camassia quamash*), and various mariposa lilies (genus *Calochortus*) emerge as part of the plant community. In addition, still other weedy species are reintroduced into burned-over areas, persisting for several seasons until eliminated with the regeneration of advanced growth of chaparral shrubs (Sampson 1944; Sweeney 1956).

In areas of mixed chaparral cover, scrub oak and interior liveoak are among the principal broadleaf trees, and both are non-deciduous and both sprout vigorously after fire. However, on the lower margins of the chaparral belt blue oak becomes dominant and at the upper margins black oak (*Quercus kelloggii*) is dominant. Both blue oak and black oak are deciduous, with the blue oak being somewhat less responsive to fire. All four of these oaks are important as sources of food for deer in the form of leaves and acorns, with oaks of the lower margins being especially important during the period in which deer are on their winter range (Biswell and Gilman 1961).

Leopold (1950) has emphasized the significance of the lower edges of the chaparral belt where woodland-oak forest and grasslands meet as having been areas of special abundance for game animals during the early historic period of California:

> Prior to settlement, deer seem to have occurred principally along "edges" where forest and grassland met or on recent burns in the forest. Neither dense timber nor extensive prairie supported many deer. The woody shrubs and/or tree reproduction which constitute staple items of deer diet are characteristic of subclimax ecological conditions (in other words, of early stages in a forest successional cycle), such as occur even today on prairie borders where woody plants encroach on the grass only to be pushed back periodically by drought or fire...the borders of the Sacramento Valley were maintained in young brush by recurrent fires, some of them probably set by Indians for the specific purpose of producing more game [Leopold 1950:572].

The broad ecosystemic features of California chaparral described above apply (though always with local environmental exceptions) for all of the state's foothill regions. However, because we lack specific detailed information on practices of Indian burning, it is with respect to the more general considerations governing chaparral ecosystems that the questions are here directed. At the same time, the recommendations suggested by Biswell (1967) for the use of fire in wildland management are also applicable to the same general considerations governing chaparral ecosystems.

Studies in California wildlife management have shown the significance of various relationships between animal populations and environments subject to fire succession (Biswell 1959a, 1961, 1963, 1967; Biswell and Gilman 1961; Biswell et al. 1952; Humphrey 1962; Komarek 1963; Leopold 1950; Leopold et al. 1963; Miller 1963). Depending upon local environmental factors and the conditions under which fire takes place, it has been shown that deer in recently burned-over chaparral cover show marked increases in numbers, size, and improvement of health:

> An area of prescribe-burned chamise chaparral was compared with a similar unburned area as a control. Counts of deer in the burned area showed a summer population density of about 98 per square mile after the initial burning treatment. This rose to 131 in the second year, and dropped to 84 in the fifth and sixth years. In the dense, untreated brush the summer density was only 30 deer per square mile. Ovulation rate in adult deer was 175 per cent in treated brush and only 82 per cent in untreated brush. Deer weights were higher in prescribe-burned brush than in the untreated area [Biswell 1967:81].

Small game populations are similarly effected. Research in the chaparral regions of Lake County (Biswell et al. 1952) has shown that valley quail are found in numbers two-and-a-half times greater in burned areas than in unburned areas, jackrabbits two to four-and-a-half times as great, with the number of doves simply noted as having increased:

> It seems evident that the generous amounts of herbaceous vegetation, along with the edge-effect supplied by the scattered clumps of brush encourage the build-up of most resident small game species. In the opened brush are found not only the densest populations of most small game, but also cover which is most suitable for upland hunting [Biswell et al. 1952:164].

Not all small game species increase as a result of fire and some may in fact be reduced in total numbers. However, the actual potential for the hunting of all animals may be greatly improved:

> Even species such as the brush rabbit and mountain quail, which seem to be more numerous in the heavy brush than in the opened brush, may be hunted more successfully in the latter areas. It is almost impossible to hunt small

game in heavy brush, especially after the first fall rains [Biswell et al. 1952:164].

The above-mentioned studies recommend that opened brushlands be maintained by a pattern of spot burning rather than the removal of brush over large expanses. The argument is that this would provide an optimum environment for both protection against the adverse effects of wildfire and as an improved habitat for game. The overall area is characterized by brush-enclosed openings at early stages of secondary succession. This would be quite different than the solid stands of chaparral which now cloak foothill regions and are periodically swept by wildfire:

> Burned spots should usually be small, 5 to 10 acres or so in size, in order to form as much edge as possible.... Spot burns of about five acres scattered here and there are probably sufficient for initiating a program of managing chamise brushlands. The spots should be scattered evenly over the whole area rather than clumped [Biswell et al. 1952:472].

It is recommended that spot burning be accomplished during the fall or spring when the fire hazard is reduced, since destructive wildfires are more likely to occur in the hottest and driest summer months. At the same time, soil erosion is reduced:

> Fires in grass are less intense than those in brush; the grass seeds and residue are not all destroyed; the grass begins growth following fall rains and soon covers the soil; the soil is firm following fire. In dense brush, on the other hand, the fires are intense; the soil is loose and bare the following winter; the shrubby vegetation recovers slowly [Biswell et al. 1952:159-460].

The dangers of wildfire and erosion are not the only factors important in the timing associated with fires. Of direct importance for hunters and gatherers would be the more immediate impact on the available cover of herbaceous plants for both animals and man. Late fall burning results in an earlier winter growth of herbaceous plants eagerly sought by animals, and the maintenance of such winter grass areas would directly benefit local populations of hunter-gatherers. In addition, fire differently affects the stands of chamise chaparral from those of mixed chaparral, the difference being especially significant between sprouting and non-sprouting species. Burning, it is suggested, should take place in late fall when the greatest number of species are positively affected:

> The greatest number of new seedlings come in the spring after fall burning. Apparently spring burning favors sprouting shrubs over non-sprouting species. Since some of the better shrubs (i.e., for browse) are non-sprouting species perhaps a combination of spring and fall burning is preferable to burning only in spring [Biswell 1967: 811].

The frequency of fires is also significant in that sprouting species tend to be favored by repeated fires and non-sprouting species adversely affected, if seeds have not been produced between the period of burning.

Coniferous Forest Belt

The coniferous forest areas of California include the Sierra Nevadas, timbered portions of the Coast Range, and the higher elevations of the smaller mountain ranges in southern California. In the lower zones of the Sierra coniferous forest, this mixed-conifer type includes the western yellow pine (*Pinus ponderosa*), sugar pine (*P. lambertiana*), incense cedar (*Libocedrus decurrens*), white fir (*Abies concolor*), and the Sierra redwood (*Sequoia gigantia*). At higher elevations ponderosa pine may be replaced by red fir (*A. magnifica*), followed at still higher elevations by lodgepole pine (*P. murrayna*).

Within the coastal coniferous forest two broad subclasses are distinguished: the redwood forest and the pine-fir forest. Redwood forests characterize the cool and damp regions along the coast with relatively heavy precipitation levels of up to extremes of 100 inches per year. The dominant tree vegetation includes the coast redwood (*Sequoia sempervirens*), Douglas fir (*Pseudotsuga menziesii*), and tanbark oak (*Lithocarpus densiflora*). Within the higher and/or drier sections of the northwest coastal area the pine-fir forest includes those regions made up of increasingly large numbers of Douglas fir. In addition, greater numbers of tanbark oak are found with admixtures of madrone (*Arbutus menziesii*), chinquapin (*Castanopsis chrysophylla*), sugar pine (*Pinus lambertiana*), maul oak

(*Quercus chrysolepsis*), and black oak (*Q. kelloggii*). Finally, on the drier and eastern margins of the pine-fir forest the plant community will grade into and eventually give way to a ponderosa pine forest, effectively the same as that found in the Sierra Nevadas.

Variations of the principal subspecies occur to make up numerous subtypes, along with local admixtures of other cone-bearing trees (most notably the two species of sequoia) and certain broad-leaf trees. Throughout the mixed conifer forest there is visible evidence of the fact that fire has been a significant force in natural selection. In no single species has this been more dramatically demonstrated than with the giant sequoia (Biswell 1961; Biswell et al. 1966; Hartesveldt 1964; Hartesveldt and Harvey 1968; Kilgore 1970, 1972; Rundel 1971).

While fire is a fundamentally important selective agent in the coniferous forest regions of California, there are basic differences between patterns of fire succession within a conifer forest and that within chaparral. Whereas in chaparral succession there are "fire type" plants which occur only on recently burned-over areas, the herbaceous cover in a burned-over forest is like that of surrounding unburned areas. Within the coniferous forests there are no herbaceous plants which are inseparably adapted to fire (Sweeney 1968:120).

Wildfires have often resulted in the development of brushfields with almost totally degraded forests, the process of recovery to a mixed coniferous forest being greatly impaired. However, the conditions which now exist with respect to succession following wildfires are as unnatural as the conditions which contribute to major conflagrations in the first place. In the primitive forests of California wildfires, certainly crown-fires, were rare whereas frequent ground fires of low intensity, ignited by lightning or Indians, were a common feature. The problem of wildfires is essentially related to the large and unnatural accumulations of fuel with the result that crown-fires of holocaust proportions develop, and the succession pattern which follows is markedly different from that which follows light burns. Fires are a natural feature of mountain environments and frequent burning serves as a negative feedback, preventing the longterm destruction by wildfires at some later time:

> California's primitive forests were kept open and park-like
> by frequent surface fires set by lightning and by the
> Indians. The forests were in a stable equilibrium, immune
> to extensive crown fires [Biswell 1968:61].

Thus, unlike the overly protected debris- and tree-choked woods that characterize most coniferous forests today, parklike primitive forests were maintained and perpetuated as a result of frequent small burns. Such forests were characterized by uneven-aged stands, each individual stand dominated by even-aged groups of trees. The general effect of fire was to check succession, reduce competition, and remove aged and diseased trees.

In describing ponderosa pine forests of the Southwest, C.F. Cooper notes that

> ...they used to be open, park-like forests arranged in a mosaic of discrete groups, each containing 10 to 30 trees of a common age. Small numbers of saplings were dispersed among the mature pines, and luxuriant grasses carpeted the forest floor. Fires, when they occurred, were easily controlled and seldom killed a whole stand ....

> Today, dense thickets of young trees have sprung up everywhere in the forests. The grass has been reduced, and dry branches and needles have accumulated to such an extent that any fire is likely to blow up into an inferno that will destroy everything in its path....

> Lightning is frequent in the ponderosa pine region, and the Indians set many fires there. Tree rings show that the forests used to burn regularly at intervals of three to 10 years. The mosaic pattern of the forest has developed under the influence of recurrent light fires. Each even-aged group springs up in an opening left by the death of a predecessor [Cooper, C.F. 1952:155-156].

Such a mosaic of even-aged stands was described in the Sierra Nevadas by John Muir as follows:

> The inviting openness of the Sierra woods is one of their most distinguishing characteristics. The trees of all the species stand more or less apart in groves, or in small irregular groups, enabling one to find a way nearly everywhere, along sunny colonnades and through openings that have a smooth, park-like surface... [Muir 1894:113].

As it is with other vegetational zones, the belt of mixed conifers has been subjected to a cycle of fires and revegetation, in some areas the fires having been as frequent as every two years (Biswell 1967). It is the idea of a coniferous "climax forest" where forest succession is seen as essentially linear and static that is unnatural. By reducing the mat of needles and debris, both shrubs and herbaceous plants become more abundant for browse, resulting in greater numbers of animals on summer feeding ranges and under conditions in which they are more easily hunted. At the same time excessive accumulations of fuel are precluded and destructive wildfire conditions do not develop.

Figure 3.5. Two years following a controlled burn at Redwood Mountain, Kings Canyon National Park, and the area is largely "fire proof." Large trees remain healthy, competition has been reduced, and litter from the forest floor has been cleared. Such frequently lightly burned forests are more productive of plant and animal life and, at the same time, are better protected against holocaust fires.

78

Figure 3.6 Eighteen years after the Cherry Gap Fire in Sequoia National Forest (1954) the area remains badly scarred, despite efforts at reforestation. Such destructive crown fires were probably quite rare in the aboriginal forests of California as a result of both man-made and natural fires.

Studies in wildlands management stress the importance of using fire for the maintenance of a "sub-climax forest," a pattern which very nearly approximates the patterns described for the primitive forests of California. Described by Biswell (1967) as "idealized management," a primary concern is with the development and perpetuation of productive timber. In general the pattern involves the cutting, clearing, and burning of various even-aged stands within a larger forest area, to be accompanied by individual thinning of trees in other areas:

> As I visualized this plan, it is almost identical with the way in which the forest reproduced itself and developed when nature was free to operate in its own fashion. During aboriginal times, the forest cover and light fires must have been in nearly perfect balance--nature's balance. From this research I have concluded that prescribed burning in ponderosa pine simulates the light fires that functioned in nature to develop a stable type of fire sub-climax forest. Thus in the judicious use of fire we are imitating nature [Biswell 1967:79].

This general outline of fire within the Sierra mixed coniferous forest is in many respects quite different from that of the northern Coast Range. Biswell has not proposed a similar model for the redwood and pine-fir forest of northwest California. However, in the discussion of the evidence available on the various Indians of that area, certain aspects of the more important differences between the Sierras and northern Coast Range will be considered and the Indian impact upon that area will be demonstrated. Because we do not have detailed evidence for the use of fire by any one California Indian community living in any specific habitat, the level of generalization which follows is necessarily broad. Consequently, the three ecosystems models used here are probably not specifically applicable to any particular local habitat; instead they represent more general abstractions of the relationships found throughout the mixed pine forests, chaparral, and woodland-grass regions of California.

THE EVIDENCE

Ethnographic studies of California Indians have demonstrated the great variety of plant and animal resources used for aboriginal subsistence. Whereas acorns, large game (especially deer), and fish constituted the bulk of available food, large amounts of herbaceous plants and smaller game were also taken in the annual quest for food. Among the more important of the secondary sources were the seeds of various grasses and bulbs of lilies, both plant families being highly productive in terms of fire successions.

As noted earlier, Stewart (1955a) maintains that there is evidence for almost every tribe in the western United States having used fire to modify their respective environments. Within California, Reynolds (1959:139) shows that at least 35 tribes used fire to increase the yield of desired seeds; 33 used fire to drive game; 22 groups used it to stimulate the growth of wild tobacco; while other reasons included making vegetable food available, facilitating the collection of seeds, improving visibility, protection from snakes, and "other reasons."

However, while the use of fire is noted for almost every Indian group in California--and in many instances the motivations for burning are given--most reports do not mention the conditions, timing, or even the plant cover in which the firing took place. Only Reynolds has attempted to deal with a body of ethnographic and biological data in a systematic way, applying perspectives and insights from fire ecology.

The data required to fit the pattern of woodland-grass, chaparral, and forest successions must contain at least some information on the location, character, or timing under which burning took place. Unfortunately, even the best documented information on the use of fire is all too brief and lies buried within a mass of general ethnographic detail, usually within sections describing subsistence activities or as part of a general description of the precontact environment. On the other hand, it is probably because the early studies were "ethnographic" and not specifically "problem structured" that we have any information at all. Yet, limited as the information may be, where statements show that fire was employed in a particular way, at a given time, and to a specified vegetation, we can assume a set of interrelationships involving consequences for a variety of species because of what we know from contemporary studies about ecology and the role of fire in woodland-grass, chaparral, and forest belts. Though in most cases we have little more than ethnographic snippets of information, the facts become greatly enlarged when seen in an ecosystemic context that goes far beyond the information originally provided.

Woodland-Grass Belt

Both because our knowledge of California's primitive grasslands is more meager than that concerning the woodland-grass, chaparral, or forest belts, and because the grass and woodland-grass belts are very similar, the areas of grass vegetation are not here treated as separate ecosystemic units. Instead, the limited evidence available on California's prairies is considered essentially as it relates to and helps explain the adjacent woodland-grass belt of the foothills.

References to Indian burning in the larger and smaller valleys of California are relatively few and not especially informative. For instance, Kroeber in writing on the Maidu of the Sacramento Valley notes only that "grass was constantly burned off because it grew too high" (1932:390), from which one might conclude that part of the reason for its growing too high was because it was "constantly burned off."

In Cook's (1960) compendium of reports on early Spanish expeditions to the Central Valley, one description of an area a few miles south of the Merced River gives a suggestion of the time of year that burning took place. However, it must be largely inferred from the date of the expedition leader's log entry, September 27, 1806:

There are at this spot about sixty oak trees and a few willows in the bed of the stream. The forage was extremely scanty, and that the country appeared to have been burned over by the Indians did not conceal the fact that the land is very poor. Consequently there is little pasturage [Cook 1960:218].

Quite obviously had the burning taken place prior to the summer, in the spring or late fall prior to the growth of forbs and grasses, more forage would have been available and there would have been less clear evidence of burning as late as September. On the other hand, a somewhat later time of burning is suggested for the Monterey area in a report dated October 3, 1771 in which a fire was described as having threatened the Presidio:

The heathens are want to cause these fires because they have the bad habit, *once having harvested their seeds*, and not having any other animals to look after except their stomachs, *they set fire to the brush so that new weeds may grow to produce more seeds*, also to catch the rabbits that get confused and overcome by the smoke [Clar 1959:7, emphasis mine].

The date of early October makes the burning period later, yet the comment that the burning occurs "once having harvested their seeds" is in keeping with other descriptions below. At the same time, the report refers to the burning of brush so that "new weeds may grow," the implication being that brush was being controlled and the production of herbaceous plants increased. As mentioned above, summer burning normally acts so as to reduce and control the growth of brush (the general impact being different upon sprouting and non-sprouting species) and, thus, favors grasses and forbs.

The reports are at best ambiguous and except for the reference to oaks and grassland near Merced, little or nothing is provided in terms of describing the environment. As the report noting the fire near Monterey points out, the interests of the Spaniards and Indians in maintaining grasslands were quite different, the Spaniards being primarily concerned with a year-round supply of forage for horses and cattle, Indians with the production of seed. The continued threat to Spanish interests was sufficiently important to result in the establishment of California's first fire regulation, a proclamation issued by Governor Arrillaga in 1793.

Comments from the *Culture Element Distributions* mentioned above are even less illuminating, as when Aginsky (1943:452} comments for the Chukchansi Yokuts and several Miwok groups: "Ground burned over." A still more parsimonious fact is given by Driver (1937:61) in referring to twenty-one different groups (from among Western Mono, Yokuts, and still others east of the southern San Joaquin Valley) with the statement in reference to hunting: "With fire." Such bare-bone facts offer nothing in the way of substantive information that can be used for ecological interpretation.

Jepson, writing from the point of view of the botanist and without the documentation of ethnographic sources, gives one of the few interpretive statements on the general impact of aboriginal burning in the Central Valley:

> The long inhabitation of the country by the Indians and the peculiar local distribution of the Valley Oak in the rich valleys is in some way connected. These oak orchards, of great food importance to the native tribes, indicate plainly the influence on the trees of Indian occupancy of the country. The extent and nature of the relations of Indian tribal culture and the habitat of the oaks cannot yet, if ever, be completely defined, although it is clear that the singular spacing of the trees is a result of the annual firing of the country... [Jepson 1923:39].

No further examples have been found which can suggest a relationship between plants, animals, and man within the prairie type grasslands of California. That burning took place in the Sacramento and San Joaquin valleys we know, but we do not have the appropriate kinds of evidence to show how the uses of fire might have fitted into the ecology of California's grass prairies except for the suggested pattern of summer burning.

On the other hand, there are references to burning in the smaller river valleys, mostly in those north of San Francisco, and in the woodland-grass margins separating the valley grass and the foothill chaparral belts. In writing about the valley of the Russian River, Barrett describes such a setting:

Except for willows and the like at some points along the
river, there were almost no trees in the valley itself. But
here was a great wide area of waving grass higher than a
man's head, with deer, bear and other big game everywhere... In the foothills were many great oaks loaded with
acorns, and farther up were the buckeyes, manzanitas, and
other kinds of Indian foods. It was up there that we found
the Indian potatoes (various bulbs of the lily family)
[Barrett 1952:47].

Describing the Redwood Valley in the same general area, Kniffen
notes subsequent changes and the earlier significance of fire:

The vegetation covering has experienced great changes.
Certainly the chaparral thickets of manzanita, madrone,
scrub oak, and buckbrush which now characterize many
sections of the Valley were formerly restricted to the
higher slopes and ridges of the mountains. A beautiful
park landscape, largely of oaks, was maintained by *annual
burning, done "when the straw was dry."* In this manner
the brush was held down; the larger trees were uninjured
[Kniffen 1939:373, emphasis mine].

With respect to the time of burning, there is very little evidence
to suggest what might have been either the differences or similarities for
the burning of grass prairies and that of woodland-grass areas. The above
quotation by Kniffen is generally in keeping with the Spanish references as
to the time for burning in valley grass areas, though the statement that it
took place "when the straw was dry" is imprecise to say the least.
However, within the foothill areas of woodland-grass the pattern of
summer burning is more evident and is in keeping with the recommendations suggested by Biswell (1967).

Stewart notes for the Pomo of Ukiah Valley--but without specify-
ing whether the area burned was valley or foothill grasslands--that "a
woman collected the grass seed from her pinole (generic term for grasses)
field and then set fire to the field..." (Stewart 1943: 44). Still another
reference to the Pomo, which quite clearly indicates that the area referred
to is woodland-grass, specifically notes that the control of brush is
involved:

As one old Pomo Indian told me: "*The grass was burned every year*. The fires were started and *allowed to burn in every place*. Burning was to make the weeds grow better and *to keep down the brush*" [Stewart 1951:320, emphasis mine].

The following comment on the Foothill Yokuts and Western Mono of the southern Sierras seems to apply to the woodland-grass belt, both from what is known of Western Mono village sites and the author's reference to "scattered bull pine, oak, etc.":

J.R. claims that when he was a boy the Indians throughout this region set fire to the brush *after the seeds had been gathered (about July)*. The men started the fire and the women watched to see that it did not approach the houses. When it did, it was beaten out. "It burned the hills, all over, clean through to the next one." The trees, which were green, did not ignite easily: however, "dead trees and logs were all cleaned up that way." The tree covering of this country, J.R. says, was about as it is now, scattered bull pine, oak, etc., and in about the same quantity [Gayton 1948:176, emphasis mine].

Certain points in the above quotation require additional comment. It is perhaps not clear what kind of seeds were being gathered; in fact the author's phrasing would seem to imply that it refers to seeds of brush and not those of grasses. However, "seed gathering" normally refers to the collection of grass seeds and not the berries of manzanita (probably *Arctostaphylos viscinda* or *A. manzanita*) which were collected for making unfermented cider and gathered at about the same time of year. Also, the quotation strongly suggests that the dominant cover was grass as a result of two comments involved. One, it is noted that when the fire approached the house "it was beaten out": grass fires are beaten out, brush fires are not. Two, the statement that "the trees, which were green, did not ignite easily" strongly implies a ground fire burning in grass and, unlike a brush fire, of insufficient heat and intensity to burn mature trees, either oak or pine.

'Bull-pine' is a local term normally used for digger pine and sometimes ponderosa pine. Ponderosa, or yellow pine, is normally found at elevations higher than that of the woodland-grass belt, the digger pine being the conifer normally found within this area. However, from the Kings River south to the Tule River, an area within which the Foothill Yokuts and Western Mono were found, the digger pine is not found in the woodland-grass belt. Instead, in a very limited way, the ponderosa pine occupies that particular niche in this part of the Sierras (Storer and Usinger 1963:149).

It should perhaps also be mentioned that, in contrast to the position taken here, Gayton is dubious about the practice of aboriginal burning, particularly in the southern Sierra. Her reasons have primarily to do with the difficulty of obtaining firewood, most of which derived from dead trees and logs. However, the argument here is based on well established evidence that aboriginal burnings did take place; the questions raised concern the more specific questions of "how," "when," and "where" such burning occurred. Her own doubts on this are referred to in Footnote 81, p. 379, of her monograph.

Within grassland areas only the pattern of summer burning appears with any kind of consistency in the references cited, with individual examples varying from July to October. However, we do know with certainty that burning within the grassland areas, both within the valleys and on the surrounding woodland-grass belts, took place following the harvests of seeds. From this we may quite reasonably infer some of the general effects described by Biswell (1967) in his recommendations for the management of wildlands outlined above.

The importance of this "single fact" regarding the time of burning has to be viewed in terms of the significance which fire has on particular ecosystems. No other Indian behaviors even remotely approached in magnitude of power that which the hunter-gatherer held in using fire to convert energy and, consequently, structurally and functionally alter local environments.

Thus, it must be reemphasized and stressed that fire is a physical factor, the impact of which fundamentally alters the entire living situation for plants, animals, and man. What we do not know with any certainty is the degree and intensity to which man influenced woodland-grass environments relative to the impact of natural fires in the same area. It should be remembered that the timing, or seasonality, of natural and man-made fires within the woodland-grass belt coincides, with lightning storms most frequently occurring in late summer and early fall.

However, the relative impact of Indian burning compared to that of natural conflagrations can be suggested in broad terms. The frequency of lightning fires in the Sierra Nevada is a function of slope and the amount and kind of plant cover: most lightning strikes occur at the higher elevations, and the vast majority of fires take place in a mature coniferous forest (E. Komarek 1968).

Consequently, natural fires occur much less frequently in the woodland-grass belt. At the same time we know that brush had increased in these areas following the nineteenth century, indicating that prior to this the woodland-grass areas were more open. Since World War 11 fire has been widely used to reestablish and manage these areas as rangeland. Thus, the fact that fire must now be artificially employed to regain and maintain a woodland-grass habitat would indicate that Indians also employed it artificially to maintain a similar environment. This does not necessarily mean that the Indians would have burned all of the estimated 7,500,000 acres of California's woodland-grass belt, either consistently or (from the point of view of rangeland management) well. The actual impact in any particular area would depend upon a number of factors, not the least important being population pressures and the multiple effects that this could have upon local resources.

Consequently, if it is accepted that during Indian occupancy of the woodland-grass areas the country was much more open than it was after the turn of this century, we can only conclude that the original inhabitants played a most significant role in the fire "management" of grasslands. Burcham (1959) and Clar (1959) have both argued to the contrary, their general argument being that the Indians lacked sufficient numbers and the technological skills to have had any significant impact on their environment. More recently Heady (1972) has argued essentially the same point, that Indian burning in the woodland-grass zone was only marginally significant.

The interpretation that I am making can not, however, be proven or refuted on the basis of a consideration of only one kind of vegetation or even several kinds of vegetation belts considered separately. It is the differential use of fire in a number of areas by a people possessing what is essentially a single, interrelated transhumance subsistence strategy that strengthens the overall argument. Again, it is not the individual facts nor the total number of such facts that is significant but, rather, how the information fits an ecological system of knowledge that has been gained from the actual study of fire in field situations.

A more distinct and, in some ways, a much more dramatic pattern of burning is demonstrated in the following evidence presented for the chaparral belt, with fairly clear indications shown of the effects of Indian "management" in California brushlands.

Chaparral Belt

For the chaparral belt the pattern of wildlands management proposed by Biswell is more complicated than that outlined for the woodland-grass zone since it involves the burning of opened areas ("spots") within chaparral stands, two different patterns of burning (in chamise and in mixed chaparral), and two different times of burning (fall and spring), both of which are different from the annual seasonality of natural fires (summer).   Correspondingly, the ethnographic evidence is also more complicated.

One of the points stressed by Biswell (1967) for the management of chamise chaparral concerns the opening up of grass enclosures, particularly in the south-facing slopes of chamise dominated brush.   Several ethnographic descriptions give clear evidence of a similar aboriginal pattern having existed.

Although specified only as some areas of "brush," the description for the Karok from the interior coastal mountain region of northern California is particularly interesting.   The following statement is taken directly from a woman consultant:

> (1) Our kind of people never used the plow, they never used to grub up the ground, they never used to sow anything, except tobacco. All they used to do was to *burn the brush at various places*, so that some good things will grow up.

> (2) That way the huckleberry bushes grow up good... And the hazel bushes, when they burn them off for hazel sticks, they pick them two years, then they are good... And the bear lilies also they burn off, they pick them in the next summer, in July...

> (3) And the wild rice plants also they burn, so that the wild rice will grow up good. *They burn it far up the mountains.*

> (4) And sometimes they also burn where the tan oak trees are lest it be brushy where they pick up the acorns. They do not want it to burn too hard, they fear that the oak trees might burn.

88

(5) And sometimes they used to set fire there long ago where they saw lots of acorns on the ground, in a tanbark oak grove they made roasted unshelled acorns. They do not set fire for nothing, it is for something that they set fire for.

(6) And where they are going to sow tobacco, too, they burn it, too. It is the best place if there are lots of logs there, for there are lots of ashes... Ashes are good on the ground, where fir logs have burned, where pitchy stuff has burned.

(7) *It is summer when they set fire to the brush,* at the time when everything is dry, *that is the time that is good to set fire, in the fall before it starts to rain. At different places behind peoples rancherias they set fires.*

(8) Tobacco was all that one used to sow. First they set fire up slope, in the summer time... set fire to logs. They do not go by the moon when they burn it. *They burn it any time in the summer.*

(9) Some kinds of trees are better when it is burned off; they come up better ones again. But some kinds of trees when it is burned off disappear, another never to come up again. The manzanita, another one does not come up, when it is burned off. An old tree bears better, too. And the tan oak is not good when it is burned off, the tree dies. When they are burning, they are careful lest the trees burn [Harrington 1932:63-65, emphasis mine].

This lengthy comment is the most extensive single statement available on Indian burning in California. By comparison with most other references it is a mine of information. Unfortunately, it also contains an apparent contradiction.

First of all, it must be recognized that it includes information relating to both chaparral and coniferous forests, and the informant is not always specific as to what areas or vegetation it is that she refers. The data must be treated piece by piece.

In paragraphs (1) and (7), her comments refer to what I conclude to be the pattern of "spot" burning within chaparral, when she notes that the brush was burned at "various places" (paragraph 1), and later, "different places behind peoples rancherias" (paragraph 7). The statement in paragraph (1) could also be interpreted to refer to the planting of tobacco, which is mentioned in the preceding sentence, and tobacco was grown--as detailed at more length in paragraph (6)--in coniferous forest areas, not chaparral. Whether "various places" refers to chaparral vegetation or coniferous forest, the comment is appropriate and the added clause "so that good things will grow up" would also apply in either the secondary succession of chaparral or with the planting of tobacco in burned over areas within the coniferous forest belt.

The informant's comments as to the time of burning mentioned in paragraph (7) seem to be clearly contradictory when she states, all within a single sentence, that "it is summer when they set fire, in the fall before it starts to rain." What may have been lost or gained in the translation from Karok to English can hardly be known, of course, but the qualification "before it starts to rain" would seem to emphasize the latter period, even into the late fall since rains are not common in either summer or early fall. In any case, the statement is equivocal.

In paragraph (2) the time of burning is not mentioned, but it is assumed that the area mentioned is within the coniferous forests since hazel (*Corylus cornuta*) is a plant characteristic of the higher forest areas, and though the huckleberry (genus *Vaccinium*) could be one of several species found at various altitudes, "bear lily" is undoubtedly *Xerophyllum tenax*, a member of the lily family known as "bear grass" or "Indian basket-grass," and characteristic of coniferous forest vegetation (Munz 1959:1327-28). The comments in paragraph (3) seem to be a continuation from paragraph (2) and the "wild rice," or grass, must refer to seeds from upland meadows with the additional remark "they burn it far up the mountains."

In paragraphs (1), (5), and (9) a different pattern of burning associated with acorns is mentioned. The only species referred to by the informant is the tanbark oak (*Lithocarpus densiflora*), a species in the lower and drier areas of the coastal redwood belt, effectively on the border between the coastal chaparral and the combined Douglas fir and redwood forests. In addition to the tanbark oak, the Oregon (*Quercus garryana*) and black oaks are also found in the same area. Twice she mentions the care taken so as not to harm the tanbark oak, a non-deciduous species more easily harmed by fire than most other species of oak.

Except for the contradiction already noted regarding the time of year that brush is burned, the information is reasonably consistent with the pattern of "spot" burns outlined by Biswell (1967). At the same time it provides valuable information on the coastal coniferous forests to be discussed below.

Still more data support the argument that Indians burned chaparral in the pattern suggested by Biswell. In discussing both redwood forest and chaparral areas of the northern Pomo, Stewart notes that "the brush was *burned at intervals,* making hunting much easier than at present" (Stewart 1943:34, emphasis mine). Driver, in his listing for *Culture Element Distributions: Northwest California,* notes for the Yurok that: "*Hunting tracts burned* to facilitate pursuit of game" (Driver 1939:375, emphasis mine). Unfortunately, whether such hunting tracts existed in chaparral or were simply opened areas within the forest is not known.

The Tolowa of southwest Oregon occupied areas ranging from coastal redwood forests to interior coastal mountain forests of both Douglas fir and chaparral. The following statement by Drucker would seem to apply to chaparral. "Informants maintain that *near-by hills were kept clear of brush by annual burning*; this also improved the grass, so that deer frequented *such clearings* and could be shot easily" (Drucker 1937:233, emphasis mine).

That this refers specifically to chaparral is not entirely clear. Baumhoff (1963:180) lists 60.5 square miles of the over 955 square miles of Tolowa territory as being in chaparral. However, because of Drucker's comment about the brush on nearby hills, followed by the remark about "clearings," and the fact that the chaparral margins and openings are primary game areas, there is good reason to accept this description as applying to chaparral and not coniferous forest.

In discussing the Nisenan, or Southern Maidu, of the northern Sierra Nevada, Beals notes both the timing and indicates the pattern of spot burning. "*In the fall* brush burned toward center of *large circle*" (Beals 1933:348, emphasis mine). Du Bois (1955:14) writes of collecting grasshoppers "by burning off large grass patches," in describing the Wintu, or Northern Wintun, residents in an environment of chaparral, wood-land-grass, and coniferous forest areas. Unfortunately, neither the specific vegetational cover nor the time of year in which the burning took place is mentioned.

In describing two methods of hunting deer, Holt notes for the Shasta:

The second method was used on *the more open hills of the north side of the river*, where the white oaks grew. *When the oak leaves began to fall fires were set on the hills* [Holt 1946:310, emphasis mine].

Then they came down...*in the late fall... It was at this time they had the big drive, encircling the deer with fire* [p.312, emphasis mine].

The "white oaks" referred to by Holt are apparently Oregon oaks which would grow along the upper slopes and ridges (Munz 1959:399). The "more open hills of the north side of the river" would also be the areas of concentrated chaparral cover. Whereas openings are only suggested, the time of burning is specifically noted.

Further south, Aginsky notes in the *Culture Element Distributions: Central Sierra* that the various groupings of Miwok, Yokuts, and Western Mono used fire for hunting deer "In the fall of the year," and that the burning occurred "toward center of circle" (Aginsky 1913:395).

In contrast to the pattern of growing of tobacco already mentioned for the higher altitude regions of the Karok territory, the growing of tobacco in the Sierra foothills involved a different time of burning. For the Nisenan, or Southern Maidu, Beals notes that "burn ground clear in winter, scatter seeds in ashes in spring" (Beals 1933:356). Barrett and Gifford mention a similar time of planting tobacco by the Miwok:

The principal supply of tobacco came from wild tobacco plants but seeds were, in some cases, planted. This was done about March... Fairly well watered and burned over ground was selected, preferably on a northern slope [Barrett and Gifford 1933:146].

Because of the timing involved, the above references on the Nisenan and Miwok must apply to areas below the snowline and probably within the chaparral belt. Spring burning, as has been mentioned, tends to reduce chamise chaparral and this displacement of brush would be necessary in growing tobacco in a particular area. It may represent a part of a pattern of mixed spring and fall burns.

A different pattern and timing of burning is suggested for the mixed chaparral cover found within the small valleys of the southern Cascades occupied by the Achomawi:

The valley center of this area is of limited extent and is
set off by steep walls. Winter brings heavy snows to the
high flat above the river; the valley has rain rather than
snow... The heavy precipitation results in a dense and
varied vegetation cover. With the pine and fire of the
hills are the manzanita, dogwood, yew, ash, maple, and
oak of the valley. *What would have been a dense undergrowth was prevented by annual spring burnings following
the retreating snow* [Kniffen 1928:313, emphasis mine].

The area described by Kniffen is apparently in the lower regions
of the Pit River at an elevation of approximately two to three thousand
feet. As his description above would seem to indicate, it is a transition
zone between brushlands and coniferous forests. Of particular interest
here is the pattern of spring burnings which tends to favor sprouting
species over non-sprouting species with a general reduction in brushy areas.
However, other than having noted that "what would have been a dense
undergrowth was prevented," nothing more is given.

Elsewhere Kniffen has suggested a pattern of fall burning in a hill
landscape of opened brush for the Kacha Pomo of Redwood Valley:

Extensive grassy openings characterized the slopes, particularly the one to the east of the valley. An association
of live oak, black oak, and Oregon oak graded with
altitude into a chaparral composed mainly of scrub oak,
manzanita, buckbrush, and chamise, with frequent addi-
tions of madrona, Christmas berry, and the like. Far up
on the western valley flank the tan oak became prominent,
and with it were the yellow pine and Douglas fir. The
mountain to the east [*sic,* surely west] showed fewer
species and numbers of trees, with chaparral assuming
greater prominence [Kniffen 1939:373-74, emphasis mine].

Acorn gatherings lasted until late November. That the
gathering might be easier, all the *dry weeds and brush
were annually burned after the seed gathering was over,*
so that there remained no underbrush in the valley or on
the lower hillsides [Kniffen 1939:378, emphasis mine].

In this instance both openings within the brush and the period of burning are specified. In a passage quoted earlier, Kniffen (1939:373) mentions the different pattern of summer grass burns within the valley itself, though in that reference no specific times were given for either valleys or surrounding slopes and the pattern of cleared spots within the chaparral was only suggested at best. Still, the pattern of autumn burning in the chaparral areas was clearly stated.

The most consistent statement of burning chaparral concerns the time of burning, particularly the pattern of fall burns. Without more detailed descriptions of the plant cover involved (chamise or mixed chaparral) the difference between fall and spring burning can only be assumed. As noted by Biswell (1967) above, spring burning favors sprouting species, whereas some of the best browse is provided from non-sprouting species, those dominating the south-facing slopes of the chaparral belt. The pattern of spring burning tends to remove, not improve, non-sprouting species. Fall burns tend to induce the early growth of some of the most palatable species for deer and this may have been extremely important to survival:

> The lean time of the year for most aboriginal Californians was the early spring, before plant growth began and before the start of the spring salmon run. It was then that the threat of starvation was most serious [Baumhoff 1963:161].

Fall burns, in contrast to spring burns, would induce plant growth, of direct benefit to both man and animals, during the most crucial part of the year. And, whereas some burning and the resultant brush removal was undoubtedly important, the pattern of fall burning with early induced spring growth appears to have been the most significant factor in aboriginal adaptations to the chaparral belt.

One of the brief comments from the *Culture Element Distributions: Northwest California* on the Mattole of the northern coast range is particularly interesting when noted with respect to Biswell's recommendations that a combination of fall and spring burning is probably desirable. Without any indication of the area or vegetation involved Driver notes:

> Annual burning in Sept. *One side of the river burned one year, other side following year.* Animal tracks visible in ashes [Driver 1939:375, emphasis mine].

Except for the fact that the burning of opposite slopes is mentioned, there is little here to support the idea of a pattern involving the burning of chamise and mixed chaparral, and nothing which suggests a combination of fall and spring burning.

Two general features of the Indian patterns of burning are of particular importance. First, the patterns of fall and, secondarily, spring burning involve, not simply an intensification of the natural pattern of fires, since lightning fires occur during the summer and early fall, but, rather, a pronounced departure from the seasonal distribution of natural fires. The pattern previously shown for the woodland-grass belt, as well as what will be shown for the coniferous forest regions, involves the intensification of the natural pattern; the strategy of fall and spring burnings involved a quite different kind of "management" of the chaparral areas by both the intensification and a dramatic shift from the seasonality of natural fires. This idea implies, of course, that Indians played a fundamental role in more than the maintenance of the chaparral belt; they were probably active, selective agents in the very evolution of California's chaparral.

Second, the pattern of spot burning very strongly suggests a rather carefully managed environment of plants and animals, a pattern only now being recognized and promoted as ideal wildland management. How this pattern within the chaparral may have developed and the specific details of how it was managed and maintained we do not know, of course. However, limited as the ethnographic data are, they strongly indicate that such a pattern of environmental manipulation and control did exist. Most important, by creating and/or maintaining openings within the chaparral, the Indians increased the overall resource potential of an area and created the enclosures, or "yarding areas," where these resources could be more readily exploited.

In many cases, though not all, the same Indian groups that exploited woodland-grass and chaparral also hunted animals and collected plants within portions of the coniferous forest belt, particularly the ponderosa pine regions of the Sierra Nevada and the redwood-Douglas fir areas of the northern Coast Range. Here, again, in both kinds of coniferous forests different patterns of employing fire existed and the evidence seems to clearly indicate that the impact of the Indian was significant in the maintenance and evolution of the vegetation types therein.

Coniferous Forest Belt

As it is treated here, the ethnographic data on the coniferous forest belt include examples from the two major forest regions of California: coniferous forest of the northwest Coast Range and the montane coniferous forest of the Sierra Nevadas. Of particular significance is the fact that both areas have been differently affected by fire, both as it occurs naturally and as fire was used by the respective Indians of the two areas. Within the northern Coast Range both the pine-fir and the redwood forest are considered; the subtypes most commonly referred to in the Sierra Nevada Range are the ponderosa pine and the white fir-sequoia forest.

The recommendations made by Biswell on coniferous forests apply specifically to ponderosa pine forests. Similar recommendations for the coastal conifer forest are not available. What is demonstrated, however, is the apparent impact that the Indians of the Redwood Coast had upon the environment in which they lived. As evidence shows, it was probably considerable but of quite a different character than that demonstrated for the Sierra Nevada.

Coastal Coniferous Forest. Unlike the Sierra Nevadas, the Coast Range is not an area of intense lightning activity and lightning fires are a relatively rare phenomenon. In the Sierra, by contrast, lightning fires are annually recorded at a hundred and more, whereas those for the northern Coast Range seldom amount to a score or more in any one year (E. Komarek 1968:26-33).

Yet, within the northern Coast Range, fire scars on the great redwoods are clear evidence of the recurrent impact and importance of fires within the forests of that region. In describing the role of fire within the redwood region Fritz has noted that "unless Indians set them, it is difficult to explain the fires of centuries ago..." (Fritz 1931:940).

The Indians of northwest California depended heavily upon the available resources of salmon and they seem to have been able, or perhaps required, to rely somewhat less on plants and game. As Baumhoff (1963) has pointed out, most Indians of this area clustered around the major fisheries available to them on the rivers, in areas which commonly included chaparral-covered slopes as well as upland forested areas. However, while they made relatively less use of forest and brushland products than did Indians from other regions, the hunting of game and the gathering of plant material remained important for all tribes. For the more interior groups (e.g., the Hupa, Whilkut, Yurok, and Karok) hunting and gathering were relatively more significant than for coastal populations.

Harrington's (1932) report of a Karok Indian woman, mentioned above with reference to the effects of Indian fires in chaparral, included several comments relating to burning within the pine-fir forest of the interior region. Specifically mentioned was the time of burning upland grass areas: summer. A similar comment referring to both the Karok and the Yurok collection of basket-making materials also points up the summer pattern of grass burning:

> Hazel sticks are conceded by the women of both tribes to be the best but are the most difficult to procure nowadays. New little shoots from a ground recently burned over are the ideal. This statement is followed, however, by the lament that fires cannot be set as they used to be by the old-time weavers, and by the regret that accidental burnings occur so seldom in places where they do basket makers any good. The lower Klamath people seem to be most fortunate in this matter of fires. Lucy Thompson recounts the burning over of the hazelnut flats as part of the program for their preservation... People on the lower Klamath *went to burn the brush during a dry summer or in the early fall.* The following spring the young shoots sprouted but were left uncut until their second year [O'Neale 1932:15, emphasis mine].

Hazel is regularly found at higher altitudes in a variety of plant communities throughout most of California.

A similar practice related to the collection of hazel sticks and the pattern of summer burning in the higher elevations is reported for the Hupa:

> For ribs (to make baskets) she goes to a place where a fire has burned over a hazel patch.... For the larger baskets she takes the shoots the second or third year after a fire. These shoots are from *Corylus rostrata* var. *californica*... [*C. cornuta*, Munz 1959:899; Goddard 1903:38].

For decorative work the leaves of bear-grass, *Xerophyllum tenax*... give a clear white, and the stems of the maidenhair fern, *Adiantum pedatum*... furnish a glossy black. The leaves of the *Xerophyllum tenax* are gathered in the late summer when the tips begin to show white.... The ground is frequently burned over and the spot visited on the second or third year after. This plant is very common on dry ridges at an elevation of from two to four thousand feet [Goddard 1903-04:39-40].

As noted above, hazel and bear lilies are found within the coniferous forest belt.

Earlier in the monograph the same author notes the time of burning in the higher grass areas of the pine-fir forest:

Late in summer the grass on Bald Hill and perhaps other places was fired and the fleeing deer taken in snares or killed with weapons while frantic from fear [Goddard 1903-04:22, emphasis mine].

Still another reference to the Hupa mentions the time of burning grass areas at the higher elevations of the Coast Range:

Madia elegans, Common Madia... This is not used as a food plant by the Karok because not enough of it grows here (in Karok territory), but they say the Hupa used it like "oat- flour" (grass seed). It grows in quantities on the Bald Hills near Hoopa. *The Hupa burn the hills while the plants are still green but after the seeds have matured.* After burning they take their "oat-baskets" (seed baskets) and gather the seed from the charred plants [Schenck and Gifford 1946:390, emphasis mine].

For the Shasta, as well, the burning of higher elevations was practiced, it too being associated with the use of hazel sticks:

The Shasta largely use sticks of hazel in making baskets. The sticks are gathered in great quantities, the best ones from ground denuded by fire of its natural growth of fir and hemlock... [James 1903:79].

Thus, for the Hupa, Karok, Yurok, and Shasta the pattern of burning grassy areas within the coniferous forest of the Coast Range is well authenticated as being in the late summer or early fall. At the same time, Driver (1939) notes the fact that in northwest California all but the Kato, Tolowa, and Karok practiced "burning for better seed crop..." (Driver 1939:314), though other references mention that the Karok (Harrington 1932) and the Tolowa (Gould, personal communication) also burned to improve plant cover. In addition to the general comment on the Indians of the northwest Coast Range, Driver also notes a frequency of burning for the Wiyot:

> Burning every 2 or 3 years to get better berry and seed crops, and to increase feed for deer [Driver 1939:314].

Drucker, on the other hand, notes a markedly different time of burning for the Tolowa:

> Late spring, when the old fern was quite dry and the new growth just starting, is said to have been the time for burning off the hillsides to improve the hunting grounds [Drucker 1937:232].

The difference here and that mentioned for the Hupa may perhaps be attributed to the fact that the Tolowa are coastal and the Hupa an interior group, or it may represent burning at different altitudes.

However, our lack of knowledge about the ecology of the coastal redwood belt as it would have affected and would have been affected by different patterns of burning in specific microenvironments makes such generalizations rough guesses at best. Drucker's comment may represent a specialized pattern of burning, an error in reporting, or a contradiction to the thesis presented here. However, the remaining evidence all supports the general pattern of summer, not spring, burning.

The significance of Indian fires within the redwood forest is recognized by Fritz as having been long established:

> Fires ran through redwood forests long before the white man arrived. Individual fires have been dated back by wound tissues on stumps to over 1200 years... It is certain that [the Indian] occasionally set the woods afire over many centuries but it is extremely doubtful that he did it

with any thought in mind for improving or safeguarding
the forest for the trees themselves [Fritz 1931:939, 940].

Fritz seems most concerned with the fact that the Indians didn't
think about the redwoods in terms of better logging and that some of the
best lumber was ultimately lost as a result of fire. He seems less
concerned with the fact that the forest survived intact as an ecological unit
and not just as a crop of marketable trees. His argument is essentially
that the redwoods were maintained in spite of aboriginal burnings and not
in any way because of it. That the Indians, as hunters and gatherers,
would or could have so abused the overall environment for such a long
period of time without immediate and recurrent adverse effects is difficult
to imagine. Indians burned for reasons no less "practical" than those of
modern-day loggers; however, both their cultural perspective and their
resource needs were more generalized.

Gould makes the observation that Indian fires were more than just
occasionally set:

> From my informants, and from a limited amount of
> archival material and circumstantial mention in published
> sources, I have the impression that burning of the forested
> areas near the coast was regular (at least once every year)
> and widespread. Burning occurred throughout the redwood
> belt...and was intended (or so I was told repeatedly by
> my informants) primarily to enhance the growth of low,
> forest floor vegetation for the purpose of providing
> materials for basket-making (i.e., 5-finger ferns, spruce-
> root, and hazel). Repeated burning kept the undergrowth
> from choking out these plants, and it also made movement
> through this area easier. The Indians kept out of the
> redwood belt as much as possible since it was the most
> unproductive micro-habitat in their area, and it was easy
> to get lost there - but they did enter it, nevertheless, in
> search of raw materials like redwood and fibrous materials
> for making baskets [R.A. Gould, personal communication].

However, given the population densities and the extent of forest
cover in the northern Coast Range (Baumhoff 1963), large areas of
redwood and pine-fir forest must have remained unburned for much longer
periods. Both the work of Fritz (1931) and research now in progress

indicate that burning was not widespread and that large fires occurred only rarely, perhaps no more than two or three times every 100 years, even less in the wettest portions of the coastal forest (S.D. Veirs, personal communication). On the other hand, localized burning was apparently well distributed and frequent.

The reports of early explorers clearly indicate that much of the redwood forest was choked with down timber. A vivid description is provided by the first overland party from the Sacramento Valley in its journey to the coastal region of the Wiyot Indians in Humboldt County:

> Through this forest we could not travel to exceed two miles a day. The reason of this was the immense quantity of fallen timber that lay upon the ground in every conceivable shape and direction, and in very many instances one piled upon another so that the only alternative left us was literally to cut our way through. To go around them was often as impossible as to go over them. We were obliged, therefore, constantly to keep two men ahead with axes, who, as occasion required, would chop into and slab off sufficient to construct a sort of platform by means of which the animals were driven upon the log and forced to jump off on the opposite side. There was not the least sign indicative of the presence of any of the animal creation; indeed it was almost as impenetrable for them as for us, and doubtless was never resorted to save for purposes of shelter [as quoted in Loud 1918:228-29].

However, as Loud (1918) has noted, the areas of deadfall-choked forest were only part of the coastal mountain habitat and it was not effectively the environment upon which the Indians depended for subsistence hunting and gathering. His following description of the selectively burned and maintained areas throughout the redwood and pine-fir forests is the most revealing picture we have of how the Indians of the northern Coast Range managed forests, brush, and grasslands through the use of fire:

> *Within the forests, at all elevations from sea level to the top of the ridges, there were small open patches, known locally as "prairies," producing grass, ferns, and various small plants. These prairies are too numerous to mention*

in detail.... Most of these patches if left to themselves would doubtless soon have produced forests, but *the Indians were accustomed to burn them annually* so as to gather various seeds, especially a species of sunflower, probably *Wyethia longicaulis.* The statement of Professor Jepson that "there is today more wooded area in Humboldt County than when the white man came over a half a century since," was confirmed by reports made to the writer that some of the old prairies had come up to young growth of forest. These prairies were of incalculable value to the Indians, not alone for their vegetable products, but also for the game found upon them. A sharp contrast is drawn between the animal life in the forests and on these prairies, in the accounts of the exploration party previously mentioned [above]. At one time the party fasted three days and lost two pack mules by hunger and exhaustion, before they came to a prairie stocked with game and grass. From there they went on for ten days without "the sight of any living thing that could be made available or useful for food." Then ascending a rocky eminence they reached another prairie where they saw on one side "little knots of deer, on another and nearer...a large herd of elk, and still in another direction both." Before reaching any of this game they met and shot five grizzly bears.

One of the men in the above mentioned party and several of the mules starved to death before the trip ended, but *the Indians were better acquainted with the location of these oases,* as it were, in the midst of desolation, *and they maintained regular trails between them* [Loud 1918: 230-31, emphasis mine].

The author then goes on to list some of the trails, with thirteen in all described and mapped. One need only imagine the problem, even after discovering the trails from one "prairie" to another, of mounted men and pack horses negotiating the foot-trails and animal tracks used by Indian hunters.

In an area in which resources in game were relatively limited--Baumhoff (963:176) rates the area as either "secondary" or "tertiary game land"--the Indians effectively provided for the plant growth and yarding areas which would attract deer and other game. Plants and game seem to have been no less managed than they are now in the contemporary programs of wildland management.

Fritz (1931) makes a passing reference to grass prairies and trail networks within the redwood and pine-fir forests when he notes:

> The stories of old residents of the redwood region concerning the acts of the Indians are conflicting. Some believe that the Indians set the woods afire every season that there was a sufficient accumulation of litter to support a fire - every four or five years - and that the course of an Indian travelling through the woods could be charted from a distance *by the succession of smokes as he set fires*. Others say that the Indian was afraid of fire and set it only to drive game or to burn out his enemies, or that his *prairie fires* escaped into the woods [Fritz 1931:939, emphasis mine].

Though much further south, the overall environment of the area occupied by the Coast, or Southwestern, Pomo living just north of the Russian River is much more in keeping with the redwood and pine-fir forests than the predominantly woodland-grass and chaparral vegetation regions inhabited by the inland Pomo. Drucker describes the area and one of the uses of fire for the Coast Pomo in the following way:

> In the deep valleys along the perennial streams, on the well-protected north slopes, tree growth is heavy. On the higher slopes with southerly exposures *there are numerous and good-sized natural openings where the vegetation cover is grass and shrubs rather than trees.... The treeless openings were formerly covered with wild oats and clover*, now rapidly disappearing in the normal plant succession of an overgrazed country.... [Drucker 1939: 383, emphasis mine].

> *To assure the permanency of the natural openings* and to maintain the quality of the oat crop, *the dry straw was burned off every few years, generally after the first good rain of fall* [Drucker 1939: 388, emphasis mine].

A more specific account of the northern region has been provided to me by Gould as a result of his studies in ethnographic archaeology in northern California and southern Oregon:

> The term, prairies, for the clearings in the redwood forest areas of N. California is really inappropriate, since most of these clearings are very small (the largest one I ever saw was only about 1/4-mile wide and about 3/4-mile long, and most are much smaller than that). I really don't know what caused these clearings, but they appear to be entirely natural in origin. The Indians (here I include Tolowa, Tututni, Yurok, Karok, and Wiyot) did burn these areas over fairly often, and I think it would be fair to suggest that this burning helped to maintain these areas by inhibiting the growth of brush and trees. These "prairies" --in all cases I have seen--did *not* contain any village or habitation sites, since they lie within a zone of extremely poor natural resources for that region. However, these clearings are frequented by elk and deer, which the Indians there hunted whenever they could [R.A. Gould, personal communication 1972].

This pattern of opened areas within the coastal mountains is similar in structure to what has already been discussed for grass openings within chaparral areas and, though environmentally quite distinct, they seem to have served the same purpose: increases in and concentrations of plant and animal resources.

The only other example of burning reported for Indians of the northern Coast Range concerns the use of fire within oak groves by the Yurok, the example being in keeping with that already described for the Karok by Harrington's woman informant mentioned above:

> Mamie Offield says the trees (tanbark oaks) are better if they are scorched by fire each year. This kills disease and pests. Fire also leaves the ground underneath the trees bare and clean and it is easier to pick up the acorns [Schenck and Gifford 1952:282].

However, the most consistent pattern to emerge is that of summer burns in the higher elevation grasslands of the coastal coniferous forest, particularly in the inland areas away from the heaviest concentrations of redwoods. Almost as consistent and certainly the most dramatic pattern to appear is that of opened grass "prairies," apparently within all elevations of the redwood and pine-fir subtypes in the northern Coast Range. What these two patterns strongly indicate is the fact that the Indians of this region had made a use of fire which involved a technologically sophisticated control of natural resources in a region in which the particular resources of forest plants and animals which they sought were not in great abundance.

The degree to which the Indians of this area affected the overall environment is certainly debatable. As already noted, Fritz (1931) has claimed that large areas within the redwood forest have gone unburned for long periods of time and current studies by the National Park Service seem to substantiate the fact that large fires were infrequent. Apparently burns were restricted to grass "prairies" within the forest and to grass-lined ridges, such as Bald Hill near Hoopa (S.D. Veirs, personal communication). Questions regarding the frequency and distribution of fires are particularly intriguing given the fact that natural fires have played such a relatively unimportant role in the evolution of plants and animals in this area.

Similar questions have been raised and at least some of the questions concerning the frequency of fires have been answered regarding the impact of Indians in the coniferous forests of the Sierra Nevadas. The effects of Indian burning, specifically in the ponderosa and the white fir-redwood forest subtypes, were much less dramatic than those just mentioned for the Coast Range. However, as research in the ecology of fire in the Sierras has recently shown, the elimination of aboriginal burning may have had much greater ecological significance.

Montane Coniferous Forest. In the *Culture Element Distributions* surveys for the southern Cascades and the length of the Sierra Nevadas (Aginsky 1943; Driver 1937; Gifford and Klimek 1939; Voegelin 1942), all of the major tribal groups, as well as the vast majority of local settlement groups, are listed as having used fire, the two reasons most commonly given being for hunting animals and for improving wild seed crops. As already noted, fire has been a significant but variable factor in the natural history and evolution of all three Sierra vegetation belts.

Within the belt of Sierra pines and firs, lightning fires have played a much greater role than in any of the plant communities previously discussed. It is in the Sierra coniferous belt that we might expect the least concrete evidence of aboriginal burning since, of course, natural fires predate man there as an important selective factor. Also, with evidence showing a close correlation between the seasons of natural and prehistoric man-made fires, we should not expect to find the more distinct departures from the natural fire pattern, such as those already illustrated for the northern redwood forest or the chaparral.

Furthermore, from the ethnographic and archaeological evidence we know that the coniferous forest region was only seasonally exploited and, equally significant, that it generally supported fewer people and contained less resources than did the chaparral or woodland-grass belt (Baumhoff 1963). Finally, it will be seen that the ethnographic data are even more parsimonious with information than they have been for the areas already mentioned.

All of this would seem to suggest that the impact of aboriginal burnings in the montane coniferous forest was in fact relatively small. Yet, just when the ethnographic record falls short, analysis from field studies in fire ecology adds an important dimension to our documentation of Indian burning with a kind of information not available on other areas of California. What we learn from these sources is that the impact of aboriginal burning within the coniferous forest belt of the Sierras was very significant.

The occasional ethnographic reference to the time of burning indicates, just as the pattern of transhumant exploitation dictates, that Indian burning occurred in the coniferous forests during the late summer or early fall. In discussing the Nisenan, or Southern Maidu, in the foothills and mountains east of Marysville and Sacramento, Beals notes the overall effect that this had on the forest cover:

> The land was apparently burned over with considerable regularity, primarily for the purpose of driving game. As a result there were few young trees and all informants were agreed that in the area of permanent settlement, even so far up in the mountains as Placerville, the timber stand was much lighter than at present.... The Indians insist that before the practice of burning was stopped by the whites, it was often a mile or more between trees on the ridges, although the canyons and damp spots held thickets of timber [Beals 1933:363].

As an indication that burning took place within the forest whenever sufficient litter accumulated to carry a fire, the same author comments in note form, "In mountains large area sometimes covered with about 3 in. pine needles in which insects hid, which then fired..." (Beals 1933:347). In an earlier report on the Nisenan, Faye describes the use of fire to surround deer and then concludes that "this practice obtained in summer" (Faye 1923:40). In a manner not uncharacteristic of ethnographic reports, he does not mention whether an undercover of brush, pine needles, or grass was involved.

In the next paragraph, however, Faye makes a most interesting statement, which suggests something of the knowledge the Nisenan possessed with respect to the pattern of fire successions:

> It was a general practice of these Indians to clear the forests of undergrowth by setting fire to it. They seem to have been able to keep the fire under control. *They claim that it prepared the ground to receive seeds. Seeds, however, were never sown by man's hand* [Faye 1923:40, emphasis mine].

This may well reflect the Indian's recognition that many non- sprouting species of brush require fire to germinate seeds and initiate new plant growth.

Without referring to the time of year involved, Kroeber gives a generalized description of the pattern and frequency of burning by the Maidu in the drainage of the Feather and American rivers:

> Like most of the Californians who inhabited forested tracts, *the Maidu frequently burned over the country often annually.* It appears that forest fires have been far more destructive since American occupancy, owing to the accumulated underbrush igniting the large trees. Of course the Indian was not attempting to protect the stand of large timber: he merely preferred an open country. This is shown by the fact he also burned over unforested tracts [Kroeber 1953:396, emphasis mine].

To Kroeber's comment it should be noted that, given the significance of fire successions, much more than simply having an "open country" was involved, whatever the specific reasons for aboriginal burning may have been.

The setting of fires in the ponderosa pine forest in the Yosemite region is also noted by Barrett and Gifford:

> Small fires, built by several men, were set in the hills around a meadow into which deer went. These men kept building new fires. The hunters were concealed behind the trees and brush. As the deer descended to the meadow, they approached the fire from curiosity. Then the concealed hunters shot them with the bow and arrows. As there was no noise, the deer took no alarm. They were also shot from ambush, as they endeavored to escape along the trails from small fires set for the purpose of driving them out. Deer were particularly sought where the deerbrush (*Ceanothus integerrimus*)...grew, and upon which they fed [Barrett and Gifford 1933:179].

Working from a different perspective than I have employed here, Reynolds (1959) shows that the twentieth century practices of fire exclusion have resulted in the disruption of the dynamic balance of plant and animal communities in and about the area of Yosemite National Park. Through the use of historical source materials, ethnographic and archaeological reports, and the study of historical photographs--illustrating the steady change from the dominance of more fire adapted species to the spread and dominance of less fire adapted species--Reynolds, a geographer and naturalist, is able to demonstrate the pronounced changes that have occurred in flora and fauna of the central Sierra since the turn of the century.

His conclusions are that "lightning was not the most significant or effective ignition agent operating in the central Sierra Nevada during aboriginal times" and that the "necessary additional frequency was furnished by the action of aboriginal cultural fires" Reynolds (1959:215).

In a similar study on Sequoia National Park, Vankat (1967) has attempted to show how the vegetation of that area has changed since the first incursions of white men into that portion of the Sierras. The conclusions of both Vankat and Reynolds are similar with both arguing that the disappearance of the Indians resulted in pronounced changes in flora and fauna, particularly in the ponderosa pine and white fir-redwood subtypes of vegetation.

Vankat claims that in Sequoia Park the populations of Western Mono were less than those reported for the Miwok in Yosemite, and that consequently the Western Mono made less of an overall impact upon their environment. However, the problems in equating the demographic data from these two areas (Baumhoff 1963:213-221) make any definitive statement comparing the two highly tenuous. In any event, Vankat provides fairly conclusive evidence to show that the consequences of Indian burning in the lower portions of the coniferous forest, specifically the ponderosa pine and white fir subtypes, were of great import for maintaining a balanced forest ecosystem.

From the pattern of vegetational change studies, Vankat is able to show that there were two developments that were essentially functions of particular historical events in the nineteenth century. With information gained from dating the age of various trees, he notes two different times during the last century in which white firs exhibited rather sudden increases in numbers relative to other species:

> The 1860 increase (which is less clear than the later increase) corresponds with the demise of the Indians in the park region, so it is probably due to the elimination of Indian cultural burning. The 1900 increase corresponds with the initiation of a fire control program in the park, so it is due to the reduction in frequency of fires [Vankat 1967:73].

Whereas various local studies (Vankat 1967:75) have indicated the general pattern of change to less fire resistant species of trees within the park, Vankat's research is the first to demonstrate the particular times in which the increase in the density and dominance of white fir began. Most significant, he has shown that there are two different periods with which he is able to correlate changes both in the patterns of land use and in the ignition of fires.

It is the first date, corresponding to the Western Mono's final abandonment of their hunting and gathering grounds within the park, which is of particular interest here. The years after 1860 and before 1900 represented a new period in which man-made fires were set by sheepmen, miners, hunters, and the like. It also involved a major change in the pattern of land use with the introduction of grazing by sheep and cattle. Thus, after 1860 both the pattern of land use and the way in which fire was employed to facilitate the pattern of land use were drastically altered.

Finally, it must be noted that the changes represented in 1900 involved the elimination of fires, particularly those set by sheepmen, and grazing was greatly reduced. It must also be emphasized that the burning practices of sheepmen and loggers represented quite different purposes from those of the Indians and they were specialized to alter the environment essentially for a single purpose. The different character of Indian and white burning was summed up by John Muir:

> Incredible numbers of sheep are driven to the mountain pastures every summer, and their course is ever marked by desolation. Every wild botanic garden is trodden down, the shrubs are stripped of leaves as if devoured by locusts, and the woods are burned. Running fires are set everywhere, with a view to clearing the ground of prostrate trunks, to facilitate the movements of the flocks, and improve the pastures. The entire forest belt is thus swept and devastated from one extremity of the range to the other... Indians burn off the underbrush in certain localities to facilitate deer hunting. Mountaineers carelessly allow their campfires to run, so do lumbermen, but the fires of the sheepmen or *Muttoneers*, form more than ninety percent of all destructive fires that range the Sierra forests [Muir 1894:199].

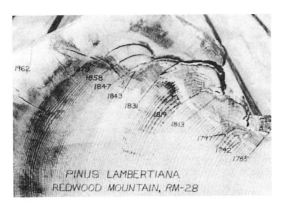

Figure 3.7. Dated fire scars on a sugar pine offer the best evidence of the frequency of aboriginal fires in the Sierra Nevadas. Prior to about 1900, fires in the Redwood Mountain area of Kings Canyon National Park averaged one in every nine years; the measured frequency of lightning fires since that time has been one in twenty-five to one in fifty.

Still more evidence has been recently made available which em-
phasizes the point made by Reynolds, and restated by Vankat, that
lightning fires were not of sufficient frequency or importance to account
for the number of fires that occurred in the Sierras during aboriginal times.
This evidence comes from an examination made of cross-sections from
aged tree stumps and downed logs in the Redwood Mountain area of
Kings Canyon National Park. By dating the fire scars from cross-sections
of trees of various ages it has been shown that prior to 1900 fires occurred
on the average of every three to fifteen years, and averaged about nine
years (Kilgore 1972:36). This is in keeping with estimates made elsewhere
which Biswell (1968) has summed up for the Sierras with frequencies as
variable as every one and two years to as infrequent as every twenty-one
years. What the new information on Redwood Mountain adds is a direct
comparison for a single area of primitive forest fires with the frequency of
lightning fires in the period since fire suppression activities began.

Since 1910 National Park Service records on lightning fires in the
Redwood Mountain area indicate that the frequency of lightning fires in
some areas is roughly one fire every 25 to 50 years to other areas in
which no lightning fires have occurred (D. Taylor, personal communication). This work very precisely demonstrates the relatively high frequency
with which Indians burned within the white fir-sequoia forest subtypes as
against the known frequency of fires ignited only by lightning.

Thus, we know that all or at least large parts of the Sierra Nevada
forests were burned on a recurrent basis considerably in excess of the
frequency with which natural fires occurred. From the ethnographic and
archaeological record we have the evidence to show that the time of
burning was in the late summer or early fall, a period which coincides
with the seasonality of natural fires. The very limited ethnographic data
suggest that burning occurred wherever sufficient ground cover and litter
existed to carry a fire through one stand to another. The most important
features of any "controls" must have been those exerted by the very
regularity and frequency with which fires were set. Joaquin Miller noted,
over one hundred years ago, just such a control of literally fighting-fire-
with-fire by the Indians of Yosemite when he stated:

> In the Spring...the old squaws began to look about for the
> little dry spots of headland and sunny valley, and as fast
> as dry spots appeared, they would be burned. In this way
> the fire was always the servant, never the master.... By
> this means, the Indians always kept their forests open,

pure and fruitful, and conflagrations were unknown [as quoted in Biswell 1968:46].

It is undoubtedly the case that when populations declined and the Indians finally disappeared that fuel conditions rapidly increased and the increases and invasions of less fire tolerant species occurred, this correlating with Vankat's estimated date of 1860. The new patterns of land use by the first whites into the area, plus the different employment of fire associated with that land use, undoubtedly resulted in a more specialized application of fire with different consequences for local habitats. The subsequent buildup of fuels suspended the controls which frequent Indian fires had built into the secondary succession pattern of the montane coniferous forest.

There is no ethnographic or historical information on the various other, higher elevation subtypes within the Sierra coniferous forest (red fir, lodgepole pine, etc.) and except for the comment that fires in the primitive forests seem to have occurred more frequently than now (Vankat 1967:77, 86), there is nothing in the written record to suggest specifically what the role of Indian burning may have been. Since the plant and animal resources are reduced as altitude increases and growing seasons shorten, we may expect that the Indian affected those environments to lesser degrees.

DISCUSSION

My own interest in the subject of aboriginal burning in California began as a consequence of having been involved in fire suppression work as a seasonal employee of the National Park Service extending over a period of twelve years. The obvious contradiction between what the State and Federal agencies were doing in fighting forest fires and what the Indian had once done in igniting them goaded me into examining the ethnographic record in an attempt to discover what it was that seemed to have made burning "work" for the Indian and not result in the desolation we expect of forest fires.

Over a period of several years the various references to Indian burning were collected and some sort of organizing principle sought to enable me to enlarge upon these facts. At first the evidence appeared sufficient for developing several hypotheses since, as Stewart (1955) has

112

maintained, there is information on almost every tribe in the West having deliberately set fires.

Unfortunately, I found little information and--except for Reynolds' (1959) and Vankat's (1967) studies--even less research which went beyond the notation that Indians had set fires in the primitive grass, brush and forestlands of California.

It was not until I examined the various works of fire ecologists that the possibility occurred to me of considering ethnographic reports as they might be projected onto a model of ecosystemic relations. It became apparent that if I wished to enlarge upon the ethnographic data at my disposal, given the fact that there was virtually no possibility of adding to that data by either interviews or observations, then I must look to other disciplines for a new system of relationships and meanings.

Biswell's (1967) recommendations on the use of fire in the management of California wildlands was the most suggestive and has provided the broad systemic outlines against which the references to Indian burnings have been examined. However, because the model proposed by Biswell contains certain requirements about the timing of burning, the vegetational cover, frequency, etc., most of the ethnographic references to aboriginal burnings were of little use since often the information stated only that fires were used.

Yet, even given the dearth of references which could be fitted to Biswell's proposals, there are sufficient data to show the broad outlines of how California Indians used fire to manipulate and exploit a variety of different environmental systems. Thus, it was possible to take isolated facts and give them new contextual meanings within a multivariate system of relationships because of what is now known--and in a sense has been rediscovered--about the human ecology of California's primitive wildlands.

I would further contend that the arguments made for any one vegetational belt or subtype are strengthened by the arguments made for other zones. Whereas we conceptually isolate and study the various zones of vegetation, there is a pronounced pattern of interdependence which links the different ecosystemic units because of the relatively great interchange of biota which occurs in mountain zones in contrast to other regions (Odum 1971: 402). This aspect of zonation and interchange has two features relating to the ecology of man that are important to consider here.

First of all, the single most important organism in the interchange which occurred between different belts, or zones, was of course the Indian. In almost every case aboriginal subsistence involved hunting and gathering in two or more vegetational belts. The ecological niche of the Indian was not restricted to his role in a particular community or ecosystem; his ecological niche was the totality of his relationships in two or more ecosystems. Like other migratory species, he was involved in the high degree of interchange characteristic of mountain zones. However, to a degree far greater than that of other species, he ranged throughout the whole variety of some fourteen major vegetation types which characterize the flora of California. The most fundamental component of this human interchange between zones was the Indian's employment of fire to intensify and even seasonally change the patterns of secondary fire succession.

Secondly, as a consequence of living in a variety of zones, Indians were able to exploit the ecotones, the transitions or "edges," between forest and brush, between brush and woodland, between woodland and grass. As we know, it is a general principle of ecology that it is the ecotone areas in which the density and variety of life are the greatest. Like men every-where--the pioneer who clears the forest or the farmer who plants trees on the prairies--the Indian did not simply take the habitat as he found it. Even though the overall environment already provided two and often more natural ecotones, the Indian was able to create a variety of local ecotones within vegetational zones. At the same time, even where natural ecotones already existed--e.g., between woodland-grass and chaparral zones--aboriginal burning pushed back the upper zones of brush or trees to favor a more productive cover of mixed trees, grass and shrubs.

In both the mature chaparral and coastal coniferous forest, California Indians maintained edges within a more generalized cover of brush or trees to both increase and concentrate resources of plants and game. However, within both the woodland-grass and the montane coniferous forests local ecotones were less distinctive in form, the natural vegetation already a mosaic of trees, brush, and grasses. Yet, in both zones a complex interface was maintained and regularly recreated between grasses, forbs, shrubs, and trees.

While the natural ecotones were undoubtedly of great significance, it was undoubtedly the case that the man-made edges both between and within vegetational zones were of much greater significance to Indian patterns of subsistence. As Odum has noted, "it seems likely that ecotones assume greater importance where man has greatly modified natural communities" (1971:159).

The term "edge species" is sometimes used to describe those organisms which occur primarily in ecotones. In the primitive wildlands of California the Indian was certainly the "superior edge species." Unlike other edge species he did not simply live at the wilderness edge, he built it.

Understanding the indigenous practices of maintaining ecotones may help answer the questions raised in the arguments which assert that Indians burned only small tracts of land, or those that maintain that the overall impact of Indian burning was negligible (e.g., Burcham 1959; Clar 1959; Heady 1972). As mentioned above, one of the most important aspects of aboriginal burning was that openings result in the local concentration and increase of resources.

Large scale burning would have reduced the complex of ecotones and, consequently, the total amount of plant and animal production. The natural pattern of fires, because of their relative infrequency and the greater intervening buildup of fuels, would select for much larger and older stands of fire climax succession. The very "spottiness" and much higher frequency of very localized Indian burning seem to have effected a much more complex overall ecosystemic pattern than would have been the case with only natural fires.

It is undoubtedly the case that Indians did not set all or even most of California to the torch in any given set of years. Despite a precontact population that is estimated to be among the highest in North America, they probably lacked sufficient numbers to burn all or even most of the vegetation on any regular and consistent basis, even had they so wanted. And in the end, the reduction in Indian populations due to disease and later genocide must have greatly restricted the areas burned annually until, by the mid-nineteenth century, Indian burning was no longer a significant factor in maintaining the primitive wildlands of California.

The overall picture presented here for the variety of vegetational belts and the impact of aboriginal burning has important implications for settlement and population densities. Baumhoff (1963) has presented the most comprehensive study of population distributions in California. In his work he notes the relatively heavy distribution of population in the areas of woodland-grass and chaparral cover (see Fig. 3.8). The highest population concentration is noted for the basins of the Sacramento and San Joaquin rivers and is accounted for in large part by the significance of fisheries being added to resources of acorns and game. Away from the main rivers of the Great Valley densities were markedly lower than either the river basin or the surrounding foothill regions. Also, he points up the different population densities for the redwood forest region, lower than that of the foothill areas, (his "Lower Klamath fish adaptation" zone). A

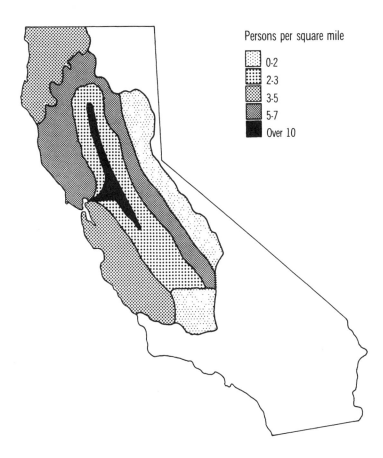

Figure 3.8. Indian population densities of central and northern California (redrawn from Baumhoff 1963).

reexamination of his data, particularly for the northern Coast Range and the Sierra Nevada, would be particularly interesting when considered in terms of the fire patterns and increased resource potentials in each of the areas.

Lastly, I have suggested that the broad strategy used in the analysis here may have applications to other problems in prehistory and ethnohistory. An ever increasing body of data is available on ecological studies on natural ecosystems. Of particular significance to anthropologists are the ongoing studies of the International Biological Program (IBP). From what ecologists say about the structure and operation of particular environments, the anthropologists may be able to pose appropriate questions as to the role which men, using certain technological strategies, played in a given system of environmental relationships during historic and prehistoric periods.

Rather than simply working from the archaeological or ethnographic evidence to construct a system of relationships, the researcher would apply the data to a system of relationships that have already been constructed from various ecological field studies. The proof of a particular hypothesis would then be demonstrated by the way in which it could be seen to fit a set of established ecosystemic relations. Thus, the single archaeological or ethnographic fact is both compounded and tested when examined and projected against a multivariate system of analysis from studies in ecology.

VEGETATION BURNING
BY THE CHUMASH[1]

Jan Timbrook, John R. Johnson, and David D. Earle

The question of whether aboriginal hunting-gathering peoples of California modified their environments by periodic burning of vegetation has been widely discussed, both by anthropologists and by geographers. Several tribes used fire in hunting, with such techniques as rabbit drives; to improve forage for game animals which would then be hunted; and to increase the availability of certain plants for direct use by humans (Lewis 1973). Bean and Lawton (1973:xxxvi) proposed that burning was part of a sophisticated technological inventory of energy extraction processes which supported the high population density and cultural complexity of aboriginal California. In their view, true agriculture was not adopted by most peoples in the state because it would have been not only unnecessary but a step backward in efficiency.

Plant geographers have suggested that the evolution and distribution of certain vegetation types in southern California have been greatly influenced by human activities, among which European introduction of plant species and grazing animals are only the most recent. It is thought by some that frequent burning by prehistoric Californians sustained a park-like landscape with grass and scattered oak trees, and that chaparral has invaded these areas since burning was suppressed after Spanish colonization in the 19th century (Aschmann 1959, 1976:41).

Actual documentation of burning of vegetation by Indians has been confined primarily to northern California (Lewis 1973; Sampson 1944), and complaints have been voiced regarding the lack of information available about southern California Mission groups or about pre-European practices (Bean and Lawton 1973:xxi-xxii; O'Connell 1974:118). Aschmann (1959) had assumed from plant distributions that these coastal groups did burn the local vegetation, but he could produce no documentation from early

[1]This paper originally appeared in the **Journal of California and Great Basin Anthropology**, Vol. 4, No. 2, pp. 163-186, 1982. It is reprinted here by permission of Malki Museum Press. Acknowledgements have been deleted.

Spanish historical sources. Jonathan Sauer (1977:383) also stated that there was no historical evidence of vegetation burning by the Chumash.

Historical accounts describing burning in early times by Indians on the southern California coast are indeed extant, although they are not widely known. They suggest that purposeful burning of some types of native vegetation was a regular occurrence among the Chumash Indians of the Santa Barbara Channel region during the late 18th century, that the practice was suppressed in the Mission Period, and that it had long faded from cultural memory by the late 19th and early 20th centuries when ethnographic data were collected from Chumash survivors.

The early accounts of vegetation modification by the Chumash are significant because they provide information useful in reconstructing the pre-Hispanic landscape. This knowledge is valuable to foresters, botanists, geographers, and ecologists, as well as to anthropologists and archaeologists.

The Chumash are of particular interest because of their high population density, sedentary existence, and complexity of socio-political organization which was far closer to the chiefdom level than to the band (Anderson 1978:6). As a relatively complex nonagricultural group, the Chumash example can serve as a way of evaluating Bean and Lawton's hypotheses about environmental manipulation and cultural complexity in aboriginal California (1973:xxxv-xxxvii). It may also provide important comparative evidence for discussions of similar human behavior in different times and places on a worldwide basis.

It is therefore the purpose of this paper to call attention to the ethnohistoric evidence which shows that the Chumash did deliberately use fire in ways which may have had pronounced long-term environmental effects, and to demonstrate that encouragement of growth of certain plant resources was the principal reason for the practice of burning.

THE COASTAL CHUMASH ENVIRONMENT

The ethnohistoric accounts are concerned with the coastal portion of Chumash territory, roughly from the mouth of the Santa Clara River in Ventura County on the south, north to the Santa Maria River at the border between Santa Barbara and San Luis Obispo counties. Much of this area is a low, flat plain a mile or so in width, lying between the waters of the Santa Barbara Channel and the steep slopes of the Santa Ynez Mountains, which rise to an elevation of over 4000 feet within about five miles of the coast. To the west, the landscape trends more toward gently rolling hills dissected by small seasonal watercourses. Turning northward from Point Conception, the terrain again flattens out into broad plains with extensive sand dunes near the shore.

The climate of this area is Mediterranean, with warm dry summers and mild rainy winters. Precipitation averages about 12 to 17 inches along the coast, more at the higher elevations. Marine air moderates temperatures in this coastal area, so that prolonged freezing is rare. Winter temperatures of $40°$ to $50°$ F. are typical. Early summer is characterized by fog; the hottest months are August and September, when temperatures are commonly 75 to $90°$ F. (Smith 1976:3-4).

The vegetation in this area today has been much altered by recent human activities (Smith 1976:15; Heady 1977:499). Outside settled areas, the coastal plain is covered with a mixture of introduced grass species, particularly *Avena*, *Bromus*, and *Hordeum*, and broadleaved introduced weeds such as filaree (*Erodium* spp.), fennel (*Foeniculum vulgare*), mustard (*Brassica* spp.) and milk thistle (*Silybum marianum*). In spots less heavily grazed by cattle, coastal sage scrub vegetation--particularly coyote brush (*Baccharis pilularis*), sages (*Salvia* spp.) and California sagebrush (*Artemisia californica*)--now extends all the way to the coast and is thickest on hillsides (Mooney 1977:476). This low, soft shrub community intergrades on its upper edges with chaparral, a dense, stiff shrub cover more typical of steeper slopes and thin, rocky soils (Hanes 1977:419). Liveoaks (*Quercus agrifolia*) are now found in rocky soils on north-facing slopes and in canyons, but formerly were more widespread in grassland-savanna or in woodland relatively free of understory (Griffin 1977:407-409). Most of these oaks were cut for feed, firewood, and building material after European and American settlement in the 19th century (Clifton Smith, personal communication 1983). Barring human interference, the distribution of these broad vegetation types is most influenced by elevation and topography, which affect temperature and precipitation, and by the soil type and character of the geological formation on which the plants grow (Smith 1976:21-25; Dibblee 1976; Minnich 1983:1289; Griffin 1977:409).

The chaparral has been extensively studied by plant ecologists because of its intimate relationship with the wildfires which occur frequently during the dry months of the year. It is often said that the chaparral community evolved with fire and has adapted to naturally occurring fires in several ways, such as sprouting from basal burls and producing seeds which germinate best after fire (Hanes 1977:432-433). The interval between fires in any one area depends on the amount and moisture content of fuel, source of ignition, and weather conditions. Two or three decades are required to build up enough fuel for large, intense chaparral fires, but smaller ones can occur more often (Minnich 1983: 1292).

In general, abundant herbaceous cover permits burning of grassland and coastal sage scrub more often than is possible in chaparral (Minnich 1983:1292). However, the effects and frequency of grass fires today are not necessarily comparable with those in aboriginal times before introduced weeds and heavy grazing destroyed the native grasslands (Stewart 1956: 318). Lightning strikes, which occur most often during late summer drought, are the major cause of natural fires but tend to be confined to the higher elevations (Burcham 1974:104). Fires do not usually burn down slope (Daubenmire 1968:214), although they have been observed to do so in southern California when fanned by Santa Ana winds (Vogl 1968:81; J. Sauer, personal communication 1983). Since just the right combination of wind, temperature, humidity, fuel, topography, fire ignition and location must coincide, it seems likely that extensive fires in grasslands along these low plains near the coast would seldom occur under natural conditions-- that is, if no humans were present.

Humans *were* present, however, and had been in the area for at least 9000 years before Europeans arrived. At the time of first intensive Spanish contact in the 1770s, an estimated 15,000 Chumash people inhabited the Santa Barbara Channel coastline and offshore islands. This population was largely sedentary, and settlements of 500 to 1000 people were not unusual on the coastal plain (Brown 1967). The area north of Point Conception and the interior valleys were somewhat less thickly settled, but the population was still sizeable there as well. Chumash culture has been well described by several authors and need not be reiterated here (see Anderson 1978). Suffice it to say that the Santa Barbara Channel coast is regarded as a culture climax area and that a very large, sedentary population with complex social, political, economic, and religious organization and a high development of material culture and the arts was supported by a hunting, gathering, and fishing subsistence base (Blackburn 1975; Hudson et al. 1977, 1978; Hudson and Underhay 1978; Hudson and Blackburn 1982).

With such a large population, it would be surprising indeed if human-caused fires did not occur in grasslands along the coast (Heady 1977:499). Village campfires must have escaped and burned out of control with some frequency. The following ethnohistoric accounts will show that grassland fires were not always accidental and sporadic, however, but deliberately and regularly initiated by humans.

CRESPI'S ACCOUNT

Fr. Juan Crespí accompanied the Portolá expedition in 1769-1770 and made detailed observations of the native culture and natural environment of the Santa Barbara Channel mainland coast (Brown 1965, 1967). The most familiar published translation of Crespí's diary, in Palou's *Historical Memoirs of New California* (Bolton 1926), is actually a composite version of the Portolá expedition. It is only partly drawn from Crespí's original diary, but with much incorporated from the more succinct journal kept by the expedition's engineer, Miguel Costansó. There are two original holograph texts of Crespí's journals which have been translated by Alan K. Brown (n.d.) but have not yet been published. Excerpts from the translation of one of these texts which deals with vegetation burning by the Chumash are reproduced here with Dr. Brown's permission, with emphases added by the present authors.

August 20, 1769. After setting out from camp on what later became known as Arroyo Burro Creek, near Santa Barbara, Crespí wrote:

We went over land that was all of it level, dark and friable, well covered with fine grasses, and *very large clumps of very tall, broad grass, burnt in some spots and not in others*; the unburned grass was so tall that it topped us on horseback by a yard.[2] All about are large tablelands with big tall live-oaks (I have never seen larger), and many sycamores as well. We have come across rose-patches in such great amounts that the plains here were full of them in many spots.

After camping the next night in the populous Goleta area, where between five and seven Chumash communities were found, the expedition set out westward toward Point Conception.

---

[2]"...clumps of very tall, broad grass...so tall that it topped us on horseback by a yard" surely refers to giant wild rye, Elymus condensatus. The grasses described as "very fine" are unidentified, but could be Stipa pulchra. Saltgrass, Distichlis spicata, is reported for the Guadalupe Dunes. Effects of burning may have differed with grass species and habitat involved (Frank Davis, personal communication 1983).

... in sight of the shore, over some low-rolling tablelands with very good dark friable soil and fine dry grasses; *in many places it had all been burnt off*. It was all flat land, excepting only some short descents into a few dry creeks. If it can be dry-farmed, all the soil could be cultivated. Shortly after we left this point, the great live-oaks at this spot dropped behind us.

On *August 24, 1769*, after camping near a large village in what may have been Tajiguas Canyon, Crespí again commented on burned vegetation:

We set out from here at San Güido, taking a due westerly course, and again going down to the shore. We were soon stopped here, and went up to some low-rolling tablelands that end in high bold cliffs near the sea, but are all very good dark friable soil, *well covered with very fine grasses that nearly everywhere had been burnt off by the heathens.*

After reaching the Chumash village at Gaviota Canyon, Crespí reported:

The mountains that have been alongside us during the last two days' march *are bold, rough and steep*; white-colored here and there, as though from white earth or stone, and, *where not whitish, well covered with dry grass.*

As the Portolá expedition continued its march toward Point Conception, Crespí--obviously interested in pastureland and feasibility of agriculture--repeatedly described treeless tablelands with good soil covered with fine, dry grasses. At one point he remarked:

... the place lacks nothing but wood, of which there is none.

On *August 27, 1769*, after leaving Chumash settlements near Point Conception, Crespí again mentioned that in some places the grassy tablelands had been burned.

Continuing northward past Chumash villages at Jalama Beach and Cañada Agua Viva, the expedition rounded Point Arguello. On *August 29, 1769*:

> ... we set out from the San Juan Bautista Village on a due northwest course, across level ground near the shore. We soon passed the second point, and made out still another afar off, making a sort of large bight. *We went almost all the way over salt-grass, all very much burnt off by the heathens*, with some descents to dry creeks. On going about a league and a half, we reached a stream [Honda Canyon] with a good amount of fresh water emptying into the sea, but no village nor soil of any worth upon it. The soldiers had scouted up to this point, and it was not a full day's march, *nor was there grass for the animals, as it had all been burned off*.... On going about three hours, in which we must have made about two leagues and a half, we came to a hollow where the heathens had said there were some pools of water, and *although it had been burned off, there were spots that had not been and where there was good grass for the animals*; a halt was ordered here....

After crossing the Santa Ynez River and continuing northward past San Antonio Creek but before reaching the plains of the Santa Maria Valley, the expedition came to a hollow in the hills. There Crespí once again noted:

> ... fine soil and *dry grass almost all of which had been burned by the heathens.*

This was the last time he mentioned grassland burning within Chumash territory on this trip.

Portolá's return journey through the Santa Barbara Channel area to San Diego took place in January, 1770. He made a second trip northward in May, 1770. Crespí's journals cover both these trips and describe the appearance of "good" grasses and wildflowers along the coastal tablelands in Chumash territory. In the spring of 1770 along the coastline north of Point Arguello, the expedition encountered fields of wildflowers such as are sometimes seen in the area today. On *May 7, 1770*:

124

... we started from the San Juan Bautista de los Pedernales
village and point here, keeping on a northwesterly course
over very grassy level land near the shore. We shortly
passed the point here, and in the distance made out
another that formed still another bight. At once after
setting out, we commenced to find the *fields all abloom
with different kinds of wildflowers of all colors, so that,
as many as were the flowers we had been meeting all along
the way and on the Channel, it was not in such plenty as
here, for it is all one mass of blossom,* great quantities of
white, yellow, red, purple, and blue ones; many yellow
violets or gilly-flowers of the sort that are planted in
gardens, a great deal of larkspur, poppy and sage in
bloom,[3] and what graced the fields most of all was the
sight of all the different sorts of colors together. On going
about a league and a half, we came down to a deep creek
in a hollow where there is a good deal of grass and a
good-sized stream of running water .... On this whole
march, three leagues from the point of San Juan Bautista
de los Pedernales, *we have seen not a bush* nor a single
heathen.

---

[3]Identification of the wildflowers listed by Crespí are difficult because he applied the
names of common Spanish garden plants to unfamiliar plants he found growing in California
(Alan Brown, personal communication 1983). The authors have discussed the matter with
Dr. Brown, who translated the passage, and feel the following identifications are probably
the best:

"yellow violets or gillyflowers"--Viola pedunculata, although "gillyflower" (Spanish
"aleli") may refer to Dianthus.

"larkspur"--possibly Delphinium, but more likely Lupinus.

"poppies"--Spanish "cardosanto" refers to prickly poppy, Argemone, in Mexico.
That plant would not be found near Point Arguello, so Crespí may have
been trying to describe California poppy (Eschscholzia californica). But
the two species are not similar in appearance, and the senior author
feels Spanish "cardo," thistle, may have referred to Cirsium brevistylum,
which is common in the area Crespí visited (Smith 1976:282).

"sage"--probably chia (Salvia columbariae) rather than any of the woody species,
since "not a bush was seen."

These spectacular wildflower displays were seen in the very same area which Crespí had noted as having been burned the previous summer.

Crespí's diaries provide both excellent descriptions of the topography and vegetative cover of the Santa Barbara coastal area at the beginning of the Spanish colonial period, and very specific evidence of grassland burning by the Chumash, or "heathens." It is apparent from these descriptions that the shrub communities of coastal sage scrub and chaparral were once considerably less extensive than they are today. For example, the mountains between Tajiguas and Gaviota--or at least their lower flanks --were described as covered with grasses in August 1769, whereas dense chaparral is found there today. In addition, "not a bush" was seen in the South Vandenberg area north of Point Arguello in May, 1770; today the vegetation there is coastal sage scrub (see Smith 1976:21-24 for a general discussion of the occurrence of these communities today). Crespí's descriptions are in fact quite consistent with the theoretical picture presented by Aschmann (1976:41) of a park-like landscape with scattered oak trees which was sustained by frequent burning in pre-European times.

It is also clear that what Crespí saw was the result of fires which were set deliberately in grasslands by the Indians, rather than escaped campfires or lightning-caused fires, since he speaks of grass being "burnt off by the heathens."

Leaving aside the reasons for setting fires for the moment, a discussion of the effects of repeated burning is in order, to account for the discrepancy between what Crespí reported and what we see in the same places today. It seems likely that the Santa Barbara coast in pre-European times was dominated by grassland and oak savanna, with perennial bunch grasses interspersed with broad-leaved native annuals (Heady 1977: 492-494). Seasonal wildflowers, such as described by Crespí, often appear to be the dominant plant cover in all natural grasslands (Burcham 1957: 27). Even where oaks are present and form a savanna or open woodland, the essential character of the community is still that of a prairie (Burcham 1957:90).

Fires which burned in grassland would not be expected to stop at the shrub line, and may have occasionally spread up-slope into coastal sage and chaparral. While these two plant communities are adapted to fire, that adaptation is not based on burning more often than about ten-year intervals--more often for coastal sage scrub, less often for chaparral. Fires at one- to three-year intervals could be expected to burn even new growth, prevent shrub regeneration, and effectively extend the area colonized by grasses at the expense of coastal sage scrub or chaparral communities.

Indian burning may also have been an important factor in maintaining the openness of oak savanna in coastal areas; mature oaks are well adapted to survive ground fires by sprouting (Griffin 1977:408-409; Sweeney 1968: 114). Some oak species may produce more acorns as a result of thinned understory after a fire (Lewis 1973:17).

A second ethnohistoric account, a few years after Crespí's visits, also mentions burning in grasslands. It is even more explicit in stating that fires were deliberately set by the indigenous peoples of the Santa Barbara Channel, and offers some clues as to the reasons this was done.

RIVERA Y MONCADA'S DIARY

Fernándo Rivera y Moncada was the military governor of California from 1774 to 1777. On his travels throughout the territory, he frequently had contact with Indian people who had for the most part not yet been missionized. His diary has been published in Spanish (Burrus 1967), but will be quoted here in translation, with emphases added by the present authors.

On *April 24, 1776*, Rivera y Moncada stayed the night near "Mezcaltitan" at the mouth of the present Goleta Slough, which he described as the most populous part of the Santa Barbara Channel coast. The following day he journeyed eastward to just past what is now Ventura.

> I passed outside the Channel. It was already dark when we stopped at the Santa Clara River. *The gentiles* [heathen Indians] *destroy and consume the pastures with their burnings* [Burrus 1967:253].

In a later journal entry, Rivera y Moncada summarized his travels between San Gabriel and San Buenaventura in the south-eastern part of Chumash territory as follows:

> Having made beforehand in this Diary extensive report of this road, [and] given information about the villages of the Santa Barbara Channel, it has seemed to me [proper] not to repeat [this], since I have not had the least novelty in my [most recent] journey. I have experienced great drought [here], therefore some of the springs along the

road I have passed [are] dry; this is something that has not happened to me since I entered these lands, and in the countryside [there has been] extreme need of pasture for the animals which in some areas has caused me difficulty in staying overnight and in stopping at midday, due to *the horses and mules not having grass, all occasioned by the great fires of the gentiles, who, not having to care for more than their own bellies, burn the fields as soon as they gather up the seeds, and that [burning] is universal, although on some occasions it happens that it may be greater or less, according to the winds or calm* [Burrus 1967:310].

Rivera y Moncada's account, like Crespí's, stresses the fact that vegetation burning by the Chumash was deliberate, widespread, and affected large areas. He also indicates that fires were not necessarily controlled, and therefore they could have spread from grassland or savanna into shrublands in the foothills and mountains. Although the open parklands thus created would provide excellent forage for game animals, improved hunting is not given as the reason the Chumash set fire to pastures.

In his descriptions of the Monterey area, Rivera y Moncada explicitly stated that the heathens burned "so that new weeds may grow to produce more seeds" (Clar 1959:5). It may be inferred from the account presented here that the Chumash were also burning to promote the growth of vegetable foods for their own consumption. The phrase "they burn the fields as soon as they gather up the seeds" indicates that seeds of grassland plants were sought-after and that burning was not done until these had been harvested. Seeds of most annual wildflowers ripen in late spring or early summer; seeds of native grasses are usually shed in June or July. This fits well with Crespí's reports of burned grasslands on his August visit, and with the usual burning of vegetation in summer or fall by other Indian groups elsewhere in California (Bean and Lawton 1973:xxi-xxii; Lewis 1973:19; Biswell 1967:82).

Springtime burning would be unusual, both because of low vegetation flammability and in terms of harvesting desired food resources. It is not clear from Rivera y Moncada's accounts of the Santa Barbara Channel whether he actually saw burning in progress or merely observed its effects. He passed through eastern Chumash territory in the midst of a severe drought. Lack of rain the previous winter would have resulted in a failure of the usual growth of new graze, which would have been particularly serious for his horses and mules if the pastures had been burned the summer before.

Small, hard seeds such as those of grasses and sage were important in the diet of many California Indian groups and were likely so for the Chumash, as will be discussed below. There is also evidence that fresh, green shoots were eagerly consumed, particularly after some months of living on stored food. This is shown in the third ethnohistoric account.

THE LONGINOS JOURNAL

Naturalist José Longinos Martínez traveled through both Alta and Baja California in 1791 and 1792. He recorded information about the flora, fauna, natural resources, and native peoples of the area, under orders from the Spanish King, Carlos III. Longinos made many valuable observations about the Chumash of the Santa Barbara Channel area, and also noted certain cultural features which seemed to be widespread or universal throughout the territory of New Spain (Simpson 1961:vii). In the following passages, emphases have again been added by the present authors.

> In this part of the Santa Barbara Channel... if a chief merely makes an attempt to pass through another's jurisdiction, fighting and quarreling result, so great is the distrust that these nations have of one another... *Their wars are frequent and always originate over rights to seed-gathering grounds*, or in disputes over concubines... The gentiles living between San Diego and San Buenaventura *store up against the winter the plants that bear the most seeds*... These nations [north of Santa Barbara] continually *keep on hand small baskets of seeds and other foodstuffs* .... In all New California from Fronteras northward *the gentiles have the custom of burning the brush*, this for two purposes: one, for catching rabbits (brush-burning being a form of hunting); two, *so that with the first light rain or dew the shoots will come up* which they call pelillo [little hair] and *upon which they feed like cattle when the weather prevents their seeking other food* [Simpson 1961: 58-59].

Thus the Longinos journal contains specific evidence that burning was carried on by many California Indian groups, probably including the Chumash, for two purposes: for rabbit drives (as opposed to improving forage for animals to be hunted later), and for promoting the growth of green shoots to be eaten by humans. Longinos also stresses the importance of seeds in the native diet, and although the connection between burning and seed gathering is not explicit in this account, it was probably a third motive for setting fires. It is unclear whether by "brush" Longinos meant shrub vegetation, hence chaparral or coastal sage scrub in the Chumash area, or merely vegetation in general. The motive for burning in any particular area would depend on several factors including vegetation type. There are several species of native annual and perennial plants which have been called "fire followers," meaning they germinate and grow much more profusely after an area has been burned (Smith 1956). Many of these are grassland species and produce seeds which were used by California Indian peoples, a fact which will be discussed in more detail below.

By the time of Longinos' visit in the late 18th century, Spanish colonization and missionization of the California Indians were already well under way. The Chumash and others were increasingly denied the right to continue many of their traditional practices, including vegetation burning, under the new administration. This is the subject of another historical document.

ARRILLAGA'S PROCLAMATION

The year after Longinos' visit, the first fire control regulation in Alta California was proclaimed by Governor José Joaquín de Arrillaga, who was in Santa Barbara at the time. Arrillaga's proclamation, the accompanying letter to the Padre Presidente of the Missions, Fermín Francisco de Lasuén, and Lausuén's reply are quoted in their entirety from Clar (1959:8-10), with emphases added.

Arrillaga's letter to Lasuén, dated May 31, 1793:

> *Because of various complaints that have reached me about the serious damage that results from the fires that are set each year in the pastures by Christian and Gentile Indians,* and having been informed not only by various officials but also by different mission fathers that the aforesaid damage is true, I have taken measures to publish the enclosed

proclamation which I am passing into your hands with the entreaty and charge that you please inform all the mission fathers that they are to contribute for their part to the observance of such a just proclamation not only by *warning the Christian Indians, and particularly the old women, not to become liable for such offense, but also by threatening them with the rigors of the law,* trying in case of fire to clear the way for corporals of the guard to have Christian Indians help them to cut off with all possible determination the fire that may threaten their vicinity, to which end *I authorize to the comandantes whatever may be expedient in carrying out this order.* Also I should notify you that on my way here from San Diego, at the Missions of San Juan Capistrano and San Gabriel, having called the natives together, I instructed them in the presence of the reverend mission fathers about this my proclamation and the penalties that would be incurred by infractions of it. I shall do the same at the missions on the way to Monterey, for *I should like to see my wishes, which are directed toward the common good, partly if not wholly carried out.*

May Our Lord Keep You, Most Reverend Father.

Mission Santa Barbara, May 31, 1793.
José Joaquín de Arrillaga

The proclamation:

DON JOSÉ JOAQUÍN DE ARRILLAGA, CAPTAIN OF CAVALRY, INTERIM GOVERNOR AND INSPECTOR COMANDANTE OF UPPER AND LOWER CALIFOR-NIA.

With attention to the *widespread damage which results to the public from the burning of the fields, customary up to now among both Christian and Gentile Indians in this country, whose childishness has been unduly tolerated,* and as a consequence of various complaints that I have had of such abuse, I see myself required to have the foresight to *prohibit for the future (availing myself, if it be necessary,* of the rigors of the law) all kinds of burning, not only in the vicinity of the towns, but even at the most remote distances, which might cause some detriment, whether it be by Christian Indians or by Gentiles who have some relationship or communication with our establishments and missions. Therefore I order and command all comandantes of the presidios in my charge to do their duty and watch with the greatest earnestness to take whatever measures they may consider requisite and necessary to uproot this very harmful practice of setting fire to pasture lands, not omitting any means that may lead to the achievement of the purpose which I propose in this order, to which effect they will publish it in their respective jurisdictions with particular charge to the corporals of the guard, commissioners, and magistrates of the towns that they exercise equal vigilance in trying to advise the Christian Indians and the Gentiles of the neighboring rancherías about this proclamation and impressing upon them that those who commit such an offense will be punished, and in case some burning occurs, they are to try immediately to take the most appropriate means to stop the fire, or failing that, to direct it into another direction which may result in less damage, apprehending the violators, of whatever class or sex, who would be punished in accordance with the degree of malice there may be on the part of the offenders; and in order that there may be no obstacle to the observance of this order, I beg and charge the Reverend Fathers, priests of the missions, that they do their part in instructing the Christian Indians not to commit such transgression. And in order that it come to the attention of all and that nobody may allege ignorance, I order that this decision of mine be published by proclamation in the presidios as well as the missions and towns of this province which is in my charge, making it be known to all classes of Indians, Christians as well as Gentiles, and repeating its publication annually, with the full understanding that whatever lack of observance may be noticed in this matter (which is) of such great interest will be worthy of the most severe punishment.

Given in Santa Barbara, May 31, 1793.
                    José Joaquín de Arrillaga

On June 2, 1793, Fr. Lasuén replied to the Governor from Mission San Carlos:

> My dear sir: I have received the proclamation which you sent me dated the 31st of last month, ordering the prevention by all possible means of the *horribly destructive fires which are experienced every year in this country.* Two days ago, after it was published here, I sent it to Mission Santa Cruz with a little corollary of mine for the other two missions of the north, advising that in all three a copy be made and put in the archives and that its publication be repeated annually as you direct. I will do the same (with God's help) in the future with the rest of the missions. *In all of them all possible efforts have been made with the greatest earnestness toward the remedy of this conspicious damage,* and from now on, by virtue of your opportune proclamation, they will be continued with greater hope for the desired effect. The mission fathers of the missions at which you have stopped must have been very grateful to you for *having deigned to instruct the Indians yourself in the obligation of abstaining from such excess and the punishment they will incur if they do not comply.* That exhortation will no doubt give great weight to our own and will perhaps make them effective. I wish to thank you now for being of a mind to extend the same favor to the remaining missions. And with the mission fathers of all (the missions) I repeat that I am at your disposition. God keep you in his Holy Grace.

> Very sincerely yours
>   Father Fermín Francisco de Lasuén

The Governor's letter and proclamation were issued in Santa Barbara, indicating that grassland fires were considered a major problem in coastal Chumash territory. It is further noteworthy that old women were particularly implicated in the setting of such fires; women were the principal gatherers of seeds.

Fire suppression was not merely confined to proclamation, but was diligently put into practice. This is illustrated by another historic document of seven years later.

MISSION QUESTIONNAIRE

In 1798 a questionnaire was sent out to presidio comandantes inquiring about the treatment of California Indians by the Spanish padres, in response to accusations of cruelty which had been made by a former missionary at San Miguel (Bancroft 1886:587-596; Engelhardt 1930: 566-600). The replies by Felipe de Coyoechea, comandante of the Santa Barbara Presidio, were especially irksome to the missionaries, so they in turn prepared their own responses to the questionnaire. The replies made to two of the questions by Fr. Gregorio Fernández at Mission La Purísima are of interest (Fernández 1800). This mission was near Lompoc, in the northwest portion of Chumash territory, not far from the Point Arguello area visited by Crespí in 1769 and 1700.

> *Question 10.* What types of diversions do the neophytes [baptized Indians] enjoy? What excursions are they allowed, so that they may gather seeds? For what length of time?
> *Answer.* The neophytes are permitted all kinds of diversions which are popular among them. Likewise, half the year, or almost one-half the year, is granted them for gathering their wild seeds, in the various seasons.
> *Question 12.* What sorts of punishments are meted out to the neophytes? Differentiate for the sexes. For what sort of transgressions are they punished? Do the fathers have shackles, chains, stocks, and lockups, or whether they only make use of the means of punishment available to the members of the guard.
> *Answer* [in part]. The misdeeds for which we fathers chastise the Indians thus are concubinage, theft, and running away. *When the transgressions are against the common good, like killing cattle, sheep, or firing pastures, which has occurred sometimes, the corporal of the guard is notified* [emphasis added].

134

Under the missions, the baptized Indians were permitted to continue gathering their wild seeds but prevented from setting the fires that (as will be shown below) promoted a more abundant harvest. The missionaries, military, and settlers understandably wished to discourage the grassland fires that destroyed grazing for their livestock and endangered settlements, although in some parts of California these same interests set fires in forests and chaparral to convert them to grassland (Heady 1977: 509; Pyne 1982:416-418). Suppression of burning by the Spanish and their successors contributed to a decline in productivity of the native grassland and to encroachment of coastal sage scrub, and perhaps of chaparral, into grassland and savanna habitats (Aschmann 1976:43-44). Invasion of European grasses, broadleaved weeds, and large herbivores, and the practice of agricultural cultivation, completed the destruction of the native grassland in coastal Chumash territory (Burcham 1957:185-199; Heady 1977:497-499). This drastic alteration of the environment probably contributed to a gradual abandonment of traditional seed foods by the Chumash, although certainly other factors came into play as well (Cook 1941).

Many other aspects of Chumash culture were lost under the mission system, but vegetation burning was surely one of the first to die out, given the stringency of military enforcement. Even though some Chumash people attempted to go back to village life after the secularization of the missions in 1834, private ownership of their former lands prevented them from reviving all their old food-gathering practices. Thus, it is not surprising that the use of fire as an important hunting and gathering technique had been forgotten by the time ethnographers began interviewing Chumash survivors in the late 19th and early 20th centuries.

THE HARRINGTON NOTES

John P. Harrington, ethnographer and linguist, was the most thorough of the several anthropologists who collected data from living Chumash people. He worked in the Santa Barbara, Ventura, and Santa Ynez areas on several occasions from about 1912 until the 1950s. In what must be over 100,000 pages of field notes on the Chumash, Harrington recorded only one mention of vegetation burning and that was in an inland area. María Solares, an Ineseño woman of Yokuts-Chumash ancestry, said that:

...some of the Indians were burning chamiso[4] one day near
Mt. Pinos to hunt cottontails and jackrabbits, and the fire
got beyond their control [Harrington n.d., cited by Horne
1981: 116-117].

It is uncertain whether this event involved Chumash people, since
Mt. Pinos was an area jointly used by several groups, including Chumash,
Kitanemuk, and Yokuts. Use of fire in this instance may have been
instigated by one of these other groups, but elsewhere Harrington (1942:
6) did report that the Emigdiano Chumash used fire in driving antelopes
into enclosures.

No accounts were found of burning as a hunting technique in the
coastal Chumash area. Neither was burning of vegetation to promote
growth of plants for human food mentioned by any of Harrington's
Chumash consultants. In fact, use of grass seeds was barely discussed by
most, at least in comparison with the details provided on acorns and wild
cherry pits (Timbrook 1982:166). This may be an indication that native
grasses had been substantially reduced in abundance by the late 19th
century (by Harrington's consultants' lifetimes), an idea confirmed by other
lines of evidence (Burcham 1957:185-199). Plant specimens were collected
in the Santa Barbara area by Chumash consultant Lucrecia García and are
now preserved in the National Anthropological Archives, Smithsonian
Institution. Of the 13 grass specimens, the only natives are three species
of *Elymus* (observation by the senior author). Introduced grasses *Avena*
and *Bromus* were said to have been pounded, leached and baked into
bread in earth ovens (Craig 1967:126). It is not clear whether the Spanish
word "avena" was used by Harrington's Chumash consultants to refer to
native grass species as well as to Mediterranean wild oats (*Avena* spp.).

Small seeds of flowering annuals were still remembered by
Chumash people after the turn of the century (Craig 1967:124-126). Chia
(*Salvia columbariae*) is one of the best known of these, and it was
frequently mentioned by Harrington's consultants as a staple food. The
seeds were harvested in quantity and stored in baskets in the home. They
were prepared by toasting and grinding into flour which was either eaten
dry or mixed with water to form a gruel (Harrington n.d.). The question

---

[4]"Chamiso" can mean just brush in general, or a particular shrub species, Adenostoma
fasciculatum. This plant does not grow near Mt. Pinos, so María probably meant just bushy
vegetation or perhaps basin sagebrush (Artemisia tridentata).

is often asked today where the Chumash got the quantities of chia they were reported to have eaten, because the plant is not common in the coastal area. *Salvia* species are among those known to occur after fire (see Table 4.1), and some California Indians burned chia gathering areas to improve productivity (Bean and Lawton 1973: xxi). Overgrazing and suburban development, as well as the cessation of burning, have probably contributed to the decline in abundance of *Salvia columbariae* on the coastal side of the Santa Ynez Mountains; the plant is still found here in certain places under favorable conditions, but is not common overall.

Another species of seed plant mentioned by Harrington's consultants in Santa Barbara, Ventura, and Santa Ynez was one of the tarweeds, *Hermizonia ramosissima*, which was also prepared as pinole. Luisa Ygnacio told Harrington about 1912 that the Santa Barbara Chumash used to eat a great deal of these seeds, but by her day this food had gone out of use. She had seen it prepared just once by her mother-in-law, María Ignacia, who had fixed it for José Venadero by toasting the seeds and then pounding them to flour. Luisa reported that the flour was black and dry, with a not disagreeable taste (Harrington n.d.). This plant is still common in fields along the coast (Smith 1976:295).

Seeds of red maids (*Calandrinia* spp.) were formerly of great importance to the Chumash. Large quantities of these small, black seeds have been found in cemetery contexts in the coastal area. Excavations by Yarrow and Bowers for the 1876 Geographical Survey expedition uncovered a child burial in an olla filled with *Calandrinia* seeds--misidentified by a Mexican worker as chia--on Mescalitan Island in the Goleta Slough (Yarrow 1879:36-37; Benson 1982:56, 307). Phil Orr found 12 quarts of red maid seeds associated with a burial on Santa Rosa Island; these were radiocarbon dated to 600 ± 70 years B.P. (Orr 1968:200). Similar finds have been made by other archaeologists in cemeteries on the mainland and channel islands (Ford 1887:11-19; Orr 1968:210; King 1969:37; Smith 1976: 131; Abbott 1879:78-80; Benson 1982:84, 329).

Harrington's Chumash consultants stressed the use of red maids seeds, called "pil" in Spanish and *khutash* in Chumash, as offerings and also as food (Harrington n.d.; Hudson et al. 1977:55, 65; Hudson et al. 1978: 138). Red maids was one of several kinds of seeds (chia, acorns, and islay were the others) which were stored in large baskets in the home (Luisa Ygnacio in Harrington n.d.). Its importance is further indicated by the fact that its Chumash name, *khutash*, was the same as that of the Earth, which was regarded as the Indian's mother, "for she gave them their food" (Hudson et al. 1977:37, 113). Coyote asked to be given *khutash* and ate it as he pounded it, according to one Chumash myth (Blackburn 1975: 204).[5] Red maids, like chia, must have been much more common in coastal grasslands than it is today; *Calandrinia breweri* is much more abundant after burns and is a definite "fire follower" (Smith 1976:131, and personal observation by the senior author). It was a food plant widely used throughout California (Heizer and Elsasser 1980:243). The seeds were parched, pulverized, and pressed into cakes for eating (Barrett and Gifford 1933:152-153).

Grassland plants were not only used for seeds, however. As already noted by Longinos, many kinds of green sprouts were eaten by the Chumash. Harrington's consultants mentioned several species consumed in this way. One of the most favored was clover (*Trifolium* spp.) Luisa Ygnacio said that the Indians used to eat it raw, "like a cow; not much--like we eat fruit now." When old María Ignacia lay dying, she wanted to eat clover; perhaps she craved the comfort offered by a food from her childhood. Simplicio Pico of Ventura said they ate clover raw, like lettuce, and María Solares of Santa Ynez said the Indians used to eat the raw leaves and the seeds of clover (Harrington n.d.). Several species of *Trifolium* are commonly found in burns and in disturbed areas (Smith 1976:177-180).

Harrington's notes reflect the changing Chumash diet in recent times. By the time of his interviews in the 1910s and 1920s, most consultants were speaking of wild seeds and greens as things the old people used to eat, but which were no longer in common use. Burning as a food procurement technique was apparently unknown. Today, over half a century later, the possibility of completely understanding Chumash subsistence is even more remote. But when the ethnohistoric evidence we have presented is combined with botanical information, an interesting picture emerges.

---

[5]The identification of ǥutaš as chia in the text (Blackburn 1975:207) is incorrect since many consultants refer to chia and khutash. The Barbareño Chumash word for chia is 'ilepesh (Harrington n.d.).

PLANTS THAT FOLLOW FIRE

A list of the most common herbaceous plants that occur today in the coastal grasslands of the Chumash area was compiled with the help of knowledgeable local botanists.[6] Plant species native to the area under consideration and that are known to have been eaten by the Chumash or by other California Indian peoples comprise 70 genera, as shown in Table 4.1. Of these 70 genera, about 35 occur after fire and an additional 15 reach their peak of abundance in areas that were burned the previous year. The latter are sometimes called "fire followers" (Smith 1956) or "pyrophytic endemics" (Hanes 1977-433).

Plants found after grassland fires, and those that probably provided significant food resources for the Chumash, included grasses--especially perennial bunch grasses--and herbaceous plants in the sunflower, mustard, parsley, pea, buttercup, evening-primrose, sage, figwort, lily, and amaryllis families. Plant parts consumed included seeds, green leaves, shoots, and corms or bulbs.

Grasses that may have been of most importance before the introduction of weedy species include California brome (*Bromus carinatus*), ryegrasses (*Elymus condensatus, E. glaucus,* and *E. triticoides*), meadow barley (*Hordeum californicum*), coast range melic (*Melica imperfecta*), bluegrass (*Poa scabrella*), needlegrasses (*Stipa pulchra, S. lepida,* and *S. cernua*), and perhaps other (Heady 1977:495-496; Wayne Ferren, personal communication 1982). Several of these species have seed heads which shatter easily when ripe, so that harvesting with a seedbeater, as the Chumash did, would be quite efficient (Bean and Lawton 1973:xxxiv; Craig 1967:125).

Bunch grasses produce more seeds if leaf growth is sufficient to manufacture food reserves which are stored in the roots of the plant (Burcham 1957:226). Burning would remove dead thatch and enrich the soil, thereby promoting plant growth and seed production (Daubenmire 1968:211; Horton and Kraebel 1955:254). The optimal burning interval for bunch grasses varies between species and geographical locations (Daubenmire 1968:250-254). Indians in some parts of California are said to have burned grasslands every year to improve the following year's seed harvest (Stewart 1951:320). In the area under consideration, it is thought that

---

[6]Mary Junak (Santa Barbara Botanic Garden), Wayne Ferren (University of California, Santa Barbara, Herbarium), Clifton Smith (Santa Barbara Museum of Natural History).

Table 4.1

COMMON HERBACEOUS PLANTS OF COASTAL GRASSLANDS IN CHUMASH TERRITORY, WITH THEIR USES BY CALIFORNIA INDIANS

Plant Genus	Family	Plant Parts Used By	
		Chumash	California Indians
Achillea	Asteraceae	roots, leaves	roots, leaves
Agoseris	Asteraceae	(SEEDS, LEAVES)	
Agropyron	Poaceae		SEEDS
Allium	Amaryllidaceae	BULBS	SEEDS, BULBS, LEAVES
Amaranthus (some I)	Amaranthaceae	(SEEDS, LEAVES)	SEEDS
Ambrosia	Asteraceae	leaves	leaves
Amsinckia	Boraginaceae	(SEEDS)	(SEEDS)
Anagallis (I)+	Caryophyllaceae	(leaves)	
Anthemis (I)	Asteraceae		leaves
Apiastrum +*	Apiaceae		STALKS
Apium (I)	Apiaceae	STALKS	
Aster	Asteraceae	(SEEDS)	
Astragalus	Fabaceae		FRUIT
Atriplex (some I)	Chenopodiaceae	SEEDS	SEEDS
Avena (I)+	Poaceae	(BULBS)	SEEDS
Bloomeria+	Amaryllidaceae		BULBS
Brassica (I)	Brassicaceae	LEAVES	SEEDS, LEAVES
Bromus (some I)+	Poaceae	SEEDS	SEEDS
Calamagrostis	Poaceae		SEEDS

Table 4.1 (cont'd)

Calandrinia +*	Portulacaceae	SEEDS	SEEDS, LEAVES
Calochortus +*	Liliaceae	BULBS	BULBS
Calystegia +*	Convolvulaceae		stalks, leaves
Camissonia +*	Onagraceae		SEEDS
Carex +	Cyperaceae		r o o t s, l e a v e s
Castilleja +	Scrophulariaceae	(SEEDS)	SEEDS
Caucalis	Apiaceae		roots
Chaenactis +*	Asteraceae		SEEDS, leaves
Chenopodium (some I)	Chenopodiaceae	SEEDS, LEAVES, roots	SEEDS, LEAVES, roots
Chlorogalum +	Liliaceae	LEAVES, roots, leaves	ROOTS, LEAVES, roots, leaves
Chorizanthe +	Polygonaceae	(whole plant)	
Cirsium	Asteraceae	STALKS, LEAVES	STALKS, LEAVES
Clarkia +	Onagraceae		SEEDS
Collinsia +	Scrophulariaceae		
Conyza (I)+	Asteraceae	leaves	leaves
Croton	Euphorbiaceae	stems, leaves	stems, leaves
Cryptantha +*	Boraginaceae	(SEEDS)	
Cucurbita	Cucurbitaceae	fruit	SEEDS, fruit
Cyperus	Cyperaceae		SEEDS
Datura	Solanaceae	roots, seeds, leaves	roots, seeds, leaves
Daucus +*	Apiaceae	(roots)	ROOTS
Delphinium +	Ranunculaceae		LEAVES, FLOWERS
Dichelostemma +	Amaryllidaceae	BULBS	BULBS
Dodecatheon +	Primulaceae		ROOTS, LEAVES
Elymus +*	Poaceae	stems	SEEDS, stems
Epilobium +	Onagraceae		(SEEDS)
Eremocarpus	Euphorbiaceae		leaves
Erigeron +	Asteraceae		roots
Eriogonum +	Polygonaceae	stems	STEMS, leaves, roots,
Erodium (I)	Geraniaceae	(SEEDS, LEAVES)	

Table 4.1 (cont'd)

Genus	Family		
Erysimum +	Brassicaceae		LEAVES, FLOWERS, roots
Eschscholzia	Papaveraceae		
Festuca +*	Poaceae		
Foeniculum (I)	Apiaceae	(STEMS)	
Fritillaria	Liliaceae		BULBS
Galium +	Rubiaceae		seeds
Gilia +*	Polemoniaceae		SEEDS
Gnaphalium +	Asteraceae	leaves	leaves
Grindelia	Asteraceae	whole plant	
Haplopappus +	Asteraceae		LEAVES, STEMS
Helenium	Asteraceae	whole plant	SEEDS, STEMS
Helianthus	Asteraceae		whole plant
Hemizonia +	Asteraceae	SEEDS	SEEDS
Hesperocnide +	Urticaceae		SEEDS
Heterotheca	Asteraceae	(SEEDS)	stems
Hordeum (some I)+	Poaceae	(SEEDS)	SEEDS
Hypochoeris (I)+	Asteraceae	LEAVES	
Juncus +	Juncaceae	stems	SHOOTS, SEEDS, stems, leaves
Lasthenia	Asteraceae		SEEDS, LEAVES
Layia +	Asteraceae	SEEDS	SEEDS
Lepidium +	Brassicaceae	SEEDS	SEEDS
Linanthus +	Polemoniaceae		whole plant
Linaria (some I)+	Scrophulariaceae		
Lomatium +	Apiaceae	ROOTS, roots	LEAVES, STEMS, ROOTS, roots
Lotus +*	Fabaceae	stems	LEAVES
Lupinus +*	Fabaceae	FRUIT, SEEDS	LEAVES, FLOWERS, whole plant
Madia +	Asteraceae		SEEDS
Malacothrix +*	Asteraceae		
Malva (I)	Malvaceae	SEEDS, LEAVES	leaves
Marah +	Cucurbitaceae	(LEAVES), seeds	SEEDS, roots, seeds

Table 4.1 (cont'd)

Scrophularia	Scrophulariaceae	leaves	leaves
Senecio +	Asteraceae	(SEEDS)	(SEEDS)
Sidalcea +	Malvaceae		PARTS UNSPECIFIED
Silene +*	Caryophyllaceae		parts unspecified
Sisymbrium (I)	Brassicaceae		LEAVES
Sisyrinchium	Iridaceae		
Solidago	Asteraceae	leaves	leaves
Sonchus (I)	Asteraceae	LEAVES	
Stellaria +	Caryophyllaceae	(LEAVES)	
Stipa +	Poaceae		(SEEDS)
Thysanocarpus +	Brassicaceae		SEEDS
Trifolium +	Fabaceae	LEAVES, SEEDS	LEAVES, SEEDS
Urtica	Urticaceae	stems	LEAVES, stems
Xanthium	Asteraceae	LEAVES, leaves	
Zigadenus +	Liliaceae	leaves	leaves

(I) introduced (non-native) plant.
+   plants that occur after fire (one or more species).
*   plants that are most abundant after fire (one or more species).

Food uses of plants are listed in capital letters, non-food uses in lowercase letters. Information that is not certain is enclosed in parentheses.

Sources: Smith 1976; Heizer and Elsasser 1980; Sweeney 1956; Clifton Smith, personal communication 1983; Mary Junak, personal communication 1982; Harrington n.d.

[A]Opuntia is thought to regenerate after fire (L. Benson 1969:168-170).
[B]Phacelia leaves reported by Curtis (1959:141) as having been eaten raw, but this seems unlikely as they cause severe dermatitis in some persons.

Table 4.1 (cont'd)

Marrubium (I)	Labiatae	leaves	leaves
Matricaria	Asteraceae	leaves	leaves
Melica	Poaceae		
Mimulus +	Scrophulariaceae		LEAVES, whole plant
Marabilis	Nyctaginaceae		leaves
Monardella	Labiatae		LEAVES, STEMS, leaves, flowers
Montia +	Portulacaeae	LEAVES, SEEDS	STEMS, LEAVES, flowers
Muhlenbergia +*	Poaceae	stalks	stalks
Navarretia +	Polemoniaceae		whole plant
Nicotiana +	Solanaceae	leaves	leaves
Oenothera +	Onagraceae		LEAVES
Opuntia[A] (+)	Cactaceae	STEMS, FRUIT	STEMS, FRUIT
Orthocarpus	Scrophulariaceae		
Oryzopsis (I)	Poaceae		SEEDS
Oxalis (some I)	Oxalidaceae		leaves
Paeonia +*	Paeoniaceae	roots	roots, seeds
Penstemon +	Scrophulariaceae		roots, stems, leaves
Perezia +*	Asteraceae	leaves	leaves
Phacelia +*	Hydrophyllaceae	(LEAVES)[B]	leaves
Plagiobothrys +	Boraginaceae		SHOOTS, FLOWERS
Plantago (some I)	Plantaginaceae	leaves	
Platystemon	Ranunculaceae		LEAVES
Poa +	Poaceae		SEEDS
Polypogon (some I)	Poaceae		
Pteridium	Pteridiaceae	whole plant	SHOOTS, roots
Ranunculus +	Ranunculaceae		SEEDS
Raphanus (I)	Brassicaceae	(SEEDS, LEAVES)	
Rumex (some I)	Polygonaceae	LEAVES, SEEDS, STEMS, roots	LEAVES, SEEDS, roots
Salvia +	Labiatae	SEEDS, (SHOOTS), leaves	SEEDS, leaves
Sanicula +	Apiaceae		LEAVES, roots

bunch grasses would thrive and produce a good seed crop if burned every 3 to 5 years (Wayne Ferren, personal communication 1982). However, an annually burned stand of *Stipa pulchra* on Las Tunas Road in Santa Barbara was reported to be one of the finest stands of bunch grass in the vicinity (Wells 1962:96).

Fire commonly favors forbs over grasses in both annual and perennial grasslands, so that herbs fill in the interstices between grass plants (Daubenmire 1968:249). Broadleaved annuals which were of greatest significance to the Chumash for their seeds were chia (*Salvia columbariae*) and red maids (*Calandrinia* spp., especially *C. breweri*). The probable abundance of these plants in the coastal grasslands of Chumash territory was discussed above, and both occur most abundantly after fires. Seeds of several members of the sunflower family, particularly tarweeds (*Hemizonia* and *Madia* spp.), were also a significant resource. Many other seed plants were probably used to a lesser degree.

Green shoots and leaves of clover (*Trifolium* spp.), miner's lettuce (*Montia perfoliata*), pigweed (*Amaranthus* spp.), and goosefoot (*Chenopodium* spp.), and probably other species as well, were eaten by the Chumash in historic times. It is questionable whether these ever formed a significant portion of the diet, and as a seasonal food consumed in small amounts, greens were probably more important for enjoyment that for actual calories or vitamin content.

Another plant type of great importance to the Chumash, although not mentioned specifically in the ethnohistoric accounts of grassland burning, is that which forms underground bulbs or corms. Several members of the lily and amaryllis families produce such bulbs and are often seen in great profusion in savanna and chaparral the spring after a fire. This is in part a matter of increased salience when surrounding vegetative cover has been burned off, but the bulbs also sprout more vigorously and more of them flower the first year after a fire (Keeley et al. 1981:1615). Because seedlings of these plants thrive in the more open post-fire vegetation, regular burning over a period of time would probably favor bulb-forming species (J. Sauer, personal communication 1983). Two such species, brodiaea (*Dichelostemma pulchellum*) and mariposa lily (*Calochortus* spp., especially *C. catalinae*), were harvested in huge quantities by the Chumash and many other California Indian groups (Harrington n.d.). Increased bulb production would be a beneficial side effect of fires set for other purposes rather than an immediate goal in itself, since it would be a gradual, long-term development.

Certain other plants used for purposes other than food are also encouraged by fire. Some are medicinal; others are basketmaking or construction material. Since the ethnohistoric accounts emphasize burning in connection with food species, these other plants will not be discussed in this paper, but they are included in the list of grassland plants in Table 4.1.

DISCUSSION

Contrasting views of the effects and frequency of fires before and after European arrival have been put forth in the literature. Some of the major points merit discussion here.

It has been stated that lightning was a far more important cause of fire in prehistoric California than humans were; that California Indians lacked both the labor force and the technological skills necessary to do the physical job of burning large tracts of vegetation in a systematic or purposeful manner; and that like all early peoples they regarded fire with a mixture of fear, reverence, and awe (Burcham 1974:106, 111). The evidence presented in this paper clearly shows that these statements do not apply to the Chumash Indians and coastal grasslands within their territory. The documents quoted also answer questions about the reasons fires were set, address criticisms that insufficient use has been made of pre-20th-century accounts to assess the impact of aboriginal burning in California, and counter statements that fire suppression is exclusively a 20th-century policy.

Some have argued that the Chumash did not deliberately burn chaparral (e.g., Horne 1981:111-123). The ethnohistoric documents quoted here should not be interpreted as conflicting with Horne's argument. We believe that grass fires could have readily spread into chaparral and had significant effects on the density and boundaries of that community, at least on the coastal side of the Santa Ynez Mountains. However, no evidence has been found to indicate that the Indians actually set fires in the chaparral itself. We cannot say for certain whether anthropogenic fires affected chaparral in interior Chumash territory; this may have been the case if inland valley grasslands and savannas were also burned, and Arrillaga's proclamation indicates they might have been. But regular burning may have had more significant effects on the distribution of coastal sage scrub than on chaparral (Richard Minnich, personal communication 1983).

Charcoal deposits in the Santa Barbara Channel have been interpreted to show that fires were less frequent prehistorically, or at least that there was less net burning per unit area, per unit time (Byrne et al. 1977:366). These data are still being analyzed. We suggest that even if precipitation and wind deposited burned material in the sea in a regular, predictable pattern after every fire, grassland burning would not produce enough ash and charcoal to be visible in the varved cores from the Santa Barbara Channel floor. Other recent research has shown that fires were probably more frequent but smaller before suppression policies were enacted in the last century (Minnich 1983). That grassland fires were frequent and widespread in early historic times is indicated by the explorers' comments about burned fields and by the necessity of a proclamation by the governor and military enforcement to stop the Indians from "firing the pastures." We suspect that the practice was one of some antiquity, but further archaeological investigation is needed to demonstrate this. Close observation of the effects of escaped campfires may have led the Chumash to experiment with deliberate burning of grasslands.

The increase in extent and density of chaparral since European colonization of southern California has been noted by many authors, and two contradictory sorts of explanations of this observed phenomenon have been offered. On the one hand it is said to be the result of more frequent fires in recent times (Burcham 1974:219-220), and on the other as the result of fire suppression (C. Sauer 1952:17; Lewis 1973; Aschmann 1976: 41; Stewart 1951:318; Minnich 1983). In the botanical literature, the debate still rages over the successional status of chaparral and its relation to coastal sage scrub and grassland after fire (Hanes 1977:447; Mooney 1977: 476-478; Axelrod 1978:1119, 1127). The ethnohistoric evidence shows that fires were more frequent in Mission and pre-Mission times, at least in grasslands. It can be argued that although some shrubs sprout after fires, if they were burned often enough they might be thinned out and eventually killed. While destructiveness of any one fire would depend on temperature and humidity conditions, a long regime of regular burning could increase the spacings between shrubs--areas that are normally occupied by herbs and grasses (Sweeney 1968:118; Hanes 1977:433; Heady 1977:501). Eventually, then, the shrubs would die out and the vegetation type in any one spot would be completely modified. Fire is widely used as a means of maintaining grass dominance in environments where in its absence woody vegetation would overwhelm grass; woody species that do not sprout from their roots can be either eliminated or reduced to a thin stand of small individuals by repeated burning (Sampson 1944; Daubenmire 1968:248;

Heady 1977:501). This process would be more likely to occur in coastal sage scrub than in chaparral (Richard Minnich, personal communication 1983).

Decreased fire frequency should allow seeds normally brought in from adjacent shrub communities by animals or by natural dispersal mechanisms a chance to grow and shade out grasses and herbs (Sauer 1952:17; Sweeney 1956:171). The result should then be recolonization, or "secondary succession" (Burcham 1957:220), of areas that had been maintained as grassland by burning, but that were actually better suited to chaparral or coastal sage scrub in terms of their soils and topography.

Perhaps future analysis of charcoal and pollen deposits in sloughs and marshes along the Santa Barbara coast will provide more information about the relative abundance of plant species and communities in prehistoric times.

The evidence presented here strongly suggests that the Chumash understood the connection between fire and the growth of certain useful plants, and that their principal reason for setting fires was to encourage the growth of seed plants, bulbs, and green shoots for human consumption. Of these food resources, seeds were most important in Chumash diet because of the quantities that could be obtained and because they could be stored for long periods of time. It is our opinion that the Chumash could have obtained the large quantities of chia and red maids seeds found as burial accompaniments and reported in the ethnographic literature only by burning the coastal grassland and savanna.

Fires were set in late summer after seeds were collected, but probably no attempt was made to burn the entire coastal plain every year. In fact, it might not be possible to burn such a large area so often. Fires require a certain amount of fuel for their spread; plant growth, and therefore fuel build-up, is related to rainfall. Fires in grassland and coastal sage scrub are at present larger after wet winters, but are more likely to spread into chaparral after dry winters (Minnich 1983:1291). Crespí's description of grass burned in some places and not in others supports the idea that some patches were burned one year, others the next. This would allow enough time for dry fuel to accumulate and support a fire, so that the optimal burning of each patch every few years was probably achieved.

The ethnohistoric evidence is less clear on the acquisition of animal foods as a motive for setting fires among the Chumash. If the coastal Chumash were using fire in game drives--and it is not certain that they were--it was most likely for hunting small animals such as rabbits or rodents, which are abundant in grassland (Burcham 1957:189). Deer do not aggregate in herds suitable for hunting with fire, but the Chumash would surely have taken advantage of any opportunity to hunt deer and smaller game attracted by increased green forage resulting from fires. The usual methods of bow hunting with the aid of deer disguises would be most appropriate in grassland-chaparral ecotones where shrubs and herbs sprouting after fires provide succulent browse for the animals (Wirtz 1974: 17; Bell 1974; Lewis 1973:28), and also provide both camouflage and ease of movement for the hunter.

CONCLUSIONS

Increased plant food yield and improved hunting were probably both seen by the Chumash as good reasons for burning vegetation. Both involve the significant process of performing an activity at one point in time in order to obtain desired results at another point in the future, some months or a year away. That the Chumash regularly engaged in long-term time reckoning and advance planning is shown by their development of a calendar system based on astronomical observations keyed to cycles of earth and sky (Hudson and Underhay 1978). As mentioned above, the Chumash could have developed the idea of burning to increase plant and animal resources from observing the effects of escaped fires near their settlements. It is arguable that, for the Chumash at least, Bean and Lawton's hypotheses about the rise of cultural complexity in aboriginal California can be taken one step farther: burning was not an "energy extraction process" in the sense of exploiting something that already existed, but truly a food production technique more efficient than agriculture in this ecological setting. Indians were allowed to continue gathering wild seeds in Mission times because agriculture could not support the neophyte population (Coombs and Plog 1974).

The probable effects of regular burning on the vegetation of coastal Chumash territory over a long period of time have significant implications for attempts at reconstruction of the aboriginal environment, both here and elsewhere. The grassland and savanna which dominated the landscape of the Santa Barbara plains and foothills when the Spanish explorers first arrived have now been replaced by coastal sage scrub as well as much non-native vegetation, and chaparral has apparently increased its density and extent, since grassland burning has been suppressed for nearly 200 years. A similar situation may have prevailed in the Santa Maria and Santa Ynez valleys as well, although specific data are lacking for these interior grasslands. On the other hand, in some places--for example the San Gabriel River to the south--very thick vegetation was described by Crespí in the same areas where chaparral is found today (Burcham 1957:94). Pollen records indicate that chaparral and coastal sage scrub have only dominated the local landscape for the last 2300 years, having succeeded coniferous forest and oak woodland; this trend may have been related to human activities as well as to climate changes (Heusser 1978:673; Schlesinger et al. 1982:76). The point is that archaeologists and others should be very cautious in assuming that plant resources available to the inhabitants of any site hundreds or thousands of years ago were the same as those found in the same area today.

Vegetation burning by hunter-gatherers was a widespread practice in many parts of the world, from Europe to Australia (Sauer 1952; Stewart 1951, 1956; Lewis 1973; Gould 1980:81-82; Pyne 1982:66ff.). In the midwestern United States, tall-grass prairies were maintained by natural fires or those set by Indians, and with fire suppression by settlers and increased grazing the prairies were later colonized by trees (Stewart 1951). The pampa of Argentina is also thought to have been a culturally-induced vegetation type (Schmeider 1927).

It has been said that the extensive records of Indians setting fire to fields and forests throughout North America should make it apparent that this activity was an important ecological factor in the development and maintenance of many types of so-called "natural" vegetation (Stewart 1951: 319; Day 1953; Sauer 1952:12; Daubenmire 1968:211), and that the general effect of their use of fire was to replace forests with grasslands (Pyne 1982:69; Sauer 1950). The practice of vegetation burning by the Chumash should be added to the list of important ecological factors in southern California.

NATIVE CALIFORNIANS AS ANCIENT AND CONTEMPORARY CULTIVATORS[1]

Kat Anderson

The California Indians were highly accomplished practical botanists, perhaps as knowledgeable about subtle differences in form, color, and behavior as some university professors who have spent their adult lives reading and making field observations. But they were also knowledgeable in a different way--a way directed at understanding nature in such a manner as to use it without destroying it [Heizer and Elsasser 1980].

INTRODUCTION

California has been sculpted by prehistoric human hands, as well as by earthquakes, lava flows, floods, lightning fires, and windstorms. Just as channel overflows revitalized the sandbar willow, California sycamore, and valley oak habitats, Native Americans--through the pattern and timing of harvests, as well as through the burning, pruning, weeding, and planting of places--favored certain mixtures and frequencies of plant and animal species.

Yet almost everywhere that Westerners have gone, they have underestimated the skill, ingenuity, and capability for shaping the landscape of the peoples they have displaced. Many of California's landscapes, which were culturally affected to a considerable extent, refute the idea that Native Americans "lived lightly on the land." However, the realization that parts of California bear the imprint of former human cultures does not necessarily imply that the land was therefore "corrupted" or "soiled." That

---

[1]This is a revised and expanded version of a paper that was originally presented at the Seventh Annual California Indian Conference, Sonoma State University, October 18, 1991. The author wishes to express her heartfelt appreciation to the Native American consultants who imparted invaluable historical information to her about the land. She also wishes to thank the Yosemite Association, Yosemite National Park, the Hardman Foundation, and the California Native Plant Society for their financial support. She is especially grateful to Scott Carpenter, former Yosemite National Park Archaeologist, and to Jan van Wagtendonk, Director of the Yosemite Research Center.

self-defeating attitude keeps us from exploring a Native American partner-ship with nature that left the resource base intact, despite the fact that there were effects from human action that were beneficial to native cultures.

The long centuries (lasting at least 12,000 years) of successful adaptation to life in California suggests that certain tribal approaches to land use were far more sophisticated than Westerners suspect. When one talks with elders in various tribes today, it becomes clear that there was a realm, pattern, and scale to human use that was suited to wild places, accessible through the ancient knowledge of those elders' ancestors. This paper attempts to look seriously at some of the possibilities for wilderness living suggested by Native American ways.

GATHERING WITH REGARD FOR PLANT REPLACEMENT AND RETURN

Native Americans harvested resources in such a way that the plants continually thrived in the same locations. Many tribes understood that there were plant-use cycles. An important rule for most cultural groups was "do not take everything". Therefore, harvesting rates were not much in excess of tribal yearly needs, and whole plants were left to ensure next year's harvest. These rules are still remembered and practiced today:

> We used to go up to the mountains and my dad would spot the brodiaea. We would only take half of the plants in a cluster. We never would pick them all in one area. You only take what you need [Hector Franco, Wukchumni Yokuts, personal communication 1991].

> Black oak acorns were the best of all. It was a sin to cut a black oak tree down. When gathering acorns, mother would leave some for seedlings [Katie Appling, Southern Miwok-Paiute, personal communication 1989].

In addition, vegetative reproductive structures were left behind. The implication seems to be that prehistoric native peoples harvested the most important plants on a sustained-yield basis. Bulbs, corms, and tubers of wild onions (*Allium* spp.), yampah (*Perideridia* spp.), lilies (*Lilium* spp.), mariposa lilies (*Calochortus* spp.) and wild hyacinth (*Brodiaea* spp.) were harvested carefully, leaving bulblets, cormlets, or tuber fragments behind to ensure a population for the following year. This gathering strategy is strictly adhered to today:

> We harvest the soaproot--break them off at the roots--so the roots grow into new plants. I've noticed they grow a lot more in the areas where we gather it [Barbara Bill, Yokuts-Mono, personal communication 1991].

> We gather bulbs and we only take the big ones and leave the little ones behind for next year's supply. We never take them all [Ron Goode, North Fork Mono, personal communication 1989].

When mushrooms are gathered, the stems are left behind so that the mycelia remain intact, thus ensuring future mushroom production:

> We were always told in gathering mushrooms to leave the stems of the mushrooms--without that nothing comes back [Mary Spears, Southern Miwok-Yokuts, personal communication 1989].

> We used to gather mushrooms under the pines. The dirt would puff up under pine needles. We'd use a knife to slice it so the root would stay in the ground. Mother said it was important to leave starters for other mushrooms [Katie Appling, Southern Miwok-Paiute, personal communication 1989].

The white roots (rhizomes) of sedge (*Carex* spp.) and the black roots (rhizomes) of bracken fern (*Pteridium aquilinum* var. *lanuginosum*) for basketry were dug in such a way as to stimulate new rhizomes, which then grew into "spur" plants. Plants are still continually harvested and managed today in ways that are self-renewing. There is a correct balance between taking and leaving alone:

> The sedge is gathered in the spring when the soil is soft and the runners are out. We thin them if there are too many plants and they don't have enough room. They take too many nutrients. By thinning it gives some of

154

them more room to grow. They're healthier [Barbara Bill, Yokuts-Mono, personal communication 1991].

One could wipe out a root supply in three years. With the white root it is important to leave the main root system. You don't cut the original stock, you cut off the runners [Ron Goode, North Fork Mono, personal communication 1989].

GATHERING ENSURES ABUNDANCE

There are still handfuls of native people today who have an intimate and respectful relationship with nature precisely because it is near at hand, and because they continually tap its creative ferment and hidden potential through the use of such materials as leaves, branches, berries, flowers, seeds, roots, horns, fur, claws, meat, organs, and bones. When gathering or hunting plants or animals, they unite the concept of "home" and the notion of "use". The distinction between nature without humans (wilderness) and nature with humans (home) is not made:

I've always wondered why people call plants 'wild.' We don't think of them that way. They just come up wherever they are, and like us, they are at home in that place [Clara Jones, Chukchansi Yokuts, personal communication 1990].

The fact that plants and animals are honored *through* human use reinforces the feeling that plants, animals, and humans all belong to a place:

When a Karok woman went out to collect pine roots, hazel stems, and bear-lily roots for her baskets, she moved in an animate and indeed passionate world. She gathered her basket materials from people--from a woman and her children who had once been dreadfully poor. By plucking roots and stems she was not harming these people but rather honoring them, transforming them into beautiful baskets that would be displayed during ceremonies, 'sitting in glory before the rich people.' The woman was thus helping the roots and stems fulfill their destiny [Margolin 1981:79].

Elders remember a time when mushrooms abounded, quail coveys were thick, and brodiaeas were dug "in a sea of blue." There is a common feeling among elders today that plants want to be used. This idea is similar to the concept that the fish and deer want to be caught and eaten. If not gathered they become scarce or disappear altogether:

> A plant with a purple flower would come out like daisies. We'd dig the bulb before it flowers and eat it like a potato. There used to be lots in those days. Nobody's digging them like they used too--that's why they're not as plentiful [Grace Tex, North Fork Mono, personal communication 1990].

> We gathered *dana* in the first part of May or the last part of April. We didn't have any stores. We'd gather it with a manzanita or mahogany digging stick. We'd go early in the morning and come back by evening because you need a lot of the potatoes to make a meal. Nowadays you hardly see them anymore because nobody goes out and gets them [Ruby Cordero, Southern Miwok-Chukchansi Yokuts, personal communication 1991].

These examples suggest a respectful, attentive concern for the source of plant and animal abundance, a complete cooperation with nature's processes, and a yielding to its limits (Berry 1981:98). They point to an intimacy and familiarity with the habits and requirements of valuable animals and plants that native peoples still continue to express daily.

NATIVE PLANT CULTIVATION

Areas where desirable plants grew were transformed into favorite gathering sites through indigenous management. Native peoples increased the potential for plant resources in these areas. Wild plant populations at favored gathering sites persisted and flourished as a result of human manipulation, technology, labor requirements, and indigenous conservation rules, rather than purely as a result of natural processes (Peri and

Patterson 1979: 42). Abundance came with thrift and restraint--but also as a consequence of human disturbance.

For example, many of the plant species that were widely used in California are "weedy" perennial species that exhibit strong vegetative reproduction in the form of rhizomes, bulblets, cormlets, tuberous root fragments, and adventitious shoots (Anderson 1991c). The most favored shrubs, grasses, ferns, and sedges for basketry, as well as the preferred herbaceous plants for edible corms, bulbs, and tubers, all evolved and thrived in a context of periodic disturbances that included flooding, rodent activity, fire, and herbivory. Human groups, through tillage, pruning, coppicing, weeding, and burning, subjected these plants to no more disturbance than they were already accustomed to receiving (Anderson and Nabhan 1991:30).

Seedbeating, Sowing, and Burning
to Maintain Native Seed Crops

Plant populations on important gathering sites could be destroyed by human mismanagement. Therefore, nondestructive gathering strategies involved technological factors as well as harvesting and management principles. For example, seed gathering was conducted in much the same manner by many tribes. Whether it involved Cahuilla women collecting chia seeds (*Salvia columbariae*), Pomo women beating the stalks of seedbearing grasses (*Elymus* spp.), or Miwok women harvesting the seeds of tarweed (*Madia* spp.), a procedure in which plants were struck with a stick or special seedbeater basket was used throughout California. Since not all seeds on the same stalk ripen simultaneously, and not all plants ripen together, seedbeating ensured that at least some seed fell at the source; in addition, perennial plants remained intact, thus ensuring next year's harvest. A strong wind will shake the ripening grain of seed culms onto the ground, thereby guaranteeing that any seeds ripening somewhat early (before harvesting) or late (after harvesting) will remain at the site.

Written descriptions of Indian women gathering seed are few. In early November, 1846, journalist Edwin Bryant observed California Indian women gathering grass seed for bread:

> This process is performed with two baskets, one shaped
> like a round shield, and the other having a basin and
> handle. With the shield the top of the grass is brushed,

and the seed by the motion is thrown into the deep basket held in the other hand. The five women appeared at a distance like so many mowers cutting down the grass of a meadow [Bryant 1985:352; actually, the seed was brushed with the deep basket with the handle--the seedbeater--and the open-mouthed "shield" basket caught the falling seed].

These gathering strategies were truly efficient. While harvesting grains with a seedbeater is labor-intensive and time-consuming, it was still efficient on a longterm basis, because it preserved the source of production--the plant population being harvested. A much more destructive method of harvest would be to break off the seed heads or uproot the plants, removing most of the seed from the site. According to the ethnohistorical record, this was rarely done (Barrett and Gifford 1933:154-155; Drucker 1939:9).

Formerly, custom often dictated that families gathered enough seeds to last through the winter, with an occasional small surplus to trade or store; however, not all of the seeds were gathered from the site. There is some record of broadcasting a portion of the collected seeds to ensure the next year's crop:

The brush in basins in the hills near the winter villages [Paiute] was burned and *Mentzelia* and *Chenopodium* seeds were broadcast. There is no question that this practice was native.... [Steward 1938:104].

Drucker (1939:11) also recorded that seeds of wild plants were broadcast by the Yuma Indians in southern California.

To stimulate seed production and/or protect the perennial stock, areas were sometimes burned by indigenous groups:

They did burning for specific things. I know that down in the low country in Yokohl Valley the Indian people would burn that whole valley. It produced grass seeds-- a type of wild rye. That grass you can eat and it was gathered and then burned [Hector Franco, Wukchumni Yokuts, personal communication 1991].

The usual California practice was followed of burning the country over in order to clear out the underbrush for facilitating acorn gathering, and to foster the growth of seed-bearing annuals [Kroeber 1925:467].

To assure the permanency of the natural openings and to maintain the quality of the oat crop, the dry straw was burned off [by the Coastal Pomo] every few years, generally after the first good rainfall [Kniffen 1939:388].

After a trip to Torrey Pines, she [Delfina Cuero, Diegueño] commented that there were more weeds, underbrush shrubs, carpets of dried pine needles, and broken branches than she had ever seen when she was young and with her family had gathered food and pine nuts there. She was afraid there was so much fuel that any chance fire would destroy the trees... She said that burning every year never let enough fuel accumulate to damage the trees. She also said that she had been told that some pine nuts had been planted to increase the size of the grove" [Shipek 1991:77--78].

Burning, Pruning and Coppicing to Enhance Native Shrubs

Previous anthropological studies of Native Americans have tended to focus on plants removed from their biological context, and have emphasized the cultural product rather than the source of the production. For example, no connection was made between the qualities of a plant used for a particular purpose and how those features were selected for or "nurtured" in the plants growing in the countryside. Even in those cases where some management information was recorded, no connection was made between use and management. For instant, how does management ensure continued plant abundance/availability for use? How is the plant harvested and/or managed to encourage the qualities considered desirable for specific uses?

In talking with weavers today, one learns that they are looking for very specific characteristics when selecting plants for making basketry. Basketmaker Norma Turner (Mono), for example, seeks the following qualities when she selects bluebrush (*Ceanothus cuneatus*) branches for the rims of a cradleboards, winnowers, and sifting baskets:

> I look for brownness, roundness, length and no lateral or side branches. We call them shoots. The old sticks are white and sometimes they have little branches on them and they're dry--not flexible. Those sometimes break [Norma Turner, Mono, personal communication 1991].

Many California native shrubs have benefited from being tended for centuries (Anderson 1990:7). Weavers today remember their elders burning bushes, often "on the sly," to augment the production of long, straight shoots with no lateral branches. Sourberry thickets were burned by the North Fork Mono for baskets; oak stands were fired by the Western Mono for looped stirring sticks; Chukchansi Yokuts fired buttonwillow patches for arrows; and North Fork Mono burned white oak and buck brush for cradleboards:

> A burn brings the sourberry and the redbud up real nice for baskets or when we prune, it comes up nice every year. If we don't there's nothing there to use for baskets [Anonymous North Fork Mono elder, personal communication 1991].

> They use the new growth of the black oak for spoons. Where it's cut or where wind has broken it and there starts new growth, that's what they would harvest. They would use the new growth of the black oak and white oak for mending cooking and winnowing baskets. These would be gathered in burnt over areas or cutover areas [Lydia Beecher, Mono, personal communication 1991].

> They used to burn for buttonwillow to help it and make it nice for arrow shafts. It will be one of the first to be gone if we don't start preserving it. Horticulture will help (Clara Charlie, Choinumni-Chukchansi, personal communication 1990].

> My uncle and grandfather burned all around the bluebrush [*Ceanothus cuneatus*] and white oaks [*Quercus douglasii*].

They'd pile brush on it and light the oaks and bluebrush on fire with a match. Mother, grandmother and my great aunt would harvest the little ones the following August to January for the tops of the baby baskets. They preferred the shoots after a burn because these are the ones that grow right from the ground and they're straight and slender [Norma Turner, Mono, personal communication 1991].

Today, weavers prune and coppice (a severe form of pruning) basketry shrubs as a substitute for their former burning practices (Fig. 5.1). These horticultural techniques not only change the qualities of the plants, leading to easier and more practical manufacturing, they are also beneficial for the plants:

We cut the redbud and it's brand new again. It's beautiful. The nice ones grow from down low. Pruning seems to make the plants better. If we don't cut them, the plants are bushy, all dried up, and have no color [Barbara Bill, Yokuts-Mono, personal communication 1991].

A long time ago Indians could go any place to pick materials for baskets. Cutting back redbud it comes back every year. It spreads from the ground. It doesn't hurt it--it grows better [Amy Rhoan, Paiute, personal communication 1989].

Hidden aspects of this human management can also be elucidated by examining finished cultural products sitting on dusty museum shelves. When carefully analyzed, the arrows, baskets, musical instruments, game sticks, and myriad of other items collected by ethnographers reveal the condition of the plants that were used at the point when they were harvested by human hands. The elderberry used for the clapper sticks, the snowberry used for the arrows, or the branches of maple used to make a basket are too straight, too uniform, and too lacking in lateral branch scars to be from undisturbed plants in the wild. The bundles of basketry rods and coils of basketry sewing material collected further substantiate the

Figure 5.1. Margaret Baty, contemporary Western Mono weaver, holding baskets made with branches from pruned native shrubs.

162

preference for a plant architecture that is the result of such forms of human management as burning, weeding, pruning, or coppicing (Anderson 1991a:149; Fig. 5.2). Branches from wild plants bear the marks of age-- they are gnarly, insect-infested, and crooked, with cracked, mottled, moss-covered bark. A cooking basket made with such branches would never hold water, a storage basket would sit lopsided, and arrows would never reach their targets.

Hundreds of straight rhizomes and thousands of straight branches were needed to make the baskets produced by a single village, yet a search in the wilds for long, straight, slender switches with no lateral branching is largely in vain. In order to gather sufficient suitable branches for making the many kinds of baskets produced by adolescent and adult females in various villages, Native Americans had to manage and maintain abundant populations of certain plants at what was virtually an industrial level (Anderson 1991c).

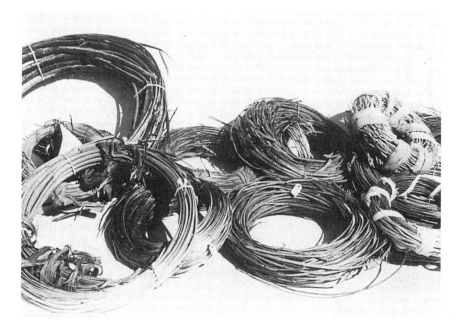

Figure 5.2. Coils of split young shoots and rhizomes to be used in the sewing (weft) of coiled and twined baskets. The coils are from the branches of maple, willow, redbud, and buckbrush, and from the rhizomes of sedge and bracken fern. Photo courtesy of the P.A. Hearst Museum of Anthropology, University of California, Berkeley.

Because of the constant need for young growth, the burning of areas for the improvement of basketry materials was frequently conducted by Native Americans; this has been substantiated by both ethnographic interviews and the ethnohistoric literature:

> Regular burning off of brushy areas [by the Karuk] produced good second-growth hazel twigs, which after two years were picked, peeled, and dried in the sun [Bright 1978:183].

> The best quality bear grass, gathered [by the Karuk] in July on dry ridges between two and four thousand foot elevations, is found in areas which have been burned over the preceding year. Only new green leaves will then be on the plants, and it is more easily picked and worked in this state [Fields 1985:51].

> When you cut sourberry it makes new shoots. They're nice and strong. Every two years I cut it. If it's not cut back it has a lot of little branches coming out of the stem and it's not good for anything. The top they used to burn it. It was filled with dried leaves [Lydia Beecher, Mono, personal communication 1991].

The extent of burning varies from setting individual plants on fire to burning "patches" of the plant to burning whole hillsides:

> My mother used to go out, pick from a maple thicket what she wanted, cut the rest down and, after spreading the leaves, set it on fire. In two years there would be a good growth of fresh shoots. In present years it becomes difficult to get the materials. The Forest Service no longer allows digging, nor can fires be made (Potts 1977:38).

Lily Baker (Maidu) stated that fires were set around individual maple trees to promote the growth of new shoots for basketry (McMillin 1956:27). According to Driver (1939:381), the Karok and Wiyot burned to make hazel and willows grow better for manufacturing baskets.

> Basketry material grows a lot better after a burn. The
> redbud and the sourberry they use for baskets. They
> know what they're looking for. They'd burn in the fall
> when the sap starts to go down. They'd light the whole
> hillside on fire [Dan McSwain, Mono, personal com-
> munication 1991].

The extent of burning may have changed through time, as laws were passed making burning illegal. For example, a procedure in which leaves were piled on individual shrubs and then lighted on fire was carried out after it was against the law to burn, and therefore may not reflect prehistoric burning techniques. According to consultants, this technique was designed to isolate the fire in one spot--thus concealing it from authorities, not allowing it to get away, and reducing the amount of smoke produced. It is highly likely that whole hillsides were fired prior to contact, so that entire clumps of redbuds, sourberries, and deer brush would have been affected, rather than just individual plants.

Ethnographic interviews, ethnohistoric sources, early photographs showing the straight stems harvested by weavers (Figure 3), and items of material culture in museums all verify the prevalence of pruning, coppicing, and burning of native shrubs by California Indian tribes. Many ethnohistoric reports hint of horticultural management when they label branches suitable for basketry, fish weirs, arrows, headdresses, structures, etc. as "withes," "sprouts," "young growth," or "suckers," thus implying that new growth was required.

Clark, for example, reported (1987:38) that the Yosemite Miwok wicker basket traps for catching fish were constructed of "long willow sprouts" loosely woven together and closed at the pointed lower end. Other statements are similar:

> Only the year-old wands (*Salix* sp.) without branches were
> chosen [by the Northern Paiute], and they were sorted as
> to size and length [Wheat 1967: 92].

> The split strands for twining the rods together [by the
> Southern Sierra Miwok] are black oak *Quercus californica*
> [*Quercus kelloggii*] (te-lay-ly), mostly young shoots which
> have great strength [Merriam 1955:111].

> The (arrow) shaft [used by the Sierra Miwok] was of the young shoot of a tree which closely resembles the willow; or young shoots of the western sweet-scented shrub, *Calycanthus occidentalis*; or apparently of elder [Barrett and Gifford 1933:217].

A survey of the ethnohistoric literature regarding burning by California Indian tribes shows that the major purposes for the burning that were recorded included (1) keeping the country open; (2) managing game; (3) stimulating the production of food crops; (4) decreasing insect pests and diseases; and (5) facilitating food gathering. The use of fire to induce the sprouting of many types of shrubs needed for making different cultural items was rarely documented. When it was recorded, it was often apparently considered unimportant, because the citation occurs as one obscure line buried in the text of a book, diary, or report.

Burning an area for the purpose of increasing or improving basketry materials was recorded by far the most frequently, probably because of the vast quantities of "straight shoots" that are needed to facilitate this enterprise. Burning on the sly or on reservation land to increase basketry material has even continued up to the present in a few places in California:

> Some of the materials for baskets [Maidu] were gathered in the valleys and some in the high mountain regions. To get good materials the bushes (redbud, maple & willow) were burned and the green and pliable shoots such as maple, that grew after the burning, were used [Potts 1977: 35].

Another example is supplied by Eleanor Beemer, a non-Indian woman and neighbor of the Luiseño people of Southern California, who recorded the following information in her diary:

> She [Juana, a Luiseño woman] promised to go with us down her trail to the river soon. She must burn the squaw bush [*Rhus trilobata*] shrubs along the way to force them to produce more canes [Beemer 1980:30].

Similar practices were followed in other geographical areas as well:

Both intentional and unintentional pruning of willows (*Salix* spp.) and lemonade berry (*Rhus trilobata*) for basketry fibers also took place in most areas [of the Great Basin]. In all areas with willows, women favored certain species and varieties in specific stands. They habitually cut first-year canes for baskets, thus in effect cultivating the patches, which in turn produced vigorous and straight canes the next year from the old root stock. Women at Walker River (Paiute) specifically recognized the efficacy of this process.... The San Juan Southern Paiute commonly burn patches of lemonade berry to promote hardy, straight growth... [Fowler 1986:94].

Many of the ethnohistoric reports of burning vegetation for the purpose of manipulating plant architecture refer to northern California; here, cultures were less disrupted at the time of early anthropological inquiry, and burning for basketry is still conducted in some areas today (Ken Peugh, personal communication 1992).

The foundation [of a Karuk basket] consists usually of carefully chosen shoots of the California hazel gathered the second year after burning the brush at the place where it grows [Harrington 1932:103].

The young shoots of deer brush that grow after a fire are gathered [by the Karuk women] and utilized in a similar fashion to young hazel shoots [Fields 1985:49].

Leaving the river, we ascended a long spur of mountain to the top of the dividing ridge between it and Redwood creek, through alternate forest and prairie land.... Prairies of rich grass [*Xerophyllum tenax*] lie on their southern slopes....The Indians [Chilula in northern California] used the stalks in their finer basketwork.... Late in the season, however, the grass is often burned, and dependence cannot always be placed upon the usual grounds [for animal feed] [Gibbs 1851:133].

Tillage and Burning to Maintain
Bulb, Corm, and Tuber Resources

Early reports describe plant populations of wild onions (*Allium* spp.), yampah (*Perideridia* spp.), brodiacas (*Brodiaea* spp.), and blue camass (*Camassia quamash*), as bountiful in California. Yet these plants were harvested by Native Americans in many parts of the state for centuries. The plants store concentrated nutrients in their vegetative reproductive parts, and were formerly an important item in the diet of many cultural groups. These bulbs, corms, and tubers are often called by the generic term "Indian potato".

What is intriguing is that the historic levels of production achieved at well-known gathering sites may have been mediated by human intervention (Anderson and Nabhan 1991; see Fig. 5.3). The vast fields of yampa recorded in early settler's diaries may have been maintained or increased through indigenous habitat management.

Figure 5.3. Photograph taken in 1931 by J. P. Harrington showing a Wintu couple, Billy George and Rosa Charles, digging for yampa (Perideridia sp.). Photo courtesy of the Santa Barbara Museum of Natural History.

Just as separating an overcrowded garden patch of daffodils is necessary to enhance growth, so selective harvesting by humans seems to cause many of these swollen underground stems to thrive. Is it possible that native groups practiced a form of tillage? The development of underground storage organs is an important means of propagation among perennial plants (Cook and Stubbendieck 1986). The digging of bulbs may have "thinned" the resource, separating small bulbs or corms and activating their growth and, therefore, increasing the size of the tract; it would also have resulted in aerating the soil, lowering weed competition, and preparing the seedbed to increase seed germination rates (Peri and Patterson 1979; Peri 1985).

Some of the various types of Indian potatoes are still highly valued or remembered by gatherers from various cultural groups, and recent interviews substantiate the fact that plant parts were and still are purposely left behind by Indian harvesters to ensure a future abundance:

> In digging wild potatoes we never take the mother plant. We just select the babies that have no flowers, just leaves. We are thinning the area out so that more will grow there next year. Also when harvesting wild onions with a little stick we would leave some of the young ones behind. They don't have a taste yet and will be ready the following year [Clara Jones, Chukchansi Yokuts, personal communication 1989].

> We gathered Indian potatoes in May or June when the leaves are green and when in flower with digging sticks. The stem and leaves are small like celery. They grow in grassy areas near ponderosa pines. You boil them just like a potato and they're eaten plain. We'd go back to the same area and gather them. My mother and grandmother would only take the best and the biggest. They wouldn't harvest the smaller ones. They also gathered two or three kinds of wild onions in the foothills along streams. The plants were harvested in spring before flowering. They never cleaned everything out. They would always leave some behind [Virgil Bishop, North Fork Mono, personal communication 1991].

The gardening or human management of bulbs and corms has been documented to a limited extent in the literature. Many of these species thrive on disturbed sites. Peri (1985) reports that the harvesting of corms, bulbs, and tubers by Pomoans in the California Coast Range aerated the soil and resulted in the severing of bulblets from the parent bulb, thus increasing the size of the plant bed. The Cahuilla Indians in southern California harvested the large corms of *Brodiaea* spp. and replanted the smaller corms to ensure a crop the following year (Bean and Saubel 1972). The Yurok, Hupa, and Tolowa still harvest the bulbs of *Lilium* spp. and selectively harvest the biggest bulbs, replanting the small bulbs for later harvest (Heffner 1984). Marie Potts (1977) said that the Maidu people steadfastly limited their gathering of the roots of wild carrot and camas, and always left some plants behind for seed.

Early reports also mention Indian potatoes growing in beds as if cultivated. Murphy, in her observations of California and Paiute Indians (1959), reported that the *Brodiaea* and *Calochortus* species grew in beds and were, therefore, easily harvested. While they seemed small for digging, one could do blind digging on them after locating even one seed stalk. Saxton Pope reported that a Yahi Indian could go out on an apparently barren hillside and with a sharp stick dig up enough brodiaea bulbs in an hour to furnish food for a good meal (T. Kroeber 1961).

The disturbance of tubers, bulbs, and corms by lightning fires can eliminate competitive shrubs and grasses and recycle plant nutrients, thus activating new vegetative reproduction and increasing the size and quantity of bulbs and corms. Various California Indian tribes took advantage of this ecological effect and burned over patches of Indian potatoes:

> A fire-glow in the distance, and then the wavy line of burning grass, gave notice that Indians were in the valley [Yosemite] clearing the ground, the more readily to obtain their winter supply of acorns and wild sweet potato root --"huckhau" [Baxley 1865:476].

> They used to burn for the wild potatoes (*Homogi* and *Dana*). We used to go where it had burned and we'd find great big potatoes. Otherwise the potatoes are little. They'd set the fires about now in August or later in the fall about September. Then by spring the plants start coming back up. It would fertilize the ground--maybe the

ashes do something [Ruby Cordero, Miwok/Chukchansi Yokuts, personal communication 1991].

Tena used to grow up in the hills. There used to be a lot of them. They grow better after a burn. When spring comes they shoot up. Fire only kills the tops, but the seeds are still under the ground [Lydia Beecher, Mono, personal communication 1991].

INDIGENOUS CONSERVATION TENETS

The various examples cited above may reflect an approach to plant harvesting that protected the desired ends. Expressed in Western terms, these examples illustrate a number of tenets that appear to have been operating within indigenous cultures to protect and conserve useful resources:

1. The quantity taken does not exceed the biological capacity of the plant population to regenerate or recover.

2. Gathering techniques sometimes mimic a parallel natural disturbance with which the plant has coevolved, thus maintaining and sometimes enhancing plant production.

3. The tool used is appropriate to the resource. It does not deplete the plant population of interest.

4. Horticultural techniques are used to give plants a competitive edge and put resources back into the system.

5. Often plants are chosen that exhibit remarkable vegetative reproduction.

6. Management is frequently at a scale that maintains the integrity of the plant community.

7. Taboos, codes, or other social constraints are in place to discourage depletion or overexploitation and avoid waste--thus reinforcing conservation-minded behaviors.

RARE AND ENDANGERED PLANTS,
ANIMALS, AND CULTURES

Public land managers have awakened to the necessity of protecting animals and plants that are potentially endangered or rare. Unfortunately, the few remaining indigenous plant-gathering sites are also often rare and endangered. Tribal needs for protected gathering sites (such as a quarter-acre sedge bed) are often minuscule in comparison to the size of the wildlife habitat required to maintain such rare and endangered animals as the spotted owl.

An Indian woman, in a letter to the Bureau of Land Management, asked that a small wild celery gathering area be kept intact. Another smaller patch had already been partially destroyed when the area around a lookout was leveled with machinery. "It is the only one in this region of any significance," she said, and "I have been going to the larger patch ever since I was old enough to make the climb with my aunt. As we went she would tell me a Shasta legend about the Coyote sisters going for Icknish on Quartz Hill."

Many of our plants and animals that are classified today as extinct, rare, or endangered appear to be so due to recent changes in the land use practices of Anglo-American settlers rather than as a result of climatic changes or Indian over-exploitation. Some of the possible factors that have contributed to the decline of these species are overgrazing, fire suppression, urban development, agriculture, recreation, mining operations, groundwater depletion, and logging. However, another possible explanation may be the very absence of human disturbance.

Plants such as the Kaweah brodiaea (*Brodiaea insignis*; Hector Franco, Wukchumni Yokuts, personal communication 1991) and western leatherwood (*Dirca occidentalis*; Kelly 1991:59) were harvested by native Californians for their edible plant parts; today they are classified as "rare and endangered" by the California Native Plant Society (CNPS 1988:17,40). There may be a causal relationship between former indigenous gathering and management practices and the rare status of these and other plant species that are disappearing.

An elderly Yurok weaver in northern California recently applied for a permit in one of California's state parks to pick five-finger fern stems for basketry material; her request was denied because "there were no known areas within state park lands where the fern grew in sufficient

Figure 5.4. The U.S.F.S. Mariposa Ranger District fire crew preparing for experimental deer grass burn, Administrative Site, Sierra National Forest. Virgil Bishop, North Fork Mono (with deer grass in hand), explains how the stalks are used in basketry.

quantity." Park officials were concerned that the amount regarded as necessary (two armfuls) would wipe out a major portion of the already limited population. Yet the collection of five-finger fern (or "black fern" as the Indians call it) was an ancient Yurok tradition. According to Yurok basketmakers, they "prune their fern patches so they might return to the same patch the following year" (Heffner 1984:73). Again, the idea that human use and tending ensures plant abundance and quality is pervasive in Native American thought.

Native peoples' interactions both past and present with native plants may offer some interesting, yet novel, approaches to wildland management. The semicultivation or other human disturbance of certain wild plant species that are threatened with extermination may prove effective safeguards against their rarity. In some cases, there may well be a connection between underuse and the presence of particular plants on lists of rare and endangered species. *Wilcoxia* spp., for example, used to be more abundant in Arizona in prehistoric times, even though indigenous groups ate the tubers. Sandfood (*Pholisma sonorae*) was savored by the O'odham or Sand Papago, and their harvesting strategies may have dispersed the seeds of this now rare and endangered plant (Nabhan 1985:55). Several case studies along the U.S./Mexico border attest to the fact that indigenous cultures in that area practiced the recurrent regeneration and consistent protection of plant populations over many human generations--and that those same populations are now threatened with extinction due to modern land usage (Nabhan et al. 1991:142).

Many public lands agencies in California have adopted a definition of natural vegetation as "vegetation that existed prior to European settlement." This, therefore, was the vegetation that was used, walked through, talked about, and manipulated by indigenous Native Americans. Ecologists increasingly find themselves working with native peoples and anthropologists to unravel former cultural practices regarding the land and establish the facts necessary for reconstructing the landscape. Native Americans today still retain a great deal of ancient knowledge concerning local areas and their ecological histories. The utilization of native expertise often leads to interesting approaches in which natural and cultural resources become synonymous.

Assisted by Kathy Heffner, and with the help of Yurok, Karuk, and Hupa elders, Forestry Technician John Hunter of the Six Rivers National Forest has conducted a series of experimental burns to enhance the quality and quantity of an important cultural resource, beargrass (*Xerophyllum tenax*). The most desirable beargrass consists of "the young shoots that come up in the center of clumps after periodic fires;" these are used in basketry, or braided on dance dresses, deer hides, and hats. Elders have complained that without fire, beargrass stands are not as plentiful and the old leaves on existing plants are weaker, thicker, and less pliable (Hunter 1988). The decline in stand quantity and quality is the result of the absence of Indian burning and the fire exclusion policies of the Forest Service.

Similar experiments are being conducted in Sierra National Forest, with the assistance of Indian elders, to measure the effects of simulated indigenous burning on the growth and reproduction of deer grass (*Muhlenbergia rigens*; see Fig. 5.4). Deer grass, a very important basketry material both historically and presently to Indian weavers, was managed with fire in order to increase flower stalk production and to increase the length and the thickness of the culms. Indian burning may have had the added benefit of causing fragmentation, a process in which portions of the plant die out and leave small fragments which then break off and become new plants, thereby increasing the size of the tract. In the absence of fire, deer grass colonies are now dwindling in areas that once were excellent traditional gathering sites.

Small-scale experimentation to test California Indian management methods is just beginning. Indigenous knowledge offers resource managers a diversity of approaches to the perception, conservation, and utilization of native plant resources. Yet one thing is already clear--as traditional plant gathering sites continue to disappear, so too will the knowledge base that keeps the ancient harvesting and management traditions of indigenous cultures alive. The perpetuation of indigenous customs and ready access to valuable resources are factors that are inextricably linked.

The indigenous systems of resource management that effectively controlled our public lands five centuries ago are now as rare and priceless a resource as the plants, animals, and rocks that these systems of knowledge were designed to protect and enhance. A future challenge for us all will be to develop viable land-management strategies for California which sustain both the resource base and the cultural integrity of indigenous peoples. We can begin by integrating fully the figure of the Native American into our ecological vision of the American wilderness (Cohen 1984:189).

'THE BASKET IS IN THE ROOTS, THAT'S WHERE IT BEGINS'[1]

DAVID W. PERI and SCOTT M. PATTERSON

The renown of Pomo basketry in the ethnographic literature has been based almost exclusively on form, fineness and evenness of stitch, symmetry, design, and, to a lesser extent, technique. Pomo basketweavers, however, have continually stressed that an essential part of learning the art of basketry is learning the art of root collection. One of the biggest complaints about new weavers, Indian and non-Indian alike, is as follows: 'They don't want to learn how to dig and prepare those roots. They can't call themselves weavers until they learn how to do that.' This paper maintains that the cultivation of basketry roots is a significant factor in the superior reputation of Pomo baskets. According to a celebrated Dry Creek weaver, 'the basket is in the roots, that's where it begins.' Consequently, we explore here the processes of basket sedge collection (i.e., cultivation) that the Pomo practice.[2] We also include the characteristics and qualities that weavers use in assessing sedge roots and comment on sedge root exchange and value.

---

[1]This paper originally appeared in the **Journal of California Anthropology**, Vol. 3, No. 2, pp. 17-32, 1976. It is reprinted here by permission of Malki Museum Press. Acknowledgements and several original figures have been deleted.

[2]All information contained within single quotation marks and not cited comes directly from consultants. These quotation marks only appear the first time the word or words are used.

SEDGE IN LITERATURE

The rootstocks of sedge (*Carex* sp.)[3] provide one of the most important basketry elements used by the Pomo (Hudson 1893:567-568; Chestnut 1902: 314). Baskets made from sedge form the basis for much of the Pomo's reputation for excellence in basketry, allowing for a fineness and evenness of stitch that is by some standards without equal anywhere (Hudson 1893:562, 576; Purdy n.d.:19; Curtis 1924:57; Kroeber 1925:144, 147). Samuel Barrett (1908:137) observed:

> The fine woody fibers make it possible to dress sewing elements down to a size hardly larger than that of a fine thread, and it is from this material that almost all of the very finest Pomo baskets are chiefly made.

V.K. Chestnut (1902:314) wrote that baskets made from sedge "are known technically as 'root baskets' and are the strongest, most durable, and most costly that are made."

Discrepancies arise in the Pomo ethnographic literature as to the species of *Carex*, or sedge, used as basketry elements. Some authors record only one species (Hudson 1893:567; Purdy n.d.:21), while others record two or more being used (Chestnut 1902:315; Mason 1904:443; Barrett 1908:137; Merrill 1923:236).

As a sewing element sedge roots were first identified by J.W. Hudson (1893:567). He reported only one species, "slough grass" "*kah-hoóm*," and identified it as *Carex mendocinoensis* (1893:567-568).

In Chestnut's (1902:315) work, the first discrepancy, and the apparent cause of all future problems of identification, arose when "*ka-hoóm*" was recorded as *Carex barbarae*. Chestnut made no mention of *C. mendocinoensis* or why he recorded "*kah hoóm*" (now written *ka-hom*) as *C. barbarae*. The possibility that Chestnut was correcting Hudson's misidentification is supported by the fact that Chestnut (1902:314fn) cited the authority upon which his identifications were based, whereas Hudson did not.

This unresolved confusion was perpetuated by later authors, some of whom recorded only *C. mendocinoensis* as the principal species (Purdy

---

[3]Sedge or Carex as used here refers to only those species of sedge whose roots are used as basketry elements by the Pomo.

n.d.:21), others recording only *C. barbarae* (Mason 1904:443): Barrett 1908:137), and still others recording both (Merrill 1923:236).

Carl Purdy (n.d.:21), writing in 1901-1902, recorded "*ka-hum*" or "*Carex mendocinoensis*" as the most important of the basketry elements, apparently having used Hudson's (1893) earlier work.

Barrett (1908:137), without citing the basis of his identification, recorded the use of *C. barbarae*. No mention was made of *C. mendocinoensis*.

Edith Merrill (1923:236,230) reported that both *C. mendocinoensis* and *C. barbarae* were used by the Pomo as a wrapping element, with *C. barbarae* recorded as one of their "chief materials." Her sources for *C. mendocinoensis* must have been Hudson (1893) and/or Purdy (n.d.), because her study was based solely on published sources (Merrill 1923: 216); her source for *C. barbarae* must have been Chestnut (1902) and/or Barrett (1908). It should be noted that she apparently misapplied Hudson's (1893:568) common name "slough grass" to *C. barbarae* (1923:236).

Two additional unidentified species are also discussed in the ethnographic literature. One of these, occurring in the vicinity of Clear Lake, was reported by Barrett (1908:137); the other, *Carex vicaria*, found in Round Valley outside of Pomo territory, was recorded by Chestnut (1902:315) and is not of concern here.

Because the confusion in the literature between *C. mendocinoensis* and *C. barbarae* cannot be resolved based solely on the literature, and because Barrett's data concerning his unidentified Clear Lake species are insufficient for identification, ethnobotanical fieldwork is needed.

According to the botanical literature (Munz and Keck 1968:1429), *Carex* is the largest genus of flowering plants in California and, with its more than 1000 species, one of the largest in the world. Though hybridization is common, it has been rarely observed or reported in California. Munz and Keck record 144 species in California; of these, 3 are introduced, 15 extend beyond North America, and 21 are endemic to the state.

The discussion of *Carex* in Munz and Keck (1968:1436-1468) reveals interesting data on its extensive distribution in California. Of the 29 plant communities recorded (Munz and Keck 1968:12-18), species of *Carex* occur in all but four.[4] *Carex* grows in all types of soils, alkaline or acidic, barren or fertile, marshy or dry, and occurs from sea level to the

---

[4]Carex is not found in Shadscale Scrub, Alkali Sink, Lodgepole Forest, and the Joshua Tree Woodland (Munz and Keck 1968:14-16,18).

timberless Sierran peaks, with *Carex haydeniana* growing at 13,600 feet maximum elevation. Some species are of wide occurrence while others are quite restricted. Of all the species recorded, *Carex rossii* had the widest range, from sea level to 12,400 feet; however, sedge is conspicuously absent in the arid desert regions and the lodgepole pine forests.

SEDGE TRACTS

Though *Carex* is widespread and common in Pomo territory, not all sites where it occurs are used as sources of basket roots. According to older basketweavers, tracts of sedge were widespread before the turn of the century, and most Pomo tribelets had a local source of roots.

The terms 'tracts' and 'beds' are used here to reflect a Pomo point of view in that they refer only to those sites known to be used. Basketweavers divide tracts into one of two types: 'river root tracts,' typically growing along the Russian River and its tributaries; and 'coastal root tracts,' growing along water courses closer to the coast. These geographical divisions overlap and refer not to individual species of *Carex* but to many species growing in the same general region. For example, coastal sedges are also found along the Russian River as far upstream as Guerneville, Sonoma County. A third type of sedge tract may possibly exist in the Clear Lake region (see Barrett 1908: 137); however, our fieldwork to date has not confirmed this.

Within coastal and river root divisions, there are three types of beds: 'sand root' beds; 'dirt root' beds; and heavy clay beds. Sand root beds consist principally of sand, and are the most preferred because they yield the whitest roots, which are used in the finest baskets. Sand root beds occur in both coastal and river tracts though principally in coastal tracts. Dirt root beds consist of a mixture in varying proportions of loosely-compacted sand and soil. It is said that these roots grow faster than those found in sand because of the additional nutrients available in the soil of dirt root beds. Dirt root beds occur along stream and river bands in low bottom land and yield a less-preferred colored root, from off-white to brown. Dirt root and heavy clay beds are most commonly found in the river region. Heavy clay beds consist of highly-compacted soil characterized by the absence of sand and the presence of clay. These beds are recognized but not used because, even with extensive use, they only yield short, kinky roots. Heavy clay beds usually occur above the flood plain and are associated with springs.

In both the coastal and river regions, there are a number of preferred tracts. The earliest record of a preferred tract, a river root tract located near Hopland, appears in Hudson (1893:568). Today's most preferred tracts yielding the highly prized river roots occur in Mahilkaune Pomo territory along Dry Creek, Sonoma County. An elderly Dry Creek weaver recalls that these tracts were used at least as early as 1875.[5] The oldest of the basketweavers remember Dry Creek as being the most continuously and most extensively used area in the Russian River basin. Indians from Mendocino, Lake, and Sonoma counties use, when given a choice, the Dry Creek tracts exclusively. Today's most preferred coast root tracts occur along the Navarro River, Mendocino County.

Although there is no record in the ethnographic literature of private ownership of sedge tracts among the Pomo, many basketweavers today establish informal 'claims' on certain beds through extended usage, though they make no attempts to prevent others from using these sites. One Ukiah Pomo weaver stated that 'in the early days' the locations of sedge tracts were kept secret: 'They only tell their relatives.'[6] After being dug, roots were coiled and carefully concealed in the bottom of a burden basket; the women then returned home, pretending their digging sticks were walking sticks. Dry Creek women were apparently unconcerned with concealing the whereabouts of their preferred tracts, and said that people who were 'stingy' with the locations of new tracts would lose their luck in finding roots.

Basketweavers today find themselves excluded from their sedge beds by fences and trespass laws. This reduced access is a sore point among weavers, since they are required to either 'sneak around' to use the few good local tracts or travel great distances to other sites. Such enforced activity constitutes not only a physical hardship and inconvenience for these elderly women, but an economic hardship as well, since the resulting increase in travel expenses reduces profits from the sale of baskets.

In addition to being denied access to collecting tracts, weavers must contend with the continuing problem of tract destruction. The earliest

---

[5]Information from consultants has been related, where possible, to the modern designations of Pomo tribelets. Where the information has not been specified, it may be construed to have general applicability for all of the Pomo tribelets.

[6]The phrase 'in the early days' as used by consultants refers to some time before 1890.

recorded description of the destruction of a sedge bed is that of one near Hopland:

> ...before the thrifty rancher found the true value of this rich alluvium in hop culture the [Indians] from rancherias far and near would come and gather these preferred roots [Hudson 1893:568].

Tracts continue to be destroyed by gravel mining operations (see Allen 1972:19), flood control, and commercial, agricultural, and industrial development.

THE COLLECTION PROCESS

Weavers possess intimate knowledge of the different functions of the sedge root systems. 'Basket sedges' are 'everlasting plants' (perennial), with grass-like triangular stems that reproduce both with flowers and through spreading rhizomes. The mature or "parent plants" have two separate root systems: one consisting of rootlets or 'foundation roots' that grow vertically into the soil, supply water and minerals; the other comprising rhizomes and yielding 'basketry roots.' These rhizomes or 'runners' grow to form an underground root network that firmly 'anchors the plant,' reducing the erosional effects of the rivers and streams along which it grows. The roots of sedge plants with multiple runners are called 'family roots': the longest root is the husband, the next longest is the wife, and the shorter roots are the children.

The new season's growth are 'spring roots' and are recognized by sharply pointed tips or 'spurs.' The second season's roots are called 'ripe roots,' referring to their maturity for basketry purposes. In later years, if not collected, a rhizome will sprout and come to the surface, eventually growing a mature crown of foliage, foundation roots, and its own rhizomes. After this original rhizome has established a new plant, it turns black with age and rots away completely in a few years.

Tract Maintenance

An essential ingredient in the development and maintenance of sedge root tracts is the recognition and modification of environmental conditions vital for yielding the finest roots. It seems reasonable to suggest that in precontact times, because sedge root elements were essential in subsistence technology and ceremonial basketry, weavers maintained tracts to insure predictable supplies. In modern times, though the emphasis of basketry is primarily a commercial one, tract maintenance is no less important.

Collectors are faced with a delicate problem: they must obtain an adequate root supply and at the same time insure the tracts' continued viability. To accomplish this, weavers today use a collection strategy regulated through supernatural sanctions and taboos that is compatible with the reproductive mechanisms of sedge. Proscriptions, taboos, and the weavers' specialized knowledge of the requirements of sedge insure not only the survival of the plants but also the supply of roots as well. For example, sexual and menstrual taboos serve in part to regulate the number of days available for collecting, thereby reducing collection pressure on the tracts.

The earliest record of tract maintenance and "primitive agriculture" was presented by Mason (1902:443):

> Mr. Coville draws attention to a bit of primitive agriculture...The Pomo women insist that the toughest and finest roots can be obtained only at certain spots. Unconsciously they have been making this true by means of their digging sticks and clam shells, during all the years loosening the ground and removing weeds.

The removal of rocks, branches, other roots, and debris from beds results in a loose, homogeneous soil that allows free expansion of the roots. Competition from extraneous plants is eliminated by 'weeding them out' (see Mason 1904:443; Allen 1972:19).

In frequently cultivated or 'easy digging' beds, the roots are removed before they have the opportunity to become tangled. In beds cultivated infrequently, obstructions cause roots to grow bent or 'kinky.' These beds are 'kinda hard digging' because they contain roots from several seasons, which usually become tangled. In beds rarely or never cultivated, the soil has a tendency to become compact, and generally contains an abundance of extraneous debris. These beds, characterized as 'rough digging,' yield very short, thick, kinky, and tangled roots. With frequent and continued cultivation, all sand and dirt root beds can in time yield finer sedge roots.

There is no need for the beds to be left fallow to restock the roots, as the plants "will make runners again next spring and [the roots will] be good in the fall" (Theodoratus et al. 1975:174). Basketmakers know that if they carefully dig out the older roots, leaving the spring runners behind to mature, that sedge beds can be harvested on a yearly basis without danger of depletion.

When digging, weavers are careful to replant short pieces of roots and accidentally unearthed young plants, and have at times transported these to other locations for the establishment of new tracts (cf. Theodoratus et al. 1975:173). Transportation of other types of plants has been recorded for areas of California (see Bean and Lawton 1973:xxvi); however, its practice is of unknown antiquity among the Pomo.

Basketweavers recognize that improper digging techniques are detrimental to the beds. According to weavers, there is definitely a right way to dig sedge roots. Because of this, they are reluctant to bring inexperienced individuals to their favored spots. Today, the collection pressure on the preferred beds is very high, as they are few in number and basketry classes are growing in popularity. Basketmakers agree that students must learn the collection process before they are considered weavers; therefore, collecting trips are required as part of the curriculum. Non-preferred beds are used for the training of novices in cultivation and collection in order to preserve preferred areas. By using less preferred beds to train weavers, basketmakers are able to 'thin out' the tangled roots and, in time, to develop these beds into preferred tracts.

In summary, through cultivation of sedge beds, weavers increase the quantity and quality of the roots in addition to extending the size of tracts. As long as sedge beds are cultivated, they supply a predictable and probably indefinite resource.

Collecting Restrictions

Today sedge gathering is not considered a wholly secular activity; for many weavers it is "spiritual" (Theodoratus et al. 1975:179). Highly specific, supernaturally sanctioned "rules" exist in two different stages of the collection process--those in force before leaving for the beds and those in force while collecting. The extent and degree of observance varies with different individuals (Theodoratus et al. 1975:179). It seems reasonable to suggest that in earlier times ritual restrictions were more extensive and more widely observed than today.

All weavers except one Ukiah Valley woman, who is also a singing doctor, agree that menstruating women and 'their men' have never been allowed to collect roots, and that violation of this rule results in sickness: 'It's just like having worms in your body; those worms look just like those short roots.' The Ukiah Valley doctor and weaver does not observe menstrual restrictions: 'This is modern times and I'm a modern Indian. It doesn't affect me. I've my own rules, I'm different that way.'

Menstruating women are said to be more susceptible to rattlesnake bite if they dig for roots: 'Those snakes are attracted by that waste blood, they'll bite that woman.' A Dry Creek weaver has said:

> There are restrictions on handling sedge roots because 'the women are afraid of the snakes.' A snake may have crawled over the root while it was in the ground, causing the weaver to become ill and require a doctor [Theodoratus et al. 1975:179].

All collectors agreed that in earlier times sexual abstinence was observed before and during root collection. 'If a man sleeps with a woman, his thing will get like those roots; it looks funny, the women won't go around him anymore, that's his punishment,' remarked a Cloverdale Pomo woman. She also commented: 'Those roots will get jealous if they [the collectors] do that [have intercourse], they'll go to somebody else, and you'll have those other people's luck.'

The singing doctor from Ukiah sings as instructed by the 'spirit' before collecting her roots. She also 'prays' for others before they collect to protect them from snakes, especially rattlesnakes.

Other observances are reported for the Dry Creek Pomo:

> While digging for sedge, a consultant was asked the Dry Creek name for the plant and replied: "I'll tell you when we get back home, if I tell you now they will go back on me," meaning she will not have any more luck in locating roots [Theodoratus et al. 1975:178].

One Cloverdale woman remarked: 'You should not brag about your roots before you have 'em, you're going to come home with an empty sack if you do that.' She also stressed the importance of complimenting or 'talking good about the roots.' She considered it proper to exaggerate the length of roots so as not to offend them even though they may be short: 'Sometimes those roots test you, they come up short to see how you're going to talk about them, hear what you're going to say. If you talk good about them they'll come up long.' She also stated that roots dug after dark will turn black, and if collectors eat acorn bread while collecting, the roots will turn 'dark like the bread.' One Upper Lake woman and her family abstained from drinking water while collecting roots.

Another weaver (a Cache Creek sucking doctor) observes the following rules:

> She only collects the roots in the morning hours when it is not raining, and eats no food prior to gathering. After she collects the roots, it is washed off in the creek and is washed again when she returns home [Theodoratus et al. 1975: 179].

Some weavers are said to have more luck in digging the roots than others. Luck is acquired by observing the rules for collecting. Certain individuals also own special songs which bring luck. Angelica is carried by some to 'make 'em lucky for the roots,' as well as to protect them while collecting.

Collecting Seasons

The season for collecting sedge roots varies between coast and river root tracts. Within river root tracts, the collecting season also varies between sand and dirt root beds. Such variation may also exist within the coastal root tracts, although this is yet undetermined.

The time for collecting river roots was reported by Hudson (1893:568) as follows:

> During the summer months and even into the fall, as long as the rising waters would permit [access to the beds]...

Chestnut (1902:317) recorded that river roots were collected during the summer and early fall. According to Allen (1972:18), in referring to roots two or more seasons old,[7] sedge is collected "generally in early spring." A Ukiah Pomo weaver, referring to river roots,[8] has commented that "sedge grass roots are at their best in the fall of the year, about October"; however, "it is possible to cut these roots any time of the year..." (Newman 1974:7). According to Theodoratus et al. (1975:176):

> Dry Creek Pomo basketmakers have recently reported that the 'old timers' gathered sedge 'after the first rains in the fall, when the ground loosens up.' The roots at this time of the year are 'seasoned up ripe, it's not too fresh.' In recent years, sedge root has been gathered during all seasons, though winter weather makes collection difficult.

Our discussion with basketmakers regarding the collecting season led to the following conclusions: (1) Sand root beds are best collected from late summer to the first rains in the fall, when the spring growth is mature. (2) Dirt root beds are best dug after the early fall rains when the soil has loosened up: 'The digging's easier then.' Basketmakers also agreed that today, with access to sedge beds limited, 'Anytime is the best time, dig them whenever you get the chance.'

Collection Method

Root digging is often a family affair, with men, women, children, and old people participating. Many times 'they'd make a big trip of it, camp a week at a good spot,' with everyone collecting and the men doing the 'heavy work.'

In the early days, a fire-hardened, single-pointed, hardwood digging stick was used to loosen the soil and expose the roots. The earliest description of sedge collection by the Pomo was reported by Hudson in 1893:

> Armed with a clam shell in one hand and a short stick in the other, he takes a bunch of this grass as a starting point, and lays bare its radiating roots. Selecting the best

---

[7]Personal communication with Elsie Allen (January 27, 1976).

[8]Personal communication with Molly Jackson (January 27, 1976).

186

of these, he grasps the root between the first and second toe, and gently lifts it a little, to indicate its hidden course under the sand to the next bunch. This fact ascertained the clam shell scoops out, while the stick carefully loosens all stones or hardened earth in its path, till soon a little trench some three or four inches deep, uncovers the beginning of this *kah hoom* gem. The work is slow and careful, lest the sharp edge of a rock cut or bruise the tender fiber, whilst in the rear like a ship's rudder the guiding foot and protecting toes keep pace [Hudson 1893:568-569].

Older basketmakers are familiar with this collection method, but are unable to contribute additional details.

Tools used in root collection have changed since Hudson's time. The digging stick was first replaced by the crowbar, and later the tire iron. The crowbar was said to be too heavy and cumbersome: 'It tired the men out too soon, it was even harder digging for the women.' The tire iron quickly found widespread acceptance, as it is lighter and more efficient than the crowbar. Allen (1972:18) noted that a "three-pronged curved fork was used in the old days, and a similar steel fork for digging can be used today." Other basketmakers refer to these as 'grubbing hooks.' They consist of three equally spaced and pointed prongs, attached like a hoe blade, at right angles to a handle (Allen 1972:18). The length of the handle and the overall weight of the 'hook' vary with different individuals. When basket-weavers find a hook that's 'right for them,' they tend to favor it above all others. In addition to the grubbing hook, "your hands and fingernails also help a lot in separating a long root from the soil (Allen 1972:18)."

The method of sedge root collection using modern tools has been described as follows:

The space between the prongs allows it to be drawn easily through the soil and when a root is reached, the tool is so constructed as to minimize damage to either the root or the parent plant. It is used to scratch the soil from around the parent plant to expose where the runners lie. Once a runner is found, it is carefully traced by digging the soil away from either side until the end is reached. The runner is then firmly grasped and pulled directly upwards. The parent stock and the root separate easily [Theodoratus et al. 1975:176].

Though modern tools have replaced those described by Hudson, the techniques as well as the approach to collection remain the same, namely, to obtain sedge roots while insuring the continual productivity of the beds.

Other tools are also used in collection (i.e., cultivation). Spading forks are sometimes used by men to thin out a patch if the roots and plants are particularly dense from lack of cultivation. As a rule, digging tools with flat prongs or blades are avoided, since they tend to cut the roots. Newman (1974:8) recently recorded the use of a "small garden fork" for digging sedge roots. Allen (1972:18) recorded the use of a trowel; however, other basketmakers regard it as awkward and prone to cut the roots.

One of the differences observed between older, experienced basketmakers and those of less experience is the individual's posture while digging. More experienced individuals sit while digging to make their work easier. Less experienced individuals stand bent over while digging: 'I guess they're embarrassed to sit like us old Indians.' Experienced basketmakers associate stooping with 'kinky' roots: 'They'll get kinky roots standing that way.' Other comments were: 'You get too tired standing that way'; 'That's the way white people dig their roots.'

It was observed that those who stand dig by hoeing and chopping rather than by gently digging: 'You can tell when somebody's been digging who doesn't know how, they chew up the ground and tear up the roots.'

Basketmakers say that men don't have enough patience to 'dig out the roots. When they get tired, they cut them off anywhere. They don't dig them out all the way. They start out good, but you know how those men are.'

A review of Hudson (1893:569-570) revealed a seeming contradiction between the number of root coils collected per day in the 1890s and today. He observed that in a good day's work a man will collect ten roots, and a woman will often double this amount. He recorded that their roots were usually four or five feet in length, depending upon the condition of the soil and the disposition of the collector, and that the "splittings from two roots make a coil convenient to handle" (Hudson 1893: 569-570). A good day's work would then yield five to ten coils per day. However, basketmakers today report that 'one good day's digging' in a preferred tract yields 'three of four coils.' This seeming contradiction is resolved by the fact that there is no standardized root count in a coil, and that modern coils are substantially larger than those reported by Hudson.

The structure and efficiency of the grubbing hook appears to have revolutionized root digging. This tools allows greater ease of manipulation and greater soil moving capacities than were ever possible with a digging stick. The three prongs of the cultivator can be compared to having the efficiency of three digging sticks simultaneously, and it would therefore represent a three-fold increase in effectiveness over the digging stick. It seems reasonable to estimate that the cultivator could reduce digging time up to one-third of that required by either digging sticks or tire irons. In other words, a root formerly uncovered with the digging stick in 30 minutes (Hudson 1893:569) could now be uncovered with the cultivator in only 10 minutes. Women who once gathered 20 roots per day (Hudson 1893:569) could now be collecting 60. Men who formerly gathered 10 roots per day (Hudson 1893:569) could now collect 30.

ROOT QUALITIES

Five interrelated qualities are recognized by basketmakers in assessing sedge roots: length, color, straightness, strength, and pliability. The importance of these qualities varies according to the intended use of the basket, which in turn determines the basketry technique required.

Root length varies, depending upon where the plant occurs. Roots under 15 cm. are generally avoided: 'They're not good for much; too short.' As a rule, the longer the root, the better. Sand beds yield the longest roots; the longest observed during our fieldwork was over 2 m. and was dug in Dry Creek, Sonoma County. Sand roots over 1.75 m. are not uncommon, but the average length is between 60 and 90 cm.

The color of sedge roots varies from white to pale lemon (Hudson 1893:573), to cream colored (Hudson 1893:569), to tan, to a rich brown. The term 'white roots' refers to roots pure white in color. This term is also applied to the whitest of the cream-colored roots. Though all colors of sedge are used, white is by far the most preferred. Sand beds produce the whitest roots, their color being attributed to the 'white color of the sand.' Dirt roots are a rich brown, reportedly taking on the color of the dark soil. 'Old roots,' regardless of the soil they grow in, are also brownish in color.

A rich brown color is additionally associated with 'under the leaf roots,' which typically occur along stream beds in well-shaded, moist areas under trees. After a sufficient leaf cover has developed, the sedge roots grow above the ground and 'run under the leaves.' The color of under the leaf roots, like dirt roots, is brown. This is attributed to the brown color of the fallen leaves.

Straightness is an important root quality because it affects root strength. Roots growing in beds that contain obstructions in the soil have a tendency to kink or bend: 'The root goes along until it comes to a hard place, then it turns and make a kink.' It appears that roots seek lines of least resistance and grow straighter in soil that they can easily penetrate. These kinky or bent roots are the least preferred because the kinks must be cut out, yielding a series of lengths rather than a single long root. Additionally, each kink causes a weak spot, which is compounded to the point of breaking when the root is split and cleaned. In addition of their proneness to splitting unevenly, the split sections are narrower at the point of the kink, and the overall section needs to be sized to the width of the kink. Oftentimes the kink can be reduced by 'thinning it out,' i.e., reducing the width and thickness of the overall element. Although the result is a fine, threadlike root, when used as a sewing element the kink causes an uneven stitch that does not lie flat as 'straight roots,' and is therefore avoided in the finer-coiled baskets. In the majority of instances, the bent section of the root is simply cut out, resulting in two shorter pieces. As one weaver commented, 'You only go through all that work if you're hard up for roots.'

Roots that are particularly short and kinky are called 'old-lady roots.' 'When the ladies get old, they get shorter and bent over. That's how these roots get their name.' Kinky roots are more preferred over the old-lady roots because the sections between the kinks are longer.

In general, the more pliable roots are preferred; however, the lack of pliability can to some extent be compensated for by splitting, sizing, and soaking. Coast roots are said to be by far the most pliable of the roots.

Age effects length, strength, pliability, and color. The ideal age for roots is between one and three years. Age as a selective factor in collection usually refers to roots three or more seasons old, large in circumference, and brown in color. These old roots have specialized uses. Each new season's growth is 'spring roots' and is gathered in the fall. As a rule, approximately 15 cm. near the tip are removed because of softness. Immature spring roots, 'young roots,' are avoided because the inner tissue is too soft and easily broken. As new growth matures in the fall, this soft tissue becomes dense and woody, i.e, 'gets seasoned.'

There is no doubt that basketmakers recognize different types of sedge roots and are aware of the special properties of each. They consider these properties in the weaving technique, in the preparation of the element, and in the subsequent use of the basket (cf. Merrill 1923:228)

Sand roots, because of their color, are used for the fine coiled ceremonial or gift baskets (see Theodoratus et al. 1975:171), since these whitest of roots are preferred as background to the black or red designs. White is also the preferred background for twined gift baskets. 'White roots' are used in feather baskets where the inner surface is readily apparent, e.g. in 'sun baskets' and plate form baskets. Because these baskets are used in ceremonial exchanges and as offerings, it is important to use only the finest of roots.

In earlier times, a basketmaker of any repute would strive to have all her baskets made from the whiter sedge roots. When asked why, since with age and use all sedge roots baskets darken, a basketmaker recently told us that the basket will darken evenly all over and will not 'spot,' i.e., not darken unevenly.

Dirt roots, because of their color, are used to repair older baskets whose elements have darkened with age and can be used on either twined or coiled baskets, being especially preferred for the latter. Dirt roots tend not to be used in fine baskets; however, they can be used in baskets where the elements are concealed by feathers. Dirt roots are not used, however, in 'sun baskets' or plate form feather baskets where the inner surface is readily visible.

Although longer roots have a more generalized use in Pomo basketry, shorter roots are also used. The short, straight sections between the kinks of the old lady roots and kinky roots are used for making miniature baskets; however, longer roots are preferred for these miniatures since 'the baskets go faster' (i.e., they do not require as much weaving time). Shorter roots require continual sizing and replacing of new sewing elements as they become too short: 'For those little ones, longer roots are best; you can go all the way with one or maybe two roots.' Another use of shorter roots is for the white contrast between the black design elements: 'Sometimes you need just a few white stitches--those short ones are good for that.' Shorter roots are also used in repairing coiled baskets.

Old roots, because of their age, are 'thicker' or larger in circumference than other roots. The shortest and thickest of these are called 'chubby roots.' Because old roots are 'wide when you split them, ' they yield a wide, strong 'flat root.' Because of their pliability and strength, flat roots are particularly well-suited for use on plain twined work baskets:

'They make a strong weave, a strong basket.' Also, the wide elements obtained from flat roots 'make the weaving go fast.' Old roots become fibrous with age and, for this reason, are only soaked a short time. If oversoaked, they tend to split apart into fibers. Old roots are brown and, like dirt roots, are used to repair old age-darkened baskets.

Coastal roots, due to their pliability, are preferred by some weavers for use in miniature baskets: 'It makes weaving the tiny stitches easy.' Because of flexibility ('you can cinch it up tight'), coastal roots are also preferred for lattice and other twined weaves, i.e., close twining that demands a rigid warp material and a very flexible woof (cf. Merrill 1923:229).

According to weavers, the major drawback of baskets woven with coast roots is their inability to be used with water for any length of time, since the elements break up into individual fibers. One basketmaker has reported that coast roots were not used for cooking baskets or 'mush baskets.'

River roots, in contrast to coast roots, are known for their dense, tough strands which range in color from white to tan. These tough elements yield very strong and durable twined and coiled baskets. They require comparatively lengthy soaking to soften, but the fibers do not break apart and are therefore suited for most purposes. River roots are more widely available and used than coastal roots and are far more common in modern Pomo baskets.

EXCHANGE AND VALUE

Although sedge occurs throughout the Pomo and adjacent territories, this did not preclude exchange for roots, though Davis (1966) recorded none. Since certain types of sedge not found locally are preferred for specific basketry techniques, exchange is required. Today, exchange becomes even more important as preferred tracts in local areas become destroyed or access to them is denied, forcing weavers to travel to new beds or to purchase roots.

Hudson (1893) recorded the value of sedge in terms of clam shell disc beads and other basketry roots. It seems reasonable to advance the hypothesis that sedge roots formed a part of the intra- and inter-tribelet exchange system of the Pomo.

Since 1893 there has been a gradual increase in the price of sedge coils (Table 6.1). The period just before and after the turn of the century was a period of intensive selling or trading of baskets by Pomo weavers for money and/or goods. Pomo baskets were in great demand by ethnographers for museum collections, serious collectors, and those who collected because it was stylish for the times (Mason 1904:187-188). The rise in prices between 1893 and 1920 reflects this interest and, possibly more important, is indicative of the decreasing number of preferred sedge beds.

Table 6.1

THE VALUES OF SEDGE ROOTS[9]

Date of Value	Amount of Sedge Roots	Equivalent Value	Source
1893	5 bunches	100 clam beads sm. bunch bulrush 6 bunches redbud	Hudson (1893:572)
1899	1 bunch	65 clam beads	Mason (1900:347)
c. 1900	1 coil	50¢	Cloverdale Pomo
c. 1920	1 coil	$1.00	Cloverdale Pomo
c. 1940s	1 coil	$1.25	Dry Creek Pomo
1962	1 coil	$5.00	Cloverdale Pomo
1970s	½ cleaned root	25¢ to 50¢	Kashaya Pomo
	¼ coil	$5.00	Cloverdale Pomo
	1 coil	$20.00	Cloverdale Pomo
1974	1 coil	$15.00	Cloverdale Pomo
1975	1 coil	$20.00	Cloverdale Pomo
	1 coil "coast roots"	$35.00	Cache Creek Pomo
	1 coil	$25.00	Coyote Valley Pomo
1976	1 coil	$25.00	Cloverdale Pomo

Weavers are forced to go outside of their local areas to purchase or trade for roots. According to weavers, the years before World Wars I and II marked a low point in the sale of baskets and sedge coils. The post-war period brought a renewed interest in the sale and collection of Pomo

---

[9]Coils as used here consist of cleaned and split root elements.

baskets. According to weavers, this was also the period of extensive land development that contributed to the demise of collecting tracts. Reduction in the number of preferred tracts and the declining number of experienced weavers brought about rising prices for sedge coils and subsequently the baskets themselves. When recently asked about the prospects for the future in terms of sedge root and basket prices, a weaver replied: 'Like the white people say nowadays, prices are going up.'

CONTEMPORARY CALIFORNIA INDIAN BASKETWEAVERS AND THE ENVIRONMENT[1]

Bev Ortiz

The Indian's preservation of the land and its products for the ten thousand or more years of their undisputed occupancy was such that the white invaders wrested from them a garden, not the wilderness it salved their conscience to call it [Kroeber and Heizer 1968:24].

INTRODUCTION

In modern California the concept of wilderness "uncultivated and uninhabited by human beings" (Gove 1971:2614) has been widely popularized, negating a very different, thousands-of-years-old human relationship with the land. Mihilakawna Pomo elder and weaver Lucy Smith described this relationship, as she recalled her mother teaching her as a child that:

We had many relatives and that we all had to live together; so we'd better learn how to get along with each other. She said it wasn't too hard to do. It was just like taking care of your younger brother or sister. You got to know them, find out what they liked and what made them cry, so you'd know what to do. If you took good care of them you didn't have to work as hard. Sounds like it's not true, but it is. When that baby gets to be a man or woman they're going to help you out. You know, I

---

[1]This is a revised and expanded version of a paper that was originally presented at the Seventh Annual California Indian Conference, Sonoma State University, October 18, 1991.

196

thought she was talking about us Indians and how we are
supposed to get along. I found out later by my older
sister that mother wasn't just talking about Indians, but
the plants, animals, birds -- everything on this earth. They
are our relatives and we better know how to act around
them or they'll get after us [Peri and Patterson 1979:43-
44].

Complex social and religious traditions have long guided the land
management techniques used by weavers. Both spiritual and practical, old-
time "rules" or "prohibitions" continue to be followed by many contemporary weavers. Foremost among them is a commitment to give back
something for whatever is taken:

We never go out without thanking the Creator for
providing us with whatever material we're getting [Norma
Turner, Mono, personal communication 1991].

You thank the place that you picked it--that it will come
back, and that you'll be able to gather it, [and that] it will
be plentiful... You're always thankful that you're able to
pick [Henrietta Lewis, Yurok, personal communication 1991].

We take from the earth and say please. We give back to
the earth and say thank you [Julia Parker, Kashia Pomo,
personal communication 1988].

The giving back is accomplished through songs, prayers, and
offerings:

I remember being out in the sedge beds with Laura
[Somersal] before the [Warm Springs] Dam was built. We
went way up on the Dry Creek side, and when we sat
there at lunch, she would say this little prayer. She didn't
make a big deal out of it. She said, "Thank you." (She'd
say, "Yahwiy.") And she pulled a little piece of her bread
off and threw it in the plants... [Kathleen Smith, Mihilakawna Pomo/Olemitcha Miwok, personal communication
1991].

When my grandmother went out and gathered, she
respected the plants. She would pray before she gathered
them... [Barbara Bill, Dunlap Mono, personal communication 1991].

I know that there are songs. No one told me that I
should say things to these plants...[but] I sing to the plants
as I approach them, and then just before I pull them, and
then as I pull them, and then afterwards to the area. I
don't know how accurate that is, but if intentions mean
anything-- Some innate feeling; something has come forth
[L. Frank Manriquez, Tongva/Ajachme, personal communication 1991].

Some rules establish a means of honoring the basket as alive,
which in turn honors the plants from which the baskets come and, by
association, the land which nourishes the plants:

I don't know what I'd do if I had to sell one of those big
cooking baskets. They're a part of the family. They're
just like one of the children. And these baskets are alive.
That's what the old people always said. These baskets,
just like the rocks, are alive... These materials that we
make baskets with are alive... There's a connection
between the ancestors, the people, the basketmakers, and
these baskets [Norma Turner, personal communication
1991].

The main thing, if you're doing basketmaking, is to have
good feelings and thoughts. That's why they have basket
songs; and that's why people are laughing and enjoying
themselves together... If you're feeling sad--if you're angry
or something--you better not even touch the basket,
because the basket is part of you [Vivien Hailstone,
Karuk-Yurok and member of Hupa Tribe, personal
communication 1991].

It's more than just rules for making baskets. A lot of
them are rules for living--good sense things for your well-

198

being [Kathy Wallace, Yurok-Karuk and Hupa, personal communication 1991].

Other rules are based on supernatural sanctions:

All aspects of the [Mihilakawna Pomo and Makahmo Pomo] collection process are regulated by very specific rules... Each of these rules is supported by supernatural sanctions, and violations result in negative supernatural consequences. The extent that these rules are observed today varies among individuals. In earlier times, the ritual restrictions were more extensive and were widely observed...

By far the most important of all collection restrictions are those which pertain to menstruation. Consultants unanimously agreed that menstruating women and their men are never allowed to collect roots, and this taboo is strongly upheld by most weavers today. Violation of the taboo is believed to result in serious illness. In addition to causing personal harm, the presence of "unclean" (menstruating) women in the area is believed to result in the destruction of the sedge beds [Peri and Patterson 1979:64-66].

While many old-time basketry rules continue to be observed by contemporary weavers, some have fallen to the changing circumstances of modern times:

If there's a reason for it that I can see, and it makes sense, then I'll go with it... They used to say don't weave at night--only certain times of the day. Well, way back when, you had to weave when there was plenty of daylight. Now we have lights... Some of the rules change with the times [Sharon Tate, Karuk, personal communication 1991].

Whatever the changes, respect for the land remains. The horticultural techniques used to ensure a good harvest embody the respectful relationship between weavers and the land. As expressed by Julia Parker, such techniques are the result of "making friends" with the basketry plants (Ortiz 1991:27). They acknowledge a positive interaction between the plant and the weaver which is beneficial to both. As explained by Cache Creek Pomo elder Mabel McKay in the 1970s:

> When people don't use the plants they get scarce. You must use them so they will come up again. All plants are like that. If they're not gathered from, or talked to and cared about, they'll die [Peri and Patterson 1978:17].

HORTICULTURAL METHODS USED BY WEAVERS

California Indians have often been labelled "hunters and gatherers." However, this label belies a much more complex reality which continues to the present time. As will be shown, California Indian basketweavers utilize many of the same horticultural methods used by gardeners in their yards: judicious harvesting, pruning, cultivation, and debris clearing. They also utilize controlled burning.

Judicious Harvesting

Judicious harvesting is critical to managing the resources gathered by weavers. For instance, there are prohibitions against taking more than can be used:

> [As a beginning weaver], you see all these plants, and you're almost going crazy trying to gather all you can. And my aunt said, "Don't be greedy. Just take what you need and what you can fix" [Barbara Bill, personal communication 1991].

> They usually don't pick all of them. They just pick some, and then they leave some... We never, ever believed in picking it all [Alberta Sylvia, Yurok, personal communication 1991].

> You never take it so that you damage the area. It's like you're reserving that place so you can come back to it.

So if you destroy it in any way, it won't be there for you. Or if you take more than you're going to use, or you don't respect it...next year it won't be available for us... So always take care of it [Sharon Tate, personal communication 1991].

Knowing the proper time in the plant's life cycle to gather is part of judicious harvesting:

You have to learn the different times to pick your materials. It's not just there... You can't just go get them anytime you want [Alberta Sylvia, personal communication 1991].

Specific gathering times apply to nearly all California Indian basketry materials. Following are a few examples from Northwest California.

Fern Stems. Woodwardia fern (*Woodwardia radicans*) stems for overlay are gathered from the latter part of August until the first frost. Maidenhair fern (*Adiantum pedatum*) stems for overlay are gathered in late May through the first part of August. If gathered too early, the stems will break from lack of firmness; if gathered too late, they will break from brittleness (Henrietta Lewis, personal communication 1991; Alberta Sylvia, personal communication 1991; Ortiz 1988b:28).

Roots. Willow roots are harvested after flood or high waters have washed away soil and exposed the roots for easy gathering. Spruce (*Picea sitchensis*) root digging takes place in November, when the root attains its greatest strength and pliability (Henrietta Lewis, personal communication 1991; Alberta Sylvia, personal communication 1991; Ortiz 1988b:28).

Shoots. When they are to be peeled, willow (*Salix spp.*) and hazel (*Corylus rostrata californica*) shoots are "picked" (cut) in early spring after the buds have broken, but before they fully leaf out. Not only are the shoots flexible at this time, but the bark also easily slips. When hazel shoots are not to be peeled, they're picked in winter after the sap drops. (Henrietta Lewis, personal communication 1991; Alberta Sylvia, personal communication 1991; Ortiz 1988b:28).

Elevation and altitude affect gathering times. For instance, maidenhair fern stem is picked in May at low elevations; it is picked later at higher elevations (Henrietta Lewis, personal communication 1991; Alberta Sylvia, personal communication 1991):

> If you're going up the hill, it's going to be later than things down closer to the valley where it's warmer... Where you go...from the Central Valley up to Northern California the gathering time will change [Kathy Wallace, personal communication 1991].

Growing location is also important.   Picked from mid-April through July, bear grass (*Xerophyllum tenax*) needs a shady location to produce good shoots for basketry.   When growing in the sun, it becomes brittle and bleached out.   When growing in the shade the stems are comparatively pliable.   They also lay flatter during weaving (Gendar 1991/92:24; Newman 1974:32).
Weather is another factor that must be taken into consideration:

> We went to get bear grass last year. They usually harvest it in early July from the year before, when they burn it... [But] it was such a hot year, we should have gathered it almost a month and a half earlier. So you really need to keep an eye on the area where you're gathering [Elsie Griffin, Yurok, personal communication 1991].

Judicious harvesting includes knowing how to gather alder (*Alnus rhombifolia*) bark without harming the tree. A riparian tree which grows adjacent to stream banks, alder is adapted to battering by river stones carried by floodwaters. If a piece of bark is removed, the adjacent bark grows over the wound.

> With the alder dyes...a lot of people say you cut the inner bark away, but you don't. You take a piece of the inner bark, not the whole tree. And then it won't scar the tree [Elsie Griffin, personal communication 1991].

Pruning

Willow (*Salix spp.*) and redbud (*Cercis occidentalis*) are among the plants that benefit from pruning. Pruning occurs as an indirect outcome of harvesting individual shoots and as a purposeful result of cutting individual branches back and coppicing (cutting the plant back to its base). Basketry plants are pruned back and coppiced while the plants stand dormant (after the sap has dropped).

Undertaken at the proper time of the year, pruning increases the vigor and productivity of the plant, while at the same time stimulating the growth of the desired long, straight, and flexible shoots (Peri et al. 1985:88) Pruning also serves to control insect infestations, as with the larvae that inhabit grey willow (*Salix hinsiana*) shoots, which are used as warp and rods in Pomo baskets (Mabel McKay, personal communication 1983; Arlene Anderson, personal communication 1983).

> The gatherers don't go out and hurt the woods... We're not taking the whole tree or the whole forest. We're just taking a piece of it, and we do our best not to damage it. I've been to areas where there have been many gatherers, and...you can't tell that they were ever there, because we're just pruning the trees. We're not taking the taproot that holds the tree down. I think that it's really important for people to know that [Elsie Griffin, personal communication 1991].

> We're always saying that when we gather, we prune at the same time. Then the shoots will grow again...and now and then when we do that, I sometimes clip more so that more will come up... And it does. It comes right back up [Barbara Bill, personal communication 1991].

Cultivation and Debris Clearing

Sedge (*Carex* spp.), bulrush (*Scirpus maritimus* and *S. pacificus*), bracken fern (*Pteridium aquilinum*), and woodwardia fern are among the plants which produce underground stems (rhizomes) used for weft; willow and spruce among those that produce roots used for warp and weft. The sandy loam soil of a floodplain allows rhizomes to grow long and straight (Mabel McKay, personal communication 1983). By cultivating the same roots and rhizomes in the same place every year or two, weeding (both indirect and purposeful), and removing debris, weavers improve the growing conditions. The benefits of digging and debris clearing were described by Peri, Patterson, and McMurray in 1985:

> The direct results of such soil cultivation are increased aeration, water condensation, the stimulation of new root growth, and increased plant vigor. While cultivation loosens the soil, at the same time it mixes surface nutrients into the ground; it improves the drainage during winter months and allows better absorption of moisture during the growing season. Summer cultivation interrupts the capillary action of water to the soil surface, allowing water to remain in deeper, cooler soil layers where roots thrive. Loose soil at the surface also insulates because of its air content. When the root of root crops is not impeded by compact soil, they increase in size and quality. The removal of mature or older roots in a tract also stimulates the growth of new roots, and actually increases the tract's size...
>
> Collecting areas are kept "clean" by weeding and removing debris... The elimination of unwanted plants interrupts the natural process of plant succession and insures the continual presence of a particular plant by reducing competition for nutrients and moisture. Collecting areas were also raked to clear away dead branches, rocks, and excessive leaf litter from the plants, in order to reduce the potential of the plants' being crowded out [Peri et al. 1985:88-90].

In 1972, Elsie Allen (Makahmo Pomo, 1899-1990) described the benefits of cultivating sedge rhizomes ("white root"):

> One advantage of going back every second year--or at least every third year--to a good root-digging place is that you keep the roots from getting over abundant and tangled and thus hard to dig. When the roots are tangled--as they are in most long-untouched places--they are very hard to untangle, especially as you must try to keep them long,

not allowing them to break into short pieces. When you run into roots of other plants, you should take them out so the sedge roots can grow without competition, much as you weed a garden. When there are many mixed roots, the Indian women must labor for hours to get out the long good roots [Allen 1972:18-19].

In Northwest California, where spruce root is an important basketry material, care is taken not to disturb the layer of moss which covers the ground over the roots:

Madge Twedall taught us about respecting the land when we went out--to always thank the earth... [When digging spruce roots] we'd dig up the [moss] layer, and then fold it back and get the roots, and then put it back; and so when we left the area it wasn't noticeable that anybody had ever been there [Sharon Tate, Karuk, personal communication 1991].

You make sure you cover the [spruce] roots back up... You peel up the moss. The ground beneath the spruce trees is soft. It's wonderful to walk on. You can take it and pull it back all the way... The roots lay right there on top. You hardly ever have to dig for them. Then you take a little bit from that root. Then you cover it back up and go to a different tree [Elsie Griffin, Yurok, personal communication 1991].

Controlled Burning

Not only are California's ecosystems adapted to fire, but controlled burning has long been used to enhance the growth of certain basketry plants, such as bear grass and hazel. Natural fires similarly benefit many of the plants that are pruned.

Controlled burning results in the growth of pliable, straight, new shoots (Ortiz 1988b:28). It returns important nutrients to the soil, eliminates unhealthy plants, reduces pests, and keeps understory vegetation sufficiently spaced, assuring that each plant will get the optimum light, water, and nutrients (Peri, et al. 1985:91).

[Controlled burning] wasn't just done for the gatherers. It was done for the good of the forest [Elsie Griffin, Yurok, personal communication 1991].

In my mom's days they would burn all the brush.... They would burn under the trees, and that way things came back naturally, and there weren't forest fires. There's a lot of old ways, if they were brought in, that would be less damaging to the land [Yvonne Jolley, Yurok, personal communication 1991].

CONTEMPORARY LAND MANAGEMENT ISSUES

Modern land changes have affected the relationship between the weavers and the basketry plants they use. Buildings, roads, reservoirs, and parking lots have covered gathering sites used for generations. Stream channelization, overgrazing, agricultural and mining practices, and pollution have also taken their toll.

Such widespread environmental changes have caused a further entrenchment of the popular view of wilderness, and land untouched has become a gauge against which weavers are judged. In 1972, Makahmo weaver Elsie Allen wrote about the quandary presented by such attitudes:

Even one white gentleman came and told me I should not [gather] because it would destroy a lot of plants. He did not understand what I knew very well that the cutting out of roots and trimming of shrubs actually helped spread the growth and there was no danger as long as the digging and cutting was not overdone at any one place [Allen 1972:14].

In addition to environmental destruction, private and public property restrictions, permit procedures, herbicide and pesticide spraying, competition with commercial collectors, non-existent or ineffective burn policies, improper waste disposal, and safety considerations all have an impact on contemporary weavers.

Private and Public Property Restrictions

Access to basketry materials has been limited by private property boundaries, as well as by public land laws and management practices which preclude gathering. Sometimes a procedural change is all that is necessary to correct the access problems. For instance, when CalTrans prunes redbud along certain roadsides, they inadvertently choose the proper time to produce good shoots for basketry the following year (Jennifer Bates, Northern Mewuk, personal communication 1992). With notice, local basketmakers would be able to gather the resulting shoots before they're pruned again (Gendar 1991/92:24).

Elsie Allen has discussed the need to get a landowner's permission:

> Permission may be needed to dig roots in some areas, but you can assure the landowner that you are actually improving his land by doing the digging, as the sedge roots grow back quickly after being taken out--as long as you leave some in the ground--and they are of great help in holding the soil along creeks and rivers.

> The sedge roots are hard to find now in quantity or of good quality because they have been disturbed by too many roads and buildings, but man needs to learn that the sedge root is a vital part of the harmony of nature and preserving of the soil. It is especially useful in preventing creek banks from washing away, and can be encouraged to grow by all property owners. Digging of the roots, when correctly done and leaving behind about half of those found, actually strengthens the growth and soil-holding properties of the roots [Allen 1972:19].

Despite the benefits, Allen found it difficult to convince public and private land owners to let her dig. Once, she and a companion were chased away from a park for digging root. That same fall, the creek they had been chased away from was dredged and the root was covered with four feet of gravel, which completely destroyed the bed (Ortiz 1991/92-:17).

When a gathering site is lost to development, it may take a year or more of pruning and cultivation before a new site will yield usable shoots and roots. As explained by Pomo weaver Susan Billy, "...[It's] a lot of energy...to go out and get the materials, and to prepare them and to spend months, [or] years, making your baskets..." (Ortiz 1991/92:17).

Permit Procedures

Where gathering is permitted, special permits may be needed. At times, elderly weavers have been left waiting at locked gates for an official to let them through at a prearranged time; or they have been expected to walk up roads instead of drive (Kathleen Smith, personal communication 1991; Mabel McKay, personal communication 1983). Access and permit procedures sometimes exclude members of non-federally recognized tribal groups (Gladys McKinney, Dunlap Mono, personal communication 1991).

Such procedures are also humiliating, dehumanizing, cumbersome, or serve as a complete barrier for weavers:

> ...[It's] really hard for us to sometimes go out there on the side of the roads and sneak... There's no reason we should go out there and feel this way... Do we get little cards? What should we do that we don't have to go out there and feel like we're going to get arrested, or shot at? Should we wear little tags? Or special hats? ...In the millions of people in California, we're just a grain. We're not out there to destroy the roadsides or anything; we're out there to hold on to a tradition. And unfortunately we are up against a lot of obstacles [Jennifer Bates, in Gendar 1991/92:30].

> I hear a lot of talk about getting permits. Why should we have to do that? If they can see what we're doing, and see that we're Native American, why should we have to get permission...to gather what is rightfully ours... Think of it... You'll be just covered with permits before your life is over... Think of [public land] as your own... We don't own it, they don't own it, but it was given to us as special people to use [Bertha Mitchell, Yurok, in Gendar 1991/92:30].

> We've been regulated for so long that when we go into offices--I know it's not intentional--but they treat you like

a child. It's just a mentality that has existed for so long, that it's going to take a long time to get rid of that mentality... They say you're hurting the trees, but everybody I've ever been with takes great care so that they don't harm the trees. We seem to get blamed for everybody that goes down and chops a tree [Elsie Griffin, Yurok, personal communication 1991].

Herbicide and Pesticide Spraying

Since basketry materials are often placed in the mouth when being split, herbicide and pesticide spraying on public and private lands where weavers gather presents special concerns:

It concerns me because the spray...is cancerous. I myself don't want to die a slow death [Susan Burdick, Yurok, in Gendar 1991/92:28].

Some Paiute weavers have developed blisters after placing sprayed materials in their mouths (Marion Steinbach, personal communication 1988), as have weavers from other areas.

When I tried to split my redbud, it poisoned my lip, and it made blisters, and it got into my gums. So I had to have my "splitting tooth" (I call it) pulled [Norma Turner, Herbicides Panel, California Indian Basketweavers Gathering, June 27, 1992].

My niece also had problems with her eyes after gathering hazel. A burning sensation...and they're saying, "We really can't do anything about this spraying because it's privately owned." In Klamath people were complaining about diarrhea, vomiting, a number of things after the spray... There has to be some type of an alternative... [Susan Burdick in Gendar 1991/92:30].

Competition from Commercial Collectors

Contemporary weavers also face competition from commercial collectors:

We have a lot of florists that come up into the area and old time hippies that pick the redbud, and they make those wreaths... [We'll] go up and we'll say, "Uh-oh look, someone's already been here" [Florence Dick, Dunlap Mono, in Gendar 1991/92: 26].

[We] have to fight with the florists...that come up and take...the maidenhair and the woodwardia ferns [Verna Reece, Karuk, in Gendar 1991/92:26].

[Some non-Indians] go into the mountains in vanloads chopping all the bear grass in sight... They want to find some factory or something where they can have it all sold... They're just wiping it out... They don't even know what it's used for or what they want done. They just want to make money off of it... It's out of the reach of the Indian people where they're going with it... They're totally demolishing the whole plant [Terry Tripp Rompon, Karuk, personal communication 1991].

Nonexistent or Ineffective Burn Policies

Since some basketry plants require burning, modern fire suppression policies have created particular difficulties for contemporary weavers:

In my area there's a lot of underbrush, and now it's so bushy that you can hardly get off of the road. They don't let the Indians continue burning in their own way [Henrietta Lewis, personal communication 1991].

Where burn policies are established, they can be ineffective for weaving purposes. At times, burns are located in inaccessible areas difficult to find by map. Other times they aren't timed or located for optimal plant growth. For example, to produce soft and flexible weaving strands, bear grass must be burned every year in the fall (Josephine Lewis, Karuk, personal communication 1992). The U.S. Forest Service, however, prefers to burn later in the year. While this satisfies local air quality control board standards for cool, slow burns with little impact upon on-the-ground vegetation, it leaves the weavers without a reliable supply of high quality materials. The resultant bear grass shoots are less pliable, and the weavers lose a whole season's growth (Susan Burdick, personal communication 1992; Josephine Lewis, personal communication 1992). While bear grass is more pliable when picked from a shady place, the Forest Service burns logging slash in open areas (Gendar 1991/92:24, 25). Likewise, burns need to be spaced so weavers have enough time to gather before a site is burned again:

> [It] was really hard for us to get our sticks, because they'd burn, and we planned to pick the following year...[but they burned] it over again. That's happened for three years at one place [Alberta Sylvia, Yurok, personal communication 1991].

Improper Waste Disposal

Gathering spots are often contaminated with garbage and human waste. Camper septic tanks are thoughtlessly emptied into the sand near willow stands. Weavers also find disposable diapers and toilet paper at gathering sites (Gendar 1991/92:28).

Safety Considerations

Rattlesnakes have long been a concern for weavers (Mabel McKay, personal communication 1983):

> [My grandmother] was always praying, and she was always talking to the rattlesnake, because the rattlesnake likes to be under the sourberry sticks--the plant that we get... I remember when I went out with her, she would pray, and then she would talk to the snake and say in her dialect, "I'm coming to gather sticks, and I'm not bothering you. Please don't bother me" [Barbara Bill, Dunlap Mono, personal communication 1991].

> [When] momma was younger than I am now [85], she couldn't see too good. So I had to get a stick and hit the ground [to see if there's] something there--a snake or lizard [Lucy Smith, Mililakawna Pomo, personal communication 1991].

In addition to snakes, contemporary weavers face unique safety concerns. Some have been shot at (Ortiz 1991/92:16). Others have unwittingly encountered marijuana fields:

> It's not safe to gather. I've walked into a pot field in the woods trying to gather, and we've actually had people try to stop us on the road [Terry Tripp Rompon, Karuk, personal communication 1991].

CONCLUSION

> ...[The] weavers are there to gather to make baskets, not to trespass on land that probably was theirs before boundaries were put up, whether it's a park or private property [Linda McGill, Makahmo Pomo/Paiute, personal communication 1991].

Contemporary basketmakers are working to resolve the land management issues which they face, and some progress has been made. For instance, as a result of meetings with California Indian basketweavers, the Forest Service has begun to take weavers' needs into account when conducting controlled burns.

Critical to the resolution of these issues is a broader public understanding of California Indian weavers as land managers who continue to utilize broad-based horticultural and controlled burning techniques. Such techniques belie the modern concept of untouched wilderness.

MANAGING OAKS AND
THE ACORN CROP[1]

Helen McCarthy

INTRODUCTION

It is well established that foods made from acorns originally provided an essential dietary component (i.e., a staple) for the First People of California (Kroeber 1925; Gifford 1939; Baumhoff 1963; Basgall 1987), and *acorn*, as many now refer to it, still continues to make an important contribution to the contemporary expression of traditional culture. It is offered as a specially featured dish at family celebrations, at tribal gatherings, and at Big Times, and it is also often served as a healing and soothing food to elders or others who are ill. Thus it is worthwhile, in considering the role of Native Californians as environmental managers, to examine the strategies and practices that pertain to their management of the acorn crop, since it may readily be assumed that people will develop the means to both maximize and protect those resources and products which are critical for their survival. This paper explores a number of such potential strategies, and at the same time reviews the relevant biological characteristics of oaks in order to better understand and evaluate the potential effects of these strategies. The data are drawn from both the statewide ethnographic literature and from my own research, which has been carried out in the southcentral Sierra Nevada region with Mono and Chukchansi peoples.

There are several potential, interrelated goals which may be pursued in the management or manipulation of tree crops: managers can seek to achieve (1) an optimal growing environment; (2) a maximum number of producing trees in a suitable location; and/or (3) a maximum

[1]This is a revised and expanded version of a paper that was originally presented at the Seventh Annual California Indian Conference, Sonoma State University, October 18, 1991. The author wishes to take this opportunity to thank the many elders who graciously and generously shared their expert knowledge, and accepts full responsibility for any inadvertent errors. The research upon which the present paper is based was carried out between 1984 and 1992.

crop production. In a contemporary orchard, these objectives are achieved through such techniques as planting, irrigation, soil enrichment, pest control, pruning and thinning, and the elimination of competitors such as weeds. Precontact Native California peoples knew and used several of these strategies for resources other than oaks, including planting (e.g., tobacco; see Schenk and Gifford 1952; Harrington 1932; Kroeber 1925:88), weed control, and pruning and thinning, all of which are well documented, particularly with reference to basketry resources (e.g., Peri and Patterson 1979, 1976 and this volume). It is suggested here that the use of fire or burning (Harrington 1932; Schenck and Gifford 1952; Lewis 1973 and this volume) was both the most frequent and the most effective tool used by California peoples to manage the environment in general and oaks and the acorn crop in particular, although the effectiveness of other strategies (such as planting and pruning) will also be evaluated. In addition, it must also be recognized that there were other important but non-environmental management strategies employed by California societies to distribute and apportion the acorn crop. These included trade between groups, ownership of trees and groves, and the use of extensive storage facilities (McCarthy n.d.). Discussion of these topics is beyond the scope of this paper. Finally, it is crucial to recognize the importance of the ceremonial component which was an integral part of the environmental management system.

THE RESOURCE

Oaks are widely distributed throughout California, and may even be said to be characteristic of the California Floristic Province (Barbour and Major 1977). The California oaks include 18 species of the genus *Quercus* and one representative of *Lithocarpus* (previously classified as *Quercus*), with eight of the tree-size species supplying the major economic contribution to the native diet. There were clear dietary preferences for several of these species (Baumhoff 1963:163-164; Kroeber 1932a; Barrett and Gifford 1933). Tan oak, *Lithocarpus densiflora*, was usually preferred where it was available, but it has a relatively restricted distribution in comparison to other oaks; it is found in only 7.8% of the state's area, in the Coast Range (Plumb and McDonald 1981:2). Black oak, *Quercus kelloggii*, was the preferred species in many localities; it is available across a much larger range--about 18.4% of the state--and is mainly a mountain dweller. Blue oak (often referred to as white oak), *Quercus douglasii*, a foothill species; valley oak, *Quercus lobata*, found (as its name implies) in valley and lowland areas; and Oregon oak, *Quercus garryana*, another mountain species found primarily in the northern portions of the state, also contributed significantly to the acorn reserves. Three live-oak species might also be used if yields from preferred types were inadequate; these were the canyon live oak, *Quercus chrysolepis*, which is quite important in some areas (e.g., San Diego County [Harrington n.d.]); the interior live oak, *Quercus wislizenii*; and the coast live oak, *Quercus agrifolia*.

A great deal of confusion exists in the literature concerning the common names used for oak species; unfortunately, many (perhaps most) of the early ethnographers got species thoroughly mixed up, and consequently created innumerable problems for later researchers. For instance, valley oak is commonly known as water oak, mush oak, or white oak, but the term white oak also refers to blue oak and Oregon oak, while the latter may be called Garry oak or post oak. Fortunately, both tan oak and black oak are easily distinguished from the others in the field, and the common terms for them are not confused. The native terminologies are, of course, explicit, clear, and unambiguous, and the native peoples have a detailed knowledge of the characteristics of each species. The basic problem was (and often still is) that the ethnographers were not sufficiently familiar with their own Western classification system to be able to establish the correct correspondences--thus Kroeber, Barrett, Gifford and most other ethnographers all had problems making accurate identifications. The only exception to the rule was C. Hart Merriam, who was a trained botanist and often carried specimens with him; he was also aware of hybrids and was able to identify them (Merriam n.d.).

There is a significant overlap in the distribution of oak species, so that in many areas several species are available; thus people usually have a range of acorn choices. For instance, the members of one Mono family in the North Fork area of the central Sierra Nevada have five species growing within sight of their home: black oak, blue/white oak, valley oak, live oak, and canyon live oak. This circumstance can be especially important in years when the crop fails in a preferred species, since it does not usually fail totally in all species in the same year; therefore, at least some acorns should be obtainable every year. A species of oak tends to produce good crops in several-year cycles, bearing well once every two or three years in a specific region (Plumb and McDonald 1981); a bumper crop may be followed by one to three years of light or even no crops. In other geographical areas, however, only one or two species may be available; this can lead to a situation in which potentially serious shortages can occur during a year of crop failure. For example, a simultaneous failure in both valley and blue oaks (which is quite possible since they show a tendency to cycle together in production) might have a major impact on a population. This kind of potential difficulty was ameliorated by trade between groups in different ecological zones, especially trade eastward and westward across elevational zones; however, that is properly considered economic or social management rather than environmental management.

It would be extremely useful for this examination of resource management to understand basic levels of acorn productivity of California oaks, but "long-term quantitative records are not available" (Griffin 1976:429), so that at best only anecdotal information exists on this important issue. There is no question that most species sometimes produce "heavy crops but with great tree-to-tree and place to place variability" (Griffin 1976:429). The "yield is related to tree age, crown diameter and bole diameter" (McDonald 1978:147), but some individual trees never produce a single acorn (McCarthy n.d.; McDonald 1978:109). Reports of bumper crops, however, reveal the range of potential productivity; e.g., 500-600 lbs. per tree have been reported for *Q. garryana* (Smith 1929:160), while comparable amounts have been noted for *Q. lobata* (Wolf 1945) and *Q. kelloggii* (McCarthy n.d.). On the other hand, a number of widespread crop failures have also been recorded (Wolf 1945), including the recent (1990) failure of *Q. kelloggii* in the Sierra (McCarthy n.d.). The problem is not so much one of identifying the potential yield that could be produced in a specific year, but rather one of determining how often levels of high productivity are actually realized and what the long-term average level of productivity (i.e., the predictable yield) might be. In a 17-year study of *Q. kelloggii* (which, however, did not focus on nor systematically collect productivity data), McDonald observed that there is a good seed crop every five or six years, and that the tendency is for there to be either a good crop or none at all (McDonald 1978:147), although every year there are always a few trees which bear at least some acorns (ibid.:109). In addition, *L. densiflora* is reported to be a more consistent producer than other oaks (McDonald 1978:61). Even on the basis of this minimal evidence, it is clear that acorn productivity is erratic, and thus a consummate subject for management.

PLANTING

Planting is a potential environmental strategy for managing distributional problems, as well as for increasing the number of desirable trees in an area or bringing the most preferred species closer to home. It is well established that native peoples planted tobacco prior to contact (Harrington 1932; Kroeber 1925), and at least a few other plants were possibly sown as well; this is particularly likely in the case of soaproot, which was spread by corm and/or seed, and basket grass (*Muhlenbergia rigens*), which was transplanted as a whole plant (McCarthy n.d.). So would people have also planted oaks? How effective might the planting of oaks be, and what obstacles have to be overcome, particularly in the case of black oak, the preferred species in the Central Sierra foothills?

First, oaks are slow growing and long lived. Slow growth is also correlated with late maturity, so that it is many years before a planted tree attains crop-bearing age. For instance, it takes a black oak 30 years to start producing even a small crop of acorns, at least 80 years to yield a bumper crop, and it is not fully mature until it is 175 years of age (McDonald 1978:275). During a discussion of planting I had with several Mono, one woman responded with a laugh: "I'd be dead before it was grown. Let the blue jays do the planting, it's their job" (McCarthy n.d.).

A consideration that is perhaps even more important than growth rate is the fact that oaks exhibit tremendous variability in acorn production, from place to place and from tree to tree, both in terms of the size of the crop and the size of the acorn (McDonald 1978:109). The capacity of a particular tree to produce many or few acorns, or large or small acorns, is an inherent characteristic of that individual tree--a good tree produces a generous crop of fat acorns, some trees produce only small acorns, and others do not bear a crop at all. Significantly, even choosing acorns from a "good tree" apparently does not necessarily guarantee the future productive characteristics of trees grown from them. Thus, not only would a woman have to wait many years for a tree to mature, she could not be certain that it would be a good producer until it did in fact bear a crop. One Mono woman, for example, has a black oak in her yard that was a young tree when she moved there some 60 years ago as a bride. When the tree finally began bearing, the family was disappointed to see that the acorns were too small to be desirable, so that although the tree often bears a prolific crop, the woman and her daughters gather elsewhere (McCarthy n.d.). Many people were dislocated from their traditional homes during the contact period and resettled in rancherias located in areas that lacked

218

important plant resources. A number of Mono and Chukchansi people have told of having established such species as soaproot, basketgrass, redbud, and sourberry near their new homes, and have even discussed trying to plant grey pine, but oaks have not been mentioned as part of these efforts (McCarthy n.d.).

It is suggested that the characteristics of late maturity and unpredictable yield strongly diminish the probability that the planting of oaks could ever have been a systematic strategy employed by indigenous California peoples, although there may well have been other--as yet poorly understood--biological factors that prevented the predictable and successful planting of oaks. It is worthwhile to ponder here why almonds, pistachios, and acorns are all found in pre-Neolithic Natufian hunting-gathering sites, in the Near Eastern cradle of domestication, yet only almonds and pistachios were subsequently brought under cultivation (Henry 1985:371). Furthermore, contemporary botanists, foresters, and ecologists have had very poor results in their numerous, diverse attempts to regenerate oaks (Standiford 1991).

In addition, acorns were undoubtedly distributed on occasion (and later grew into trees) as a result of women carrying basketsfull home from the gathering grounds; however, a critical stage in acorn processing may have prevented this from occurring too frequently: it is essential to dry acorns before storage so they won't become moldy. This is often done at the gathering grounds before people return home, if they are camping there for several days; otherwise, it may be accomplished at home. Acorns are actually quite fragile with regard to moisture loss, and drying is an extremely effective means of preventing germination (McDonald 1978:64, 148). Thus, most acorns lost from already dried reserves would not be viable, which greatly reduces the probability that the distribution of oaks was significantly affected by the accidental loss of gathered acorns. It may be suggested, therefore, that neither purposeful nor accidental planting played an important role in the management of oaks and the acorn crop.

KNOCKING

Another management strategy involves knocking, in which the ripe acorns on the tree are knocked from the branches with a long pole, both from the ground and by men or boys from the tree itself. Peri and Patterson (1979:37-40) have cogently argued that this constitutes a form of pruning, a pruning which is accomplished when the poles hit the limbs and not only knock the acorns off, but break off the ends of numerous branches as well. Like pruning, this would encourage lateral growth and increase the area of the canopy, thus creating more locations for acorn generation in successive years. In addition, this activity clears dead wood from the tree. Since dead wood harbors disease, decay, and pests, it is definitely beneficial for the tree to have these reservoirs of contamination removed.

In some species of oaks, however, knocking may endanger the subsequent year's crop. In white oaks such as valley, Oregon, blue/white, Engleman, and coast live oaks, the acorns mature in one year --i.e., they are pollinated in the spring and are ripe by fall--and knocking would not present a problem. However, in black oaks such as black, interior live, canyon live, and tan oak (two of the most highly preferred), acorns take two years to mature--i.e., acorns from blossoms pollinated in spring will not be ripe until a year later (Munz 1959:902). The tiny acorn buds are on the new wood, at the tips of branches, which are the very parts that are most likely to be pruned off by knocking; consequently, the next year's crop would be extremely vulnerable to damage by this process.

In spite of the potentially negative consequences of knocking on some oak species, it must be considered an effective management strategy for other reasons. For example, it effectively advances the harvest season so that gatherers have more time available in which to collect the whole crop. Thus a tree might be harvested by knocking a week or two prior to the acorns falling on their own, thereby giving the collectors more time to gather from more trees, or to travel to a more distant grove. An even more important reason, however, is that knocking gives people a competitive edge, particularly against birds--jays, woodpeckers, and band-tailed pigeons. For a perspective on the magnitude of this problem, consider the following statement: "...at Hastings [Reserve in Carmel Valley area] scrub jays have [been reported to] remove acorns from individual valley oaks at rates exceeding 400/hour," and in a poor year "they may harvest all the crop before it falls" (Griffin 1980:242). Clearly, it behooves anyone interested in gathering acorns to get there before the birds! A line of a Hupa song performed to bless the new acorn crop addresses this problem: "Birds must not like the food" (Goddard 1904:233). Of course, birds are not the only creatures who like acorns. Competition is also fierce once the crop does fall, since acorns are relished by deer, bears, squirrels, gophers, and other animals (Griffin 1976). In summary, it is not hard to see how important knocking may be to managing the crop and maximizing the gathered yield.

BURNING

The use of fire, through burning portions of the landscape, was one of the most effective management tools available to California peoples, and its application and careful control were particularly important to the manipulation of the oak/acorn resources. The record is clear that tribes up and down the state burned systematically and with purpose (Lewis 1973, and this volume; Stewart 1955c; Kroeber 1925, 1932a). Burning is known to be beneficial to grasslands throughout the world, and some chaparral plants are even pyrophitic; i.e., they actually require burning in order for seeds to germinate. However, what specific effects does fire have on oaks? Fire not only affects individual plants, it affects the overall structure of the ecological community, and influences the composition and distribution of species within that community. It is this level that is of initial concern.

Many studies have shown that the California landscape (especially the woodlands) is fire adapted, which means that it could not have attained the composition and structure it exhibits without frequent fires (Lewis 1973, and this volume; Reynolds 1959; Vankat 1970; D. Todt, personal communication 1990). Black oaks in particular would not have either their present distribution or their frequency without fire, and studies have shown that fires begun by natural causes (i.e., lightning) would not have occurred frequently enough to create that distribution. Reynolds, in research carried out in the Central Sierra (Stanislaus National Forest, Yosemite National Park, and in Calaveras and Mariposa counties), found that

> natural ignition [is] inadequate to explain the vegetational
> relations that existed at contact time. Therefore, fires
> stemming from aboriginal practices must have played a
> very important role in this region [Reynolds 1959:136].

His research also showed that there is "more old growth black oak than one would expect" to find, "in open places or former openings in the coniferous canopy particularly on southern exposures" (Reynolds 1959:150). Reynolds, noting that village sites are often found near mature black oak stands, argued that cultural factors played a role in maintaining the stability of these black oak areas, and that the "age and size of the oaks suggest that burning was pursued aggressively by the Indians" (1959:150). This suggestion is based on the fact that oaks, especially black oaks, need considerable light for optimal growth and concomitantly good acorn production; if they are left to compete freely with conifers in the woodland, the conifers will overtop and shade out the oaks, and eventually take over (McDonald 1978; Plumb and McDonald 1981). When an oak or mixed community is burned, however, conifer seedlings (cedar, fir, pines), which might grow to be competitive adults, are destroyed by the fire, and are thus prevented from establishing a foothold in the grove or opening. Oaks and oak seedlings, on the other hand, are capable of resprouting and reestablishing themselves, thus maintaining their dominance in that locale. This ability to resprout is a critical adaptive characteristic in a fire-structured landscape, and is the essential factor underlying the effectiveness of fire in promoting an optimal environment for oaks. However, under the current policy of fire suppression, conifers and brush are encroaching on many meadows, openings, and stands of oak. An examination of old photographs of Yosemite (Fig. 8.1) clearly shows this process of replacement, which was kept in check by systematic burning in precontact times (Reynolds 1959). Miwok burning in Yosemite Valley is well documented (e.g., see Clark 1904, 1927; Johnston 1970b).

In addition to promoting a favorable distribution of oaks in the woodland community, the use of fire may positively affect individual trees and their yield. Karuk women, for example, reported that "the trees are better if they are scorched by fire each year. This kills disease and pests" (Schenck and Gifford 1952:382). Two pests in particular may infest an acorn crop: the Filbert Weevil (*Cucurlio occidentalis*) and the Filbert Worm (*Melissopus latiferreanus*). The latter drops out of the tree and goes through a reproductive cycle in the ground beneath the tree, emerging later to reinfect the acorns (P. Kirsch, personal communication 1991). Some botanists have observed that there is often a particularly heavy infestation during the year following a bumper crop (D. Todt, personal communication 1990). Indian peoples clearly understood this relationship, as the following statement by Klamath River Jack in a letter to the Fish and Game Commission demonstrates:

> Indian have no medicine to put on all places where bug and worm are, so he burn; every year Indian burn. ... Fire burn up old acorn that fall on ground. Old acorn on ground have lots worm; no burn old acorn, no burn old bark, old leaves, bugs and worms come more every year. ...Indian burn every year just same, so keep all ground

222

Figure 8.1. Upper: lower Yosemite Valley from Union Point, 1866. Photograph taken by C. E. Watkins. Lower: lower Yosemite Valley from same location, 1961. Photograph take by R. P. Gibbens. The rock slide at upper left that was apparent in 1866 has been nearly covered by vegetation. Photos courtesy of the Yosemite National Park Research Library.

clean, no bark, no dead leaf, no old wood on ground, no old wood on brush, so no bug can stay to eat leaf and no worm can stay to eat berry and acorn. Not much on ground to make hot fire so never hurt big trees where fire burn [Jack 1916:195].

Consultations with entomologists specializing in non-chemical pest control methods have confirmed the fact that burning the debris under oaks would destroy not only the reserve of wormy acorns but significantly control the pest population breeding and developing in the ground; therefore, it would indeed be an effective technique against these particular pests (P. Kirsch, personal communication 1991).

Fire also keeps an oak stand clear of undergrowth, so that it is protected from the effects of a large, intense fire, which might cause severe damage. A brush fire can be very hot, increasing the likelihood that a fire in mature brush will spread to the nearby tree canopy, resulting in heavy destruction to the trees. An annual burning of vegetation, usually after grass seeds have been gathered (Kniffen 1939; cf. Kniffen 1928, for burning in the spring), can effectively inhibit the growth of brush, and thus prevent intense, damaging fires from occurring later. In some areas, such as in the foothills of Madera County, brush control was even more aggressive according to one Chukchansi/Mono woman:

Large acrages [sic] were burned over twice to kill the brush. The first time the brush was burned in the spring; the second time it was burned in the fall. The following spring, the grass, berries and wild barley came up [Teaford 1930].

A number of elders in the southcentral Sierra Nevada report that in the early days the forest floor was clear and you could ride a horse anywhere through the woods (McCarthy n.d.).

An additional benefit of burning stems from the fact that the elimination of competitors such as brush and conifers means that more groundwater is available to oaks, which again has the effect of enhancing acorn production and favoring the growth of oak seedlings. And finally, since burning keeps the ground under the oaks cleared off, gathering acorns is easier (Schenck and Gifford 1952:382), a point immediately appreciated by anyone who has ever picked acorns out of bear clover (kit-

kit-dizzy) or other dense ground cover--or from poison oak. The faster a gatherer can pick, the more acorns she can collect.

In spite of fire/burning being a *necessity* for the maintenance of a favorable environment for oaks, and despite the fact that oaks respond adaptively to fire damage by resprouting even after they have sustained a considerable amount of damage, fire can be a double-edged sword that is potentially very damaging to oaks. The First People were also aware of this, as the following statement from a Karuk woman demonstrates:

> Some kinds of trees are better when it is burned off; they come up better ones again. But some kinds of trees when it is burned off disappear, another never to come up again. ... An old tree bears better, too. And the tan oak is not good when it is burned off, the tree dies. When they are burning, they are careful lest the trees burn [Harrington 1932:63-65].

The objective of planned burning, then, is a low-intensity fire (see also Jack 1916 *supra*), but even low-intensity fires can cause damage, and some foresters maintain that every fire damages an oak to some degree. Oaks have rather thin bark, which heats up and burns relatively quickly, damaging the cambium beneath and leaving scars. Scars of this sort do not heal well and readily become diseased and decayed, leaving the tree vulnerable to heart rot (Plumb 1980; Plumb and Gomez 1983; Parmeter 1977). Coast live oaks have the thickest bark and are the most resistant to fire damage, while canyon live oaks with thin, scaly dry bark that ignites readily are the most vulnerable. In addition, seedlings will not thrive if they are subjected to repeated burnings, even if they will resprout, so that some protective measures must have been taken to shield them from the flames and heat. In the final analysis, since we know from numerous reports that the native peoples did in fact burn, and that the forest structure and composition at the time of contact required systematic burning to attain its characteristics (including more oaks than it would otherwise have supported), we must conclude that native groups had developed burning with low-intensity fires into a fine art, in order to promote the growth of oaks without endangering these most vital resources.

SPIRITUAL AND CEREMONIAL PRACTICES

Thus far we have seen how important knocking and burning are for the management of oaks, but from the perspective of the First People, these objective strategies can only be effective within a climate of positive spiritual relationships between themselves, the land, and the resources it provides. These spiritual relationships are varied in nature, and involve a number of significant practices and beliefs that need to be explored.

The first point that needs to be emphasized is that these relationships operate on a daily basis and can and must be fulfilled by each person individually. These relationships require the *regular use of and respect for* plants and resources. I have often heard it expressed that many plants are gone today and that oaks do not bear good crops any more because the people no longer use them (McCarthy n.d.). There is a strong interdependence between plants and people. The acorns--and other resources as well--were put here on earth for people to use, for people's survival. The people need the plants in order to live, but the plants also need the people; they need people to gather their seeds, and leaves, and roots, and to talk and sing and pray to them. Peri and Patterson's research also strongly supports this interdependence (Peri and Patterson 1979:37-40; 1976, and this volume). If plants are not used by people, the spiritual relationship is broken, and the plants no longer have a place. A painting by Dal Castro, Maidu artist and traditionalist, gives contemporary expression to this dilemma: in the painting, the spirit of the Nisenan returns to earth as a bird spirit and wonders sorrowfully where all the people are, and why grass is growing in the bedrock mortar (Castro n.d.). The people are not preparing acorn, the ultimate symbol of traditional ways, so that the essential link between the people and their spirit world is broken.

Another level of ritual practice that we must be aware of requires a spiritual specialist and involves weather control, particularly control of that element so necessary in California, rain. Perhaps not surprisingly, the clearest statement concerning this factor comes from Southern California, specifically the Cahuilla, and describes the relationship between weather and rain and the acorn crop. Bean and Saubel report that

> ...a bad acorn crop was a serious matter of concern. In some years, it was said that cold weather came too early and trees failed to produce well. Dry seasons also were responsible for sparse crop yields. In particular, the timing

of rainfall was said to be critical to a good crop. With
the proper amount and timing of rainfall, acorns would
double in size [Bean and Saubel 1972:130].

Bean and Saubel explain, however, that rain is undesirable at harvest time
because it spoils acorns on the ground, turns them black, and splits those
still on the trees. This creates bad spots which must be removed, thus
wasting potential food as well as increasing the processing time (1972:125).
The Cahuilla shaman, therefore, performed rain-producing rituals at the
appropriate times to promote a maximum yield, and carried out prevent-
ative rituals just before the harvest to protect the crop from rain damage
(Bean and Saubel 1972:130).

However, a concern for rain with specific reference to the acorn
crop was not limited to Southern California. Dixon reports that among the
Northern Maidu, the Secret Society leader (who was chosen for his ability
as a spiritualist) was responsible for making rain when it was needed to
insure a good crop of acorns (Dixon 1905:330-131). In addition, according
to Kroeber, the River Patwin had a winter ceremony dedicated to the *wai-
saltu* or North Spirits that was expressly designed to promote a good crop
of acorns and seeds. During the course of this ceremony, the leader left
the roundhouse at night with a basket of acorn meal, which he smeared on
the oaks to make them bear a good crop. This ceremony stopped the rain
when it was held and brought the northwind (Kroeber 1932a:320-321).

Finally, many of the people up and down the state held, and
continue to hold, a ceremony in the fall for the acorns. While each group
carries out the ceremony in its own way, there are some striking similarities between these important observances. First, the performance of the
ceremony is understood to be an expression of thanks from the people to
the creator and spirit world for the acorns. The preparation of some of
the acorns, and a blessing of the new acorns and of the people, is also
likely to be a part of this observance. It was--and in some cases still is
--a serious offense among some groups for anyone to gather or eat acorns
from the new crop before this ceremony was performed, and persons who
broke this rule might suffer debilitating illness or even death (Bean and
Saubel 1972:126), or the society as a whole might suffer.

This ceremony, which expresses a group's collective thanks, is
analogous in many ways to the respect and thanks an individual gives to
a plant for its daily use. The relationships between the people, the land,
and the spirit world are recognized, reiterated, and confirmed. The
importance of this idea has been expressed again by a contemporary

Maidu artist, Frank Day, in a painting entitled *Whirlwind.* In the painting, Day depicts a whirlwind blowing apart the roundhouse and throwing the people out. This drastic event has occurred, Day says, because the people did not give thanks for the gifts received:

> I have given to you and you have received; but you have denied me, your giver. They neglected their duty of giving thanks to the spirits for the bounty they received [Day n.d.].

As a result, the people suffered dire consequences. Thus it is critical to maintain the relationship with the spirit world, in order to continue to receive gifts such as acorns and to maintain health and well-being.

CONCLUSIONS

In conclusion, it is clear that the First People of California took an active role in managing oaks and their acorn crop by employing a variety of strategies. Some of these strategies and techniques achieved more than one goal, and had objectively demonstrable efficacious results. An examination of the information on the planting of oaks suggests that this was probably not a successful, systematic strategy in California, nor probably elsewhere either. On the other hand, knocking acorns from the trees significantly reduces the serious competition for acorns that stems from birds and animals and additionally may encourage maximum future crop production for selected species by acting as a pruning technique; however, it may be counterproductive in this regard for other species. Knocking also extends the length of the harvest season.

Burning has been shown to promote and maintain an optimal environment for oaks by reducing the number of such competitors as conifers, thus altering the structure and composition of the ecological community and increasing the distribution of such preferred oak species as black oak. Burning also reduces the fuel load in the forest, greatly diminishing the probability of severe damage from intense fires, and concomitantly increases the available water for oaks by eliminating competitors. Further, burning acts to restrict the major pests which spoil the acorn crop, and establishes an uncluttered ground surface which facilitates the gathering process. The strategy involved is to burn with a low-intensity fire in order to minimize potential damage to the oaks.

228

Finally, rituals were seen as generating the favorable rain and weather patterns necessary for a good crop, and spiritual and ceremonial observances, at the level of both the individual and group, promoted the proper relationships between the people, the land, and the spirit world, thus maintaining the continued giving and receiving of the life-sustaining acorns.

QUALITY FOOD: THE QUEST FOR PINE NUTS IN NORTHERN CALIFORNIA[1]

Glenn Farris

INTRODUCTION

The material in this paper is largely derived from my unpublished dissertation (Farris 1982a), which originally grew out of an interest in learning how Indian people used pine nuts in northern California; that interest, in turn, developed from a summer spent conducting an archaeological survey at the crest of the northern coast range in Mendocino National Forest. The survey identified many archaeological sites with manos and metates at elevations of 6000-plus feet. Trying to determine possible uses for these tools led to a consideration of the sugar pine trees which dotted the high country. What was actually known about gathering sugar-pine seeds or those of their cousins, the low-elevation gray pine? While a great deal of attention had been paid to the fact that the peoples of the Great Basin, the Transverse Ranges, and the border with Baja made good use of piñon nuts (from *Pinus monophylla* and *P. quadrifolia*, for the most part; see Bettinger 1976; Lanner 1981; Shipek 1968; Wheat 1967:12-14), no systematic study of pine-nut use in California north of the Tehachapis had been undertaken. Of course, there were certainly many relevant comments in the ethnographies, in Indian folktales, and even in the observations of some of the early European visitors to California. However, facts as basic as the nutritional value of these seeds had yet to be determined. With the assistance of Dr. Vic Rendig of the University of California, Davis, it was determined that these seeds were more like those of the high protein, high fat two-leaf piñon (*P. edulis*) of the Four Corners area, than those of the relatively low protein, high carbohydrate single-leaf piñon nuts (*P. monophylla*) of the Great Basin and Tehachapis (Farris 1980; also see Farris 1982a, 1982b).

---

[1]This is a revised and expanded version of a paper that was originally presented at the Seventh Annual California Indian Conference, Sonoma State University, October 18, 1991.

Table 9.1

COMPARISON OF NUTRITIONAL ELEMENTS FOR SELECTED FOODS

FOOD	WATER	PROT.	FAT	CARB.	FIBER	ASH	Kcal/100g
		----g./100 g. Edible Portion----					
Pinus lambertiana (seed) [Sugar Pine]	3.3	21.4	53.6	17.5	----	4.2	594
P. sabiniana (seed) [Gray Pine]	3.6	25.0	49.4	17.5	----	4.5	571
P. coulteri (seed) [Big-cone or Coulter pine]	3.7	25.4	51.0	14.4	----	5.5	574
P. pinea (seed) [Italian Stone Pine]	5.6	31.1	47.4	11.6	(0.9)	4.3	556
P. monophylla (seed) [Single-leaf Piñon]	10.2	8.1	23.0	56.3	(1.1)	2.4	450
Quercus lobata (meal) [California Valley Oak]	8.7	4.8	18.6	65.9	----	2.0	440
Q. kelloggii (meal) [California Black Oak]	11.3	3.8	19.8	64.8	(2.1)	0.3	443
Corylus spp. (seed) [Hazel]	5.8	12.6	62.4	12.2	3.0	2.5	616
Corylus spp. (meal) [Hazel]	2.7	11.7	65.6	17.8	----	2.2	656

Table 9.1 (Cont'd)

Juglans nigra (seed) [Black Walnut]	3.1	20.5	59.3	14.8	---	628
Corn flour	12.0	7.8	2.6	76.8	---	361
Wheat flour	12.0	13.3	2.0	71.0	---	352
Salmon (smoked)	58.9	21.6	9.3	0	---	153
Venison (lean meat, raw)	74.0	21.1	4.0	0	---	106

(Above data from Farris 1982a:78)

The data in Table 9.1 demonstrate what a concentrated food pinenuts are. This characteristic was well-known to Ramsay Blake, an Apwaruge man of Fall River Mills, who stated that gray pine nuts were the kind preferred by his people. They made quite a rich food: "Eat ten or twelve, makes you strong" (Blake, quoted in Rivers 1980).

The high fat content found in *P. sabiniana* and *P. lambertiana* seeds is primarily of the polyunsaturated variety. The great reliance placed upon salmon in northern California (Baumhoff 1963) may have fostered a need for fat to accompany the lean salmon (Table 9.1). Mark N. Cohen, for example, has suggested that this combination was an important transition food in the shift from big-game hunting to a more mixed meat-vegetable subsistence:

> ...the fish-nut combination which replaced or increasingly supplemented large mammals in the prehistoric diet of so many regions is an attempt to duplicate the dietary contribution of these animals once the latter were exhausted, extinct, or simply too scarce to provide a reliable food supply for a growing population [Cohen 1977:193].

When I first proposed a study of the Indian use of pine nuts, the invariable academic query was, what is the volumetric return for labor expended for pine nuts? After all, current theory insisted that the Indian peoples would only invest their precious food-collecting time in activities that produced the highest return for the effort, such as hunting large animals and collecting volume foods like acorns and buckeyes. However, references were continually being made to the importance of pine nuts in the diet. Ultimately, it became clear that this food was considered such a treat that people would spend weeks in its gathering, travelling far from their winter homes to the high elevations of the Sierra Nevada, the Coast Ranges, and the Cascades to find it. Native peoples were doing a very human thing, enjoying a quality food which the mini-max theorists were only too ready to deny them.

Members of the first Spanish expeditions that penetrated the mountains of California in 1769-1770 made frequent mention of the fondness that the Indian peoples they met had for pine nuts. Fr. Juan Crespí mentioned on at least four occasions that people they had encountered offered his group pine nuts as food (Bolton 1927:156-157, 193-194, 197). The Spanish were no doubt especially quick to take note of this fact because eating pine nuts was a long-established custom among Mediterranean peoples. Early botanists on the Pacific Coast also noted the native preference for pine nuts. David Douglas (1833; 1959), who named the sugar pine and gray pine for two of his benefactors, first realized the existence of the stately sugar pine tree when he noticed that an Indian who had travelled up to the Columbia River had a pouch filled with its seeds.

The other main pine nut source was a lowland, foothill tree, the digger pine, a term which of course is a variant on a pejorative name that the whites gave to the Indians themselves. Some people have chosen to call these trees the gray pine, but most old-timers hold on to the term that they have heard all their lives.

PROCUREMENT AND PROCESSING

There is a significant difference in the way in which the sugar and gray pines are harvested. The cones of the gray pine are tightly attached to the branch, and must either be knocked off with a stick or twisted off by hand. A hooked stick is often used to bring them into reach. Once the cone is brought close enough, it can be either twisted off or cut off the branch. The Patwin were said to have used a "flint" knife for this purpose (Kroeber 1932a:296).

Twisting the cones off exposed one to the problem of dealing with the extremely sticky pitch. Contact with the pitch made it hard for the individuals involved to keep clean during such outings (cf. Muir 1977:148; Wheat 1967:29). Among the Paiute, basketry hats helped prevent the pitch from getting into the hair.

Sugar pine trees, by contrast, are tall, and the cones hang out on the ends of limbs, often in clusters. The pendulous nature of their attachment and their great weight give the person seeking their seeds the opportunity to use a different technique. The climber will stretch his foot out on a branch laden with cones and, by pressing on it, will get the branch moving in a rotary manner. Eventually the cone will snap off of its own weight.

Agility was a basic requirement for the tree-climber. He was often recognized as a specialist and was afforded much honor (Goldschmidt 1951:410). He was normally exempt from the onerous work of processing the cones; instead, other men, women, and children would perform this task (Willoughby 1963:28-29). Children were especially adept at retrieving cones which had rolled down the hillside (Harrington 1932:212). Prudent people would wait until the tree climber had finished knocking the cones down before moving in to collect them; one can imagine the devastating effect that a three-foot cone dropping from a height of 100 feet or more would have.

Different groups used various methods to encourage the climbers. There was a special individual among the Nomlaki called a *olhehit* who chanted a repetitive call from the base of the tree (Goldschmidt 1951:410), while among the Karok the women and children shouted encouragement, a favorite cry being "Old man turtle, bite it off" (Harrington 1932:212). Certain traditions were also observed at the time of gathering. Among the Nomlaki it was considered a serious breach for someone to break pine nuts open on wood; it had to be done on stone or it might cause the next climber to fall (Washington 1976:31).

After the cones had been gathered (and quantities as large as 1000 pounds have been recorded for the Central Sierra Miwok), the nuts were then removed:

> They were collected by the women and stood together upside down, sometimes in two tiers. Dry pine needles were then spread over them and ignited to burn off the pitch, a process called *hiñatci mulu*. Sugar pine needles were used for no other purpose.
>
> The sugar pine cones were next hammered top down on a rock so that they split down the middle. The nuts were then removed by pressing down each projecting point on the cones so that the nut would roll out. The nuts were still warm and some might be eaten at once, although pressing and blowing of the eater was regarded as necessary at first, as with most first fruits among the Miwok.
>
> The nuts were next shaken in a winnowing basket to get rid of the chaff or empty shells. The wind was the draft of air that removed the waste. As a rule, the man who climbed the tree divided the nuts among the men and women of his party [Barrett and Gifford 1933:150].

In order to appreciate what 1000 pounds of cones would mean, a little calculation is necessary. It has been estimated that an average of 3.7 pounds of clean seed is obtained from every 100 pounds of sugar pine cones (USDA 1974:623); thus the day's activity mentioned above would have produced about 37 pounds (16.8 kg) of clean seed. Discounting the 39.7% that consists of the shell portion (Farris 1982a:89) leaves 10.14 kg (22.31 pounds), yielding 60,240 kcal--enough to provide 30 people with 2000 kcal each.

When the seeds were out of the cone, they were ready to be prepared for eating or storage. Perhaps the most common form of processing involved roasting the seeds in a parching basket using live coals, which were then tossed around to mix with the seeds and to avoid burning the basket. The roasting also acted to enhance the taste. In the case of sugar pine nuts, these were sometimes placed in an earthen oven to be steamed. A pit would be dug and filled with heated rocks; the pinenuts, wrapped in leaves, would then be placed on top and the pit would be covered again with earth. Water percolating down over the rocks then created steam. In order to impart a stronger flavor, the pungent leaves of pepperwood (*Umbellularia californica*) would sometimes be used for the wrapping. Harrington (1932:213) has also mentioned grape leaves being used.

If the pine nuts were to be stored, they were dried after steaming. They could then be placed in storage baskets and either kept in the house or, as is specifically mentioned for the Maidu (Duncan 1964:29) and Paiute, placed in underground granaries. Despite their high fat content, the problem of rancidity does not seem to have been too severe, although there was an occasional complaint about "old pine nuts." Even after some years of storage, the pine nuts were often quite edible (Anonymous 1896:93). Storage of excess seeds was one of the numerous ways the Indians managed their food supply.

The soft seed-coats of these seeds allowed for easy removal. Another method involved pounding up the seeds shells and all; fiber would thus be added to the high nutritional value of the seeds. In some cases, the soft shell would apparently be ingested whole, as demonstrated by the discovery of human coprolites in archaeological sites in the Southern California desert which contained the shells of *P. monophylla* (the Single-leaf piñon) seeds (Wilke 1978:79).

The Sierra Miwok are the only people who have been specifically mentioned as having pounded sugar pine seeds in a mortar to produce a pine nut butter; it was called *lopa* (Barrett and Gifford 1933:151). This pinenut butter was in particular demand at feasts and could be eaten with the fingers like acorn mush.

Yet another way of preparing pine nuts was to grind them up to make a flour, which could then be baked into pinenut bread or mixed with water to form a gruel. In a Yuki creation myth, the hungry Coyote is provided by the creator with "sugar pine nut bread, digger pine nut bread, and hazel nut bread" (Kroeber 1932b:908).

Gray pine nuts offered other problems. The hardness of their shells required that they be cracked with a hammer stone. This would be done on an anvil stone, which often had a roughened or even pitted surface to keep the seeds from slipping. Once the shell was removed, the kernel could be eaten raw, ground to make flour for bread, or included in a gruel as was done with sugar pine seeds.

By the time the formal ethnographers began asking questions about food collecting around the turn of the century, many practices had been disrupted. It was rare indeed for an ethnographer to have actually witnessed the collection of sugar pine nuts (actually, seeds), with all its attendant drama and derring-do, as the best tree climbers, fearless men who would ascend a 200-foot tall tree to bring down the cones, risked their lives for the general good. Thanks to Lucy Thompson (1916), whose wonderful book *To the American Indian* records the passing of an era among the Yurok, we have the following description of a process that was part and parcel of a broader cultural destruction:

> In the early days when a white man arrived among the Indians, he took an Indian woman, and in the fall of the year she would want to gather some pine nuts, the white man would go with her, taking his axe, and cut down the tree, as he could not climb it, and told the woman there they are, what are you going to do about it? At first the woman complained and finally said the white man would spoil everything. Then the Indians began to cut the trees. In the last few years, these trees have become very valuable in the eyes of the white man, and it has become the complaint of the white man that the Indians ought to be shot for cutting down this fine timber for the nuts. I leave the reader to decide which one ought to be punished for the cutting of the great number of these fine sugar pine trees [Thompson 1916:28-29].

Of course, this shift in the way in which the pine cones were procured eliminated the need for expert tree climbers, as well as the tree climbing contests that had so entertained the people. Only a few elders passed on the traditions and the knowledge of the old ways in which sugar pine seeds were gathered.

Gathering sugar pine nuts involved a major movement of whole families into the high country where the sugar pines were to be found. Camps would be established for periods of as long as two months (Goddard 1903:29-30; Sapir 1910b:141; Barrett and Gifford 1933:151; DuBois and Demetracopoulou 1931:339-340). In the fall, there would be ceremonies held to pray for all kinds of food, including pine nuts (Powers 1877:237; Roberts 1980:25). The fact that it usually takes about two years for a pine cone to mature was not lost on the Indians. Wuzzie George, a Paiute, commented:

> when the Indians were gathering pinenuts in the fall, they watched for the little cones that would be the next year's crop. When they found some immature pinenuts they put a small pine bough bearing the cones into a mountain spring. Sagebrush was placed over the bough, 'because sagebrush is a medicine,' and weighed down with a rock. We talk to it and say, 'Don't get dry. We are going to eat you next fall' [Wheat 1967:116].

Because the tradition of pine nut collecting was so severely disturbed by the coming of the whites, it is often in the actions described in folktales that one can still discover the details of how it was done. The Yana, for example, have a story about a couple who went out collecting gray pine nuts. The husband climbed the tree and threw down a few cones and asked his wife if the nuts were big. She replied that they were indeed big and that he should continue throwing down cones (Sapir 1910b:123-124). In fact, there was a need for quality control in gathering pine nuts, because many of them might have a fully developed outer seed coat, but be quite empty inside. Rather than wasting time, a sample would be collected, and if it looked good, the harvest would continue.

In another story, called "The Drowning of Young Buzzard's Wife," it is sugar pine nuts which are being sought. It is a group affair in which Buzzard's son admonishes his people:

> 'Now dig for roots! They are ripe already. Let us climb sugar pines. We shall move tomorrow and you will settle down there. Now I shall climb for sugar pine nuts, they

are ripe already. The people will all come there, and we
shall settle down there where there is a nice spring. I
think the people will come here. We shall wait for them.
Many were the people who came together' [Sapir 1910b:
140-141].

The importance of pine nuts is often emphasized in creation stories as
well, as for example in the Yuki myth cited earlier in which Taikomol
provides the hungry Coyote with pine nut and hazel nut breads (Kroeber
1932a:908).

The mention of hazel nuts also brings to mind an observation
made by Alfred Kroeber concerning the Yurok:

If the child during the first five or six days of its life were
to take nourishment from its mother, the Yurok believe its
jaws would become affected and it would soon starve.
During this period it is fed only a little water in which
hazel or pine nuts have been rubbed, and which looks
milky [Kroeber 1925:45].

This substitute formula was particularly useful when a mother died in
childbirth, as Lucy Thompson has mentioned. Although I know of no
other such use of pine nuts by other California Indian peoples, there are
parallels in the Southwest where "a soup was made from the nuts of *P.
edulis* to give to babies" (Sweet 1962:9). Pine nuts have been described as
"being not only a nutritious food but very digestible and especially suited
for delicate stomachs" (Havard 1895:117-118).

Pine nuts often figured as special foods to offer as welcoming gifts
to visitors (Goddard 1903b:110, 129). Catharine Holt, for example,
recorded a rather specialized use of pine nuts among the Shasta:

Neither were pine nuts eaten at meals, except when mixed
with dried salmon. They were eaten at any time between
meals, and were also, like the mixed *ipos* and service-
berries, offered a guest upon his arrival [Holt 1946:309].

Another useful characteristic of the seeds of *P. sabiniana* was the
fact that they have very hard shells, which could be made into beads.
Pine nut beads are very prevalent in the northern part of the state and
extend beyond the area where the trees themselves are found; in fact, they

extend well up into coastal Oregon and into the Great Basin. By contrast, they are virtually absent south of the area of the Athapaskan and Wintu peoples in the Coast Ranges and, though found among the Maidu, their use seems to stop abruptly when one moves into Sierra Miwok country (Farris 1982:97-119). Why people such as the Pomo, who clearly treasured beads, did not use this common seed in their own backyard is a question that has yet to be satisfactorily answered.

CONCLUSIONS

Aside from the seeds of the sugar and gray pine, virtually all pine seeds can be used for food, but some were probably eliminated from consideration because they were too small to be worth the trouble. Large seeded species such as the Coulter pine and the Torrey pine were certainly valued for food. Ponderosa and Jeffrey pine seeds were also eaten. In fact, California is blessed with an amazing variety of pine species, far more than is found in any similar area north of Mexico. Elsewhere, I have compared the seeds of *P. sabiniana* with those of the Italian Stone Pine (*P. pinea*), which for thousands of years has been the major source of pignolia nuts from the Mediterranean region (Farris 1983).

The theme of environmental management by native Californians manifests itself in their intensive use--one might even say cultivation--of pine species. The techniques used to obtain the pine seeds were pointedly non-destructive (notably so in contrast to the approach taken by the white man in Lucy Thompson's story). Ways of ascertaining the degree of development of seeds before time was invested in their procurement are mentioned in various narratives. By selecting for good seeds, the subsequent act of removing the cones to other locations for storage and/or further processing would have increased the probability that some of the good seeds would be lost to the food-making process but would take root to expand the range. The major effort involved in procuring this tasty morsel further belies the image of the California Indians as living on the edge of subsistence. Although their food availability did go through cycles of feast and famine, they made adjustments to these by intensifying their social interaction and by increasing their range of storable foods. Pine nuts fortunately did not require the intensive leaching process which characterized so many of the other primary foods (e.g., acorns, buckeyes, and islay). Pine nuts were often used as social welcoming gifts and so enhanced the interrelations between villages.

Whether the fact was explicitly realized or not, pine nuts were useful in balancing a diet that was heavy in the carbohydrates that were obtained from many of the other plant foods. The availability of abundant, high-quality oils in pine seeds obviated a reliance solely on animal fats. Overall, pine seeds represented an excellent contribution to the native quality of life, and were certainly one reason why the people of this region could truly be described--in a recent conference comparing the successful native economies of California and Japan--as "affluent foragers" (Koyama and Thomas 1981).

BOW STAVES HARVESTED FROM JUNIPER TREES BY INDIANS OF NEVADA[1]

Philip J. Wilke

Investigation of numerous scarred juniper (*Juniperus osteoperma*) trees in western Nevada, from which it is concluded Indians took wood for the manufacture of archery bows, necessitated a review of the literature on Great Basin bows and the materials from which they were made. The goal was to better understand the significance of these trees and the relationship of the industry represented by them to the manufacture of bows in the area as a whole. Use of horn, antler, and bone for bow stave material is discussed elsewhere (Wilke 1988). In this paper, I discuss the use of various woods for bow staves in the Great Basin and adjacent regions. I then discuss the harvesting of wood for bow staves from still-living juniper trees in western Nevada, and offer ideas about the exchange of wooden bow staves or completed bows from this region to other regions. Finally, I speculate on the relationships between bowyers and the trees from which they took their bow staves, and assess stave harvesting and tree regrowth as these phenomena relate to the concept of aboriginal resource management.

THE CONTEXT OF INQUIRY

The short sinew-backed bow was of widespread distribution among the ethnographic Northern Paiute, Western Shoshoni, Northern Shoshoni, Eastern Shoshoni, Southern Paiute, and Ute groups of the Great Basin of western North America. Examples of such reinforced bows are preserved in museum collections, and descriptions of them are found in historic and ethnographic accounts.

[1]This paper originally appeared in the **Journal of California and Great Basin Anthropology**, Vol. 10, No. 1, pp. 3-31, 1988. It is reprinted here by permission of Malki Museum Press. Acknowledgements have been deleted.

Most existing Great Basin bows, whether of wood, horn, or antler, are less than a meter in length, and when at rest (unstrung) many are strongly reflexed in the handle and recurved at the ends. The backing on all reinforced Great Basin bows is of sinew, which is the extremely strong fiber of dried, shredded tendons. Sinew fibers were applied lengthwise along the back of the bow with glue made by boiling horn, hide scrapings, fish skins or swim bladders, or other animal protein, depending on the material available. The favored material for bowstrings was sinew, although various vegetable fibers were also used.

Because sinew and native-made animal glues soften when exposed to moisture, in aboriginal contexts these bows often were carried in a slipcase of animal skin to protect the string and backing (Mason 1894; cf. Coues 1897:714). Among some northern tribes,[2] rattlesnake skins sometimes were glued over the sinew backing of bows. Decoration is the usual reason given for such coverings. But the skin also camouflaged the bow and, perhaps most important, it protected the sinew backing from moisture. Usually the grip was wrapped with buckskin or other material to protect the backing from the sweat of the palm.

Most aspects of Great Basin archery technology have been reported only in very general terms. Such information as is available tends to describe the finished weapons rather than the steps involved in their manufacture. The reasons for this are several, but they mainly involve the selective survival of traditional crafts, and the biased nature of ethnographic recording.

In aboriginal western North America, crafts and technologies associated with women persisted longer in the last-century period of intensive acculturation than did those associated with men. Women continued to practice traditional crafts such as basketry and pottery, and traditional foodways such as seed and root collecting, well into the historic

---

[2] Accounts that describe the practice of covering the sinew backing of bows with snake skin (usually specified as rattlesnake) are: Northern Shoshoni (Wyeth 1851:212; Lowie 1909:192; Steward 1943:314, 370); Northern Paiute/Bannock (Steward 1943:314); Gros Ventre (Kroeber 1908:161); Crow (Maximilian 1904-07, XXII:352-353); Kutenai (Turney-High 1941:83; Ray 1942:149); Okanagon (Teit 1928:241); Flathead (Teit 1928:344); Klikitat, Umatilla, Kalispel, Shuswap, Chilcotin, Flathead, and Coeur d'Alene (northern Rocky Mountains and Plateau tribes extending into British Columbia and Alberta [Ray 1942:149]; denied for the Coeur d'Alene by Teit [1928:98]; Nez Perce (Teit 1928:99); and other unspecified tribes west of the Rocky Mountains, probably the Nez Perce, Northern Shoshoni, and neighboring groups (Coues 1897:713-714; Ferris 1940:300).

period. Aspects of this culture still survive in some regions (Wheat 1967; Couture 1978; Fowler and Walter 1985; Couture et al. 1986; d'Azevedo 1986). The ethnographic films *Tule Technology* (Smithsonian Institution 1983) and *The Earth is Our Home* (Great Basin Films 1979) emphasize the retention of traditional crafts and skills by women. In contrast, the advent first of the fur trade and then of widespread mining and ranching enterprises brought employment opportunities and new technologies, including firearms, to Great Basin Indians (Hattori 1975). In many regions these factors combined to significantly reduce big game populations. As a result, male-oriented technologies, such as flintworking and archery, and hunting as a regular subsistence pursuit, rapidly declined.

Equally significant is the fact that Great Basin ethnographers who collected information on native culture in the first half of the twentieth century were trained primarily in social anthropology. While information on traditional archery did not persist to the extent that many nonmaterial aspects of native culture did (such as language, marriage and kinship patterns, myths, etc.) ethnographers also were less able, or less likely, to elicit the vestiges of such information.

By the time ethnographers seriously concerned themselves with recording the details of traditional archery, the bowyer's art had vanished from the Great Basin. All that remained were a few museum specimens (often of questionable origin) and some reminiscences of what might have been seen long ago, or more likely what had been heard about the manufacture of archery equipment. Traditional Great Basin archery is now a lost art. The task of describing it, let alone replicating it for performance experiments, is therefore difficult.

WOODEN BOWS IN THE GREAT BASIN

Without question, the most common material for bow staves in most of the Great Basin was wood. It was more generally available and much easier to fabricate into bows than either horn or antler. Various wood species were used. Mountain mahogany (*Cercocarpus*), serviceberry (*Amelanchier*), juniper (*Juniperus*), chokecherry (*Prunus*), oak (*Quercus*), maple (*Acer*), birch (*Betula*), willow (*Salix*), mesquite (*Prosopis*), and "locust" (*Robinia*?) are all identified as bow woods.[3] While all of these woods may have been used for self (unbacked) bows, especially in expedient situations, all but possibly willow were made into sinew-backed weapons.

Availability of species largely dictated which wood was used in a given region. Juniper (*Juniperous* spp., "cedar" in historic literature [Powell 1875:128]) is identified as the favored bow wood among nearly all Northern Paiute, Western (Nevada) Shoshoni, Owens Valley Paiute, Southern Paiute, Ute, and Gosiute. The Tübatulabal and Kawaiisu of the southern Sierra Nevada also used juniper. Its popularity probably was due to its widespread occurrence and the general absence of the wood species used elsewhere (Coville 1892; Curtis 1926; Steward 1941, 1943; Stewart 1941, 1942). For most of this territory, the species used was the Utah juniper (*J. osteosperma*).[4] Julian Steward (1941:236) reported that among

---

[3] The reference to "locust" is in Kelly's (1964) "Southern Paiute Ethnography." Probably it refers to the New Mexican locust (Robinia neomexicana), which occurs throughout the Southwest in Utah and southern Nevada (Elias 1980:668). For information on bow woods among various Great Basin tribes, consult Coville (1892:360), Sapir (1910), Chamberlin (1911:346), Hooper (1920:358), Lowie (1924:245-246), Curtis (1926, XV:61), Steward (1933:259-260), Driver (1937:70), Voegelin (1938:27), Stewart (1941:384, 1942:266), Steward (1941:236, 289; 1943:313, 370), Kelly (1932:142, 1964:72), Fowler and Matley (1979:61-62), Zigmond (1981:35), and Callaway et al. (1986:350).

[4] Beckwith (1855:43) commented on the "superior bows of cedar" (probably the western Juniper, J. occidentalis) he saw among the Indians on the Pit River in northeastern California in 1854. This usually is considered Achomawi territory, although the Indians insisted they were "Pah Utahs." Their pierced nasal septa, ornamented with bars of bone or shell, suggest they were Achomawi (Steward and Wheeler-Voegelin 1974:100 [repaginated]. In the Sacramento River drainage of northern California, western juniper was sometimes used for bows. Saxton Pope (1925:14-15) described one of Ishi's bows:

> It was a short, flat piece of mountain juniper [J. occidentalis] backed with sinew. The length was forty-two inches [107 cm.].... It was broadest at the center of each limb, approximately two inches, and half an inch thick.... The wood was obtained by splitting a limb from a tree and utilizing the outer layers, including the sap wood.... Held in shape by cords and binding to another piece of wood, he let his bow season in a dark, dry place. Here it remained from a few months to years, according to his needs. After being seasoned, he backed it with sinew.

Ishi was the last Yahi (Southern Yana) of northern California. From this description (and it must be accurate, given Pope's [1918] knowledge of Ishi's archery), it appears that the

the Western (Nevada) Shoshoni, "the sinew-backed bow was generally of juniper (Juniperus utahensis) [sic], the best material in most of the territory, but sometimes of serviceberry in the northern regions where it grew." Across the area, some use may have been made of other juniper species, including the Rocky Mountain juniper (*J. scopulorum*), favored by most northern Plains tribes (Grinnell 1923,I:173), or the one-seeded juniper (*J. monosperma*).

In the Great Basin, wooden bows always were made from a single piece, or stave, of wood, not from two shorter pieces joined in the center as is the case with most horn and antler bows. They usually were reinforced with a backing of sinew. Most ethnographic accounts indicate the length of such bows was three to four feet (91-122 cm.). Drawing on unpublished notes of Willard Park, Fowler and Lilijeblad (1986:439) reported that, among the Northern Paiute, bows for large game were up to 4 or 5 ft. (122-152 cm.) long, for small game only about 3 ft. Fourteen sinew-backed wooden bows (wood not identified) of Southern Paiute and Gosiute attribution in the Powell Collection of the U.S. National Museum average only 97.5 cm. in length (Fowler and Matley 1979:62-64).[5] A sinew-backed bow of reddish-colored wood, possibly juniper heartwood, is in the collections of the Eastern California Museum in Independence. Its origin is believed to be the Owens Valley. It is now strongly reflexed and recurved and measures about 104 cm. around the curve of the belly exclusive of the nocks, which are formed of sinew. Another, apparently of juniper heartwood, is in the collections of the Lowie Museum of Anthropology (Berkeley). It is attributed to the Panamint Shoshoni (the southernmost division of Western Shoshoni), and is 101 cm. long. The nocks are

---

bow was roughed out from green juniper wood, in contrast to the situation discussed in this paper. Use of juniper species is indicated, however, west of the Sierra Nevada in California. Most Indians of northwestern California, Western Oregon and Washington, and on up into British Columbia made bows of Pacific yew (Taxus brevifolia; Driver 1939:326; Barnett 1937:169, 1939:245), a material Ishi used after he abandoned his traditional lifeway.

[5] Excluded from this group are three wooden self bows 88.5, 95, and 144 cm. long and one Uinkarets Southern Paiute wooden bow 96.5 cm. long said to have a sinewed belly. Some old bows in museum displays, and some illustrated in the literature, appear to be sinew-bellied or to have the string on the sinewed side, due to the strong reflex they have acquired with age. Only examination of the nocks might reveal that these bows have "reversed." Sinew on the belly would do nothing to protect or strengthen the bow, or to improve its cast; it would only weaken the bow and almost assure its breakage if drawn.

formed by a wrapping of several turns of rawhide near the ends of the limbs.

As with the manufacture of horn and antler bows, information is sketchy on the methods by which wooden bows were made. With access to published ethnographic information, but without the benefit of observations made on museum specimens and the experiences of modern bowyers who have successfully replicated traditional bows, it probably is not possible to make such a bow and have it perform well. Few details are known concerning the selection of trees for stave removal, the care given to trees that supplied bow staves, the proper characteristics of such trees, their ecological requirements, or their distribution. Neither is there much recorded information on the extraction of bow staves from trees or on their fabrication into finished weapons. Likewise, of the exchange of bow staves we know almost nothing. Interesting information on the manufacture of wooden bows among the Paviotso (Northern Paiute), although brief, was recorded by Edward S. Curtis (1926,XV:61):

> The bow was about three feet long, recurved at the ends, and made of a piece of cedar taken from the trunk, not from a branch. The better ones were strengthened with a reinforcement of sinew glued to the back.

These comments are useful for understanding how bow staves were extracted from juniper trees, as we shall see below.

NEW INFORMATION ON SOURCES AND EXTRACTION OF WOODEN BOW STAVES

Recent field investigations in western Nevada provided information on the aboriginal exploitation of Utah juniper (*Juniperus osteosperma*) trees for bow staves. These studies reveal some of the decisions involved in tree selection, wood inspection, stave preparation and seasoning, stave removal, and on the care and possible management of favored trees. Considerable field time spent searching for Utah juniper trees from which bow staves were harvested in aboriginal times made it apparent that trees of this species suitable for stave extraction were few and far between. They do not occur everywhere the species grows.

Forty-seven[6] juniper trees were found that clearly show the removal or isolation and growth arrestment of a total of 150 linear billets of wood for bow staves. The only other item in the native tool kit that conceivably could have been fabricated from such pieces is the digging stick, but this use is discounted for the following reasons. Digging sticks could have been made of wood lacking the specific arrangement of growth rings (tangential grain) typical of such wood; these tools could be made from various straight branches. Only persons seeking bow staves would have given such careful consideration to the quality of wood in billets removed from the trees. Consistent attention was given to length, width, thickness, absence of damaging knots, straightness of grain, lack of twist in the grain, perhaps a combination of both heartwood and sapwood,[7] and growth-rings typical of flatsawn lumber where the outer ring or rings formed a gentle arc extending across the back of the bow from one side or edge to the other.

Discovery of these trees came about while searching for timber to be used in replicating the short sinew-backed juniper bow of the Great Basin. Frederick Coville (1892:360) described the use of dead, seasoned juniper wood for the manufacture of bows by the Panimint Shoshoni:

> The bows are made from the desert juniper, *Juniperus*
> *californica utahensis* [= *J. osteosperma*]. The Indian
> prefers a piece of wood from the trunk or a large limb of
> a tree that has died and seasoned while standing.

In all cases where such wood was examined in the field, it proved to be weather-checked and cracked and unsuitable for bow manufacture. George Frison kindly pointed out that the wood was cut from living timber, and described stave-removal scars he had seen on juniper trees in Wyoming. That description led to the discovery of the trees reported here.

---

[6] Editors' Note: approximately 100 such trees are presently known to exist; they have been found in Wyoming, Colorado, Nevada, and eastern California. They appear to have had a wide distribution in the western United States (Philip Wilke, personal communication 1992).

[7] Traditional archery literature stresses the importance of combining heartwood for the belly and sapwood for the back of a bow. The compressive strength of the heartwood and the tensile strength of the sapwood complement one another for maximum strength and cast (Pope 1925:61).

248

The trees are all in Mineral County at elevations between 1,890 and 2,135 m. (6,200 to 7,006 ft.). The ones found represent the result of about 15 person-days searching for and recording information on such trees. Their actual distribution and abundance in the Great Basin is unknown, although several days' efforts to find them in central Nevada, and elsewhere in Nevada, Idaho, and eastern California yielded negative results. The work reported here represents an expansion of investigations on aboriginal big-game wing traps, and all of the specimens found are within 2 km. of these features or camps associated with them.

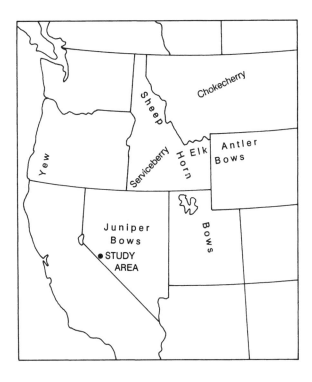

Figure 10.1. Location of the study area in western Nevada.

Thirty-three trees occur in the Excelsior Mountains east of Little Whisky Flat in an area bout 2 km. across (Fig. 10.1). Here they grow in Pinyon-Juniper Woodland (sites 26Mn738, 26Mn739) near a large wing-trap built to capture pronghorn (*Antilocapra americana*) and in and near a similar structure apparently constructed for capturing deer (*Odocoileus hemionus*) (site 26Mn685).[8]

Fourteen trees occur about 18 km. to the south, in an area of unnamed uplands partially timbered with open Pinyon-Juniper Woodland south of Huntoon Valley, east and south of Huntoon Spring. Again, all were found in an area less than 2 km. across. The trees occur near several aboriginal camps (sites 26Mn737, 26Mn740, 26Mn741) and near another large wing-trap (site 26Mn589) built by Indians for capturing pronghorn.[9] These trees show the growth arrestment or removal of one to several bow staves each, and one tree (Huntoon-1) bears the visible scars of at least 16 bow stave removals (Fig. 10.2).

The typical scar from bow stave extraction is a rough, trough-shaped groove split out and following the grain of the wood, somewhat over a meter long, about 6 cm. wide, and 2.5-3 cm. deep. The ends of the scar are marked by transverse V-shaped cuts made by the bowyer to isolate the stave, arrest its growth, and split it from the tree. The scars occur alone, or they flank one another in a series. In some cases they occur on opposite sides of a trunk, separated by branches or knots. In one case (Huntoon-1; Fig. 10.2) a series of seven adjacent stave-removal scars girdles the base of the trunk approximately one-half the way around. The same tree has a second series of stave-removal scars on the main trunk high in the crown.

Among all the trees, observed scars from stave removal vary from 89 to 187 cm. long. While the longer ones may indicate construction of longer bows, as suggested for the Northern Paiute by Fowler and Liljeblad (1986:439), it appears more likely that maximum stave length was sought to enable selection and use of the best portion thereof. The lengths of

---

[8] Reports on these traps are in progress. Sites with recorded bow stave trees east of Little Whiskey Flat are as follows: 26Mn685 (Excelsior-1 through -6); 26Mn738 (Excelsior-7 through -10, -15 through -30); 26Mn739 (Excelsior-11 through -14, -31 through -33).

[9] This trap will be reported elsewhere by R.E. Parr. Sites with recorded bow stave trees south and east of Huntoon Spring are as follows: 26Mn740 (Huntoon-1, -2, -7, -8 through -14); 26Mn589 (Huntoon-3); 26Mn741 (Huntoon-4); 26Mn737 (Huntoon-5, -6).

250

Figure 10.2. Juniper tree (Huntoon-1) with 16 stave-removal scars in two tiers. The lower series girdles the tree more than halfway around. Recently killed by lightning.

Table 10.1

CHARACTERISTICS OF 47 UTAH JUNIPER TREES SCARRED BY REMOVAL OR GROWTH-ARRESTMENT OF BOW STAVES

[Culturally scarred trees in the northern Excelsior Mountains; all work done with stone tools. Excelsior-1 through Excelsior-6 are associated with an aboriginal historic deer corral.]

Tree Number	Number of Removals, Attempts[a]	Stave Lengths (cm.)[b]	Comments
Excelsior-1	2	129, 147	Two staves removed. Removal scars partially grown over. One stave would have had a natural reflex. Figure 10.11.
Excelsior-2	3	104	Aged juniper with a massive straight trunk. Two removal scars much grown over by younger wood and of indeterminate length.
Excelsior-3	1	120	Stunted little juniper with two trunks. Stave removed from regrowth partially obscuring a natural scar. Figure 10.3.
Excelsior-4	1	143	Aged juniper with a stave-removal scar almost obscured by regrowth. Stave apparently had two bad knots.
Excelsior-5	6		Long dead, standing juniper. At least six removals; heavily weathered and no stave lengths determinable. Worked half-way around trunk.
Excelsior-6	1	>117	Small juniper, with single removal scar almost healed over. Length of stave inferred by measurement from growth-arrestment cut down to present ground surface.
Excelsior-7	5	93, >103, 115, 123, 132	Moderate-sized juniper with removals from both sides of the main trunk. Longest stave was isolated by cuts but was an apparent failure as it split out short of its intended length. Figure 10.4.
Excelsior-8	1		Wedge-shaped strip of bark removed and upper cut made to arrest stave growth. Neither remaining bark nor stave removed. Figure 10.5.

Table 10.1 (cont'd)

Excelsior-9	2	113, 186	Much regrowth evident over the shorter of two staves. Substantial twist to shorter stave.
Excelsior-10	4	110, 110, 110, 149	Enormous juniper with massive trunk; removals on west side. Massive regrowth since removal makes observations a bit uncertain.
Excelsior-11	1	98	Aged juniper with one prominent trunk: straight wood begins 85 cm. above the ground. Regrowth from left side of cut has resulted in straight-grained wood suitable for removal now. Cuts 6 cm wide, 2.5 cm. deep, northwest side. Stave detached upward from bottom cut and split out thin at the top.
Excelsior-12	2	>105, >105	Aged juniper with much regrowth. Staves removed from the east side.
Excelsior-13	3	114, 126, 145	Enormous juniper with staves removed from west side.
Excelsior-14	2	121, 121	Juniper with multiple trunks. Staves removed from the north side of the southeast trunk.
Excelsior-15	6	>104, >104, 113, >117, >123, >132	Aged juniper with several massive trunks. Staves removed from two trunks down to decayed wood at the present duff.
Excelsior-16	4	>100, 103, 113, 133	Scraggly tree with multiple trunks; much regrowth. Short slab (fireboard?) 70 cm. long also removed.
Excelsior-17	7	>94, 103, 104, 113, 128	Tall, straight, old juniper with removals from trunk and from undersides of two rather horizontal branches. Longest stave is from underside of branch and shows much regrowth at trunk end; a knot at the other end of this stave would have shortened its effective length to 114 cm.
Excelsior-18	1	113	Enormous tree with two trunks. One removal from one trunk yielded straight wood between bad knots.
Excelsior-19	4	99, 111, 112, 121	Great juniper with large branches. Much regrowth.
Excelsior-20	2	94, >127	Very old large juniper with recumbent trunks to 60 cm. diameter.
Excelsior-21	1		Single cut on one branch arrested growth at upper end of a potential stave, which was never removed but would have been ca. 108 cm. long.
Excelsior-22	5	89, 98, >115, >140	Aged juniper with removals from trunk and main limb.
Excelsior-23	1	109	Removal was attempted from the bottom cut but failed (split out) two-thirds the way to the upper cut.

Table 10.1 (cont'd)

Excelsior-24	3	114, 172	Very old juniper now largely dead. Longest stave was removed from the underside of a limb and has a pronounced curve at one end; remainder straight. One stave of uncertain length due to regrowth, but likely ca. 114 cm. long.
Excelsior-25	3	120, 120	One stave of indeterminate length; two staves removed from the same cuts.
Excelsior-26	1	187	Very old, half-dead juniper.
Excelsior-27	2	113, 116	Scraggly, twisted juniper. Longer stave was a failure.
Excelsior-28	2	106, 108	Large juniper with removals from a very difficult area between two trunks.
Excelsior-29	2	>110, 127	Old, short juniper with several trunks.
Excelsior-30	7	110, 114, 114, 119, 124	Very old, crooked juniper with massive regrowth over stave removal scars; two additional limbs removed that may have yielded additional staves. Some staves removed from this tree would have required considerable straightening, or, more likely, the trunks from which they were removed have become curved since stave removal.
Excelsior-31	7	117, 135?, >155	Large juniper with partial regrowth over 135-cm. long removal scar. Figure 10.4.
Excelsior-32	1		One very old, eroded, growth-arrestment cut on the upper side of a major limb of a very large tree.
Excelsior-33	5		Massive, ancient juniper growing only 2 m. from the floor of the canyon. Five removals, but lengths of none are determinable. Two staves removed from north side of a trunk ca. 90 cm. in diameter. One of these perhaps was wide enough to have yielded two bows. Three staves removed from a major limb. All of the straight-grained peripheral wood in this tree was harvested.

[Bow trees in uplands south of Huntoon Valley, east and southeast of Huntoon Spring. Huntoon-3 is associated with an historic pronghorn wing-trap. Evidence of use of metal tools as noted.]

Huntoon-1	16	110, 118, >120, 123, 125, 126, 126, >130, >130, >130, >130, >130	Dead juniper with straight trunk and two tiers of stave removals, one above the other. Tree more than half girdled. Staves removed from the trunk and from a branch cut from the tree with a metal axe and now lying on the ground, but all stave removal, or at least growth-arrestment, on the tree itself appears to have been done with stone tools. Shows evidence of stave removal, regrowth of wood into the stave removal scar, and later stave removal from straight-grained regrowth. Two large basalt cleaver-like

Table 10.1 (cont'd)

			Description
Huntoon-2	2		spalls (Fig. 7), apparently used to make stave-removal cuts, were found at the base of the tree. Tree recently died as a result of a lightning strike. Figure 10.2. Very old juniper. Two staves isolated and growth-arrested by cuts. Arrestment cuts at the upper end of one stave, at the lower end of the other, made with some stone tools. Neither stave removed. Figure 10.6.
Huntoon-3	1		One stave growth-arrested, but not removed, on the south side of the tree. Growth was arrested by a cut, made apparently with stone tools, 147 cm. above ground surface, toward which the stave would have been split out. This cut both arrested the growth of the stave and would have been used to split it from the tree. Partially obscured by regrowth. Straight trunk suggests intentional pruning while the tree was young. Figure 10.10.
Huntoon-4	1	110	Aged juniper. One stave removed from a fairly small (ca. 15-cm. diameter) straight (now dead) trunk among massive twisted ones.
Huntoon-5	4	105, 107, 107, 123	Aged juniper with a large straight-grained limb removed with a metal axe. Limb lies on the ground and staves were removed from it, with metal tools, apparently while on the ground.
Huntoon-6	6	103, 108, 108	Aged juniper with multiple trunks. Three staves were removed by cuts made with stone tools at their lower ends and split upward; upper extent is not observable, so lengths are not determinable. Three staves were removed with a metal axe from a limb lying on ground after this limb was chopped from the tree. Shorter axe-cut slab may have been a fireboard.
Huntoon-7	2		Juniper with rosette form of about 16 trunks. Stave(s) removed with metal tools from the central side of one trunk 15 cm. in diameter. One of the smallest trunks seen to have been used on any tree. Staves were split out upward, and are of indeterminate length.
Huntoon-8	2	>104, >104	Metal axe cuts mark the upper ends of staves removed from one of several trunks. Measurements indicate length to the present ground surface, the staves having been split out downward below the present duff. Small knots were present in both staves. Figure 10.9.

Table 10.1 (cont'd)

Huntoon-9	1	104	Stave was removed from a single straight vertical branch in the middle of a tree with a rosette form. Removed with stone stools and has a pronounced twist.
Huntoon-10	2		Growth-arrestment cuts on facing trunks, both of which have massive regrowth. Neither stave removed. One stave growth-arrested at the upper end, the other at the lower end, both with stone tools.
Huntoon-11	2		Large, lightning-struck trunk shows long cut made with stone tools. Two staves of perfectly straight-grained wood, but of indeterminate length, taken out next to one another. Possibly taken from naturally seasoned wood.
Huntoon-12	12	99,101,>106,112, 117, 120, >160	Enormous, very old juniper with several trunks and many large branches. Staves were removed from both trunks and branches. Regrowth all but obscures very old removal scars. Clear evidence of stave removal, regrowth of straight-grained wood into the resulting scar, removal of that straight-grained regrowth wood, regrowth into that scar, removal of that wood, and continuing regrowth today (Fig. 13) All removal done with stone tools. Hammerstone apparently used for stave removal remains caught among small branches where it was placed atop a large limb.
Huntoon-13	3	103	Very large, crooked tree. Two removals of indeterminate length.
Huntoon-14	2	112	Staves removed with stone tools from central straight trunk among several massive, crooked ones. Only straight wood in the tree. One stave of indeterminate length.

[a] Number of stave removals or growth-arrestments actually visible on any given tree. Actual number removed from any given tree may be greater because older removal scars may be obscured by regrowth. If stave growth was arrested but the stave not removed, so indicated.
[b] Measurement between cuts or from such cuts down to the ground surface. In the latter cases, length is indicated as greater than the value given (>). Where stave length is indeterminate because of a broken limb or trunk, or for other reasons, it is not indicated in column three.

many staves cannot be determined because they split out longer than was intended or needed, or in some cases because the end of the branch or trunk from which they were removed is no longer present. In 77 cases where stave lengths can be determined, the median value is 113 cm. This is a slightly conservative figure since it does not include "greater than" measurements of stave length; some stave removal scars extend down into the duff and others are of indeterminate length for other reasons. Table 10.1 lists the 47 trees and provides information on each.

In the course of recording field data, each tree was marked with a small metal tag nailed to the trunk or branch. Identifying numbers, the date of recording, and the name and institutional affiliation of the investigator were embossed thereon. Measurements were made of the length of the staves isolated or removed, and notes were recorded on all aspects of cultural modification visible on a given tree.

INFERENCES ABOUT EXTRACTION OF BOW STAVES FROM JUNIPER TREES

The sequence of decisions and actions involved in stave removal can in part be inferred from examination of the cuts and scars on the 47 trees. It probably involved selecting the proper tree, assessing the quality of the wood, arresting stave growth, seasoning the stave on the tree, and removing the stave from the tree.

Selecting the Proper Tree

Tree selection involved locating a suitable tree that reliably could be located again at a later date. The trees thus seem to cluster around places where people camped or worked on a fairly regular basis. They have not been found randomly distributed on the landscape where they might have proven difficult to relocate. The importance of being able to relocate the trees is evident by the fact that the staves were removed only after they had been isolated and seasoned for some time on the tree (see below).

The selected tree contained harvestable wood with the proper grain characteristics (Figs. 3, 4). Most of the junipers in the region are crooked, twisted, and full of knots and branches. The straight-grained ones, or those that had proper grain on at least one side of a trunk or branch, were the only ones used. Overall straightness of the stave was desirable, but curves in the wood, if radially (as opposed to laterally) oriented, and if not too severe, apparently could be overcome by heating and bending. Small knots were avoided where possible, and large ones always were avoided. In most cases, this required selecting older trees on which small branches had long since dropped from the lower part of the trunk and clear wood had grown over the remaining knots. Young trees tend to have numerous small branches, and hence knots, in the surface wood. Peripheral wood on such trees or on smaller limbs also would yield staves with a more pronounced lateral curvature along what would become the back of the bow. Consequently, staves were not removed from young trees of small diameter, and when smaller limbs (10-15 cm. in diameter) were used, which was seldom, they generally had grown in shaded spots and retained few or no minor branches in the area from which the stave was taken. The available evidence shows a definite preference for peripheral wood on larger trunks or limbs.

Many trees in the region lack a primary trunk. They have instead a rosette growth form with as many as 20 or more separate trunks or major limbs of approximately equal size, none of which apparently is dominant over the others. Most such trunks are more heavily knotted and branched on the perimeter side than on the side central to the overall tree. In one case (Huntoon-7) a stave was removed from the central side (with respect to the overall tree) of one of many such trunks. Better wood can be found on the central side of any of the several trunks of such trees. Small branches in these shaded places on the lower part of the trunk tend to die while still small and drop off. The knot then becomes overgrown by straight-grained wood. Adequate work space for stave removal is lacking on most such trees, however, and they seldom were used. Without metal saws or axes, it was not practical to remove certain trunks from rosette-formed trees in order to better expose others for stave removal.

In two other cases (Excelsior-17, -24), wood was removed from the bottom sides of nearly horizontal limbs, again places where small branches generally die and drop off and the resulting knots are overgrown by straight-grained wood.

Examination of Utah juniper trees in various areas reveals that most of them have badly twisted grain. Bowyers engaged in replicating traditional archery equipment refer to this as "wind in the log (wind twist)" (Alcock 1941:5). They believe prolonged exposure to prevailing winds causes twisted grain in the trunks of trees with asymmetrical arbors. While the basic tendency to develop spiral or twisted grain is genetically controlled, it can be induced by wind, and not all trees in the same grove will manifest the phenomenon (Telewski and Jaffe 1986; Frank Telewski,

258

Figure 10.3. Small, aged juniper tree (Excelsior-3) with one stave-removal scar from straight-grained wood on the facing side of the right trunk. The right photo is a close-up of the right trunk showing the scar. The straight grained wood from which the stave was removed had partially grown over an old natural scar. The stave was 120 cm. long.

Figure 10.4. Straight-grained junipers showing stave-removal scars. Left, Excelsior-7, with scars 123 and 132 cm. long on the center of the trunk (the right one was a failure, having split out short of its intended length); right, Excelsior-31, with the left scar partially obscured by regrowth.

personal communication 1988). Several trees (e.g., Huntoon-4) show evidence of stave extraction from an isolated, straight central trunk or limb surrounded by more massive, badly twisted ones. This suggests use of straightgrained wood grown in a sheltered environment in the central part of the tree. Evidence on a number of trees clearly shows that they grow in locations sheltered from the wind by other trees or, more commonly, by topographic features. Favored locations seem to be in canyons or in the lee of rimrock formations. In any event, it is apparent that some regions simply produce few or no trees suitable for bow stave extraction, all the trees present having badly twisted grain.

No preference was noted for removing wood from one side of a given tree with respect to the slope on which the tree grew. The only objective was straight-grained, knot-free wood of suitable length.

Assessing the Quality of the Wood

Wood quality sometimes was assessed by removing a strip of bark over the area where the prospective stave was sought (Fig. 10.5). In some cases (e.g., Huntoon-3), it is evident that a strip of bark the full length of the prospective stave was removed, because the growth-arrested stave was fully exposed but never was removed from the tree. In another case (Excelsior-8), only a triangular strip of bark was removed in the course of making the growth-arrestment cut at the upper end of a prospective stave. Perhaps a small area was cleared of bark and the growth-arrestment cut made, and the remaining bark over the prospective stave stripped off only after the wood had partly seasoned on the tree. Whether or not the bark was completely removed over the area of the intended stave may have depended on the season in which the growth-arrestment cut was made. Complete removal of bark over a prospective stave without risk of weather-checking may have been possible during colder months when growth was restricted.

Removal of the bark allowed visual inspection of the wood for straightness of grain, absence of twisted grain (not always evident under the rough and shaggy bark), and absence of potentially damaging knots. Many trees that lack bark in a strip on one side, but otherwise appear natural, may show the effects of such bark removal by bowyers prospecting for quality staves. Most trees exposed to such treatment will simply heal and, with the passage of time, escape detection.

Figure 10.5. Bark partially removed and growth-arrestment cut completed (Excelsior-8). No further work was ever done on this potential bow stave, and the scar has partially been obscured by regrowth.

Arresting Stave Growth

Growth arrestment was accomplished by cutting into the wood at the upper or lower end of the stave, or at both of these points.
This cut took the form of a chiseled-out V-shaped notch averaging about 6-8 cm. wide and 3 cm. deep (Fig. 10.6). In most cases the cut is quite clean and apparently was chiseled out by pounding large, sharp tools of fire-spalled local basalt into the wood. Two such tools (Fig. 10.7), each markedly stepfractured near the working edge, were found lying on the ground at the base of Huntoon-1. A basalt cobble (maximum dimension, 15 cm.), apparently a hammerstone (Fig. 10.8), was found where it had been set between branches on the upper side of a limb of Huntoon-12. These items, together with observations on the nature of the cuts themselves, suggest the means by which staves were isolated and their growth arrested. The precision of the cuts suggests these large stone chisels were carefully positioned and driven with hammerstones, rather than wielded in the manner of an axe. One might conclude the opposite from the comments of Edward Curtis (1926,XV:60) concerning manufacture of wooden bows by the Paviotso (Northern Paiute): "Their axes for cutting cedar to make into bows were made of serpentine."

It is recognized that serpentine is not widely distributed in Northern Paiute territory, and may not have been widely used for axes. The fact that the tools in question are identified as having been used for cutting bow staves suggests some degree of functional specialization, more so than one would expect for such a generic tool as an axe. The tools may, in fact, have been of a more specialized nature, such as that suggested by the chisel-like tools of fire-spalled basalt discussed above. Where steel axes were available, as they obviously were in some cases in the Huntoon group (Table 10.1, Fig. 10.9), the cut usually is more erratic and ragged, and a stray blow or two usually is evident where the point of strike missed the point of aim.

Seasoning the Stave on the Tree

Isolating the potential stave by a cut into the tree at one or both ends severed the conductive tissue and caused the wood between the cuts to cease growth and season naturally on the tree, presumably with a minimum of splitting and twisting.

It is apparent from the evidence in a number of cases that prospective bow staves usually were growth-arrested and seasoned on living trees. Seasoning the wood might have taken several years, and only replicative experiments will provide information on this point. Whether or

263

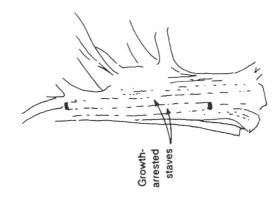

Growth-
arrested
staves

Figure 10.6. Small, aged juniper (Huntoon-2) with two growth-arrestment cuts. The cuts isolated two staves, the left one at the lower end and the right one at the upper end, but neither was removed. All the bark is now gone from this side of the tree.

not green wood ever was removed from the trees for use as bow staves cannot now be determined. It is apparent from the junipers studied that stave removal frequently was accomplished only after the wood had been growth-arrested and seasoned for some time on the tree.

Not all growth-arrested and seasoned staves actually were removed from the trees. In such cases, better staves may have been obtained. The staves not removed from the trees may be those judged inferior for reasons of configuration or grain characteristics. Perhaps they developed weatherchecks or otherwise did not dry properly. Perhaps the staves not removed represent the culls from an industry that involved sale or exchange to regions lacking trees suitable for bow stave extraction. Or, perhaps most likely, they may mark the end of an industry that was replaced by firearms or that ceased with the demise of the traditional lifeway.

Figure 10.7. Stone tools found under Huntoon-1. They are simple thermal-spalled pieces of local basalt with pronounced step-fractures at what was once a sharp edge (shown here at the bottom). They probably were used as large chisels, driven with hammerstones, to make the growth-arrestment and stave-removal cuts. Both are fractured at the end opposite the cutting edge. Length of left specimen, 16 cm.

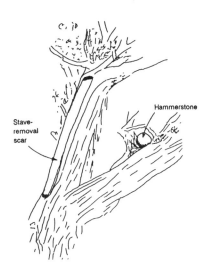

Figure 10.8. Hammerstone, 12 cm. in maximum dimension, where it was left atop a limb on Huntoon-12. A stave-removal scar 101 cm. long is visible on the more vertical limb to the left of the hammerstone.

Figure 10.9. Metal axe-cuts at the upper ends of two bow staves on Huntoon-8. The metal tag is 8 cm. long.

As noted above, one ethnographic source (Coville 1892) indicates that dead wood was used for the manufacture of sinew-backed juniper bows. The notion that bow wood was growth-arrested and seasoned on the tree is not recorded. Dead juniper trunks always have many cracks and weather-checks, and are inappropriate for bow manufacture. Perhaps Coville misunderstood or inadvertently misrepresented his informant on this point.

Removing the Stave from the Tree

Stave removal was not accomplished by the expected means of driving wedges of antler or bone under the cured wood and thus splitting it from the tree. There is no evidence in any observed cases of bruising or compression of wood fibers that would have resulted from the use of wedges. Whereas a simple *growth-arrestment* cut usually was more or less symmetrical and V-shaped, the *stave-removal* cut was V-shaped but strongly asymmetrical. The stave apparently was split from the tree by prying some sort of lever in this specially cut notch. Whether this notch was made when stave growth originally was arrested or whether it was made when the stave was removed is unknown and probably varied from case to case. The notch design to facilitate stave removal is seen on Huntoon-3 (Fig. 10.10), where the stave never was removed, and on Excelsior-1 (Fig. 10.11), where the stave was removed. The side of the stave-removal cut that bore straight into the tree described the actual end of the bow stave. Insertion of a chisel-ended lever, such as a digging stick tipped with horn or antler, into the very apex of this asymmetrical notch apparently enabled the bowyer to engage the end of the intended stave and wrench it from the tree. Freeing the stave may have been accomplished with a tool of hardwood, stone, or antler, used as a simple lever, or the tool may have been bound to the tree with wet rawhide and the stave pried free as the binding dried and shrank. Perhaps seasoning the wood on the tree resulted in formation of a crack between the main body of the trunk and the isolated stave, facilitating removal of the latter. The postulated mean of stave removal is shown in Figure 12.

The stave thus removed had grain very close to that referred to in the wood industry as tangential or flatsawn grain (Hoadley 1980:5-8). In reality, the stave probably had no flat surface on what would become the back of the bow, but rather this surface merely followed the gradual curve of the outer growth-ring. The outside growth-rings of the stave became the back of the bow, the interior wood the belly. This concentric arrangement of growth-rings, a recognized aspect of the traditional

268

Figure 10.10 Unremoved bow stave on Huntoon-3. The growth habit of this tree is atypical for Utah junipers and apparently is not a result of browsing by animals. The tree may have been pruned when young. The detail shows that the bark was removed over the intended stave, a crack formed under it at some time, and it has been partially obscured by undergrowth. Growth of the stave was arrested by a stave-removal cut made at the upper end.

Figure 10.11. Detail of stave-removal cut at the upper end of a stave-removal scar now partially overgrown on Excelsior-1. Note the preciseness of the cut and its asymmetrical configuration. A second scar is fully overgrown at the left below the crotch.

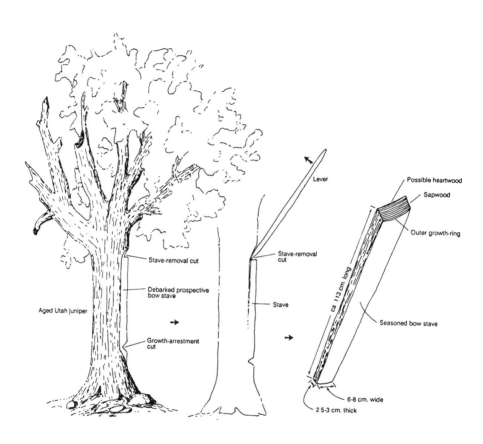

Figure 10.12. Suggested method of stave removal, and grain configuration and measurements of a typical stave.

bowyer's art (Pope 1925:61), distributed the stress evenly as the finished bow was drawn. Care had to be taken to ensure that the growth-rings on the back of the bow were not cut, or the finished bow might fracture at that spot.

All of the bows made from these staves would have had natural backs of sapwood over heartwood, or they would have consisted entirely of sapwood. This situation recalls a statement made by Stephen Powers (1877:373) regarding cedar (juniper) bows obtained by the Yokuts of the San Joaquin Valley of California, from the "mountaineers" (Monache or Western Mono): "The bow is taken from the white or sap wood, the outside of the tree being also the outside of the bow." The extraction of juniper wood by the Cheyenne, as reported by Grinnell (1923,I:173) was of a similar nature:

> A certain juniper tree (*Juniperus scopulorum*, Sarg.) was regarded as furnishing the best bow wood used in later times. Usually a small upright tree was chosen, or a stick was split from a larger tree if the grain of the piece was straight. The heart wood was not used.

Sinew laminated to the back of the bow would have provided additional reinforcement. Reinforcement is essential to prevent breakage in such a short bow and also would have increased its elasticity and recovery speed (and hence its cast).

REGROWTH AND RECOVERY

Most of the trees show healthy regrowth. Regrowth is indicated by a gradual laying-in of wood from the edges of the stave-removal scar, and in a number of case ancient scars of this nature are all but obscured by more recent growth. It is possible that many trees were exploited for staves at remote points in time but only the most recent stave removals are now detectable. Cross cutting the trunks of individual trees would be necessary to reveal the full history of bow stave removals in many cases.

Trees from which staves were removed had straight grain, at least in that area where the stave was removed. Healing of the scar resulted in the inlaying of new straight-grained, knot-free wood from either side of the scar. The straight scar served as a template for subsequent regrowth of straight-grained wood. If this straight-grained wood subsequently was harvested, and clearly it was in some cases (such as Huntoon-1 and -12), the continued removal of wood from a favored tree actually guaranteed the continued availability of wood with the proper grain characteristics (Fig. 10.13). The intervals between such removals were, however, quite long, perhaps longer than a human lifespan. Where wood of straight grain could be found around a substantial part of a trunk, it was essential that sufficient time elapsed between stave removals that the tree was able to recover and was not excessively girdled and killed.

DISCUSSION

The extraction of food substances (other than seeds, nuts, or fruits) or raw materials from living trees is well documented. Thain White (1954) and Thomas Swetnam (1984) reported the peeling of outer bark from ponderosa pines (*Pinus ponderosa*) and other trees by native peoples of Montana and New Mexico, respectively, to obtain the "inner bark" for food. Studies of the growth-rings of such trees document the practice to nearly 200 years ago. Mary Schlick (1984) discussed the extraction of bark from western red cedar (*Thuya plicata*) and the fabrication of it into bark containers by Columbia River tribes. Hilary Stewart (1984) and Russell Hicks (1985) discussed the extraction of planks from western red cedars by various Northwest Coast tribes. In all these cases, the result was scarred trees that are still recognizable on the landscape. An argument has even been made that prehistoric pueblo peoples of the Four Corners area cultivated Douglas fir trees for construction beams (Nichols and Smith 1965). Culturally altered trees ("CATs"), or culturally modified trees ("CMTs"), are recognized as important archaeological resources in various parts of the West.

The arboreal archaeology reported here is based on data not normally recorded in the Great Basin. Archaeological survey as commonly practiced, with eyes on the ground surface, simply fails to discover evidence of this kind. Doubtless many other examples of culturally modified trees have been passed undetected at close range by careful and well-trained field archaeologists. A better understanding of the significance of these trees, the bow stave harvesting industry, and the relationship of this industry to the broader picture of Great Basin archery technology, depends on the search for similar evidence elsewhere. Only then will we understand to what extent the Excelsior-Huntoon region may have supplied

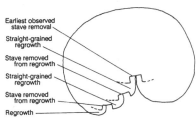

Earliest observed
stave removal

Straight-grained
regrowth

Stave removed
from regrowth

Straight-grained
regrowth

Stave removed
from regrowth

Regrowth

Figure 10.13. Huntoon-12, with its very complex history of stave removals, the nature of which is interpreted as shown in the drawing in an idealized cross section just below the metal tag. This tree has the longest and most complex visible history of cultural modification of any found, apparently dating back several centuries. It shows evidence of stave removal, regrowth of straight-grained wood into the old scar, stave removal from that regrown wood, and subsequent stave removal, regrowth, stave removal, and regrowth. At least 12 staves were removed from the limbs and trunk of this tree. The hammerstone (Fig. 10.8) was found atop the large limb that rises from the base at the lower right of the photograph.

bow staves or finished bows to other regions lacking straight-grained trees suitable for stave extraction.

Throughout much of the upper midwestern United States, including the Northern Plains, short wooden bows are thought (on the basis of very little actual evidence) to have been developed in protohistoric and early historic times to facilitate hunting on horseback. Favored woods included Osage orange (*Maclura pomifera*, acquired by exchange from eastern Oklahoma and Texas [Record and Hess 1943:389]), serviceberry (*Amelanchier*), chokecherry (*Prunus*), perhaps hickory (*Carya*, also imported from the east-central U.S.), and other superior bow timbers. The short length of the sinew-backed juniper bow of the Great Basin, throughout most of which area the horse never had a significant impact on native culture, is due instead to the limited length of staves available. The short bows of mountain sheep horn and elk antler also reflect the length practical with those materials (Wilke 1988). Similarly, along the coastal strip, from northern California northward, bows of Pacific yew (*Taxus brevifolia*) were short, broad, and flat. Their length also probably reflects the character of the raw material. In the observed cases of bow stave removal from juniper trees, median stave length was 113 cm. When split ends were removed and the bow actually was fabricated, a length of a meter or so, as described in literature, was about the longest generally obtainable.

Why so many trees in the localities studied reveal evidence of aboriginal bow stave extraction is unknown. Perhaps few places in the region have juniper trees that produce straight-grained wood, and those areas that did have such wood exported either bow staves or completed bows to areas lacking quality wood. In any event, ethnographic records suggest that the sinew-backed Utah juniper bow commonly was used by most Western (Nevada) Shoshoni and by the Northern Paiute, with some representation among the Southern Paiute, Ute, Kawaiisu, and Tübatulabal. Serviceberry (*Amelanchier*) wood commonly was used for bows in the northern Great Basin and in the northern Rocky Mountains. The mountain sheep horn bow was more common among the Northern Shoshoni, Eastern Shoshoni, Ute, and Southern Paiute. Manufacture of elk antler bows appears to have been limited to the Northern Shoshoni and Eastern Shoshoni and to other tribes of the northern Rocky Mountains and the northern Plains. A lack of suitable wood in some regions, and the availability of horn and antler, even if more difficult to work with, may have favored or necessitated use of these materials for bow staves in regions where such bow were common. Perhaps juniper bow staves or finished bows were exchanged from the study area to neighboring regions that lacked suitable material.

Export of juniper staves or bows across the Sierra Nevada into California is reported. Floristically, the latter region is more diverse, and suitable bow timbers may have been more readily available. However, several accounts (Powers 1877:373; Gayton 1948: 73; Latta 1977:285) indicate that Yokuts groups of the San Joaquin Valley and adjacent Sierra Nevada foothills obtained juniper bows from the Western Mono. Latta (1977:285), speaking of the Yowlumne (= Yawelmani, a Southern Valley Yokuts tribelet [Wallace 1978]) of the lower Kern River, stated:

> The finest bows made by the Yowlumne were made of juniper. They were backed with sinew. Juniper staves were traded from the Monache and Pah-ute to the east, or were secured in Yokuts territory in the upper Coast Range of Mountains. Bows of juniper were shorter than those made of other woods. The making of them required more skill and labor to produce than those made of other woods. They were very highly valued.

The Monache (Western Mono) occupied the headwaters of the San Joaquin, Kings, and Kaweah rivers. They were bordered on the east by the Owens Valley Paiute, or Eastern Mono, and the Mono Lake Paiute. The latter in turn were located just west of the area with the scarred trees reported here. Exchange of bow staves from the study area to the Yawelmani by way of the Monache would have involved a distance of perhaps 300 km., much of it extremely difficult terrain fully impassable during six months of winter. If Latta's account is correct (and he knew the group he called Yowlumne very well), a widespread exchange network involving several linguistically distinct groups is indicated.

Based on tree-ring counts on juniper wood grown in the immediate region (up to 50 tree-rings per centimeter, or 130 per inch), some of the trees from which bow staves were removed may be at least a thousand years old. If the last staves were removed about a century ago, the trees still seem to document an observable history of stave removals dating back perhaps as much as 400 or 500 years. Thus, the evidence suggests an ancient practice.

THE QUESTION OF RESOURCE MANAGEMENT

Current anthropological research among hunter-gatherers stresses the concept of resource management (Williams and Hunn 1982). Numerous examples around the world document the purposeful management of natural resources by aboriginal peoples. Evidence from the trees studied here indicates that individual trees were carefully exploited for bow staves over long periods of time, probably for centuries. Whether this pattern of exploitation constitutes resource management is, in my view, open to question.

By carefully removing only the desired billet of wood from a given tree, a straight template remained over which straight-grained wood would be emplaced through normal regrowth processes. Such regrown wood could then be harvested decades later. Given that long periods of time elapsed between the removal of staves from some trees, favored trees must have been well known, and tales may have been told about them and about particularly fine bows made from them. Important trees may have been named and figured prominently in local traditions.

One bow stave tree (Huntoon-3) is located along the drift fence of an enormous pronghorn wing-trap in the uplands south of Huntoon Valley. Except for this tree, which has particularly straight grain (Fig. 10.10), most junipers in the immediate area of the trap appear to have been eliminated in the course of obtaining timbers for construction. The form of this tree is so aberrant as to suggest that while still young it was pruned to remove branches on the lower trunk and thus ensure knotless wood for future bow stave extractions. This, however, is the only known tree whose configuration suggests intentional pruning.

While the cultural practice of stave extraction can be seen to have resulted in the continued production of straight-grained, knot-free wood, it is likely that no bowyer ever lived long enough to reap the benefits of his actions. The continued production of straight-grained wood for bow staves, as seen in greatest detail on Huntoon-12, was a natural, rather than intentional, result of normal regrowth processes following stave harvest. I do not believe the evidence warrants a strong argument for resource management or for the intentional cultivation of bow staves. The factor of consistent intent and payoff within an appreciable time is lacking.

THE FUTURE

Museum specimens of composite bows built on staves of sheep horn and elk antler stand with a few brief and scattered ethnohistoric and ethnographic accounts of their distribution and manufacture. No record of them is preserved on the landscape to provide additional information. Only replicative experiments of the kind discussed by Laubin and Laubin (1980:Ch. 5) and Holm (1982) will broaden our understanding of the design and performance of these weapons. With reinforced juniper bows, the situation is different. Evidence of the harvesting of wood for such bows is found on still-living trees, some of which document a history of such activity that must stretch back hundreds of years. Examination of these trees has provided substantial information on aspects of archery technology never recorded in written records.

Growth-arrestment cuts have been made to isolate a series of potential staves on Utah junipers in the study area. In some cases cuts 3 cm. deep (about that seen on many of the trees studied here) encountered no heartwood at all. Bows made from such staves may have no heartwood on the belly side, and may consist entirely of sapwood with a backing of sinew (cf. Powers 1877:373; Grinnell 1923, I:173). Further studies will concentrate on replicating the short, sinew-backed, juniper bow of the Great Basin, employing the observations and inferences presented here. The objective will be to better understand the manufacture, design, and performance of these weapons and the arrows they cast.

FUEL USE AND RESOURCE MANAGEMENT: IMPLICATIONS FOR THE STUDY OF LAND MANAGEMENT IN PREHISTORIC CALIFORNIA AND RECOMMENDATIONS FOR A RESEARCH PROGRAM[1]

Chester King

INTRODUCTION

Wood was used for fuel by California Indians and was an important resource. Wood was burned to process food in hearths, ovens, and parching trays, to heat rocks used to boil water in baskets, and to heat houses and sweat lodges. During some time periods and in some regions, wood was also used to fire grave pits, to cremate the dead, and/or to burn offerings. Wood fires were also used to provide light and heat for outdoor ceremonies.

The use of wood fuels and the management of wood fuel resources by protohistoric and prehistoric societies are topics which have not as yet been adequately studied. Obtaining and using wood fuels was of vital importance to most human societies in the past, and significant amounts of time and effort were expended by the members of such societies. Many archaeological sites contain large quantities of charcoal from wood that was carbonized when plants were burned as fuel. Although prehistoric and protohistoric wood fuel use and management have recently been studied using ethnographic, historical, and archaeological data in the highlands of Peru (Johannessen and Hastorf 1990), I know of no systematic studies of the prehistoric use of wood fuels by North American groups.

The use of wood as fuel by prehistoric Californians can be studied by employing ethnographic, historical, and archaeological data; by developing experiments and models to measure sustainable yields of fuel woods from different landscapes; and by designing experiments to measure

---

[1] This is a revised and expanded version of a paper that was originally presented at the Seventh Annual California Indian Conference, Sonoma State University, October 18, 1991.

the amounts of wood used for different purposes. The management of stands of fuel sources by California Indians may have caused significant changes in the size and composition of vegetation communities. This paper presents some of the background to fuel uses of wood by the Chumash and Yokuts Indians of southcentral California and discusses lines of research which will allow us to measure the effects of fuel management strategies on native vegetation.

ETHNOGRAPHIC AND ETHNOHISTORIC BACKGROUND

Ethnohistoric and ethnographic documents should be systematically studied to obtain information concerning fuel use by prehistoric California Indians. A brief review of the literature concerning the Chumash and Yokuts provides insights concerning the uses of wood as fuel in California. The ethnographic literature contains descriptions of cooking in yucca ovens, hearths, spit roasting, parching with coals in basket trays, heating rocks to boil water in baskets, and boiling in steatite and ceramic pots. Women apparently gathered wood for use in houses. Poor people brought wood to fiestas, and men probably gathered wood for heating sweathouses. The Chumash also used fire to manage seed fields, but their use of fire was apparently not indiscriminate. They were apparently concerned that fires should not burn unrestricted and endanger supplies of firewood. Henshaw, for example, noted:

> Ceremonies similar to the above [an incantation involving
> the use of magician's stones] were held to cure sickness,
> to cause rain, to put out fire in the mountains, to call fish,
> when a war expedition was to be undertaken, etc. [Heizer
> 1955:158].

Some villages were located in areas which contained little wood, and wood was imported to them. This was apparently the case at the village of Muwu at the western end of the Santa Monica Mountains:

> Everyone who attended the celebration was required to
> bring an offering. Some brought wood for they knew that
> at Muwu there would be no wood [Hudson, Blackburn,
> Curletti, and Timbrook 1981].

The Wowol Yokuts, who lived on Atwells Island in Tulare Lake, "had to cross on their tule rafts to the timbered or brushy stream outlets on the mainland to obtain firewood" (Kroeber 1925:483). There is little information concerning the distances traveled to obtain firewood or on trade for firewood in California.

Gayton's Chukchansi Yokuts consultants provided the following information concerning the acquisition of firewood:

> Pine, oak, manzanita, chaparral, live oak, "any kind" of wood, was used for making fire, said N.W. [Nancy Wyatt]. To fell a tree, it was burned around its base. Baskets of water were kept at hand to control and eventually to quench the flames. No stone axe was used. Both sexes carried wood, which was bundled up with string and then ported by tumpline. A piece of flat bark was laid on the back and held in place by the load, to protect against bruising. A person could carry about five logs, four feet [long] and eight inches in diameter, or more if the logs were smaller, N.W. [Nancy Wyatt] thought.
>
> Dead trees were felled by putting live coals at the base. When a tree burned through and fell, the fire was extinguished with earth. Logs were severed by burning through, leaving lengths suitable for transport. House, assembly, and sweathouse fires were banked, so coals were readily available for relighting, said J.R. [Jack Rowan] [Gayton 1948:185].

Gayton provides a more detailed description of using fire to fell trees and to remove limbs among the Wukchumni. At the end she notes:

> Felling or severing limbs by fire was best done on dead or already fallen trees, but since these were not always obtainable, live trees were attacked in winter when they were drier and there is less danger of brush and grass fire. Old trees are easier to fire than young ones. Both men and women packed wood, but only men did the firing [Gayton 1948:78].

Jack Rowan [80 years old in ca. 1930] also told Gayton that when he was a boy, the Indians throughout the Chukchansi region set fire to the brush after the seeds had been gathered. He went on to state that the fires cleaned up dead trees and logs. Gayton noted :

> The aboriginality of this practice seems dubious. Getting firewood was sufficiently laborious for the Indians to discredit their deliberate destruction of "dead trees and logs." The practice is frequently attributed to early settlers, cattlemen, who wanted better forage for their stock, i.e. land free of underbrush, with improved grazing. On the other hand , there is evidence that the shrub seeds, such as the Indians wanted, germinate better when subjected to scorching and it is possible that the result was known to natives and motivated the practice.... Powers mentions aboriginal firing of the forest "all along the Sierra".... Dr. Kroeber informs me that firing of natural growth was practiced from Yosemite northward; perhaps this is about the southern limit of this custom [Gayton 1948:176, footnote 81].

The diarists of the early Spanish land expeditions noted areas that had been burned by Indians throughout littoral California. It appears that seed fields were regularly burned to encourage yields of valued seeds, and it appears that all groups burned off seed fields on an annual basis. The burning of seed fields did not regularly involve the burning of perennial woody plants used for firewood. Wood sources may have been seldom burned off intentionally and may have been protected by fire breaks formed while collecting wood. Gayton's contention that valuable firewood was not intentionally destroyed is probably accurate, especially when the wood was in the vicinity of settlements or oven processing sites.

ARCHAEOLOGICAL BACKGROUND

Archaeological data include remains of features associated with fuel burning, carbonized remains of incompletely burned wood, and physical properties of soils and rocks associated with features used to cook food. Carbonized wood from archaeological contexts can be analyzed to determine both the species of plants which were burned and the sizes of the stems which were burned.

Analysis of Cooking Features

Types of cooking features found in archaeological sites include slab-lined cooking ovens, several types of yucca ovens, piles of rocks used for boiling water in baskets, stone lined hearths, unlined hearths, and roasting areas.

Slab-lined cooking ovens. Slab-lined cooking ovens have been found in many Santa Barbara Channel area Middle period village sites. These ovens were probably used for baking many types of food. Slab-lined ovens were constructed by excavating a parabolic pit between 0.75 and 2 meters in diameter and lining the depression with either sandstone slabs or large flat sandstone cobbles. A fire was built on the ground near outdoor slab-lined oven pits and rocks were heated on the fire. Once heated, the rocks were placed in the slab-lined pit along with food which was to be baked. An absence of evidence of any high heating of lining rocks indicates that fires were not built in these ovens (Gamble 1983:109--110, 117). Figures 11.1 and 11.2 illustrate a slab-lined oven found at the Pitas Point site (CA-Ven-27).

Yucca Ovens. In 1990 at CA-Ven-1020, a site on the southern slopes of the Simi Hills, two yucca roasting ovens were excavated to expose complete sections. These features were constructed and used in different ways, although they were similar in size and in the types of rocks they contained. It is possible that the differences between them reflect changes over time. The carbon dates listed in Table 11.1 indicate that Feature 1 was used during the late Middle period and Feature 9 was used during the protohistoric period.

The more elaborate Feature 1 consisted of a pit 90 cm. deep. The pit has a parabolic profile to a depth of 50 cm. Below 50 cm. there is a straight-sided shaft which extends to 90 cm. below surface. A fire was first built in the bottom of the shaft; the coals were then covered by a layer of rocks. Another fire was built on top of this layer of rocks. The coals of the second fire were then covered by another group of large rocks which rested on the top edges of the shaft. A third fire was built on top of this rock layer (Figs 11.3-11.5). The distribution of yucca carbon indicates that most yucca hearts were placed in these coals and then covered with a final layer of rocks which capped the oven. The rocks in

284

Figure 11.1. Pitas Point (CA-Ven-27), Area 2 west, Feature 1. Exposure of rocks at top of oven fill. All rocks except oven-lining rocks were fire-altered.

Figure 11.2. Pitas Point (CA-Ven-27), Area 2 west, Feature 1. Exposure of oven with most fill rocks removed. Area of oxidized soil and areas of high ash concentration exposed in foreground.

Figure 11.3. CA-Ven-1020, Feature 1, Unit 658. Exposure of the upper part of a yucca oven; two quadrants have been excavated below the rocks, which were at the top of the oven fill, and the oven pit outline is apparent in these quadrants.

Figure 11.4. CA-Ven-1020, Feature 1, Unit 658. Exposure of northwest quadrant showing rocks and oven fill in the east wall (compare with north-south profile in Fig. 11.5).

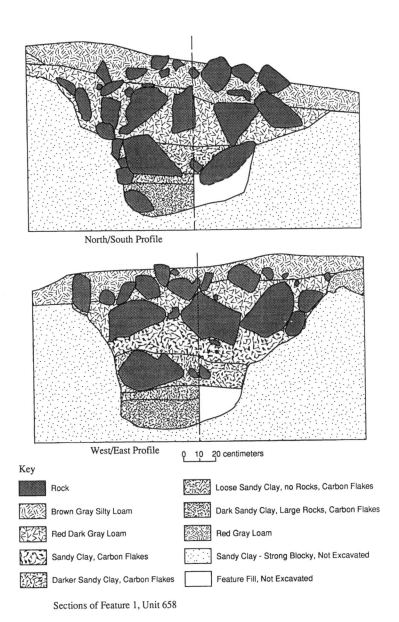

North/South Profile

West/East Profile

0 10 20 centimeters

Key

Rock

Brown Gray Silty Loam

Red Dark Gray Loam

Sandy Clay, Carbon Flakes

Darker Sandy Clay, Carbon Flakes

Loose Sandy Clay, no Rocks, Carbon Flakes

Dark Sandy Clay, Large Rocks, Carbon Flakes

Red Gray Loam

Sandy Clay - Strong Blocky, Not Excavated

Feature Fill, Not Excavated

Sections of Feature 1, Unit 658

Figure 11.5. CA-Ven-1020, Feature 1, Unit 658. Sectional views of oven fill.

288

the top layer were generally smaller than the rocks used in the lower levels of the oven. The presence of carbonized soap plant bulbs and corms indicates that corms and bulbs were also roasted in the oven. Pollen from the upper part of the oven indicates that greens may have also been baked or steamed in this oven (King et al. 1991:228-234).

Table 11.1

CARBON-14 DATES FROM TWO YUCCA ROASTING OVENS AT CA-VEN-1020

Sample No.	Unit	Feat. No.	Feat. Type	Level	Carbon Type	Date	Approx. Cal. Date
B-39956	658 NW	1	Yucca oven	40-50	Chamise, un-differ. wood	1090 ± 60 BP	AD 745
B-39957	869 A	9	Yucca oven	30-40	Wood	280 ± 50 BP	AD 1710

The other oven, Feature 9, was constructed by excavating a lens-shaped pit to a depth of 50 cm. in the center (Figs. 6-8). Carbonized yucca is concentrated in the bottom of the pit. It appears that the yucca hearts may have been placed in the bottom of the pit and the fire built over them, or they may have been placed under the coals after the flames were gone. Carbonized corms and soap plant bulbs were also found in the fill of this oven. After the firing of the pit, a layer of large rocks was placed over the coals. It appears that only one fire was built when the oven was fired (King et al. 1991:235-238).

Figure 11.9 shows the differing distributions of fire-altered rocks and carbon in the two ovens. These differences may be related to differences in fuel availability and fuel efficiency. They may also be related to different strategies for storing food. Crespí observed that the Portolá expedition was given half-baked heads of yucca in the Thousand Oaks area in January, 1770 (Brown n.d.). This may indicate that during the protohistoric period yuccas were first partly baked for storage and then later cooked in hearths or other features immediately prior to consumption. It is possible that during earlier periods yucca was more completely processed

289

Figure 11.6. CA-Ven-1020, Feature 9, Unit 869. Exposure of rock layer.

290

Figure 11.7. CA-Ven-1020, Feature 9, Unit 869. East sidewall of oven fill.

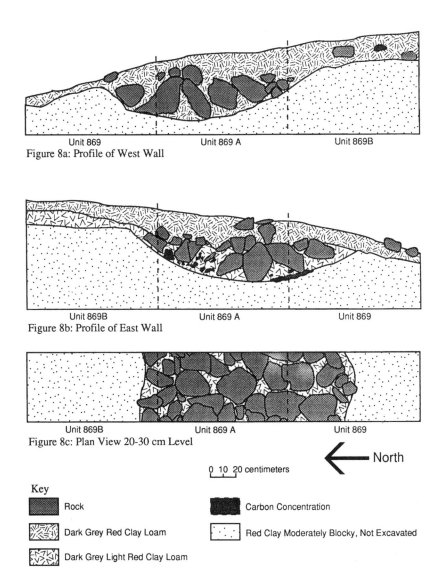

Unit 869   Unit 869 A   Unit 869B
Figure 8a: Profile of West Wall

Unit 869B   Unit 869 A   Unit 869
Figure 8b: Profile of East Wall

Unit 869B   Unit 869 A   Unit 869
Figure 8c: Plan View 20-30 cm Level

← North

0 10 20 centimeters

Key

Rock

Carbon Concentration

Dark Grey Red Clay Loam

Red Clay Moderately Blocky, Not Excavated

Dark Grey Light Red Clay Loam

Figure 8: CA-Ven-1020, Feature 9, Unit 869. Profiles and Plan View of Oven fill.

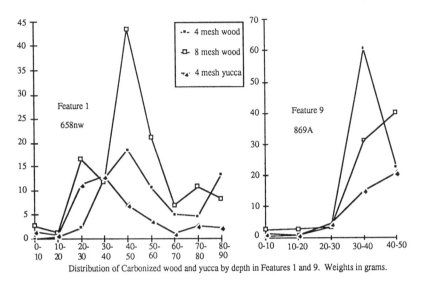

Distribution of Carbonized wood and yucca by depth in Features 1 and 9. Weights in grams.

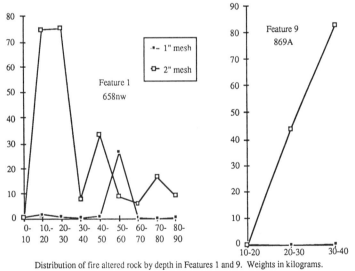

Distribution of fire altered rock by depth in Features 1 and 9. Weights in kilograms.

Figure 9: Comparisons of distributions of carbon and fire altered rocks in Features 1 and 9, CA-Ven-1020.

in ovens. The excavation and dating of additional ovens should aid in clarifying the significance of the differences between ovens observed thus far. It appears that ovens were used more at village sites during the late Middle period than they were during the protohistoric period. It is possible that changes in cooking procedures were influenced by either the availability of fuel or by changes in community organization.

Types of Carbonized Wood Found in Sites and Features

A small portion of the 4-mesh wood carbon from CA-Ven-1020 was identified by Julia Hammett and classified by species or larger taxon. Four types of wood were identified; each comes from plants that grow in the vicinity of the site and are good sources of fuel. Chamise (*Adenostoma fasciculatum*) is today the most dominant plant in the project area; its associations indicate that it was an important source of fuel in both the late Middle period and the protohistoric period. Ceanothus is common in the project area and was probably used as fuel, as was Sugar bush (*Rhus ovata*), which also grows in the project area. Burned manzanita (*Arctostaphylos* spp.) wood was identified from a midden feature at the site. The small samples of wood which were identified indicate that the woody plants which presently grow in the CA-Ven-1020 area were present in the

Table 11.2

IDENTIFIED WOOD SPECIES

Unit and Level	Chamise	Rhamnaceae	Rhus ovata	Manzanita
658nw, 40-50	1.47	0.92		
658nw, 80-90	0.94	0.98	0.27	
869A, 40-50	1.78	1.37		
665, 10-20				0.43
Totals	4.19	3.27	0.27	0.43

past and were an important source of fuel. Plants used for fuel may have been managed by the Chumash so that fuel would have been consistently available for processing yucca and other foods (King et al. 1991:157-160).

The use of yucca as food required the use of wood for fuel. Strategies of plant resource management probably changed--as the use of yucca increased--towards a greater emphasis upon the maintenance of adequate stands of woody stemmed plants which could be used to fire yucca ovens. The collection of wood to fire such ovens probably resulted in the maintenance of fire breaks. The search for wood for ovens probably kept the amount of dead wood in chaparral stands to a minimum. It is probable that grassland areas also continued to be burned. These conditions possibly resulted in firebreaks where the chaparral could grow to a size that was adequate for firing ovens without being burned in brush fires. The pieces of chamise charcoal that were found in Feature 9 indicate that the chamise which was available in the past was as large as the largest chamise growing in the area today.

ARCHAEOLOGICAL RESEARCH GOALS

The frequencies of the types of wood used for different purposes can be determined by analyzing carbonized wood from various kinds of features, such as ovens, hearths, spit roasting fires, etc. Charcoal should also be studied from sites in or adjacent to different environmental settings (oak woodland, riparian woodland, chamise chaparral, Ceanothus chaparral). Samples from documented contexts which are stored in museum collections can be used to obtain much of this information. Future archaeological excavations should also be designed to collect charcoal samples from cooking features and from other contexts. Data concerning the types of wood that were burned will aid in the reconstruction of prehistoric environments and in the determination of the distances traveled to obtain fuel. The data will also aid in the discovery of the types of fuels used for different purposes. It is expected that dense woods which produce long lasting coals would be preferred for baking and roasting. Bay wood was probably not used for roasting because it imparts an undesirable flavor to food, and cottonwood was probably not used to heat houses because of its undesirable odor.

The technique of thermoluminescence could be used to date the last time an oven was heated to temperatures above 500° C. In addition to dating the use of ovens, studies of thermoluminescence can provide information concerning the temperatures which were reached during the firing of the oven. Jon Ericson has also recommended the use of an experimental technique called hearth thermal gradient reconstruction (King et al. 1991:410); ovens should be studied using this technique to measure the temperatures reached during use. Materials from different parts of a feature should be carefully studied to enable a reconstruction of the firing and operation of the feature to be carried out.

Data concerning the temperatures reached during firing will provide information which can be used in experiments designed to determine the amounts of wood used to fire different types of ovens.

ESTIMATION OF YIELDS

Yields of firewood can be estimated using information and models concerning the growth rates and the carbon cycle of woody plants. Yields can also be measured using replicative experiments. Important issues which should be addressed in measuring yields are optimum sustainable yields, the time necessary to obtain optimum sizes of plant stems for use in firing ovens and other heating activities, and the effort required to obtain fuel from stands of different ages.

Forestry Management Literature

The growth rates of chaparral plants have been studied by foresters and botanists because the rates are important for measuring fuel loads in relationship to brush fires, the production of browse for herbivores, and the protection of land from erosion. These studies, however, have not emphasized the rates of production of useful fuels. Mooney has studied the carbon cycle in chaparral (1977b); his and other studies can be used to estimate fuel yields of chaparral stands of different ages.

Keeley and Sterling, in a more recent discussion of chaparral communities, make the following observation:

> After fire, there is a rapid increase in above ground shrub biomass that continues for several decades. The estimated annual biomass ranges from 840 to 1750 kg ha^{-1}, with the lower values being from southern California. After the first 20 yr, primary production slows, although the living biomass remains stable for 60 yr or more [1988:191].

Unburned old chaparral stands probably provided the highest yields of fire wood. It appears that the optimum harvesting strategy would be to clear the oldest stands which were available. Because old stands contain large amounts of dead wood, they are apt to burn during wildfires. The harvest of old stands may have reduced the spread of wildfires.

Replicative Experiments

To measure fuel yields from mature and less mature stands, it is necessary to gather wood from measured areas and weigh the wood from those areas according to species and size. Different types of areas should be studied. The areas which are studied should be different in age of plant stands, steepness of slopes, directions of exposure, soils, and plant species. Repeated harvesting of wood from experimental plots at different intervals is necessary to measure sustainable yields of wood fuel and discover optimum harvest rates.

REPLICATIVE EXPERIMENTS TO MEASURE USAGE

To estimate the amounts of fuel needed for cooking using the types of features found in prehistoric sites, it is necessary to use various woods to cook different types of important foods. The amounts of wood fuel necessary for heating sweat lodges of various sizes, for operating hearths, for lighting, for ceremonies, and for the cremation of individuals of different sizes should be determined. Replicative experiments should be conducted to measure the amounts of fuel needed for these and other purposes. Mathematical models should also be developed to determine the amounts of energy needed to heat different volumes of air or rocks to particular temperatures. These models could be used to extrapolate the values determined from experiments to features of different sizes.

PALEOBOTANICAL CONSIDERATIONS

The need to burn fields to enhance annual seed crops and grasslands had to be balanced with the need for wood for fuel. In the vicinity of settlements, wood was probably harvested at a high rate. It appears that camp and oven sites were often located in areas where wood fuel was available. Clearing areas for fuel to fire ovens probably encouraged the development of stands of chamise chaparral. One effect of breaking the branches off of root crowns (which can be done with the feet or hands) would be to prune or crop the plants and thus increase the rate of growth of the biomass which could be used as fuel. Changes in the amount of chaparral cover have been traditionally explained as a result of climatic variations. However, it is possible that some of the observed changes in plant cover were actually due to changes in the human management of prehistoric landscapes.

Changes in fuel use may be associated with changes in the distribution of plant communities. For example, changes in the proportions of chaparral and grassland communities may reflect a greater emphasis on management strategies which encouraged the growth of woody fuel plants needed to roast other plants such as yucca and soap root.

The most common chaparral species have the characteristics of a fuel crop. They are relatively easy to harvest, especially when dead. Chamise (*Adenostoma fasciculatum*) often snaps off at the top of its root crown. *Ceanothus megacarpus* and many other ceanothus species have minimum root supports, and senile or dead bushes can be harvested without tools. Most chaparral woods were probably broken off and limbs separated by the use of hands and feet. Fire was also probably used to cut larger pieces of wood, as has been described for the Yokuts. Other important characteristics of chaparral include the fact that it grows to maturity rather rapidly, fires made from its wood burn quite hot, and chaparral coals remain hot for a long time. Yucca is frequently found in chamise chaparral, and chamise is therefore often the most readily available wood for processing it.

Grasslands are likely to have been much more extensive 3,000-6,000 years ago, before the widespread appearance of chaparral. Annual burning was probably a land management technique that was used to increase the production of nutritionally valuable plants (Timbrook et al. 1982:175). However, further research to measure the frequencies in sediments of fine particles of carbon from grassland fires versus particles from fires in stands of woody plants is necessary in order to discover the antiquity of different burning practices.

Widespread stands of chaparral, such as occur today, are relatively recent. Pollen records from the Transverse Ranges (Heusser 1978) indicate that chaparral was of limited occurrence until about 2500 years ago, about the time that the archaeological record indicates a frequent use of woody plant stems as fuel to process yucca and bulbs in ovens. It is probable that management practices changed at this time and stands of woody plants were encouraged to grow to maturity for use as fuel. Earlier practices may have discouraged the growth of woody stemmed plants through the use of frequent burns.

RITUAL MANAGEMENT OF SALMONID FISH RESOURCES IN CALIFORNIA[1]

Sean L. Swezey and Robert F. Heizer

Ethnographers at times are more concerned with reporting data than interpreting them. As a result, ethnographies often have the appearance of being little more than collections of facts organized by a generally standardized topical outline. Synoptic surveys may result from an effort to synthesize a particular trait, custom, or complex, and from these there often results a deeper insight into the function and purpose of what, in unanalyzed form, seem to be cultural practices which are illogical or meaningless. We attempt here to review native ritual, belief, and ceremony connected with anadromous fish in the northern part of the state in the effort to determine what logical and functional significance these had in terms of Native California life and survival.

The importance of anadromous fish resources to aboriginal societies inhabiting the major freshwater river drainages of Northern California is well-documented in the ethnographic literature. Hewes (1942, 1947), Rostland (1952), and Kroeber and Barrett (1960) have summarized these data in studies aimed at defining the cultural and geographic distribution of material subsistence techniques applied to the seasonal movements of important migratory fish species. Devices and techniques which allowed for efficient harvest of anadromous fish runs included fish weirs, basketry traps, dip, thrust, arc, and A-frame nets, toggle harpoons, and application of botanical fish poisons.

Whereas the material aspects of fishery technology form a basic and informative part of the ethnographic record, the potential importance of specialized ritual procedures undertaken at the inception of anadromous fish runs has generally been overlooked. Through much of Northern

[1]This paper originally appeared in the **Journal of California Anthropology**, Vol. 4, No. 1, pp. 7-29, 1977; it is reprinted here by permission of Malki Museum Press.

300

California, ritual injunctions and social control mechanisms were instituted by specific "ritual specialists" (formulists, shamans, and moiety chiefs) at the onset of the first major seasonal migrations of salmon. In Northwestern California, ritual specialists also directed the construction and use of large, fixed weirs designed to intercept the upstream movements of fish.

A synthesis of ethnographic accounts of first salmon ritual reveals a remarkable similarity of form and function throughout Native California, particularly with respect to the seasonal occurrence of these rites and the central regulatory role assumed by various ritually empowered personalities.[2]

The present study entails a brief examination of the functional interaction between ritual and certain ecological aspects of anadromous fisheries, including seasonality, periodicity of migratory fish behavior, and harvest potential. The data can be topically divided into two broad categories: (1) *The anadromous fish resource in aboriginal California*: What major anadromous fish species were important to aboriginal economies? When did the seasonal influx of important fish species occur? In what freshwater systems did fish annually run in sufficient quantity and regularity to exist at a major food resource? What distinctive characteristics of the annual spawning runs made them an important "ecological event" to aboriginal resource economies and allowed them to be efficiently harvested with aboriginal technology? (2) *Ritual regulation of fishing activities*: What was the basic form of the "first salmon" or other anadromous fish ritual in Native California and at what time of the year was it observed? How was this rite culturally and geographically distributed? What was the role of specific ritualists in initiating and supervising "first salmon" observances? What aspects of these ritual functions were overtly managerial, conservational, or organizational in effect? Did these prescribed ritual behaviors encourage efficient harvest and maintenance of anadromous fish resources?

The hypothesis that successful adaptation of aboriginal populations to riverine resources in California, in this case the seasonal spawning runs, may have included not only technological strategies but ritual procedures designed to manage and organize the harvest of the resource remains largely theoretical due to the qualitative nature of the ethnographic information. However, the widespread occurrence and basic similarity of

---

[2]The widespread functional similarity of first fruit, fish, and game observances, and the important regulatory position of ritualists in these rites in Native California has been previously discussed by Swezey (1975).

large-scale fish rituals indicates similar cultural responses to environmental pressures presented by the major anadromous fisheries in aboriginal California.

The Anadromous Fish Resources in Aboriginal California

As a seasonally concentrated and annually available food resource, freshwater anadromous fish were an important part of aboriginal subsistence economics in northern Native California. Of the five species of Pacific salmon in the genus *Oncorhynchus*, only two are abundant in the freshwater systems of Northern California, and these species undoubtedly dominated aboriginal fish harvests. The king or chinook salmon, *Oncorhynchus tschawytscha*, and the silver or coho salmon, *O. kisutch*, regularly migrate and spawn in California rivers at distinct seasonal intervals.[3] *O. tschawytscha* is normally more prevalent in larger rivers, while *O. kisutch* does not migrate as far upstream and frequents smaller streams (Shapalov and Taft 1954:57, 264). In addition to these salmon species, large spawning populations of steelhead or rainbow trout, *Salmo gairdnerii*, are seasonally common in nearly all coastal streams of California. Except in those areas near large freshwater lakes, the greater part of the aboriginal fishing effort was directed toward these three anadromous taxa.

Various environmental factors and species characteristics determine the distribution, seasonal behavior, and potential availability of salmon and steelhead in California. The anadromous adaptation involves the migration of maturing adults from the sea to freshwater streams and their smaller tributaries. After migration upstream to the spawning grounds at the headwaters of the larger streams, eggs are deposited in suitable shallow gravel beds. The mature salmon then die. The eggs hatch during the

---

[3]The three other species of Pacific salmon in the genus Oncorhynchus, O. Nerka (the sockeye or red), O. gorbuscha (the pink or humpback), and O. keta (the chum or dog) are rare or uncommon in large numbers in Northern California. Distributional data for Pacific salmon in California and on the western coast of North America may be found in Jordon 1896:474-483); Davidson and Hutchinson 1938; Evermann and Clark 1931 [see especially the references therein]; Fry 1973:58-84. Two other anadromous taxa of local importance in California streams were the sturgeon (Acipenser transmontanum and A. medirostris) and the "eel" or sea lamprey (Entosphenous tridentatus), both of which were freshwater resources of secondary importance to salmon (Kroeber and Barrett 1960:5; Baumhoff 1963:170; Fry 1973:24-31, 32-39) but, at the same time, much exploited.

following months and the "fry" remain in freshwater for a variable length of time and then migrate to the sea where they develop to maturity over a period of several years. Upon maturation the adults return to the freshwater systems (often the same "parent streams") where they spawn and die, thus completing the migratory cycle. The natural maintenance of this cycle depends upon free access to both freshwater spawning grounds and the sea (determined by stream depth and flow volume), lowered headwater temperatures suitable for spawning and early development, and clean, unobstructed gravel beds which provide a free flow of clear, well-aerated water for incubation (Davidson and Hutchinson 1933:673; Rostland 1952:15). Across California, these conditions normally occur in the early fall. However, in several river systems, notably the Smith, Klamath, and Sacramento-San Joaquin, headwaters sufficiently cold for spawning activity occur not only during the normal autumnal temperature drop, but also during the spring, when early snowmelt from surrounding mountain ranges creates headwater temperatures and stream level appropriate for spawning activity of the king salmon (Rostland 1952:19-20). Thus, in aboriginal California, the king and silver salmon both entered larger stream systems in the latter half of the year, and the king salmon also entered in the early spring, creating an important spring-fall cycle of runs.

    Oncorhynchus tschawytscha originally ranged as an important resource as far south as Monterey Bay on the coast and the San Joaquin River and its main tributaries inland, with individual fish found as far south as the Ventura River (Evermann and Clark 1931:48). It entered the Smith, Klamath, Trinity, and Sacramento-San Joaquin systems (including the major *eastern* tributaries of the Sacramento and San Joaquin on the Sierran slope) in large numbers during the spring, between the months of March and June (Rutter 1907:150; Clark 1929:27-46; Snyder 1931:9, 18-32; Baumhoff 1963:174).[4] Of the spring salmon run in the Sacramento River, L. Stone noted that the king salmon remained scarce until the first of March,

> ...when they pour up the river in great numbers. This flood of salmon lasts through March, April, and May, making these months the harvest months of the river fishermen, both because the salmon are plentiful and in good condition [1873:180-181].

---

[4]Tributary streams on the western side of the Central Valley are generally less suitable for spawning due to greater aridity (Van Cleve 1945).

A similar influx of king salmon is noted for the Klamath by R.D. Hume:

> In 1850 in this river during the running season, salmon
> were so plentiful, according to the reports of the early
> settlers, that in fording the stream it was with difficulty
> that they could induce their horses to make the attempt,
> on account of the river being alive with the finny tribe
> [quoted by Snyder 1931:19].

Stephen Powers reported:

> There are two runs of salmon in the Klamath: one in the
> spring and one in the autumn, of which the former is the
> better, the fish being then smaller and sweeter [1872: 53-
> 3].

A summer or fall migration of king salmon occurs in the same
rivers as the spring run, and there were runs into the smaller tributaries
of the Klamath (such as the Salmon, Scott, and Shasta) and the coastal
streams south of the Klamath, including the Mad, Eel, Bear, and Mattole
rivers, and Redwood Creek. There is some historical evidence which
suggests that an additional, winter run of king salmon may have occurred
in the Sacramento River (Rostland 1952:22).

A fall or winter run of *Oncorhynchus kisutch* occurs in most coastal streams north of Monterey Bay, but this species does not enter the
interior Sacramento-San Joaquin system in significant numbers. The timing
of the silver salmon run on the coast overlaps the fall run of king salmon
in the North Coast Ranges, *O. kisutch* entering freshwater and moving
upstream in September when early rains facilitate permanent opening of
coastal streams to the sea. Spawning is usually completed between November and January, the young migrating to the sea the following year
(Shapalov and Taft 1954: 57).

The sea-running steelhead trout enters nearly all coastal streams
of California north of Ventura County to the Oregon border for spawning
purposes (Evermann and Clark 1931:49). Unlike the native salmon, *Salmo
gairdnerii* does not die after spawning. The surviving adults return to the
sea after running in freshwater. In the larger rivers, such as the Klamath,
Sacramento, and Eel, some steelhead enter nearly every month of the
year, but the major migration occurs in the late autumn or winter when

rising stream levels allow their upstream movement and spawning.[5] The run lasts for several months during the winter, usually from December to March (Shapalov and Taft 1954:108-109).

In summary, an initial description of the aboriginal anadromous fish resource in Northern California may be based on the seasonal occurrence of spawning runs in streams across the northern half of the state. Although Baumhoff (1963:173-174) has utilized stream size in "fish-miles," species occurrence, and season of migration as indices of aboriginal salmon availability, the present discussion proposes *seasonality* as the single most important factor in determining aspects of the cultural impact of the anadromous fish resource. Based on this criterion and on the ethnographic and biological data available, there were essentially *two* types of anadromous fish streams in aboriginal California: (1) *Biannual streams*; the larger river systems (or sections of these systems) such as the Smith, Klamath, Trinity, and Sacramento-San Joaquin in which an early *spring* run of king salmon as well as summer or fall runs of king and/or silver salmon, and a winter migration of steelhead occurred. (2) *Annual streams*; the smaller streams, generally the north coastal streams south of the Klamath and the smaller tributaries of the Klamath and Sacramento, in which a spring run did *not* occur, but in which some mid-year migration of king salmon and/or fall run of silver salmon as well as a winter steelhead run did occur.

The foregoing distinction is of importance for several reasons. Those native populations to whom anadromous fish were either the most important or a major staple in the food economy almost exclusively inhabited river drainages in which the spring salmon run occurred. The principal foci of major anadromous fisheries centered in Northwestern California (the Smith, Klamath, and Trinity rivers) and the Central Valley (the Sacramento-San Joaquin and their major tributaries) (Rostland 1952:149-150, 207-208; Baumhoff 1963:169-170).[6] With the exception of the

---

[5]A distinct run of steelhead enters the Klamath with the summer run of king salmon in July (Snyder 1931:23).

[6]Although ethnographic accounts have been generally used in assessing the importance of the salmon resource to native economies (see Rostland 1952:207-208), attempts have been made to quantitatively estimate the original, pre-contact salmon resource in terms of potential catch weight, available stream length, and/or spawning grounds. Hewes (1947:228) cites tribal estimates that place the total yearly aboriginal consumption of salmon in California at over 15 million pounds. This compares with an average modern-day salmon catch (data

coastal streams south of the Klamath, it appears that the most important and productive fishing areas in Native California were those which could rely upon an assured and abundant *early spring* run of king salmon.

The critical importance of the spring salmon run to native fresh-water fishing economies has been noted by Gunther (1926:605; 1928:135) and Rostland (1952:23). The spring runs provided abundant fresh salmon in the most excellent condition of the year (the late-season fish being of generally poor condition) at a time when stored provisions were dwindling or exhausted after a long winter of use. The spring salmon season may have been the most critical juncture in many native fishing economies, so great was the seasonal range from the previous fall abundance (which was largely dried and stored while the weather permitted) to the scarcity of good quality fish in the winter months. Powers makes note of the impor-tance of the spring run on the Klamath in his ethnographic essay on the Yurok:

> Then there is the vernal Salmon dance, which is something different from the formal and solemn ceremonial of the Cahrocs. We can well imagine with what great joy the villagers engage in this, when--after a dreary and desolate winter of rain, during which the wolf has been hardly kept away from their doors, and the housefather has gone down many and many a time to peer into the Klamath, if

---

from the years 1936-1960) of somewhat below 10 million pounds, most of this catch composed of king salmon produced in the Sacramento River, the populations of which have been increasing in recent years (Atkinson et al. 1966:46, 76). Rostland (1952:51) has estimated that 580 lbs./mi^2 represents the average aboriginal yield of anadromous fishes in the Pacific salmon region, noting that this figure was undoubtedly higher among fishing tribes inhabiting the lower reaches and mouths of rivers. Few historical data are available which are specific as to the actual size of the aboriginal fish resource. However, Living-stone Stone, who established the first federal salmon hatchery in California in 1872, states that 16,394 river salmon, weighing approximately 300,000 lbs,, were sent from the lower Sacramento to San Francisco in one month of March, 1872, and that 10,000 fresh salmon a week were sent to San Francisco in August, 1872, from the San Joaquin and Sacramento rivers "at a time when they are cheapest and most abundant" (1873:180, 197). That the Klamath River was also a productive source of salmon to its native inhabitants is evinced by Stephen Powers' statement of the same year concerning the Yurok fish catch: "By all these methods they catch an enormous quantity of fish: William McGarvey says he has often seen a ton of dried salmon hanging in the smoky attic of a cabin" (1872:533). The fact that salmon in the large rivers of Northern California were originally a highly abundant and readily available resource cannot be doubted.

perchance he might see the black-backed finny rovers shooting through the water, but in vain, and has turned on his heel and cursed with bitter cursing the White Man (the *waugeh*), who muddies the water so he can no longer see to spear his necessary meat--when, at last, as the ferns are greening on the mountain-side and the birds of spring are singing, the joyful cry resounds through the village, "*Maypoot, Maypoot*" ("The salmon, the salmon!"). They are coming at last! [1872:536].

In addition to the importance of the spring run of king salmon and the postulated dependence of native fishing economies upon the successful harvest of this particular resource, the significance of the seasonal spawning runs to aboriginal populations may be established along two other lines of reasoning. The number of strictly fluvial, nonanadromous fish species (excluding the trouts) in the freshwater river systems of Northern California is small and not of high quality or quantity, consisting of perch, suckers, pike, chub, river perch, and several species of minnow (Snyder 1908:155; Rostland 1952:15, 74; Kroeber and Barrett 1960:5). The comparative abundance of anadromous fish and the paucity of permanent freshwater fauna surely determined the emphasis placed upon the salmon harvest. Finally, the annual salmon runs were basically recurrent events, rarely failing entirely, and the long-term stability of productive fishing sites along major stream courses was generally assured in pre-contact times. Although significant migrations of salmon were seasonally concentrated and might last for only a variable period of weeks or months in the spring or fall (during which the quantity of fish fluctuated from abundance to scarcity), a well-organized fishing effort at the appropriate seasonal interval gave a comparatively great return:

> The high concentration of individuals in confined sections of a river, or massed in the surf, makes the effort expended by the fisherman extremely low in proportion to the effort required to obtain equal amounts of other edible products, agricultural products not excepted. In exchange for a few hours of heavy muscular effort, a single fisherman, in many cases equipped with the simplest gear, may land several thousand pounds of fish, considerably more than he could consume in a year. Compared to the weeks or months of heavy labor required by a primitive

farmer to produce a year's food supply, fishing is a highly
efficient technique [Hewes 1947:34].

When native technology, ranging from the large-scale, communal building
of a salmon weir to the efforts of a single individual with a salmon spear,
was utilized at the seasonal maxima of the fish migrations, the effort/yield
result was maximized to such an extent as to make salmon fishing perhaps
the most efficient subsistence undertaking in Native California.

We have, up to this point, reviewed ecological and ethnographic
data on fishing resources in aboriginal California in order to develop
several basic premises concerning the adaptation of native cultures to
anadromous fish resources. The salmon and steelhead resource was above
all an abundant, but seasonally variable, source of food for aboriginal
economies, and those native groups which inhabited the courses of the
major, biannual salmon streams in Northern California relied upon these
anadromous fish as a basic part of their diet. The spring immigration of
king salmon into the major streams was the most important run of the
entire fishing season in that it supplied critically needed fresh food when
stored supplies from the previous year were apt to be nearly exhausted. Of
final significance is the fact that a salmon run was essentially a locally
predictable natural phenomenon which could be efficiently harvested year
after year if a well organized fishing effort took place at the appropriate
time interval, usually at the peak of the seasonal migration.

With these basic premises stated, the following section will review
the ethnographic evidence which indicates that the coordination of
aboriginal fishing economies with the ecological contingencies of the spring
or summer salmon run in California may have been accomplished through
large-scale ritual organization and management of salmon fishing, and that
specific ritual specialists played a central role in ritual procedures undertaken at the beginning of the fishing season.

RITUAL REGULATION OF FISHING ACTIVITY IN
CALIFORNIA: AN ETHNOGRAPHIC INTERPRETATION

Throughout much of Northern California in the pre-contact past
(i.e., before 1848), the arrival of the salmon run in the spring was a time
during which the "first-salmon" rite and associated ritual behavior took
place. The intent of this observance was to recount the oral traditions
concerning the origins and travels of the first salmon, and to encourage the

immortal culture-hero to again ascend the rivers and streams. The salmon was thus ritually honored and induced to allow himself to be caught. If the first salmon was properly treated, he would act as the "leader" of the run to follow and supply an abundant catch.[7]

When the spring runs first began, procurement and casual consumption of fresh salmon was strictly forbidden. The first salmon was caught by, or given to, a ritualist who was knowledgeable as to the ceremonial details. The ritual preparation and eating of the first salmon followed, undertaken by the ritualist and his assistant or an assembled group. Upon completion of the ceremonial period, which lasted a variable number of days, the fishing season was "opened," and salmon fishing was allowed for the first time.

In the following analysis of ritual practices surrounding spring salmon fishing in Northern California, native tribes will be divided into two categories based on the ritual procedure and ceremonial specialist involved in the salmon rite, as follows:

(1) Those groups, inhabiting Northwestern California along the Smith, Klamath, and Trinity rivers, where formulistic ritual dependent upon special knowledge of mythic formulae by a priest or formulist was a basic feature. This is the region of greatest dependence upon the salmon resource (Rostland 1952:149; Baumhoff 1963:169-171). The Yurok, Karok, Hupa, Shasta, and Tolowa will be considered as ethnographic examples.

(2) Those groups, living outside the Klamath-Trinity area, along the Eel River in the North Coast Ranges and in the Sacramento-San Joaquin drainage system, where first-fish ritual involving shamans and other ritualists is a basic feature. This is the region where salmon was a staple of equal importance to plant foods or game (Rostland 1952:149-150, 207-208; Baumhoff 1963:169-171). The Maidu, Yokuts, Western Mono, Plains and Central Miwok, Achomawi, Sinkyone, and Kato comprise the ethnographic examples.

For reference purposes, details in the accompanying maps (see Figs. 12.1, 12.2) indicate the freshwater river systems, localities, and ethnographic groups to be discussed.

---

[7]The general distribution and characteristics of the first-salmon rite in Native North America are discussed by Gunther (1926, 1928) and more briefly by Driver and Massey (1957:254,256). The basic elements of the ceremony appear to have a wide distribution throughout those regions of western North America where salmon were available.

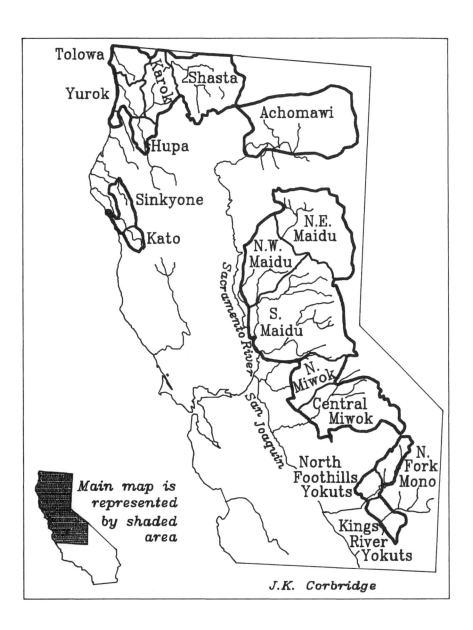

Figure 12.1. Location of tribes having first-salmon or dam-building ceremonies.

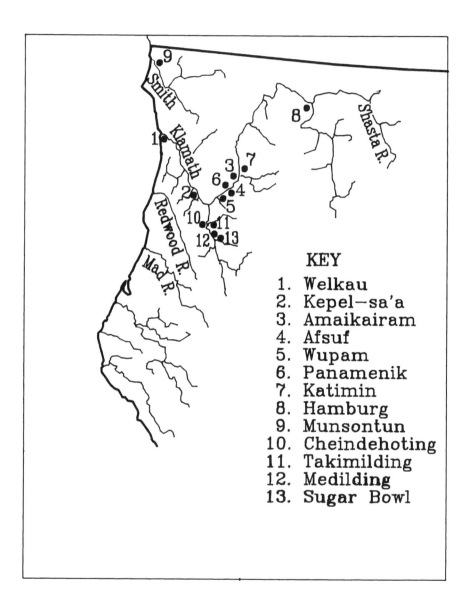

KEY

1. Welkau
2. Kepel–sa'a
3. Amaikairam
4. Afsuf
5. Wupam
6. Panamenik
7. Katimin
8. Hamburg
9. Munsontun
10. Cheindehoting
11. Takimilding
12. Medilding
13. Sugar Bowl

Figure 12.2. Klamath river villages mentioned in text.

The spring salmon run was most intensely ritualized in Northwestern California, where a central core of tribes (Yurok, Karok, and Hupa) practiced the formulistic first-salmon rite, each group undertaking one all-important spring ceremony at a specific site. Although superficially similar in initial procedure to the New Year, or World Renewal, celebrations held by these groups, the first-salmon ceremonies appear to have been held independently of these other public display dances (Kroeber and Gifford 1949:105). The salmon ritual among these three tribes incorporated several common features. The "first" salmon was always procured and ritually eaten by a priest or his assistant, who prayed, fasted and sweated for a prescribed length of time. Fresh salmon could not be consumed by any member of the community until the first spring salmon ritual took place. Supernaturally induced illness or death would occur if the taboo surrounding the capture of salmon was broken. Throughout the period of days over which the ceremony was performed the oral delivery of esoteric formulae, or myths, intended to induce and renew an abundance of salmon, was the main responsibility of the formulist. The formulist's personal knowledge of the proper content and sequence of these narrative recitations, which were treated as private property and considered to be of supernaturally creative power, established his position of primary importance in the rite.

The Yurok first salmon ceremony was held annually in April at Welkwau, a small village at the mouth of the Klamath River. It was a smaller and less important village than Rekwoi which stood directly opposite on the north bank of the Klamath River. Some ancient event may have established Welkwau as the proper place to conduct this important ritual, and, once begun, tradition fixed it as the essential spot for the ceremony. Although mentioned by Kroeber (1925:60-81; Driver 1939:314, 380) and Kroeber and Gifford (1949: 99-100), the rite is described in detail by a Yurok informant, Robert Spott, in *Yurok Narratives* (Spott and Kroeber 1942:171-179). An old formulist who lived in Welkwau performed the *"helku menekuni ne'pui"* ("the salmon spearing from shore"). Prior to the rite, no salmon caught at the mouth of the river could be eaten. The formulist prepared for seven days before the rite. He arranged for and instructed his ritual assistant (who was to perform the actual first eating of the salmon), and cleared a path from the ceremonial house to the mouth of the river. On the day before the ceremony, he prayed for the well-being of the world and an amplitude of food resources. On the day of the ceremony, the formulist told men fishing on the bank (for species other than salmon, such as sturgeon and lampreys) to watch for the "first salmon." The formulist was notified when the "first" salmon was seen.

Reciting a formula, he feigned the act of spearing a fish with his harpoon, and allowed the fish to pass up the river as the "*ne' po'wo kewononoro' apin*" ("the first salmon that goes up to the head of the river"). When the next salmon was seen, it was captured, a recitation ensued, and the fish was taken to the ceremonial house where it was cooked and ritually consumed. The assistant ate the cooked fish, and it was believed that if he could consume it in its entirety (presumably not including the bones) he would become wealthy. The formulist prayed the entire night in the sweathouse, and the next day officially sanctioned salmon fishing for all upstream Yurok villages.

The Karok first salmon rite (described by Powers 1872:427; Kroeber 1925:104-105; Harrington 1932:7; Roberts 1932a:426-440; Driver 1938:214, 380; Kroeber and Gifford 1949:35-47) was held in March or April at the village of Amaikiaram on the west bank of the Klamath several miles below its confluence with the Salmon River. A formulist and his assistant, reciting formulae, kindled a sacred fire, and cooked the first salmon for ritual consumption. These activities were not to be witnessed by any other persons, and the community as a whole was obliged to leave the village and remain secluded in the surrounding hills. Roberts (1932a: 430) mentions that salmon fishing might occur before completion of the rite, but any fish caught were saved and not consumed before the completion of the ceremony. When ritual eating of the salmon was accomplished, the people returned to the village, and all Karok were allowed to begin fishing for and eating fresh salmon.[8]

Each spring on the west side of the Trinity River, near the upstream end of Sugar Bowl Valley, a Hupa formulist would go to a selected site before anyone had engaged in fishing activities and there recite a formula over the first salmon procured (Goddard 1903:78-79; Driver 1938:314, 380; Kroeber and Gifford 1949:56-61). His formulae were narrations of the mythical creation and journey of the salmon down the river and back. Having cooked and eaten the first salmon, he prayed for an additional ten days, while he continued to catch salmon which were smoked and dried in preparation for a feast on the last day of the rite. A Hupa formulist's prayer is recorded by Driver:

---

[8]Powers (1872:427), in describing the "Dance for Salmon" of the "Cahroc," differs with this version of the Karok first-salmon restriction. He states: "No Indian may take salmon before this dance is held <u>nor for ten days thereafter, even if his family are starving</u>" (emphasis added).

Figure 12.3. Karok scaffold for A-frame net fishing. Photo courtesy of the P. A. Hearst Museum of Anthropology, University of California, Berkeley.

314

> May the fish come to Rekwoi; and may they think there
> is only one passage direct to "Sugar Bowl." May they not
> go up the Klamath beyond the junction of the Trinity.
> May they always hear the roar of the falls at Sugar Bowl
> [1939:380].

During this ten-day period the formulistic restrictions to be observed in fishing were recited, and fishing was not permitted to the public. On the tenth and final day, a community feast was held and the salmon season was declared officially "open."[9] After the performance of these spring rites, the ritually supervised construction of large fish weirs was undertaken along the Klamath and Trinity rivers, usually during the month of July, when stream levels were sufficiently low. Originally, these dams were built to harvest a new summer migration of king salmon, the beginning of which coincided with the waning period of the spring run (Snyder 1931:23). In each case a formulist directed the construction of these "fish dams" and supervised their use. Undoubtedly the best known of these communal dam-building efforts was that undertaken by the Yurok at the site of Kepel on the Klamath River. The elaborate 10-day ritual of building this fish dam is described by Thompson (1916:44-54; Kroeber 1925:58-60; Waterman and Kroeber 1938:49-80; Erikson 1943:277-282; Kroeber and Gifford 1941:81-85). The large dam structure consisted of a framework of poles, logs, and small stakes extending across the entire width of the Klamath at a relatively

---

[9]The Hupa also performed a "first-eel" (lamprey) ceremony on the Trinity River: The ceremony for first eels took place in March in Hoopa Canyon toward Weitspus. There was no special place for it, any satisfactory spot for eel fishing would do. The formulist sweated himself for ten days, drank no water, and ate alone. At the end of ten days he fished one night for eels, with the usual fine-mesh net. Whatever he caught he saved. He took the catch out and called it "one-hundred eels," a saxel, "one burden basket" full. If he caught fifty or more, he brought them home and invited people to come and eat. He could give away his catch. The woman who cooked, cut the eels for the people who came. All the eels were eaten fresh; none was dried. The night after that anyone could go eel fishing; the eels were for all to take. After that the formulist would go downstream, but he must not go upstream for five days. The reason for this prohibition was the fear that all the eels would follow him upstream. If the formulist stayed home, the eels would remain there [Kroeber and Gifford 1949:61].

Figure 12.4. Upper: Karok plunge net fishing platform at Amaikiaram, ca. 1900. After Kroeber and Barrett (1962:127, Plate 27). Lower: Amits, assistant to Lo', the Kepel fish dam builder and formulist, 1907. He provided an account of his experiences at the Kepel dam construction (see Waterman and Kroeber 1938:62-67). After Kroeber and Gifford (1949:154, Plate 7). Photos courtesy of the P. A. Hearst Museum of Anthropology, University of California, Berkeley.

shallow even-bottomed section upstream from the village of Sa' or Sha'a where the formulist's sacred sweathouse was located (Kroeber and Barrett 1960:12). The cutting of the wood to build this framework required the coordinated efforts of several hundred men from many Yurok villages along the Klamath. As many as seventy individuals were responsible for constructing the actual weir at the dam site (Waterman and Kroeber 1938:54-55). At various intervals along the downstream side of the dam, nine openings, each leading into a large enclosure or pen, were constructed. During the ten days of fish collecting at the site, large quantities of salmon were harvested and dried. The entire construction, use, and eventual dismantling of the dam was directed by a formulist, who supervised in every detail the work involved. The Kepel fish dam probably represents the largest mechanical enterprise undertaken in Northwestern California, and was clearly the Yurok's most extensively organized communal subsistence effort (Waterman and Kroeber 1938:78). The considerable amount of caloric energy derived from fish caught at Kepel is paralleled by the large amount of organized energy expended by the workers to build the dam.

The Hupa constructed a "sacred" fish dam under the direction of a formulist on the Trinity River at Chiendehoting (Kroeber and Gifford 1949:61). Built "about May" when "the thimbleberries were ripe" (Gifford speculated that it was probably built somewhat later in the year) the formulist procured the first materials for construction, and upon completion of the structure,

> ....the formulist walked across it and back, carrying a basket of water in his right hand, supported by the fingers as a waiter supports a serving tray. In his left hand he carried pebbles, which he scattered in the river, saying: "May as many fish jump."
>
> Piers were built out on the downstream side of the dam for the fishermen to stand on as they scooped up the fish. The night after the formulist crossed the dam, he and his helper took the first fish with a dip net [Kroeber and Gifford 1949:61].

Another Hupa weir was also built, in alternating years at Takimilding and Medilding on the Trinity River, under the direction of a formulist who cut

317

Figure 12.5. Upper: Hupa weir, 1906. After Kroeber and Barrett (1962:170, Plate 1). Lower: Salmon drying in rafters of Karok house, 1901. Photos courtesy of the P. A. Hearst Museum of Anthropology, University of California, Berkeley.

the first pole and directed the post driving and binding (Kroeber and Barrett 1960:18-19).

The Karok also constructed a salmon weir in July near Afsuf or Wupam (Red Cap) on the Klamath River. The formulist for the weir at Afsuf remained in the sweathouse at the upstream village of Panamenik for a period of five days. If the dam was built at Wupam, the formulist stayed in the sweathouse there for a period of five days (Kroeber and Barrett 1960:20). Further details of the ceremony surrounding these dams are not known.

Although not all fish weir construction on the Klamath and Trinity was attended by formulistic ritual, it is significant that the construction of many of the larger, communally built weirs was supervised by a formulist. The effectiveness of these structures as harvest tools and the ecological implications of their use were undoubtedly well understood by their makers. Gibbs (1853:146) and Wessells (1853:64) note that fish dams on the Klamath were effective in obstructing the salmon run and preventing passage of fish to tribes living upstream from these structures. This interference with the run was said to be a constant source of complaint and dissatisfaction among the upper Klamath River groups. The Kepel dam was deliberately torn down after ten days of use to allow the run to proceed to upriver tribes and prevent potential inter-group conflict over the critically needed salmon resource (Waterman and Kroeber 1938:50). According to Roberts (1932b:288), the abundant salmon at the height of the summer run endangered the stability of the Kepel dam by crowding against it, so the traps were opened after each day's fishing to allow the salmon to go through until the next morning. Lucy Thompson describes this procedure at Kepel:

> In these traps, there get to be a mass of salmon, so full that they make the whole structure of the fish dam quiver and tremble with their weight, by holding the water from passing through the lattice-work freely. After all have taken what they want of the salmon, which must be done in the early part of the day, Lock [the dam formulist] or Lock-nee [his assistant] opens the upper gates of the traps and lets the salmon pass on up the river, and at the same time great numbers are passing through the open gap left on the south side of the river. This is done so the Hoopas on up the Trinity River have a chance at the salmon catching. But they keep a close watch to see that there are

enough left to effect the spawning, by which the supply is kept up for the following year [1916:135-136].

A similar practice is also mentioned by Powers:

> The Whites along the [Klamath] river compel the Indians to open their weirs a certain number of days a week during the spring run, that they may participate in the catch [1872:533].

Karok weirs, when not actually in use, were also opened to allow fish to continue their migration upstream (Kroeber and Barrett 1960:20).

A final note about first-salmon ritual among the Klamath River tribes concerns the ceremonial practices and beliefs of the Klamath River Shasta. Geographically situated immediately upstream from the Karok, the Shasta believed

> ...that the first fish to ascend the streams annually brought the "salmon medicine" put on by the Indians at the mouth of the river. This first fish must therefore be allowed to pass unmolested. As soon as it passed, fish might be caught; but the first one taken from the water had to be split and hung up immediately to dry, and no salmon might be eaten till this salmon was completely dry and a portion eaten by all those fishing at that point [Dixon 1907:430-431].

When the spring salmon reached Shasta territory in April, the owners of small fish pools or "resting places" fished for several days with dip nets at these spots, then held feasts for invited guests on an appointed day. No one else ate or fished for salmon until after this ceremony (Holt 1946: 310). However, the western Shasta also depended upon a first-salmon rite performed by a man in the downstream village of Hamburg on the Klamath.[10] This man caught the "first salmon" in the spring and performed the necessary ritual, thus opening the season for catching of the

---

[10]It is unclear as to whether Hamburg was a Shasta or Karok village in aboriginal times, but this man was almost certainly a Shasta, belonging to the Kammatwa group. The territorial affiliation of the village remains in doubt (Voegelin 1942:174).

spring salmon. Notwithstanding the performance at Hamburg, the Shasta did not eat fresh salmon or steelhead until the Karok performed the White Deerskin dance at Katimin, on the Klamath just above the mouth of the Salmon River. This World Renewal ceremony was held in August, and many Shasta attended it as spectators (Voegelin 1942:174-175). This appears to be the only formal example in Native California of one tribe regulating the consumption of fish based on the ceremonial calendar of another downstream group. Informally, of course, the building of the several weirs or dams by the Yurok and Karok must have materially delayed the arrival of the salmon run in Shasta territory.

Outside of the Klamath-Trinity River area, only one other coastal stream in Northwestern California, the Smith River, had a spring influx of king salmon. At the onset of the spring runs, the Tolowa of the Smith River held a first salmon rite (DuBois 1932:258-259; Barnett 1937:190, 193, 198; Drucker 1937:261; Driver 1938:324, 380). A formulist performed the "*ha' guCLi xa'c Renic*" ("salmon-go-out-to-catch") rite during which he entered the sacred sweathouse or "salmon's home" to fast for five days and recite prayers. On the last day of his fast, the formulist caught the first salmon, built a fire, and cooked the fish, placing it upon a basketry tray on which were represented examples of the roots, leaves, and fruit of all available plant foods. He then began a long formulistic recital, requiring several hours to narrate, describing the origins of the world and the salmon's primeval journey up the Smith River. The "first foods" were divided by the formulist among the adult spectators and consumed: "After this, everyone could catch and eat the salmon; he opened the season" (Drucker 1937:261). In late spring at the village of Munsontun on the Smith River, a fish dam "boss" performed this formulistic rite over the first salmon taken in the weir there, and additional formulae accompanied the driving of the first two stakes of the weir (Drucker 1937:261; Barnett 1936:198).

In general, the procedures of the first salmon ritual in Northwestern California, and the control functions of the formulist in determining the proper time for the beginning of the fishing season, were an extension of the need for careful maintenance and harvest of this essential resource. However, among native groups outside the Northwestern culture-area, the ritual activities surrounding the spring salmon were of a different nature. The formulist and his oral recitations are absent, and in his place as the central ritualist is the shaman, who derives his power from special, personally acquired supernatural forces. Among the Yokuts, a ritually obligated moiety chief served this function.

Northwestern foothill Maidu groups on the Feather River, mountain Nisenan (Southern Maidu) along the Yuba and American rivers, and Valley Maidu along the Sacramento River held first salmon ceremonies when the spring run arrived. In the northwestern foothills, where "salmon were caught in considerable quantities in the early days," the first salmon had to be caught by a shaman, and no one else could catch or eat salmon until a first salmon ceremony was performed (Dixon 1905:184; 198; Kroeber 1925:437; Voegelin 1942:57, 175). The shaman, after catching the first salmon, cooked it, and distributed morsels of the food to all persons in the community. This ritual "communion" opened the fishing season for the year. The foothill and mountain Nisenan first-salmon rites were similarly structured, with a "dreamer or singing shaman" conducting the ceremony and opening the season on the Yuba River (Beals 1933:354; Voegelin 1942:57, 175). The Valley Maidu spring ceremony involved restrictions upon fishing and consumption until salmon were ritually eaten by secret society members in the assembly house (Voegelin 1942:57, 175).

Northern Foothills Yokuts on the San Joaquin River, Western Mono tribes on the North Fork of the San Joaquin, and Yokuts tribes on the lower Kings River held first salmon ceremonies (Aginsky 1943:398; Gayton 1948:165-166, 1946:256). An example of this rite was practiced among the Kechayi and Gashowu Yokuts on the San Joaquin River. "When the Pleiades were on the western horizon at dusk it was time to watch for the first salmon," and the chief of the Nutuwich moiety (the moiety totemically associated with salmon and ritually responsible for the fish harvest) sent "all Nutuwich men out to catch salmon." The first salmon was placed on a basketry tray, over which the Nutuwich chief spoke and prayed. A general salmon feast followed during which the moiety was allowed to partake of the salmon for the first time. Gayton (1946:256) states that the moiety chief himself speared, cooked, and ate the salmon, praying to the salmon spirit for an abundant supply of fish. Following the salmon feast the fishing season was officially opened.

Northern and Central Sierra Miwok groups on the Stanislaus, Mokelumne, and south fork of the Cosumnes rivers also held a first-salmon rite after which fishing was permitted for the first time. The first salmon was divided and eaten in a public ceremonial accompanied by dancing and offerings thrown in a fire (Aginsky 1943:398). Further details as to the structure of this ceremony are not recorded.

A brief description of first-salmon ritual among the Achomawi on the Pit River is recounted by Powers:

After the vast crystal volume of Fall River enters and
overcomes the swampiness of the snaky Pit and it begins
to descend over rapids, there salmon are caught, although
the Americans assert that salmon do not ascend above a
certain tremendous cataract which is said to exist on the
lower river. When the salmon season arrives, a band of
aged priests or "medicines" abstain from fresh fish, flesh,
or fowl for certain days, which they believe will induce a
heavy run and a bountiful catch. Even the women and
children at this time, if they wish to eat fresh salmon,
must carry it back, in the forest out of sight of the river.
Like the Meidoos [Maidu], on the Sacramento, they call
the salmon, by sitting in a circle on some overlooking
promontory, while a venerable "medicine" stands in the
midst and earnestly addresses the finny multitudes for two
or three hours, urging them to ascend the river [1874:413].

Two final examples of the first-salmon ritual in Native California
are offered. These are among the Athapaskan Sinkyone and Kato of the
Eel River. These ceremonies are of particular interest because they are the
only salmon rites recorded for a river system which did not have a
significant run of king salmon. They were probably associated with the
midsummer or fall run of king salmon into the Eel, this being the first
salmon run of the year in north coastal streams south of the Klamath.

Among the Sinkyone, fishing was at least as important as hunting
for supplying winter food, and during the seasonal salmon run the entire
tribe camped near the streams for the duration of the run, usually lasting
about two months. When the run began, anyone might catch the first
salmon, but after it was captured, it was given to a shaman who prayed,
danced, and ritually scaled and cleaned the fish with a special obsidian
knife. After cooking the first salmon at the edge of the stream where it
had been caught, the shaman ate the first morsel, then each person in
attendance ate a piece of the flesh "to ensure the increase of salmon for
the succeeding years as well as personal and tribal safety" (Nomland 1935:
153, 154). After the completion of the ceremony, a general feast of new
salmon was held. It is suggested that the essential pattern of the Sinkyone
first-salmon rite was an extension of the more prevalent first-acorn rite in
Central California (Nomland 1935:154). The shaman's prayer "*Ensongkū'
tsē ja*" ("Let us eat well") was the same as that spoken at the first-acorn
rite, and perhaps indicates a transfer of acorn formulae to a more recently

introduced salmon ceremony, the source of the salmon ritualization complex being undoubtedly the Northwestern core area to the north (Yurok, Karok, Hupa). Archaeologically there is no evidence which proves either that salmon-eating or acorn-eating are of the same antiquity. Where both acorns and salmon were eaten the two rituals may have borrowed from each other and by ethnographic times lost some of their earlier distinctiveness. The northern concentration of salmon rituals is detailed by Treide (1965).

When the first quantity of any food plant or animal was obtained in its season, the Kato celebrated a first-fruits ceremony in which several "old men" would sing over the produce and eat of it, after which all persons could eat the particular food. A salmon ceremony took place in the spring (summer?), apparently incorporating these elements (Driver 1939:314, 380).

This final section summarizes the variety of regional and cultural contexts in which a "first salmon" rite was practiced in Native California. Two principal foci of this type of ritual activity emerge, one in Northwestern California (along the Klamath, Trinity, and Smith rivers), and the second in Central California (throughout the Sacramento-San Joaquin system and major tributaries). The rites differ in that among the Northwestern tribes (Yurok, Karok, Hupa, Shasta, and Tolowa) a formulist or "priest" is the central pragmatist in an elaborate ritual performance. Outside of Northwestern California such formulistic ritual is absent, and the first-salmon ceremony is commonly performed by a shaman or moiety chief, apparently with less ceremonial elaboration. However, the basic operational features of the first-salmon rite appear consistent throughout Native California. With the exception of the Eel River Athapaskans (where the first-salmon rite may have blended with elements from similar ritualizations of the acorn harvest), the first salmon ceremony was held at the onset of the spring king salmon run, a fish migration of major importance to the aboriginal economy. At the beginning of the run, salmon fishing and/or consumption were strictly enjoined and a ritual specialist supervised this observance. Supernaturally induced illness, death, or loss of fishing luck would befall those persons who disregarded this ritual injunction. The "restraining effect" exerted by ritual restrictions concerning salmon fishing appears to have been a widespread phenomenon in aboriginal times, especially in Northwestern California (Roberts 1932b:290). After the period of restriction was lifted (following prayer and ceremonial behavior by ritualist and/or a public rite in which the first salmon is eaten by all those present), the salmon fishing season was "opened" for the first time. All persons were then allowed to catch and consume salmon for the rest of the year.

The widespread structural similarity of salmon rites in the varied cultural contexts of Native California is sufficient cause for reexamining contentions that the first-salmon rite was "merely the local object of ritual" or an expression of a psychological "attitude of veneration" (Rostlund 1952: 155; Gunther 1928: 136, 149). Alternatively, several levels of functional and adaptive importance may be assigned to the first-salmon rite in Native California, in addition to those of spiritual, psychological, or other origin:

(1) By overtly (also, it seems, covertly) regulating the beginning of the salmon fishing season, first-salmon rituals may have served a distinct conservational or management purpose. In allowing the salmon to run freely during the initial period of ritual restriction (the duration and timing of which was controlled by the formulist, and generally appears to have lasted from several days to two weeks), riverine tribes maintained a productive inventory of spawning salmon each spring, which ensured successful reproduction and return of the king salmon runs in following years. Intensive salmon fishing after the period of ritual restriction, by large numbers of individuals initiating this subsistence effort at the same time, probably benefited the production of salmon by preventing over-crowding at the spawning beds (Rostlund 1952:16). The opening and/or purposeful dismantling of weirs built and operated under ritual supervision along the Klamath also allowed the summer run to proceed to upstream tribes (and eventually the spawning grounds), this run being of major importance for winter storage (Roberts 1932b:289). Potential inter-group conflict stemming from over-use or blockage of the salmon run by downstream tribes was thus prevented. The maintenance and conservation of the salmon subsistence base on a year to year basis was perhaps the most important function of the first-salmon observance, and there is no evidence that native populations ever seriously overfished the salmon runs (Rostlund 1952:17).

(2) Ritual observances called attention to the onset of the spring runs at a time when an efficient, organized fishing effort was crucial to the successful procurement of a spring food supply. The proper timing of individual fishing or communal dam-building (during periods of maximum availability of salmon) allowed the run to be harvested with less overall output of energy and greater total yield. Maximum community energies were directed toward the run by restrictions which "opened the season" for all individuals at the same time, and premature harvest early in the season was prevented.

(3) Publicly-held first-salmon feasts, which often followed the lifting of ritual restrictions upon fishing activity, effectively decentralized the concentrated nature of the salmon run, facilitating distribution of fish resources to all members of the community. It is further possible that until the run was well underway there would not be enough fish to be caught by the numerous fishermen, and that the intense competition might lead to altercations which would be socially disruptive. Thus, "feed or fight" need not have been the only alternative if there was some ritually compulsive regulation or control for a sufficient period of time (usually not more than one or two weeks) until the fish run was abundant enough for everyone to partake of it.

We have proposed here that the "first-salmon" and fish dam-building ceremonies were essentially ritual activities arising from the need to carefully manage the anadromous fish resources and to regulate the fishing activities of large human populations which intensively utilized this resource on major Northern California streams during a limited seasonal interval. However, large-scale first-salmon rites are conspicuously lacking among native groups in the North Coast Ranges and south of San Francisco Bay. This apparent lack of ritual practices associated with the salmon run may be in part due to the paucity of ethnographic information available (especially concerning the Coast Miwok and Costanoans), non-availability of high yield, biannual salmon streams, prevalence of personal rites undertaken only by individual fishermen, or as proposed by Kroeber and Barrett (1960:148), greater emphasis placed upon ritualization and use of other food resources, particularly the acorn. Notwithstanding the absence of the first-salmon rite in these areas, the co-occurrence of the spring salmon run and some form of associated ritual activity which regulated and organized large-scale fishing activity at the outset of this run, is a common relationship in the ethnographic record.

Of final, and perhaps more reflective, note is some mention of the ultimate ecological fate of the once prolific spring salmon run in Northern California. In the latter half of the nineteenth century, California was the scene of massive cultural and environmental devastation, principally at the hands of gold miners who overran the northern half of the state in the two decades following the discovery of gold in 1848. By the year 1873, the salmon-producing potential of the Yuba, Feather, and American rivers (the latter two formerly "prolific" salmon rivers) had been largely destroyed by the smothering effects of mining silt on the upstream spawning beds (Stone 1873:177,178,193). Similar destruction of spawning grounds due to mining activities occurred in other Sierran tributaries of the Sacramento and San

Joaquin, as well as on the Klamath and Trinity rivers. In addition to the effects of mining, large-scale damming and diversion of water flow for irrigation and water supplies (which resulted in the cutting off of spawning beds, lowering of water levels, and raising of headwater temperatures in the summer when the spring king salmon require cooler waters for migration and spawning), as well as farmland and range erosion, soil runoff due to lumbering and deforestation, overfishing, and stream pollution from sawmills and other sources, effectively eliminated the spring run of salmon in California (Clark 1929:61; Snyder 1931:19; Davidson and Hutchinson 1938:673; Hewes 1947:233-236). Obliteration of the spawning beds of the Sacramento River system was nearly complete; of an estimated 5,500 miles of original spawning grounds, only 300 linear miles remained in 1929, constituting a reduction of 80% from original conditions (Clark 1929:61). These factors, operating simultaneously with the complete destruction of native lifeways, made ritual management of the spring salmon run a practice of the aboriginal past by the early twentieth century, when much of the ethnographic data were collected in Northern California. Lucy Thompson provides the most prophetic insight into the encroachment of white civilization upon the salmon management practices of the Yurok:

> The whites have often said that the Indians ought not to be allowed to put in the fish dam and thereby obstruct the run of salmon to their spawning ground, and it has been published in the papers that the fish dam ought to be torn out. One year it was published in the county papers that it had been torn out by the wardens; this was a false publication, as it was never torn out by the Indians or whites. On the other hand after the salmon cannery was established at Reck-woy, which is at the mouth of the river, the whites and the mixed bloods commenced to fish for the cannery; the whites have laws that no one is allowed to let a net extend more than two thirds the distance across the river, and the wardens are paid to see that the law is obeyed, yet the whites set one net up from one side two thirds across, and then just a few steps up another net from the other side, and which extends two thirds across in distance, and in a distance of sixty yards, there will be eight to ten nets making so complete a network that hardly a salmon can pass. *Will the whites preserve the salmon through all the ages, as the Klamath*

Indians have done, if they should survive so long? [1916: 136; emphasis added].

Today, the spring run of king salmon is of such little consequence in the major California salmon streams that it is considered of no commercial value to fishermen.

In conclusion, the anadromous fish resource in Native California was originally a seasonally abundant and renewable commodity which required intelligent and competent organization and control of fishing practices to ensure efficient harvest, especially during the spring migration of king salmon. Through the spring or summer salmon ceremony, ritual specialists directed and controlled fishing and dam building activities, regulated the opening of the salmon fishing season, and managed the use of the spawning runs, in many ways increasing the potential effectiveness with which native populations utilized the salmon resource. The anadromous fish resource was perhaps the most intensely managed and ecologically manipulated food resource among these aboriginal societies, and as a functional mechanism for the adaptation of native fishing economies to the movements of anadromous species, salmon ritual was an important cultural feature in Native California. It is further possible, we think, that the ethnographers from 1872 to 1940, in dealing not only with decimated native populations, but also at a time when environmental changes had occurred, may simply have not grasped the true importance of salmon as a basic dietary resource element. They thus failed to communicate in their reporting what we can at the present time only speculate about. What we have proposed here is a new interpretation, but it is at the same time ethnohistory through the back door.

AGRICULTURE AMONG THE PAIUTE
OF OWENS VALLEY[1]

Harry W. Lawton, Philip J. Wilke, Mary DeDecker, and William M. Mason

> ...To search for the 'first domestic plant' is to search for an event.
> It is poor strategy, it encourages bitter rivalry rather than coopera-
> tion, and it is probably fruitless. We should search instead for the
> processes by which agriculture began.
>
> --Kent V. Flannery (1973)

In 1973, Kent V. Flannery in a masterly review article asserted that no aspect of prehistory had received so much attention from archaeologists, botanists, geographers, and anthropologists over the preceding 15 years as the origins of agriculture. "Surely at this stage," Flannery observed wryly, "we could declare the origins of agriculture a bandwagon." Indeed, one can scarcely keep abreast of new literature on agricultural origins. Yet throughout the voluminous writings on this subject over the past few decades there are only fleeting references to the practice of irrigation of wild plants among the Paiute of Owens Valley.

Almost a half century has passed since Julian Steward (1930) first brought to scholarly attention ditch irrigation of wild plants by these Great Basin people of east central California. Steward (1930:156) suggested this anomalous subsistence practice might have arisen as "simply an artificial reproduction of natural conditions" existing in the swampy lowlands of Owens Valley. One reason little attention has been given since to Paiute irrigation of wild plants appears to lie in Steward's belief that these people were "on the verge of agriculture without achieving it." In fact, Steward (1930) titled his first paper on the subject "Irrigation Without Agriculture." Almost no one who has written on the subject has taken Steward's discovery very seriously or challenged his conclusions. In part, this may be because there was some wavering by Steward over the years as to whether irrigation was truly aboriginal with the Owens Valley Paiute or acquired from contact with the Spanish or later American settlers who penetrated

[1] This paper originally appeared in the Journal of California Anthropology, Vol. 3, No. 1, pp. 13-50, 1976. It is reprinted here by permission of Malki Museum Press. Acknowledgements have been deleted.

330

the region after 1850 (Steward 1930:248-249; 1938:53). Also, Treganza (1956) argued that irrigation reached Owens Valley through Caucasian contact after 1850, although he presented no data adequately defending this hypothesis. Eventually, Steward (1970:123) reconsidered the problem and somewhat cautiously returned to his original position that irrigation of wild plants in Owens Valley was probably of aboriginal origin. A third factor standing in the way of more intensive scrutiny of Owens Valley irrigation has been semantic confusion over the concept of "incipient agriculture" as opposed to true agriculture. That problem will be discussed later in this paper.

Undoubtedly, the importance of Steward's pioneer research on irrigation in Owens Valley has been obscured by his own coining of the phrase "irrigation without agriculture." Apparently researchers have taken Steward's phrase literally, since no one has added significant new insights on Paiute irrigation, and no one seems to have considered the possibility that true agriculture could have existed in Owens Valley. For this reason, recent summaries of agricultural origins (e.g., Harlan 1975) have been unable to adequately evaluate its significance. Recent archaeological work in Owens Valley (Bettinger 1975) has been directed at other problems.[2]

FRAMEWORK OF INVESTIGATION

Bean and Blackburn (1976:6) called attention to a "renaissance of sorts" that has occurred in recent years in the study of California Indians. They noted a dramatic increase in papers reflecting a commitment to the development of theory applicable to a wider arena than California or providing "significant reinterpretations or syntheses of older data that greatly alter previously accepted views on aboriginal life." Kearney (1974:5) linked this renaissance to a growing recognition that aboriginal California was probably "more representative of the non-urban stage of human

[2] Bettinger (1975:353-354) briefly considered the problem of Owens Valley irrigation and suggested that it may have begun around A.D. 1000. He based his suggestion on a change in artifact distribution which he believed indicated a decline in hunting of large game in upland areas and a presumed diversion of the labor force into construction and operation of irrigation facilities. This was in contradiction to Steward (1930) who reported that except for initial dam construction only one person was in charge of irrigation. Bettinger's archaeological investigations in Owens Valley are continuing, and it is hoped that further attention will be given to some of the information presented in this paper.

prehistory than the 'band-level' societies of contemporary hunters and gatherers in marginal environments which are relatively over-represented in the literature."

In particular, there has been a focus in the past few years on the technological processes associated with subsistence patterns of California hunters and gatherers. Heizer's (1958:23) hypothesis that the peoples of California were in a "Preformative Stage" defined as "semi-agricultural" at the time of Spanish contact has had a stimulating influence on a body of researchers who have fanned out looking for supporting data among various Indian groups. Much of their research has concentrated on southeastern California, where an increasing array of circumstantial evidence indicates that aboriginal agriculture diffused west of the Colorado River prior to European contact and was adopted by the Cahuilla, Kamia, interior groups of Southern Diegueño, certain groups in Baja California, and quite possibly some Indian groups on the Mohave Desert (e.g., Forbes 1963; Lawton 1968; Lawton and Bean 1968). Another area of primary concern has been the extent to which California Indians engaged in environmental manipulations such as burning of woodland-grass, chaparral, and coniferous forest zones to enhance plant and animal food resources (Lewis 1973). In this latter field of study, scattered data have also been assembled indicating the presence of incipient agriculture among many Indian groups (Bean and Lawton 1973). Fairly comprehensive reviews of the literature on such research may be found in Bean and Lawton (1973)[3] and Lawton (1974). Winter (1975) provided a bibliography covering aboriginal agriculture within the broader contexts of the Southwest and the Great Basin. More recent research touching upon the problem of aboriginal agriculture in southeastern California is reported by Wilke and Lawton (1975), Wilke, King, and Hammond (1975), and Wilke (1976).

Such research has made it necessary to reconsider Spinden's (1917) hypothesis that the acorn economy of California prevented the westward dispersal of agriculture from the Colorado River, where it was practiced in the pre-hispanic era. Similarly, hypotheses developed by Kroeber (1925, 1939), Sauer (1936), and other investigators that certain specific cultural or environmental factors constituted barriers to the spread of agriculture across California have been shown to be invalid or not sufficiently comprehensive in resolving this problem (Bean and Lawton 1973:viii-xvii).

---

[3] This paper also provides a general summary of most of the research which has been carried out on aboriginal agriculture in California.

In a recent review of Lewis (1973), David R. Harris commented as follows on the new research data coming out of California:

> ...What emerges most forcefully...is confirmation from California for the view that 'primitive' man's ability to manipulate his environment was much greater than conventional opinion supposes. It reinforces my belief that it is high time we rejected the simple-minded opposition between 'farmer' and 'hunter-gatherer' and sought instead to devise new and more ecologically and socially sophisticated categories in our investigations of aboriginal subsistence [Harris 1975:686].

Eventually, new directions in California research may make it possible to satisfy the demand of O'Connell (1974:120) that a clearer understanding be provided of the complex processual relationships of California hunters and gatherers to their environment and those grey areas of phenomena that shade from hunting and gathering into the domains of "semi-agriculture" or agriculture.

It was within the framework of the research outlined above that the authors determined to conduct a serious re-examination of the problem of irrigation among the Owens Valley Paiute. Our research over the past three years has brought to light previously overlooked or unpublished documentary materials indicating that irrigation was of far greater importance to Owens Valley subsistence than heretofore recognized. We will show that the Owens Valley Indians developed a complex system of irrigated vegeculture unique to North America. Some evidence will be presented that ditch irrigation of wild plants may have extended over a broader area of the Great Basin than simply Owens Valley. Field research combined with our literature survey has made it possible also to identify with considerable certainty the primary plants irrigated by the Owens Valley Paiute and to correct some misconceptions held by Steward. We will suggest that the practice of irrigation among these Indian people was almost certainly of indigenous origin and that they were engaged in agriculture by definition. Finally, we will present our conclusion that "wild" plant irrigation by the Paiute of Owens Valley offers a more exemplary model of the origins of agriculture than any yet revealed by archaeological studies of early deposits containing already domesticated plants.

NATURAL AND CULTURAL SETTING

Owens Valley is a deep structural trough in east central California (Fig. 13.1). The valley is over 75 miles long, averages 6-10 miles in width, has an average elevation of about 4000 feet, and runs generally southeast to the Mojave Desert. High mountains rise like vertical walls within a few miles on either side of the valley. The Sierra Nevada to the west and the White Mountains to the east exceed 14,000 feet in elevation, making it the deepest valley in the United States. The valley is watered by the Owens River and its numerous tributaries which take their snowy origin high in the Sierra Nevada (Fig. 13.2). Precipitation on the valley floor averages only 5-6 inches yearly due to its position in the rainshadow of the mountains. Annual snowfall averages about 12 inches. Summers are hot, and winters are moderately cold. The average growing season is 144 days (Felton 1965:120).

Although formerly classified as Eastern Mono, the Indians of Owens Valley are now recognized as the southernmost division of Northern Paiute. A definitive ethnography has been published by Steward (1933; see also Steward 1938). There were probably at least thirty permanent villages clustered into a lesser number of land-owning districts between Round Valley to the north and Owens Lake to the south, making Owens Valley one of the most densely settled regions of the entire Great Basin. The aboriginal population of Owens Valley was probably at least 2000 (Wilke and Lawton 1976:46). Many plant foods were collected in season in recognized territories, including a section of the valley floor and the adjoining mountain slopes. Especially important were pine nuts (*Pinus monophylla*) and the seeds of Indian rice-grass (*Oryzopsis hymenoides*), wild-rye (*Elymus cinereus, E. triticoides*), love grass (*Eragrostis*, probably *E. orcuttiana*), and many others (see Steward 1933:242-246). Hunting for mountain sheep (*Ovis canadenis*), deer (*Odocoileus hemionus*), and jackrabbits (*Lepus californicus*), and fishing in both the Owens River and its tributaries were also very important subsistence activities.

STEWARD'S FINDINGS ON OWENS VALLEY IRRIGATION

Before presenting the results of our research, it is necessary for purposes of further discussion to review Steward's findings on irrigation among the Owens Valley Paiute. Steward (1930:149-156); 1933:247-249)

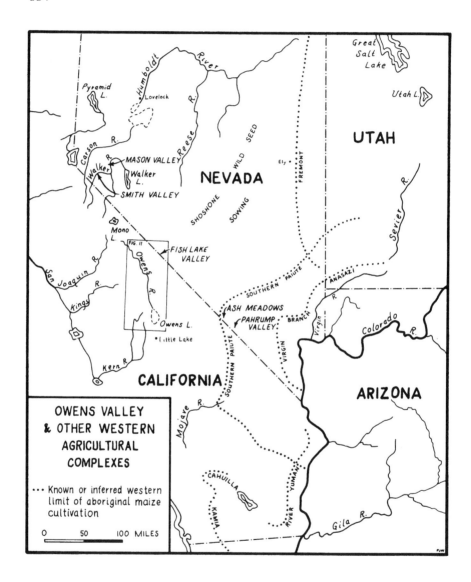

Figure 13.1. Location of Owens Valley and other western aboriginal agricultural complexes.

Figure 13.2. Environment of Owens Valley. Above: View to the southwest across Round Valley. Horton Creek in center background. Irrigation was reported by Von Schmidt just below the center of photograph. Photo by P. J. Wilke. Below: Owens River just southwest of Bishop. View to the southeast with the Inyo Mountains in the background. Photos by P. J. Wilke, October, 1975, and Copyright © 1976 by Ballena Press.

336

fully accepted his informants' statements that the practice began in aboriginal times. Steward's data were entirely ethnographic, however, and he furnished almost no historical documentation shedding light on the antiquity of the practice. The following information on Owens Valley irrigation is summarized from Steward (1930, 1933, 1938).

Irrigation Technology

Steward (1930:15) reported ditch irrigation had been undertaken "upon a considerable scale" in Owens Valley with its greatest development occurring at the northern end of the valley near the present town of Bishop, where population was most dense and "natural facilities were greatest." On each side of Bishop Creek at *pitana patü* was an irrigated plot, a northern one measuring 4 by 1 to 1-1/2 miles, and a southern plot approximately two miles square. The irrigation system for these fields consisted of a dam on Bishop Creek about a mile below the Sierra Nevada Mountains and a main ditch leading to each plot. The northern ditch was over two miles long and the southern more than three miles long, both immense earthworks the size of modern canals (Fig. 13.3) (Steward 1930:151, 157). According to Steward (1933:247), dam and ditch construction "involved no problems but entailed considerable labor." Elsewhere, Steward reported, Freeman and Baker creeks were dammed for irrigation of wild plots, and irrigation occurred from Pine Creek in Round Valley to Independence Creek about midway in Owens Valley. Steward provided no data on acreage involved in irrigation at localities other than *pitana patü*. The Northern Paiute of Mono Lake, about forty miles to the northwest of Owens Valley, did not irrigate.

The position of head irrigator (*tuvaijü⁸*) was honorary at *pitana patü*, and he was elected every spring by popular assembly. The district head man announced the time to begin irrigation, and it was approved by the people.[4] South of Bishop at Big Pine, the head man also served as

---

[4] Wittfogel (1957) argued that large-scale hydraulic works such as the digging and maintaining of canals were only possible in a hierarchically ordered society which could control the entire labor force through a central point of authority. Woodbury (1961:556) in a reappraisal of Hohokam irrigation challenged this concept. Certainly, Wittfogel's term "oriental despotism" scarcely applied to the means by which the Owens Valley Paiute selected their head irrigator and carried out their agricultural tasks. Ho (1975:47-48) reported that the first famous irrigation network in China was completed by the Wei state between 424 and 296 B.C. in the Chang River area in northern Hunan. This whole irrigation system was only 20 li in length, a little over five miles and therefore comparable to the longest

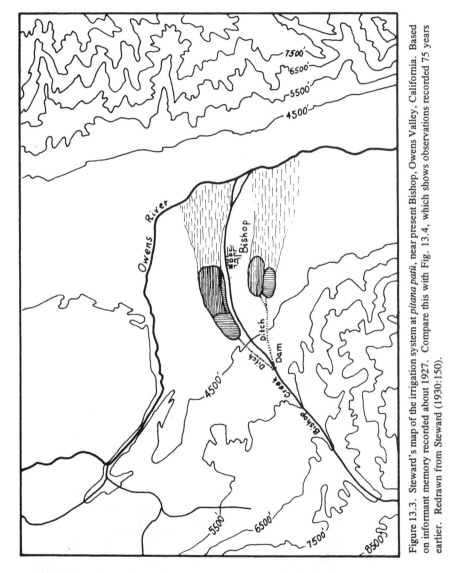

Figure 13.3. Steward's map of the irrigation system at *pitana patü*, near present Bishop, Owens Valley, California. Based on informant memory recorded about 1927. Compare this with Fig. 13.4, which shows observations recorded 75 years earlier. Redrawn from Steward (1930:150).

irrigation ditch of the Owens Valley Paiute at <u>pitana patü</u>. In reply to the Wittfogel hypothesis, Ho (1975:48) wrote: "Insofar as ancient China is concerned the theory of the 'hydraulic' genesis of culture or of 'despotism' is completely groundless." The same may be said to apply to the Owens Valley Paiute, who chose their head irrigator in popular assembly.

338

head irrigator, but he had an assistant. Irrigation was communal at *pitana patü*, and all men might assist in constructing the dam of boulders, brush, sticks, and mud. Once water was turned into the main irrigation ditch, the irrigator had sole responsibility for watering the plot by a system of small ditches and dams of mud, sod, and brush. His irrigating tool (*pavodo*) was a pole, 8 feet long and 4 inches in diameter. After water was turned into the ditch, fish were recovered from the dry stream bed. The overflow water from irrigation was permitted to take its course and wander on to the Owens River. In the fall, before harvesting of the wild plants, the dam was destroyed and the water allowed to flow once more down its main channel. Again fish were gathered, but this time from the irrigation ditch.

An interesting feature of Owens Valley irrigation was that the northern and southern plots at *pitana patü* were alternated for irrigation annually. Water was turned into one plot in the spring, and the next year the other plot was irrigated. This is a form of fallowing. Steward (1933:-247) was told by one informant that alternate irrigation was employed to "prevent soil exhaustion," but suggested a more likely explanation might be that it "enabled the plots to reseed themselves." We shall discuss below why neither explanation seems acceptable. Whether alternate irrigation was practiced at settlements other than *pitana patü* was not recorded by Steward.

Wild Crop Plants Harvested

An important aspect of early Owens Valley irrigation is that it was applied to plants other than those known to have been cultivated by aboriginal farmers in the American Southwest. Steward (1933:247) implied that the two plots at *pitana patü* were irrigated to increase the "natural yield" of two primary plants: *tüpüsi* and *nahavita* (see also Steward 1930:150).[5] He reported that the western half of the northern plot at *pitana patü* abounded in *tüpüsi*, and the eastern half in *nahavita*. The southern plot had a large stand of *nahavita* and a smaller one of *tüpüsi*. While Steward (1930:150) noted that other "wild seeds and tubers" existed in the plots, he emphasized (1930:152;1933:247) that the overflow water below the plots irrigated land bearing *mono*, *sünü*, *pauponiva*, *waiya*, *pak*, and *tsikava*, which were also harvested as food plants. The principal purpose of irrigation, however, appears to have been directed at two chief plants in the irrigated plots, *tüpüsi* and *nahavita*.

---

[5] The linguistic rendering of these terms follows Steward (1938).

Steward (1930:150) identified the plant known as *tüpüsi*[^x] as a "small bulb of the lily family." Later, he suggested (1933:245) that it was "probably *Brodiaea capitata* Benth., grassnut or blue dicks," the species currently classified as *Dichelostemma pulchella* (Salisb.) Heller. The second primary wild crop plant was *nahavita*, which he believed to be a member of the genus *Eleocharis* (spikerush). We will suggest below that Steward's identification of these plants was in error.

The seed-bearing wild plants primarily associated with the irrigation overflow below the plots are identified as follows: *mono* (also called *tsikava*, love grass, *Eragrostis*, probably *E. orcuttiana*); *sünü*[^u] (wheat grass, *Agropyron*, probably *A. trachycaulum*); *pauponiva* (?); *waiya* (Great Basin wild-rye, *Elymus*, probably *E. cinereus* or *E. triticoides*); and *pak*[^u] (sunflower, *Helianthus*, probably *H. nuttallii*) (based on Steward 1933:242-245, unpublished ethnobotanical notes of Mark Kerr, and floristic notes of DeDecker). Steward's (1933:242-245) ethnography also lists several other plants which grew on the irrigated plots or on the overflowed land. These are *atsa* (western yellow cress, *Rorippa curvisiliqua*), *sigüv*[^u] (an unidentified grass), *wocava* (another unidentified grass), *pawai* (water grass, *Echinochloa crusgalli*),[^6] and *wata* (white pigweed, *Chenopodium berlandieri*).

Harvesting of the irrigated plots was communal, and all women might assist in the effort. The intensity with which the fields were harvested is not known, but total harvesting would have required a tremendous amount of communal labor with such extensive plots.[^7] Steward does not say whether harvesting of certain plants occurred in various stages between spring and fall (when the dam at *pitana patü* was destroyed). He does say that *tüpüsi*[^x] and *pak*[^u] were harvested in the fall.

Digging sticks of mountain mahogany or buckbrush were employed in digging up *nahavita* and *tüpüsi*[^x] during the harvest. A ladle-shaped

---

[^6]: It is possible that a variety of E. crusgalli, native to the Owens Valley, named pawai by the Paiutes, has hybridized with the introduced varieties. Hitchcock (1971:712) does not indicate that E. crusgalli is native only to the Old World. An indigenous New World variety would explain the presence of a Paiute term for this plant. We are reminded by Jack R. Harlan (personal communication) that a species of Echinochloa was cultivated in China, and species of Chenopodium were cultivated in various parts of both the New and Old Worlds (J.G. Waines, personal communication).

[^7]: The plants involved are not easily dislodged from the soil, and the tubers of tüpüsi, as will be seen later, are part of an extensive root system.

340

basketry seed-beater was employed with seed plants, which were collected in a conical carrying basket. It has been shown elsewhere that harvesting with seed-beaters militated against genetic modification, which, through planting (which some Great Basin groups engaged in), would have resulted in increased yields and consequently a tendency toward increased sedentism and other cultural complexities (Wilke et al. 1972).

Theoretical Discussion

Steward (1933:248) firmly emphasized that the Owens Valley Paiute were "on the verge of horticulture but did not quite achieve it for planting, tilling, and cultivating were unknown." Earlier, Steward (1930:149) used the word "agriculture" instead of "horticulture." The term "horticulture" as used by Steward is misleading, since irrigation as practiced in Owens Valley was on the agronomic scale of field crops, which is the chief business of agriculture (e.g., Taylor 1961). Part of the misunderstanding that exists here is the result of a disagreement over terms and concepts and of conceptual changes since Steward's research appeared.

Steward (1933:248-249) presented three possible hypotheses for the occurrence of "irrigation without agriculture" in Owens Valley, which he recognized as having "an important bearing on the origins of agriculture in America." The three hypotheses may be summarized as follows:

(1) An ancient practice of irrigation may have preceded the diffusion of cultivated plants in the Southwest and survived in eastern California. Steward considered this hypothesis highly improbable, with no known evidence to support it.[8]

(2) Irrigation may have diffused from a horticultural complex of the near or remote past in the Southwest. Steward considered it unlikely that such a borrowing had occurred in recent times, since none of the crop plants grown among peoples to the east and southeast of Owens Valley had entered the Paiute irrigation complex. If diffusion from the Southwest explained Paiute irrigation, Steward (1933:249) stated, then it did not "operate in the conventional manner, for there was a differential borrowing in which a close-knit horticultural complex was broken down and the seemingly dependent or secondary element, irrigation, diffused without the carrier or *raison d'etre* of the complex--the nucleus of cultivated plants."

---

[8] The authors cannot completely rule out the possibility that agriculture became established among the Owens Valley Paiute before the concept of ditch irrigation had reached southwestern Nevada.

(3) Paiute irrigation may have been of local and independent origin. Steward considered this explanation a distinct possibility. He hypothesized that the original idea for irrigation might have come from the "swampy lowlands of Owens Valley where it is obvious that moist soil--a natural irrigation--produces a very prolific plant growth" (Steward 1933:249). Irrigation would then represent "simply an artificial reproduction of natural conditions." Kowta (1965) and Appleton and Kowta (1969), in a reappraisal of Steward's data, concluded that Owens Valley irrigation may have been of independent origin.

As mentioned earlier, Steward (1938:53) several years later admitted the possibility that irrigation was introduced by the Spanish or Americans who penetrated the valley after 1850.[9] Finally, Steward (1970: 123) returned to his original view that irrigation was probably of aboriginal origin. With the above summary in mind, we can begin our reexamination of the problem of irrigation among the Owens Valley Paiute.

SURVEY OF HISTORICAL AND ETHNOGRAPHIC LITERATURE

Early Expeditions

The earliest known expeditions into Owens Valley were those of Joseph Reddeford Walker, who traversed the valley four or five times, first, we believe, in 1834. Walker's party was on a beaver-trapping expedition to California for Captain Benjamin Bonneville. The route west from the Humboldt Sink region of Nevada over the Sierras is not known precisely, but the return route was over Walker Pass and north through Owens Valley, and is documented in the narrative of Zenas Leonard (Ewers 1959). In the fall of 1843, Walker guided the J.B. Childs (Chiles) emigrant party to California by way of Humboldt Sink, Walker Lake, Owens Valley, and Walker Pass. In the fall and winter of 1845, the route was used again when Walker joined Theodore Talbot on Frémont's so-called third exploring expedition. This passage to California was documented in Edward M. Kern's diary (1876), which unfortunately has little to say of Owens Valley. In the spring of 1846, Walker left the Frémont expedition and retraced his route. He later explored the country around

---

[9] His reservations about aboriginal irrigation were probably prompted by the publication of Chalfant (1933), who wrote the first history of Owens Valley and reported its penetration by white settlers in the 1850's.

Mono Lake, and may have once more passed through Owens Valley (Watson 1934). Leonard provided no description of Owens Valley, and Walker appears to have kept no diaries (Ewers 1959). Due to its position, well removed from emigrant routes into California, Owens Valley escaped the devastating effects of the Gold Rush of 1849.

The Von Schmidt Survey

The oldest documentary records on Owens Valley irrigation that we have been able to locate are those compiled by A. W. Von Schmidt, who surveyed and mapped the region under contract with the U.S. Government from 1855-1856. The survey consisted of laying out township and section lines, establishing corner markers, noting the character of the terrain and quality of the soil, and recording the work accomplished on plat sheets and in accompanying notes. Since the surveyors worked their way around each section (1 square mile) of the valley floor, the plats and notes give some idea of the distribution and nature of irrigation in Owens Valley. Careful study of the record indicates that irrigation was described from Rock Creek, at the north end of Round Valley, to Independence Creek, midway down Owens Valley.

Figure 13.4 shows the data on irrigation in the vicinity of Bishop and in Round Valley as recorded by Von Schmidt largely in late October and early November, 1856. In Round Valley, irrigation was observed on Rock Creek, Pine Creek (also reported by Steward), and Horton Creek, although these streams did not have their present names in 1856. Near Bishop (at *pitana patü*) the irrigation system is indicated to be of at least the extent described by Steward, as can be seen by comparing Figs. 3 and 4, which are shown to the same scale. If anything, the Von Schmidt notes indicate that irrigation was more extensive at *pitana patü* than reported by Steward.

There is little information in Von Schmidt's notes on the plants irrigated except that "fine grass" and "roots" are frequently mentioned, and "sabouse" (taboose, *tüpüsi*) is identified as the "principal article" of food in Round Valley. Seeds are not mentioned, but all of these data on irrigation are incidental to the problems addressed by the surveyors, and we must base our conclusions on what limited information they recorded in passing. Acreage of irrigated land is not given, but distances across it were recorded in chains. In this system of linear measurement, 1 link = 7.92 inches, 100 links = 1 chain (66 feet), and there are 80 chains to the mile. Just north and east of present Bishop, irrigated lands crossed on the section line were thus 1584 feet (1/3 mile) and 1972 feet (nearly 2/5

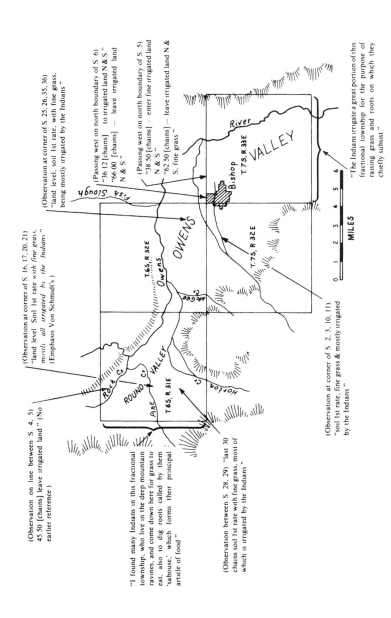

Figure 13.4. Observations made by A. W. Von Schmidt in upper Owens Valley, from the northern end of Round Valley to the vicinity of present Bishop. Mostly late October and early November, 1856. Compare this with Fig. 13.3, which is drawn to the same scale. The main channel of Bishop Creek, as indicated here based on present maps, appears to flow in the northern main ditch. The former main channel ends in modern canals which are not shown.

mile) across, respectively. The Indians in the vicinity of Bishop and Round Valley were clearly involved in large-scale food production.

Steward reported irrigation in the vicinity of Freeman Creek and Keough Hot Springs (*ütü'ütü witü* 'hot place'), but no information was recorded on it by Von Schmidt. He did unknowingly record irrigation in some detail near present Big Pine (*tovowah matü* 'small natural hill place'), where Steward indicated that a major development occurred on Baker Creek. Figure 13.5 shows many small "creeks" recorded by Von Schmidt at the spot Steward stated irrigation was practiced. It is apparent from the

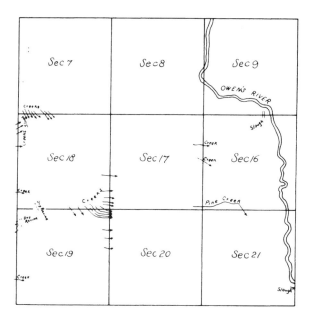

Figure 13.5. Paiute irrigation system at *tovowaha matü*, on Baker Creek near present Big Pine, Owens Valley, California. Unknowingly mapped by A. W. Von Schmidt, 1856. Compare this with Figs. 13.6 and 13.7. Note that canals or ditches ("creeks") are carrying water approximately along the contours, rather than across them.

345

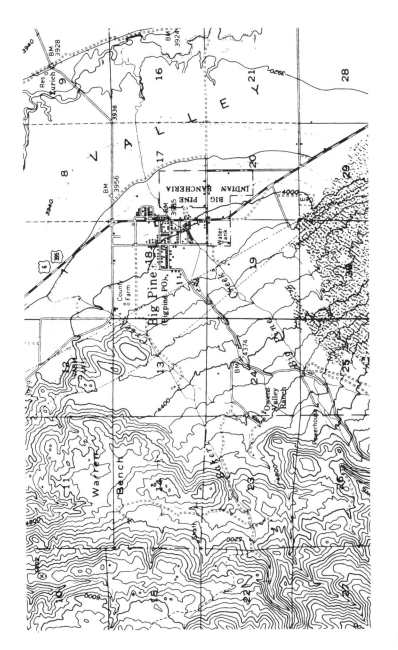

Figure 13.6. Big Pine locality as depicted on U.S.G.S. Big Pine 15' quadrangle, 1950. Note direction of the contours and compare with direction of flow of irrigation ditches shown in Fig. 13.5.

size and spacing of these "creeks" that they are irrigation ditches or canals representing the much-divided stream of Baker Creek. Also indicated on Von Schmidt's map are some "dry ravines," one of which is apparently the dry channel of Baker Creek. Von Schmidt recorded these "creeks" only where they crossed the section lines he was surveying. He clearly indicates them entering the northwest corner of S. 18, T.9S, R.34E M.D.M. and exiting the southeast quarter of the section a mile away. The irrigation system here was apparently so large that he did not recognize it for what it was. These are not natural stream channels; it is not the pattern of braided stream channels to be so evenly spaced or so uniform in size as Von Schmidt indicates (Table 13.1). Besides, they are shown carrying water across the natural slope of the land, not down it (Fig. 13.6). There is no question that the channels are man-made ditches or canals and that Von Schmidt mapped and recorded portions of the irrigation system at *tovowah matü*. The notes are dated October 18, 1856, indicating that the dam was still intact and irrigation still being carried out that late in the fall. Apparently the harvest had not yet occurred.

Figure 13.7 shows the irrigated area near Big Pine as recorded by Steward on the basis of informant knowledge. The figure is based on Steward's "Ethnographical map of Owens Valley" (1933:Map 2), and is in close agreement with the map of Von Schmidt drawn 75 years earlier. Figure 13.8 is most informative since it clearly shows the irrigation system west of Big Pine as drawn by Steward's informant Jack Stewart (Steward 1933:326). Clearly indicated in Stewart's map is a vast irrigation system along a north tributary of Big Pine Creek (Baker Creek) involving main canals and many small laterals. The significance of this map has remained unrecognized for more than 40 years, but it provides some of the best information on the distribution of water by means of small ditches or canals in irrigated plots in Owens Valley.

The next reference to irrigation in the Von Schmidt survey records is at *panatü* 'waterplace' (?), just west of Owens River in the vicinity of Fish Springs and Tinnemaha Creek, about eight miles south of Big Pine. Steward did not specifically report irrigation there, but he did indicate (see Fig. 13.7) that *nahavita* and *tüpüsi*[a] were abundant. We believe from examination of the records that irrigation was carried out with water from Tinnemaha Creek. Figure 13.9 shows "creeks" recorded by Von Schmidt in the area to the south of Fish Springs and just west of Owens River. The field notes contained no information specifically describing ditches, but, as in the case of Baker Creek, the creeks are probably irrigation ditches. Table 2 gives the widths of the ditches and the distances between them.

Table 13.1

EXTRACTS FROM THE NOTES OF A.W. VON SCHMIDT DESCRIBING IRRIGATION DITCHES OR CANALS ON BAKER CREEK, NEAR BIG PINE, OWENS VALLEY, CALIFORNIA, OCTOBER, 1856

(1 chain = 66 feet; 1 link = 7.92 inches)

Chains	Notation					
	(West on boundary between S. 7, 18, T. 9S, R. 34E)					
52.00	creek		5 links wide, course SE			
54.50	"	10	"	"	"	S by E
56.25	slough	20	"	"	"	"
64.70	creek	5	"	"	"	"
67.00	"	3	"	"	"	"
69.00	"	2	"	"	"	"
72.30	"	5	"	"	"	"
74.20	"	10	"	"	"	"
	(West on boundary between S. 18, 19, T. 9S, R. 34E)					
4.51	creek		5 links wide, course S by E			
10.00	"	"	"	"	"	E by S
13.70	"	12	"	"	"	"
16.80	"	5	"	"	"	"
18.71	"	8	"	"	"	"
24.71	"	20	"	"	"	SE
33.71	"	8	"	"	"	"
	(North on boundary between S. 17, 18, T. 9S, R. 34E)					
3.60	creek		15 links wide, course E			
5.75	"	14	"	"	"	"
9.60	"	5	"	"	"	"
15.50	"	8	"	"	"	"
28.37	"	31	"	"	"	"
	(North on boundary between S. 19, 20, T. 9S, R. 34E)					
48.10	creek		3 links wide, course E			
56.20	"	5	"	"	"	"
63.00	"	3	"	"	"	"
73.40	"	5	"	"	"	"
74.60	"	5	"	"	"	"
75.95	"	5	"	"	"	"
76.20	"	5	"	"	"	"
79.00	"	5	"	"	"	"

348

Here, then, would appear to be the record of another irrigation system of sizeable proportions. Moreover, there appears to be a clear understanding on the part of the aboriginal engineers of the proper size of the irrigation ditches, since many of them are about 40 inches wide. There are also regularities in the spacing of ditches, as can be seen in Table 13.2. A dry stream channel, perhaps representing that from which the water was diverted, is also shown.

Table 13.2

EXTRACTS FROM THE NOTES OF A. W. VON SCHMIDT
DESCRIBING IRRIGATION DITCHES OR CANALS
AT TINNEMAHA CREEK, OWENS VALLEY, CALIFORNIA,
OCTOBER, 1856

(1 chain = 66 feet; 1 link = 7.92 inches)

Chains	Notation	
		(North on boundary between S. 14, 15, T. 10S, R. 34E)
14.10	creek	10 links wide, course E
23.30	"	5 " " " "
29.00	"	5 " " " "
31.80	"	5 " " " "
		(East on boundary between S. 15, 22, T. 10S, R. 34E)
13.60	creek	5 links wide, course NE
15.40	"	5 " " " "
17.60	"	5 " " " "
28.20	"	5 " " " "
31.15	"	5 " " " "
33.00	"	5 " " " "
39.20	"	5 " " " "

Irrigation is again described by Von Schmidt in the vicinity of Black Rock Spring. While passing east on the boundary between S. 12 and 13, T. 12S, R. 34E, on October 1, 1856, Von Schmidt commented: "Note: These swampy places are *coursed* by the Indians by turning the larger streams descending from the mountains into the level plains for the purpose of raising grass to eat" (emphasis ours). The mention of coursing the swampy places recalls the situation on Baker Creek, where the

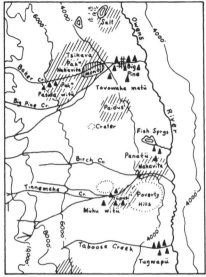

Figure 13.7. Location and extent of irrigation on Baker Creek, near Big Pine, as indicated by Steward (1933:Map 2). Irrigated land indicated by vertical hachure. Redrawn from Steward (1933:Map 2).

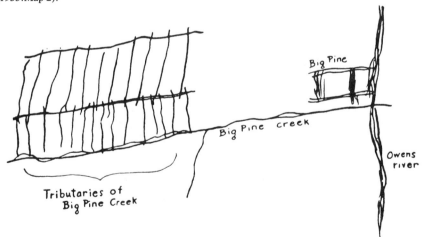

Figure 13.8. "Map of Big Pine Drawn by Jack Stewart." Steward was an informant of Julian Steward and drew this map, which clearly shows the irrigation system on Baker Creek as he remembered it about 1930. The "Tributaries of Big Pine Creek" are the irrigation ditches representing the divided channel of Baker Creek. Copyright © 1933 by the Regents of the University of California; reprinted by permission of the University of California Press.

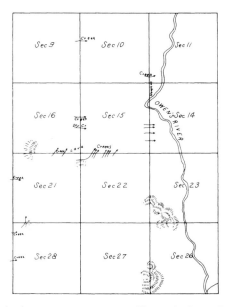

Figure 13.9. Paiute irrigation system at *panatü*, near Tinnemaha Creek, Owens Valley, California. Unknowingly mapped by A. W. Von Schmidt, 1856.

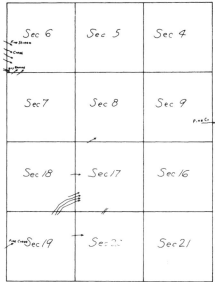

Figure 13.10. Probably irrigation system unknowingly mapped by A. W. Von Schmidt on Oak Creek (Old Fort Independence), Section 6, and Independence Creek, Section 18, T. 13S, R. 35E. Redrawn from 1856 township plat.

surveyors recorded no less than eight "creeks" (irrigation ditches) running parallel to one another and carrying water across the slope, rather than down it. It is not clear from the notes whether irrigation water was derived from Black Rock Spring or from Sawmill Creek, which reaches the floor of Owens Valley at this spot.

Proceeding down the valley another half-dozen miles to the site of Old Fort Independence, we find another apparent record of irrigation with four well-spaced streams, as well as a "dry ravine" entering the SW quarter of S. 6, T. 13S, R.35E. This would seem to document irrigation on Oak Creek (*tsak:'ca witü* 'oak place'), as indicated by Steward (1938:51) (see Fig. 13.10).

Two miles south in the SE quarter of S. 18 of the same township, at Independence Creek (*natakà: matü* '[unidentified plant] place'), four parallel streams are indicated. Steward (1938:51) reported that irrigation was practiced at Independence Creek.

Fig. 13.11 presents a summary of the findings of A.W. Von Schmidt as interpreted here and the additional occurrence reported by Steward in the vicinity of Freeman Creek and Keough Hot Springs. It can be seen that from Independence Creek on the south to Rock Creek on the north, a total distance of 57 miles along the axis of Owens Valley, there are 10 recorded and nicely spaced instances of irrigation from tributaries of Owens River. All of these developments occurred on the western side of the valley, where the many streams brought down abundant water from the snows of the Sierra Nevada. In elevation, the localities range from 4000 to 5000 feet. These data fully corroborate the reports of Steward on the distribution and extent of irrigation in Owens Valley. From the discussion above, it is apparent that whatever the plants irrigated ("grass," "roots," and *tüpüsi* are indicated), the entire Owens Valley irrigation system involved large plots totalling multiples of square miles. Dams must have been used in all instances to divert the water out of the stream beds into canals, which were further divided and carried across the plots to be watered. Where information is available, it indicates that many of the canals or ditches were about 40 inches wide, but they were often much wider, and sometimes narrower. Whether additional laterals were used to further distribute the water is not known, but the map drawn by Steward's Paiute informant, Jack Stewart, would seem to suggest that they were (Fig. 13.8). This would have aided in the watering of large plots.

352

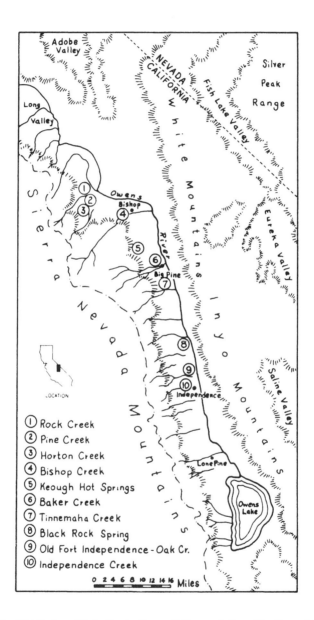

Figure 13.11. Distribution of irrigation in Owens Valley, as indicated by Steward (1930, 1933, 1938) and Von Schmidt (unpublished records). Redrawn from Steward (1933:Map 1).

Later Historical Accounts

On July 5, 1858, a party of prospectors led by David McKenzie set out from Los Angeles for Owens Valley. This group learned from the Indians that gold was being mined by prospectors at Mono Lake, and several of its members pushed on into that region. These gold ventures are described in a brief article in the *Los Angeles Star* of August 21, 1858, which provides additional recorded data on irrigation in Owens Valley:

> ...About the center from one lake to the other [between Owens and Mono lakes], there is a tribe of fine looking Indians, tall and well made, having features quite different from the Indians on Owen's Lake. They are an active, industrious race, irrigate the lands and raise a kind of pea, which is their principal food. Farther on, the party came to another tribe of Indians, resembling them, tall stalworth [sic] fellows, with nose straight. They also cultivate the land, turning the river by ditches for the purposes of irrigation. Several small streams descend from the mountains on the west and empty into the river. Where these Indians live, the land is good, and in the upper part of the valley there is plenty of clover. In this valley of Owen's River, there are probably 2,000 Indians....

The word "industrious" as applied to the Paiute of Owens Valley keeps cropping up in later accounts of these people. Throughout the nineteenth century, Anglo accounts of Indian lifeways frequently used this word to describe those tribes or groups which were engaged in agriculture.

The presence of prospecting parties in Owens Valley in the summer of 1858 may have stimulated the visit of an Owens Lake delegation of Indians to the Fort Tejon Agency. On August 20, 1858, Indian Agent J.R. Vineyard wrote to his superiors:

> A delegation of Indians from the region of Owens Lake, east of the Sierra, visited the [San Sebastian] reservation a short time since. The people of that region, so far as I can learn, number about 1500. The delegation asked assistance to put in crops next season, also someone to instruct them in agriculture, etc. I would respectfully invite your attention to the subject, as they seem to be very sincere in their solicitations [Chalfant 1933:123].

In nineteenth-century accounts, the terms Owens Lake and Owens Valley were often used synonymously. This report may therefore refer to the Indians of Owens Valley seeking to learn the culture of European crops like wheat and barley, or of native American crops like corn, which they had never grown. It would then indicate that the Owens Valley Paiute, who were themselves engaged in large-scale agronomic pursuits, felt that they would need special instruction to shift over to crops being grown by the white man. Only a people aware of the different requirements in the growing of plants would be likely to ask for specialized instruction in addition to crop seeds. Alternatively, since irrigation does not seem to have been practiced at Owens Lake, but only in the Owens Valley from Independence north, the report may indicate that the Indians of Owens Lake, who, for reasons to be suggested later, never adopted irrigation of wild crops, elected to attempt European agriculture.

Owens Valley irrigation was mentioned again in the *Los Angeles Star* of August 27, 1859, which reported that a detachment of soldiers under a Captain Davidson had marched from Fort Tejon to Owens Valley on a search for Indian horse thieves, and had vindicated the Indians of that region as not being responsible for horse raids. Instead, the *Star* correspondent, who accompanied the expedition and signed himself "Quis," reported the Paiutes to be "quiet, industrious, friendly, and altogether reliable." The *Star* account again describes the vast scope of irrigation activities in Owens Valley:

> Large tracts of land are here irrigated by the natives to secure the growth of the grass seeds and grass nuts--a small tuberous root of fine taste and nutritious qualities, which grows here in abundance. Their ditches for irrigation are in some cases carried for miles, displaying as much accuracy and judgment as if laid out by an engineer, and distributing the water with great regularity over their grounds, and this, too, without the aid of a single agricultural implement. They are totally ignorant of agriculture, and depend entirely on the natural resources of the country for food and clothing [*Los Angeles Star*, Aug. 27, 1859, p. 2].

The authors were led to the *Star* article on Captain Davidson's expedition of 1859 through an excerpt published by Guinn (1917:41-47).

Further effort led to our discovery in the U.S. National Archives of the then unpublished report of Captain John W. Davidson on his military reconnaissance to Owens Valley (Wilke and Lawton 1976). Several points should be stressed about the Davidson report. First, previous expeditions through the valley had traversed it rapidly without stopping to observe its inhabitants. Davidson's party was the first to carefully study the lifeway of the Owens Valley Paiute. His orders specifically instructed him to do so. Although these people apparently knew a few Spanish words, Davidson was unable to communicate with them except through an Indian interpreter. He found the people of the valley in a relatively pristine aboriginal state with almost no evidence of acculturation other than an awareness that they would have to come to terms with the outside forces moving in on them. (Recall the Von Schmidt survey three years earlier.) They possessed no horses, no firearms, and no metal tools. As yet there were no white settlers in Owens Valley. In his report, Davidson twice referred to the practice of irrigation:

> ...They expressed a desire to have a military post among them, as well as they could understand its nature, to live under the protection of our Government, and to have seeds and some simple instruments of Agriculture furnished them. They have already some idea of tilling the ground, as the *ascequias* [sic] which they have made with the labor of their rude hands for miles in extent, and the care which they bestow upon their fields of grass-nuts abundantly show. Wherever the water touches this soil of disintegrated granite, it acts like the wand of an Enchanter, and it may with truth be said that these Indians have made some portions of their Country, which otherwise were Desert, to bloom and blossom as the rose [Wilke and Lawton 1976:19-20].[10]

Davidson goes on to provide a rather clear botanical description of the "grass-nuts," which Steward (1930:150) believed to be *Brodiaea*

---

[10] Ascequias (sic) is Davidson's term, and was employed throughout the Southwest during this period, not only by Spanish-speaking people, but by American explorers, Army engineers, and white settlers.

capitata. He apparently described one of the two primary wild crops grown in Owens Valley, and stated that the wild crops were planted.

> These Indians subsist upon the flesh of such game as they can kill, the Deer, Antelope, & Rabbit, upon the seeds of various grasses, the Acorn, Pinon-nut, & the Tuber of a species of nutritious grass of which our horses were very fond. Whole fields of this grass, miles in extent are irrigated with *great care* [italics ours], yielding an abundant harvest of what is one of their principal articles of food. The tuber is about the size of a large marrowfat pea, has a coarse rind or covering, & tastes something like the Chincapin. They are reproduced by *planting* [italics ours] [Wilke and Lawton 1976:29]

Another botanical description of an important wild crop plant grown in Owens Valley and a second plant of apparently lesser significance is provided by Alexander S. Taylor (1861a) in his *Indianology of California*. Taylor published the report of a correspondent on the *San Francisco Evening Bulletin*, who made a trip through Owens Valley in June, 1861. At this time, white stockmen were already making inroads on the valley, and white settlers were building cabins near the present Independence and in Round Valley (Chalfant 1933:147). The *Bulletin* correspondent also referred to the Indians of Round Valley as "industrious." In describing the numerous creeks coming down from the mountains on the west side of the valley, the correspondent wrote:

> ...Some of them are large, forming branches of the river; others, mere rills, losing themselves in the dry and porous earth, irrigating a considerable patch about the place where they disappear. Most of these streams are shallow, and after leaving the mountain-ravines, have banks but a foot or two high. This admits of their being easily turned aside for irrigation, a purpose to which they are extensively applied by the Indians. These tribes cultivate a small white root of an oval shape, and the size of a cherry. It grows like an onion, sending up three blades that bear a blue lily-shaped flower. When roasted, it looks and tastes like the yam, being very palatable and nutritious. It strongly resembles the root so much in use among the Indians of

Oregon and British Columbia, called the *Camass* [*sic*]. Besides this, these Indians have a species of wild onion (amole) with a variety of other roots which they cultivate for food. In irrigating they conduct the water some distance through ditches and little acqueducts [*sic*] made of dirt. The surplus water flowing over the land below these patches of roots has caused much grass to grow along these creeks, consisting of clover, blue-joint, and bunch grass. Cattle are very fond of these and fatten upon them rapidly [Taylor 1861a:8].

Taylor (1861b) again speaks of irrigation by the Owens Valley Paiute, but presents no new data. During the Paiute Indian War in 1862, Colonel Warren Wasson (Wassen [*sic*] 1862) stated: "The Indians are fighting to hold possession of their lands, which they have irrigated and subsisted on for many years, and are jealous of white settlers coming into their country." Elsewhere, Wasson (1862) observed: "These Indians have dug ditches and irrigated nearly all the arable land in that section of the country, and live by its products" (see also Angel 1881:166). In a bloody skirmish between the Paiutes and 60 white cattle "graziers" under a colonel Mayfield on March 28, 1862, the white men lost the battle and retreated to an Indian irrigation ditch, employing it as a trench, until they could escape under cover of darkness (Wassen [*sic*] 1862; Angel 1881:166).

In addition to the historical accounts presented above, scattered data indicate that other Indian groups of the Great Basin practiced some irrigation of wild plants. Angel (1881) provided the following information on irrigation in Walker Valley, Nevada:

When the first white settlers went into the Walker Valley they found the Indians irrigating portions of it to promote the growth of an edible root which formed a great portion of their living. As far as is known this was the only cultivation of the soil previous to the operations of the Mormons in Carson Valley subsequent to 1850 [Angel 1881:131].

Catherine Fowler (personal communication) reported to the authors that she has a note from a woman of Walker River, who spent some time in the Smith and Mason valleys and was told by Indians there that a plant known as *mahavitu'u* (probably Steward's *nahavita*) was watered from a natural stream to keep it "moist." It should be noted that the Northern Paiute band that inhabited the Smith and Mason valleys and the upper Walker River in southwestern Nevada were known as the *Tövusi-dökadö*, meaning "grass-nut eaters" (O.C. Stewart 1951:363).

In the cultural elements list for the Nevada Shoshone, Steward (1941:281) recorded one informant as saying that all villages in Snake and Spring Valleys near Ely, Nevada, irrigated wild plants. A second informant stated that there were still native irrigation ditches near Ely. Steward's (1941:281) informant also reported irrigation of wild plants, the building of dams and ditches, and the election of a head irrigator among the Northern Paiute of Fish Lake Valley, Nevada. Finally, Steward (1970:123) also noted that during litigation over water rights "a few years ago" the Paiute of Pyramid Lake argued that they had irrigated with certain streams before the coming of the white man.

Patch (1951) reported discovering what he thought to be the remains of ancient irrigation ditches leading out onto a Pleistocene lakebed in Eureka Valley, which lies in the desert to the east of Owens Valley. The authors have viewed these "ditches" and believe their archaeological examination would be fruitful. Sullivan (1974) also reported the presence of rock alignments in Hidden Valley, Nevada, which he hypothesized might have been used to retard rainfall runoff and encourage the growth of grasses on the valley floor.

On July 11, 1863, following the termination of the Indian War that occurred after the white man began taking over Owens Valley and grazing his cattle in Paiute fields, more than 900 Owens Valley Paiutes were removed to San Sebastian Reservation near Fort Tejon. Many other Indians fled into the mountains. Gradually, over the next few years, many of the Indian people returned to Owens Valley. Most of their irrigation ditches were already being used by white settlers. Whether some of the Owens Valley people resumed their irrigation practices after their return to the valley is unknown. The authors have been unable to find any historical accounts of Indian irrigation of wild plants after 1863. Although irrigation in Owens Valley may have continued in some districts after 1863 on a lesser scale, it would appear that the system had largely broken down as a result of white settlement and the use of their fields for grazing and of the irrigation ditches for growing introduced crop plants.

TIME DEPTH INFERRED FROM HISTORICAL ACCOUNTS

Historical accounts of ditch irrigation in Owens Valley describe the practice as it existed from 1855 to 1862, during the period just prior to white takeover of the valley. Although apparently not realized by Steward, information provided in his own writings extends the practice back to probably at least thirty years earlier. In his *Two Paiute Autobiographies*, Steward (1934) stated that his informant, Sam Newland, born at *pitana patü*, was at the time of writing about one hundred years of age. In describing his boyhood, Newland related that the husband of one of his older sisters "had the job of irrigating *nahavita* above Bishop" (Steward 1934:432). He also said that during his early boyhood "when spring came, the people got together for a big feast, *tuwapa'it*, and elected the irrigator, *tuvaijü*, for the coming summer....They took a vote and elected my brother-in-law again, and told him to start the water" (Steward 1934:434).

Irrigation was thus fully institutionalized by 1845, and probably much earlier. The miles of irrigation ditches described in the accounts dating back to 1858 could not have been built overnight by a people lacking metal tools. When Sam Newland was still a young boy, "there was a big dance ('fandango') at *nügatuhava* just below the dam on 'Paiute ditch'" (Steward 1934:433). The ditch was thus in use by about 1845. It seems reasonable to conclude that the system of ditch irrigation as practiced up and down Owens Valley was very well developed by at least 1840. Moreover, there is no reason to assume that irrigation began in the Owens Valley simultaneously at each of the settlements as the result of some massive communal construction project. More likely it started at one settlement and was gradually adopted by other districts which lent themselves to the development and use of irrigation. Even from the most conservative point of view--assuming the technology was worked out rapidly and other settlements quickly adopted irrigation also--the system would have required a minimum of twenty years to spread out over the valley. Thus irrigation in Owens Valley has to extend back to at least 1820, almost a decade and a half before secularization of the Spanish missions, when many California Indians who had learned agriculture from the padres returned to their homelands. It seems probable, however, that Owens Valley irrigation dates far back into the aboriginal period.

TIME DEPTH INFERRED THROUGH LINGUISTICS

Lawton (1968), in presenting circumstantial evidence for the aboriginal practice of domesticated plant agriculture among the Cahuilla, reported the presence of a native agricultural terminology. He noted that the Cahuilla possessed both native crop words and words relating to the technique of crop-growing (Lawton 1968:16-20). In examining other Indian groups along the California coast, who had been under Mission influence, Lawton found that native vocabularies (e.g., Gabrielino, Luiseño, Cupeño) contained only Spanish loan words or derivatives for crop plants and agricultural practices. Thus, for example, the Spanish word *elote* for "sweet or green corn" was rendered as *looti* among the Cupeño (Hill and Nolasquez 1973:184).

In the case of the Owens Valley Paiute, Steward provides three words associated with the growing of wild plant crops: *tuvaijü^a*, head irrigator; *tüva^{ya}dut*, to irrigate; and *pavado*, the irrigator's pole. Catherine Fowler (personal communication) informs us that these are Paiute words and not derived from the Spanish. Possibly, a review of unpublished field notes of linguists working on the various Northern Paiute and Nevada Shoshone groups will elicit still more words related to irrigation of wild plants such as the words for "ditch," "fallowing," and "dam." We suggest, however, that the presence of these few recorded words in the Paiute vocabulary and the fact that the well-known Spanish term *zanjero* for irrigator did not enter their language provides at least some confirmation that irrigation did not diffuse from the Spanish missions. Whether future analyses of Paiute vocabularies can throw more light on dating the origins of irrigation in Owens Valley we must leave to linguists working in that area.

IDENTIFICATION OF THE TWO MAIN WILD CROPS

On the basis of material gathered in our literature survey, the authors set out to establish the identity of the two primary wild crop plants which Steward (1933:247) said the natives call *tüpüsi^a* and *nahavita*. Steward identified *tüpüsi^a* as *Brodiaea capitata* and *nahavita* as *Eleocharis* sp. How closely Steward worked with botanists on his plant identifications we don't know, but we immediately encountered problems with his identifications.

Steward's *nahavita*

Steward's (1933:245) *nahavita* was described by him as "having a number of bulbs." His identification appears to be in error, because *Eleocharis* sp. do not produce a number of tubers or bulbs. Such a description appears better suited to the wild-hyacinth or blue dicks, formerly *Brodiaea capitata* and currently classified as *Dichelostemma pulchella* (Fig. 13.12). This was the species Steward identified as *tüpüsi*, sometimes called "grassnuts" or "nut-grass" by laymen. Steward gave no season for the harvesting of this plant. Wild-hyacinth blooms in the spring with violet flowers and probably would have been harvested in late May or early June (Munz 1965:1385). Thus the *Bulletin* correspondent who visited Owens Valley in June, 1861 might have observed the harvest of this plant. His description of a primary wild crop plant as "like an onion, sending up three blades that bear a blue lily-shaped flower" (Taylor 1861a:8) agrees with our identification of Steward's *nahavita* as the wild-hyacinth. Catherine Fowler (personal communication) notes that an unidentified plant used by the Indians of Mason and Smith valleys, Nevada, is referred to as *mahavitu'u* and is probably the *nahavita* of Owens Valley. She adds: "It seems to me likely that this may be your Brodiaea [*D. pulchella*] and that it is probably also Angel's 'bulb root' [Angel 1881:131]."

Steward's *tüpüsi*

Steward's *tüpüsi* or taboose grass was also clearly misidentified, since his plant list showed it as gathered in the fall after the dams were destroyed (Steward 1933:245). One of his informants, Sam Newland, also mentioned his mother going to gather *tüpüsi* in the fall "after my father's death" (Steward 1934:433). Since wild-hyacinth (Steward's *tüpüsi*) is not a fall plant, it was necessary to reconsider this identification and attempt to identify the tubers Davidson saw being gathered from a grass-like plant in August of 1859 (Wilke and Lawton 1976:29).

Donald Bell of Big Pine, descendant of a pioneer family, identified the "grass-nut" of Davidson as taboose grass or taboose,[11] common names still in wide use in Owens Valley. DeDecker identified taboose grass as

[11] The common names of "grass-nuts," "nut-grass," taboose grass," and "taboose" are employed interchangeably by different writers. Steward's identification of the plant as Broadiaea capitata can probably be ascribed to the fact that it is also sometimes called "grass-nut."

yellow nut-grass (*Cyperus esculentus* L.) (Fig. 13.13), also sometimes called chufa, earth almond, and Zulu nuts (Sturtevant 1919:230).[12] Stanley Miller of the Fort Independence Indian Reservation made it possible to obtain yellow nut-grass tubers for nutrient analysis. Later, the authors discovered that Train, Henrichs, and Archer (1974:40) had identified "*too-boozie*" as the Paiute Indian name for yellow nut-grass in a report prepared many years earlier for the Works Progress Administration. Chalfant (1933:77) had also speculated that "taboose" was a member of the sedge family, but questioned its identity as yellow nut-grass. Unpublished field notes of Mark Kerr compiled by DeDecker also identified "*te-posie*" as tubers used for food and "for making milk as a beverage." Kerr's notes on Owens Valley plant names also listed "*tupu si*" as the name for wild-hyacinth.

Figure 13.12. Wild-hyacinth (*Dichelostemma pulchella* [Salisb.] Heller), from Plate 91, Fig. F of *A Flora of Southern California*, by Phillip A. Munz. Copyright © 1974 by the Regents of the University of California; reprinted by permission of the University of California Press.

---

[12] DeDecker had discovered many years previous that Steward's identification was in error and had considered publishing a short paper on this subject.

Figure 13.13. Yellow nut-grass (*Cyperus esculentus L.*) from *A Flora of the Marshes of California*, by Herbert L. Mason; plant about 1/2 to 2/3 actual size, tubers slightly reduced. Copyright © 1957 by the Regents of the University of California; reprinted by permission of the University of California Press.

There thus still appears to be some linguistic confusion surrounding the terms *nahavita* and *tüpüsi*ʸ, although we believe we have correctly identified the two primary wild crop plants. Catherine Fowler (personal communication) stated that the *tïb'uzi* (*tüpüsi*ʸ) is "really a 'food name' rather than a plant name," adding that the semantic focus among most Northern Paiute is on the product, rather than the plant.[13] Both *nahavita* and *tüpüsi*ʸ may therefore be names not for the plants themselves, but for the plant part which was eaten (i.e., corms and tubers, respectively).

It is significant that Steward's elderly informants, who recalled the period of Owens Valley irrigation, should have talked of plots containing two principal plants, *tüpüsi*ʸ and *nahavita*. Perhaps with the loss of knowledge of cultivation practices among the Owens Valley Paiute, the better-known term *tüpüsi*ʸ, adopted by white settlers as "taboose grass" and applied as a name to Taboose Creek and Taboose Pass, came to be synonymous among later generations of Indians for various tubers and corms, including that of *Dichelostemma pulchella*. Certainly, some collaborative linguistic and ethnobotanical research is needed here.

Although often treated in floras as an Old World plant, *C. esculentus*, a member of the sedge family, is known throughout the world. Professor L.G. Holms, an authority on weed control and the family Cyperaceae, informed us that it probably reached the New World very early (personal communication).[14] Often a noxious weed along irrigation ditches and in agricultural fields, yellow nut-grass has a range from cismontane California to Alaska. Like all weeds, which follow the disturbed habitations of man, it may have moved down across North America in early migrations of man over the Alaskan land bridge. During winter dormancy, this *Cyperus* species is cold-hardy and has no problem surviving in Owens Valley. A less cold-hardy worldwide species, *C. rotundus* L., is common throughout southern California and the San Joaquin Valley (Munz 1965:1426). The plant is widespread today as a weed in agricultural fields

---

[13] In her letter, Dr. Fowler notes that throughout Norther Paiute territory in Nevada the term tïb'uzi or tïpuzi is everywhere synonymous with Cyperus esculentus. She writes: "There does seem to be a common name confusion about 'nuts' or 'nut grass' or 'ground nuts,' however, which might be part of the same problem Steward was getting...". Northern Shoshone with whom she talked were unfamiliar with irrigation of the plant.

[14] Holms is currently working with other scholars on the definitive work on the Cyperaceae.

in Imperial Valley, although Castetter and Bell (1951) did not record its use among the Yumans of the Colorado River. They did report the use of *C. esculentus* and *C. ferax* L.C. Rich as a food plant among the Yuma, Mohave, and Maricopa, where in all likelihood these weeds were closely associated with the crop complexes of these agricultural peoples.

THE CONCEPT OF INCIPIENT AGRICULTURE

Anthropologists and others interested in the processes by which man moved from hunting and gathering to agriculture have created a semantic jungle of terms for initial stages in that evolution. One hacks through the literature, chopping desperately against such rarely defined terms as "incipient agriculture," "proto-agriculture," "quasi-agriculture," "semi-cultivation," "environmental manipulation," and even Heizer's (1958) "semi-agricultural," which at least had the virtue of being concrete and eminently understandable in the context in which he used it. Even the terms "horticulture" and "agriculture" are used interchangeably or mistakenly by scholars who would profit from sharing their ideas more frequently with agricultural scientists, who often rightfully view us with amusement.[15]

Domestication of plants is the result of agricultural practices and is always an on-going process. Through agricultural practices, man manipulates the natural selection factors operating in plants, favoring those genetic characteristics adapted to domestication. Nor is domestication ever complete in the sense that it stops. Although many crops such as corn are cultigens (extreme domesticates, the origins of which are obscured in antiquity), and cannot survive without planting by man, they are still being further modified by agricultural scientists (farmers, if you will) to achieve improved breeding characteristics. Other crop plants have been genetically modified by man over time without becoming domesticated to such a degree. Some of our modern crop pants (lettuce, oats, potatoes, and perhaps certain varieties of grapes and berries) under the right environ-

[15] We have found that agricultural scientists are often highly knowledgeable about anthropological concerns related to agriculture and cooperative in sharing their ideas. The authors confess that they have not always been immune to contributing to the semantic confusion surrounding "incipient agriculture" and similar terms. Sometimes it has been easier to use those terms as employed by one's predecessors than to try to clear up the confusion. Several times we have been taken to task severely by our friends the plant scientists.

mental conditions would revert to the feral or "wild" state if civilization disappeared tomorrow. Both the cultigens and those plants which could continue to survive without man's efforts are "crop" plants insofar as they are products of agriculture.

The Owens Valley Indians have been viewed as practicing something called "incipient agriculture." Even Steward (1930:150) wrote that they merely "intensified by irrigation what nature had already provided." He added that they were not engaged in agriculture because they did not "till the soil, plant, or cultivate." Ignoring the problem of whether tillage is necessary to agriculture (even agricultural scientists have differing views on its value for some crops and consider tillage primarily a weed control measure), the fact is that the Owens Valley Paiute did engage in tillage. Their digging sticks were used to turn the soil over to a depth of six inches or more in harvesting the underground plant parts of their two primary crops. While they did not possess the plow, neither did any of the other agricultural peoples of the Americas.

Steward's oldest Paiute informants were very young men at the time white settlers began moving into the valley. Soon afterwards, they became embroiled in the Indian war which led to the abandonment of the Owens Valley irrigation system. It is doubtful that these informants possessed more than a rudimentary knowledge of the system of vegeculture or root-crop cultivation practiced by their people--and vegeculture entails a very complex ecosystem (Flannery 1973:273). Neither of the oldest informants had worked as head irrigators. They may have had only a vague knowledge of harvesting methods, which were always carried out by women. We cannot know, for example, to what extent the women harvesters may have engaged in weed control of intrusive plants while gathering the two primary crops in their field plots. Certainly, Davidson in 1859 speaks of irrigation as being practiced with "great care" (Wilke and Lawton 1976:29). Davidson also reported that the grass-nuts were reproduced by "planting," which contradicts Steward's informants (Wilke and Lawton 1976:29). We will probably never know whether the Owens Valley Indians engaged in planting, but it seems evident that something resembling planting took place. The smaller corms of wild-hyacinth were probably returned to the earth during harvesting to ensure continued reproduction. Many of the smaller tubers of yellow nut-grass would become detached from the roots of the plant and remain in the ground during digging. Others probably fell from the roots to the surface of the ground. One method of controlling *Cyperus* as a weed in agricultural fields is to till the ground and bring the tubers to the surface, where they die in the sun

(Lowell Jordan, personal communication). People who exercised "great care" in the irrigation of their fields could scarcely have remained unaware of this fact. In all likelihood, the soil was tamped over detached tubers and corms after digging to ensure their continued propagation. The women harvesters may even have exercised some selectivity over the plants grown, eliminating less palatable specimens and thus transmitting improved genetic characteristics to future harvests.

The authors are unsure as to what Steward mean by the word "cultivate." Certainly he did not mean tillage, because he also noted that the Paiute lacked a knowledge of tillage (Steward 1930:150). If by cultivation he meant the nurturing or tendance of plants--one definition --then it clearly existed in the care that the Owens Valley Paiute bestowed on their fields. This was exemplified in the Paiute system of alternate irrigation between plots at *pitana patü*, which Steward hypothesized as designed to "enhance natural seeding." Walter Reuther (personal communication) has suggested that alternate irrigation of the field plots probably had two purposes. First, harvesting of fields every other year would probably have ensured a higher yield of tubers and larger tubers. At the same time, irrigation every other year may have served as a means of ecological land management. It would have decreased the possibility of unwanted vegetation invading the fields and crowding out the two principal crops, thereby reducing their productivity.

It is time to assert that the Owens Valley Paiute were engaged in the practice of agriculture. They had developed a complex farming system on an agronomic scale that required substantial communal labor. This farming system involved a tremendous amount of work both in the initial phases of construction and laying out of the vast system of ditches and canals and in the annual dam-building, irrigation, and harvest. It was a farming system fully as sophisticated as that of many societies in southeast Asia and South America that are engaged in vegeculture of manioc, yams, taro, and other root crops. Whether or not the plants irrigated underwent some genetic modifications as a result of the care they received we may never know; but domestication is a result of agriculture, not its prerequisite.[16]

---

[16] The Oxford English Dictionary, the recognized authoritative work on English, defines agriculture first as "The science and art of cultivating the soil...." It has two primary definitions for cultivation. One is "tillage." The second definition is as follows: "The bestowing of labor and care upon a plant, so as to develop and improve its qualities...."

YELLOW NUT-GRASS AS A CROP PLANT

For those who may still feel some reluctance in agreeing that the Owens Valley Paiute were agricultural, it can be pointed out that yellow nut-grass (*Cyperus esculentus*) is often considered a weed, but under the common name of *chufas* it has a respectable history as a crop plant grown under irrigation since ancient times (Killinger and Stokes 1951:5). Mummified bodies in upper Egypt dating to about 3500-4000 B.C. have been found to have the remains of yellow nut-grass tubers in their intestines, along with barley chaff (Netolitzky 1911:953-956). Further studies of mummified bodies yielded remains of yellow nut-grass tubers and various cereal grasses, with the researcher suggesting that some of the plants consumed may have been cultivated (Netolitzky 1912). Schweinfurth (1884:315) reported that among a variety of offerings found in a vault at Thebes dating to the twelfth dynasty (2200 to 2500 B.C.) there were grains of barley and wheat, tubers of yellow nut-grass and other vegetable products and fruits. While it is not known if yellow nut-grass was grown as a crop plant in Egypt during this period, the plant has been cultivated from very early times for use of its tubers as a food delicacy and for its oil content (Sturtevant 1919:230).

The chufa was distributed from the United States Patent Office in 1854 for culture in gardens (Sturtevant 1911:230). Cultivation of chufas has long been carried out and is still practiced today in many parts of southern Europe, Africa, the Near East, and England. Lesant (1822) noted cultivation of chufas in southern France as early as 1822. In Germany, chufa tubers were brought to the table as a dessert in the nineteenth century (Sturtevant 1911:230). In Constantinople, the tubers were eaten raw or made into a conserve. In Italy and Egypt, the fatty oil extracted from chufas was used as a food and in the manufacture of soap (Killinger and Stokes 1951:5). In Spain, chufas are grown under irrigation even today, and a sizeable industry has developed to exploit a milky-looking beverage known as *horchatas de chufas* (Walter Reuther, personal communication; Killinger and Stokes 1951:5). This beverage may be similar to the "milk" which Mark Kerr (unpublished) reported as having been made by the Owens Valley Paiute.

The authors have been unable to find any published data comparing cultivated strains of chufas as grown around the world with the common weedy races of yellow nut-grass. Nevertheless, it seems likely that chufas cultivation over many centuries has resulted in genetic modifications of the plant, and some races may be virtually domesticated. For that matter, if Owens Valley agriculture stretches back to any considerable depth in time, it is probable that some genetic modification also took place under the agricultural system employed by the Owens Valley Paiute. An interesting area of inquiry for plant geneticists would be to make a comparative study of the genetic characteristics of cultivated races of chufas with yellow nut-grass from Owens Valley and weedy races of the plant as they have developed elsewhere.

In the United States, chufas cultivation has been carried out chiefly by small growers in Georgia, Alabama, Arkansas, and Florida, who grow the tubers mostly as a food for hogs (Killinger and Stokes 1951:5). Yield is not notably high, and approximates that of soybeans. An extrapolation from Mayo (1941:97) and Piper (1924:461) indicates that chufas yield ranges from 19 to 26 bushels per acre. So far as we are aware, only Killinger and Stokes (1951) have devoted any research attention to increasing the yield of chufas in the South. In five years of field trials at the University of Florida Agricultural Station, they succeeded in demonstrating that yield could be increased by 30.2 percent through proper plant spacing (Killinger and Stokes 1951:15).

An examination of their field studies, however, shows that they were dealing with an experimental situation entirely unlike yellow nut-grass cultivation as it existed among the Owens Valley Paiute. In the first place, southern growers of chufas plant and harvest their crop in about four months. Killinger and Stokes (1951:14-15) achieved their best yield results with a "delayed harvest" of 4-1/2 months. In contrast, the Owens Valley Paiute are reported to have harvested their fields every two years under an alternate irrigation system. No estimates are available on the effects of increased tuber size or production of a greater number of tubers under such a fallowing system. Secondly, we have no yield data on wild-hyacinth, the other major crop grown in Owens Valley. Indian groups east of the Owens Valley Paiute had acquired a partial reliance on the highly successful maize-squash-bean crop complex developed in Mesoamerica, but are not known to have engaged in cultivation of the Owens Valley crops. The combination of wild-hyacinth and yellow nut-grass may have been an ideally integrated crop complex with ramifications that could only be understood by re-establishing such a system.

A nutritional analysis of yellow nut-grass from Owens Valley was conducted for us by J. G. Waines of the University of California, Riverside. Protein content of yellow nut-grass tubers was found to be almost equivalent to rice as a staple. Plain tubers had a protein content of 6%; tubers with fiber removed (probably the state in which they were eaten by the Paiute), 7%; and tubers with rind removed, 8%. Data extrapolated from Killinger and Stokes (1951:13) showed that Florida chufas over two seasons (1944, 1945) had a protein content ranging from 4.65% to 5.24%. Killinger and Stokes (1951) also reported that chufas contained slightly more than half the oil content of peanuts.[17]

Those who may question whether the Owens Valley cultivated plants can really be considered an agricultural crop complex should recognize that one of the two primary "wild plants" has been shown here to have a long history as a "crop plant." To refuse to accept it as a crop plant in Owens Valley, or its production there as constituting agriculture, while accepting it as a crop plant elsewhere in the world is to employ a double standard of reasoning.

ORIGINS OF OWENS VALLEY AGRICULTURE

Hopefully, we have now demonstrated that by the early historic period Owens Valley Indians practiced agriculture and that the vegeculture system they originated was unlikely to have been achieved over a brief span of time. The two primary questions to be resolved are: how did a system of agriculture begin in Owens Valley, and what impelled these people to start along the path to agriculture?

As noted earlier, Steward (1933:248-249) offered three hypotheses to account for irrigation in Owens Valley:

(1) An ancient practice of irrigation may have preceded the diffusion of cultivated plants in the Southwest and survived in eastern California.

(2) Irrigation may have diffused from a horticultural complex of the near or remote past in the Southwest.

(3) Paiute irrigation may have been of local and independent origin.

A fourth hypothesis was presented by Treganza (1956:88), who argued that ditch irrigation was acquired through Caucasian contact after 1850. This hypothesis can be dismissed, however, since we have already established that Owens Valley agriculture was well developed before the beginning of the American period.

---

[17] Content of oil (ether extract) in chufas harvested by Killinger and Stokes (1951:14) in 1944 and 1945 was 20.55% and 34.40%, respectively.

A fifth hypothesis has had currency in anthropological circles for some time with reference to early historic agricultural practices among California Indians, including the Owens Valley Paiute. We will refer to it as the "renegade neophyte hypothesis." According to this line of reasoning, a renegade neophyte (Christianized Indian) ran away from a mission-- probably Mission San Jose or San Gabriel--and found shelter in Owens Valley. Having been trained in agriculture by the Spanish, the neophyte (or neophytes) applied that knowledge in Owens Valley.

Such a hypothesis presumes, however, that a non-Paiute could have persuaded an alien group to organize a vast communal effort of ditch-digging and dam construction, develop at least a two-crop agricultural complex using indigenous plants, conceive of a cropping system to increase yields of plants, and persuade the Owens Valley Paiute to abandon part of their seasonal round of activities while an untried new system was being worked out. It also presupposes that this new system reached maximum efficiency so rapidly that it quickly spread from settlement to settlement across Owens Valley and was established by 1820. All of this is unlikely and based on the assumption that a non-Paiute could achieve prestige as a leader within the tightly-knit social organization of another Indian group. The historical record indicates that when neophytes fled the missions they also took with them the Spanish crop complex. Zenas Leonard in 1834 found such a group of neophytes west of the Sierra Nevada (probably along Kern River) growing corn, pumpkins, and melons (Ewers 1959:122). They had left Mission La Purísima after the revolt there in 1834. For that matter, there is considerable documentation showing that some California Indians acquired crop plants from the Spanish, but ignored the irrigation technology and relied on rainfall (Bean and Lawton 1973:x-xi).

A more plausible version of the above hypothesis is that an Owens Valley Paiute might have emigrated to one of the Spanish settle- ments near the coast during the early Mission period and acquired some knowledge of agriculture as a worker there. Many Indians from the interior--such as the Cahuilla of the Colorado Desert--regularly visited the Spanish pueblos to obtain work during the planting and harvesting seasons from the 1780's on into the Mexican period.

Steward's (1933:248) first hypothesis, that an ancient practice of irrigation preceded the introduction of cultivated plants into the Southwest and survived in eastern California, has no evidence to support it. We therefore agree with Steward in rejecting it.

Considerable merit lies in Steward's (1933:248) second hypothesis that irrigation may have diffused from a horticultural complex of the near

372

or remote past in the Southwest. Canal irrigation was probably underway about 2000 years ago among the Hohokam of Arizona, several hundred miles to the southeast of Owens Valley (Haury 1976). Until recently, it has been believed the northwestern extension of aboriginal horticulture in later times was probably in Pahrump Valley and Ash Meadows in southwestern Nevada, where cultivation entailed planting small fields of corn and associated crops and using a little irrigation (Steward 1938:183). Since these people were within about 150 miles of Owens Valley, it seems probable that the Owens Valley Paiute were familiar with irrigation practices in southwestern Nevada. More recently, Jensen (1976:13-16) reported finding corn cobs in dunes near Lovelock, Nevada, and the remains of a possibly manmade ditch, which may prove to be "some kind of ancient irrigation canal." Partial reliance on horticulture may be of wider distribution in the Great Basin than heretofore believed.[18]

Steward's (1933:249) criticism of the diffusionist explanation for agriculture among the Owens Valley Paiute still has merit. He observed that it called for a differential borrowing in which a "close-knit horticultural complex was broken down and the seemingly dependent or secondary element, irrigation, diffused without the carrier or *raison d'être* of the complex--the nucleus of cultivated plants."

Along these lines, Eugene Anderson (personal communication) suggests to us that consideration might also be given to the possibility that Owens Valley agriculture is ultimately derived from the Fremont Agricultural complex of Utah and extreme eastern Nevada, which declined about A.D. 1300 (Jennings and Norbeck 1955). He noted that in a situation which is marginal for a particular crop or crop complex because it is beyond the normal range or climatic conditions have deteriorated, crops might perform so poorly and weeds so well that the crops are abandoned and weeds encouraged. This might have occurred with the decline of Fremont agriculture, and diffused across southern Nevada to survive as irrigation agriculture in Owens Valley. While no data are available to indicate that such an event occurred, the idea is not unreasonable. Oats originated as weeds of marginal wheat cultivation, rye may have also and there are a number of other examples of this phenomenon. Perhaps the

---

[18] Steward (1933:334) reported a Mr. W.L. Skinner of Lone Pine as saying that corn cobs had been dug up a few inches deep in a cave at Little Lake. The authors have been unable to trace these corn cobs. Steward also noted: "C.D., unreliable, said Shoshoni formerly grew 'pinto corn' and squash, but not beans."

wild seed broadcasting by the Shoshone of Nevada (Steward 1941) is in some way also connected with the decline of agriculture in the eastern Great Basin. Alternatively, they may have acquired this practice on their own.

Both the "renegade neophyte" and the "emigrant Paiute" hypotheses appear to us to be untenable. Agricultural training at the missions was with domesticated crops. To bring back knowledge of irrigation to Owens Valley and then apply it to the cultivation of indigenous plants would require an individual of astonishing leadership skills and a visionary on the order of genius. Agricultural scientists with whom we have discussed this possibility say that the plant knowledge required of such an individual--particularly the invention of a system of alternate irrigation--would necessitate a 180-degree swing in perspective. We therefore reject the idea that an Indian leader of whatever origin, combining the qualities of both Johnny Appleseed and Luther Burbank, appeared suddenly among the Indians of Owens Valley during the Spanish period preaching a native "Green Revolution."

It is our conclusion, and we believe the most reasonable one given the present state of knowledge of aboriginal conditions, that agriculture was of local independent origin in Owens Valley and probably developed slowly over a long period prior to European contact.

Because of the extensive and well-organized irrigation system that apparently developed independently in Owens Valley by early historic times, entirely lacking in the usual New World cultivated plants and involving indigenous plant species, we must ask how such a development occurred and why it occurred there and nowhere else. Although there are apparently other instances of a similar nature in Fish Lake Valley and in the valleys of the Walker River drainage, these irrigation systems appear not to have been as well developed or of as great importance as in Owens Valley. It is difficult to postulate that the people of Owens Valley adopted irrigation from the Southern Paiute bands occupying such places as Ash Meadows to the east, since this suggests that they ignored corn and other traditional cultivated crop plants. In any case, such a contention requires first demonstrating that agriculture at Ash Meadows and elsewhere was of greater antiquity than the Owens Valley system, which remains unproven. For whatever reason the people of Owens Valley began irrigation, it is easiest to imagine that they were simply expanding on natural conditions that existed there. This was the position to which Steward returned shortly before his death.

Dr. L. F. Lippert (personal communication) has suggested that occasional quick thaws of the snowpack in the Sierra Nevada could cause streams descending to the floor of Owens Valley to sometimes overflow their banks, flooding the lowlands that later became the irrigated fields of the Owens Valley Paiute. The Indians would have observed that in such years of overflow there was an expansion of yellow nut-grass and other plants that were normally confined to areas of moist soil along the Owens River. Kowta (1965) also suggested this possibility. We believe that this idea has much to recommend it.

Communal labor in Owens Valley was not limited to irrigation, but was employed in driving antelope and jackrabbits and in fishing, with whole villages or districts participating in this latter activity under the direction of a district head man and all participants sharing in the catch (Steward 1933:250). Fish were also gathered from the dry creek beds when the streams were dammed and the water diverted into the irrigation ditches. Later, when the water was returned to the stream, fish were gathered from the ditches (Steward 1930:152). Daniel Lawton (personal communication) suggests that fishing by means of diverting streams might have led to the observation that economically useful plants were watered and made more productive over a wide area. Irrigation might thus have arisen inadvertently as a result of fishing activities. Perhaps the position of head irrigator is the same as the person who directed the diversion of streams for fishing.

The Owens Valley agricultural system appears to have achieved its greatest development in the northern part of the valley. It appears not to have been practiced at the southern end of the valley near Owens Lake, although streams seemingly suited for the purpose occur there. Von Schmidt does comment on the abundance of fish in the lower Owens River and indicates that it is on these that the Indians of the area chiefly subsisted. One reason irrigation may not have been practiced near Owens Lake is because of the abundance of *kutsavi*, the larvae of a small fly, *Ephydra hians* Say., which formerly occurred in the alkaline waters of Owens Lake. When J.W. Davidson visited Owens Lake in the summer of 1859, he reported that the Indians were busy collecting, drying, and packing away for winter use "hundreds of bushels of this food" (Wilke an Lawton 1976:30). Davidson was a keen observer, and there is no evidence that he exaggerated this point. The larvae were annually washed ashore in the summer by winds and collected in broad windrows from which they were scooped up in baskets. Irrigation was not practiced at Mono Lake either, according to Steward, nor was it recorded by Von Schmidt, who surveyed that region in 1857. Mono Lake is located at about 7000 feet, perhaps too high for successful irrigation of yellow nut-grass and wild-hyacinth. However, here again, the fly larvae occur in abundance (see Heizer 1950) and would have provided a reliable winter staple that involved less effort to obtain than irrigating and harvesting wild plant foods. Steward (1933:256) indicated that the larvae were also present in Walker Lake at the terminus of Walker River Valley. Thus, the Indians in all of these regions would have had a reliable winter food resource lacking in the northern and central Owens Valley.

The agricultural industry of Owens Valley can be viewed as an attempt to insure an adequate, reliable winter food supply, one not subject to the irregularities that characterized the annual crop of pine nuts, the recognized winter food resource across a large sector of the Great Basin. Winters tend to be long and moderately harsh in Owens Valley and may be severe elsewhere in the Great Basin. For the Paiutes and Shoshones of that region, winter was always a contest to see how long the supply of stored foods would last. In most years, and always in years when the pine nut harvest of the preceding autumn was poor, which was as often as not, spring found the Indians more or less in a state of starvation.[19] When spring arrived, it was necessary to break camp and start foraging for the first greens that made their appearance. The family units into which winter camps broke up were thus the basic economic units of much of the Great Basin.

Owens Valley had one of the greatest population densities of any region in the Basin.[20] It also differed from most of the rest of the Basin in

---

[19] Steward (1934:433) recorded a famine-like winter remembered by his informant Sam Newland: "It was a hard winter with so much snow that the sagebrush was buried and you could not even see the tops of it. We ate waiya, tüpüsi", nahavita, and other seeds my mother had gathered. There had been no pinenuts that fall or we should have gone after them and spent the winter in the mountains." Newland also stated: "The fall after my father's death my mother went out to a place west of pitana patü to gather tüpüsi" for the winter" (Steward 1934:433). Elsewhere, Steward (1933:239) reported: "Pinenut expeditions of small groups wintered in the mountains in the timber when crops were good. When pinenuts failed, they wintered at valley villages, eating stored seeds gathered in summer and fall."

[20] Davidson (Wilke and Lawton 1976:29) estimated the population of Owens Valley at about "1200 souls, tho' my guide & Mr. David McKenzie, a mountaineer of great experience & judgement, make them much more numerous." McKenzie's judgement was based in part on his experiences of the previous year, when he also visited Owens Valley,

that it had permanent villages. Whether population density led to development of agriculture in Owens Valley or whether it was the result of agriculture would at present be difficult and premature to speculate upon. But the combination of irrigated crops and pine nuts would have provided as stable a winter food supply as the combination of fly larvae and pine nuts did in nearby regions.

The combination of agriculture and hunting/gathering in Owens Valley is best viewed as typical of many non-industrial societies, even though it differed in many important respects from even neighboring areas like the American Southwest. To attempt to characterize such peoples as either "hunters and gatherers" or as "agriculturalists" is to attempt to jam information into rigid categories to which it is not necessarily suited (cf. Harris 1975:686). Certainly, the Owens Valley Indians were practicing agriculture when the earliest observations were made of them, but to call them agriculturalists is to minimize the potentially greater importance of their hunting and gathering activities. Similarly, many California and Great Basin groups which are usually considered to be typical hunters and gatherers also involved themselves in activities related to food production rather than simply food acquisition (Downs 1966b; Winter 1974). With the possible exception of the Polar Eskimo, most "hunting and gathering" societies involve themselves to some extent in forms of environmental modification, manipulation, or management. With the exception of contemporary American agribusiness, "agricultural" societies, especially non-industrial ones, likewise tend to hunt and gather to some extent. If it is necessary to classify societies on the basis of subsistence practices , then it might be more realistic to view them as having progressed to a greater or lesser degree along a continuum from strictly food acquisition to strictly food production.

CONCLUSIONS

The Paiute of Owens Valley had by early historic time progressed to a substantia extent along the path toward large-scale food production. They are perhaps the best instance in North America of a group that developed its own system of vegeculture--a system carried over to include irrigation of a variety of seedbearing plants as well. The Owens Valley

---

and provided a population estimate of about 2000 Indians.

Paiute thus offer a better example of agricultural origins than any presently known archaeological cultures that already had domesticated crop plants. And this remarkable achievement of indigenous agriculture occurred in a group which, as Julian Steward (1970) concluded after nearly fifty years of study, had evolved only "proto-bands." This was a retraction of his earlier statement that they were grouped in true composite landowning bands (Steward 1938:50). Comment on that classification we leave for a future time.

Steward (1930:153) himself deserves credit for recognizing that the Owens Valley Paiute use of irrigation could contribute knowledge within the broader framework of the "origins of agriculture." Curiously, during Steward's own time, geographer Carl O. Sauer was carrying out research on the problems of agricultural origins and dispersals. Sauer believed that vegetative propagation had preceded seed cultivation and set out to develop a theoretical basis for locating the cradle of agriculture (Harlan 1975:46). Between Sauer (1952) and Edgar Anderson (1954) a model evolved suggesting that agricultural peoples were sedentary fisherfolk living in wooded lands and bringing aggressive plants back from their riverbanks that found natural places to sprout in the kitchen middens of their homes.

Evidence since has shown that some of the presuppositions of Sauer and Anderson were simplistic or incorrect (Harlan 1975:45). Nevertheless, it seems odd that Sauer, living in California, failed to note that Steward had called attention to practices that so nearly coincided with his own model for agricultural origins. Nearly fifty years have elapsed since Steward wrote his seminal paper on irrigation in Owens Valley, but as yet no anthropologists have mustered interest in closely studying the problem. It may well be too late to acquire much of the information which still remains unknown about Owens Valley agriculture--such as the dating of its origin and the conditions under which it began. Yet research in this neglected area by archaeologists, linguists, plant scientists, and other scholars could probably tell us as much about agricultural origins as current research on the subject being carried out elsewhere in the world.

KUMEYAAY PLANT HUSBANDRY: FIRE, WATER, AND EROSION MANAGEMENT SYSTEMS[1]

Florence Shipek

INTRODUCTION

In this paper, I will describe Kumeyaay erosion control systems, which included complex techniques of controlled burning. These systems were combined with several methods of water management to maintain ground waters close to valley surfaces, and to keep the many springs and surface streams at usable levels for the complex Kumeyaay plant husbandry-corn agriculture systems. These highly effective systems were probably developed over the course of several thousand years by people gradually learning to adapt to the very erratic, semiarid climate of Southern California. I will start by summarizing the Kumeyaay plant husbandry-agricultural system (Shipek 1989), and then describe its relationship to erosion control and water management. Although each technique will be presented separately, in actual operation all techniques were used jointly and coordinated to achieve the desired effects.

This paper is based upon data collected between 1959 and 1965, primarily from Kumeyaay elders and plant specialists between 80 and 110 years of age, who had avoided the European invasion as much as possible by remaining in the Alta California mountains or fleeing to the northern Baja California Kumeyaay mountain villages. Their information was corroborated by data found in accounts written by Spanish, Mexican, and early American settlers, who described the land as they first saw it, as well as the changes which occurred after they took control, believing incorrectly that they were dealing with a "wild natural land."

---

[1] This is a revised and expanded version of a paper that was originally presented at the Seventh Annual California Indian Conference, Sonoma State University, October 18, 1991.

PLANT HUSBANDRY-AGRICULTURE

An unidentified native grain, which the Spanish described as "excellent pasture," once covered the valleys and low slopes in the Kumeyaay area. In 1773, Father Palou described the Kumeyaay as gathering this native grain by cutting and binding in "sheaves as is the custom to do with wheat" (Englehardt 1920:51). In the upper portions of some mountain valleys, the Spanish saw "*acequias*" and noted that the "pasture" was "*irrigado*" (Sanchez n.d.). The grain gradually became extinct as the Kumeyaay lost control of the land, first to the missions and later to ranchers, who covered the land with sheep, cattle, and horses. Many native annuals were replaced by European pasture grasses and weeds which had evolved in conjunction with grazing domestic animals and had seeds that passed undigested through an animal's digestive tract. The native grain survived longest in the inland southern mountains, where the Kumeyaay successfully resisted Spanish and Mexican entry. Here, surviving Kumeyaay bands still harvested the grain, burning the stubble and broadcasting seed, until the late 1880s. Thus elderly witnesses could describe the process and the grain for me in the period between 1950 and 1960. The broadcast grain sprouted with the first fall rain. If drought followed, the stalk was extremely short but still carried a small head of grain. When sufficient rains fell, the stalks grew two to three feet tall and produced more grain. The grain was described as being half the size of a grain of wheat.

In the valley bottoms and on low slopes, the grain predominated; however, leafy green and/or flowering annual seeds had also been broadcast after controlled burns, along with the grain. The varieties used were generally early spring sprouters that provided spring greens and vegetables to the Kumeyaay. Some had tuberous roots which remained and were dug after the grain harvest and controlled burns.

Around the edges of valleys, and on low slopes (particularly where a side drainage entered the main valley), oak trees were planted. Generally the grain fields under the oaks were slightly slower in ripening than in the open fields. Here controlled burns occurred after the fall acorn harvest.

On steeper slopes, the Kumeyaay planted chaparral shrubs that produced useful foods or medicines (e.g., ceanothus, manzanita, yucca, and opuntia). In addition, they also broadcast some grain seeds and other annual and perennial seeds immediately after a controlled burn. Although the chaparral shrubs immediately began resprouting from the roots, they remained small for several years. During the first year after a burn, the grain was abundant and was accompanied by annual plants that provided leafy greens. As the chaparral increased in size, the grain disappeared first; the annuals and some perennials then gradually ceased sprouting. When the chaparral had greatly reduced the annual/perennial ground cover, it was considered time to reburn the slope (Lee 1931).

Kumeyaay plant specialists experimented with all plants, testing them for subsistence, medicinal, or technical purposes, and trying seeds, vegetative cuttings, or transplants in every location. Whenever a plant was useful or successful, its numbers were increased. This specifically applied to emergency food plants, which sprouted only in the unusually timed rainfalls of drought years. Some might sprout only once in twenty years and produce vegetable and seed foods when the regular staples were reduced by drought (Shipek 1977).

Each family had fields in its home valley, usually in the form of wedges extending from the valley bottom up to the crest on each side of the drainage. They also had fields in locations scattered from the coast through the mountains to the desert. Each food, in each area, sprouted and ripened depending upon elevation, distance from the coast, and orientation to sun and wind. The time of sprouting each year also depended upon that year's sequence of sun and rain, as well as on the controlled burning sequence. Thus some food was generally always ready to be harvested somewhere. Most of the year, large group-labor forces were not necessary, unless the harvesting of large oak groves, pine groves, and special desert agave locations was involved. This system of management resulted in an even distribution of the workload throughout the year, in contrast to the intermittent, concentrated efforts required in planting and harvesting European crops.

Corn, beans, and squash were grown in mountain and desert locations beneath running springs, beside wet meadows, or in places where summer rainfall runoff would spread through the fields. Some Kumeyaay went to the New River if the Colorado had overflowed into it that year. There they cooperated to build levees and diversion dams, and to clear fields for planting.

For many plants, if a controlled burn was not followed by a correctly timed rain, the seeds would remain dormant for many years until a properly timed rain did fall. Thus, even in drought years that reduced normal food supplies, some food plants would always sprout if any rain at all fell, or if it fell erratically rather than during the normal rainy season.

CONTROLLED BURNING

By carefully managing burning sequences on different terrains, only a minimum of bare earth was ever exposed to erosion. On flats and lower slopes--areas where the extinct grain was the primary Kumeyaay food--each small area of grain was burned as the stalks dried after harvest. By burning only small patches of grain as each area dried out (depending upon local ground water and sun exposure), and then immediately broadcasting seed grain and annual seeds which would sprout with differentially-timed rains, only a small patch of bare ground existed at any one time.

Oak and pine groves, from the coast to the mountains, were burned annually, after the nut harvest. Each year's fallen leaves or pine needles, broken branches, and any low growth were burned. Such burning returned the nutrients to the soil immediately; the annual flash burning also prevented the accumulation of dead material which could contribute to damaging forest fires. Then the grain or other desired food plant seeds were broadcast over the ashes to contribute to the next year's food crop. This annual burning also prevented the development of undergrowth, including poison oak, which would reduce nutrient return to trees and thus reduce the nut crop. Annual burning also destroyed plant diseases, damaging insects, and parasites such as mistletoe and dodder (*Cuscuta* sp.); all of these, if unchecked, could damage the trees, chaparral, and other important food crops.

In the desert, mesquite and screwbean groves were managed in the same manner and for the same purpose--to maintain food crops. The Kumeyaay had experimented with planting mesquite at the coast and had succeeded in growing a few trees in scattered locations. Even isolated trees such as these had each year's trash accumulation burned to keep them healthy and producing food. In the desert, the Kumeyaay--like the Cahuilla (Patencio 1943)--regularly fired the native palm (*Washingtonia filifera*) to remove each year's trash and control potentially damaging insects. In addition to increasing the number of trees around springs in the desert and along the mountain edges, they had tried the palm near the coast, and had successfully developed a small grove near Jamul, southeast of San Diego.

Only chaparral plants, which provided food or medicine, were grown on the steeper slopes. Here the burn sequence varied depending upon the growth rate of the particular desired food or medicinal plant on that slope, and upon the plant part to be used (seeds, berries, leaves, new sprouts). The average interval between burns was anywhere from 5 to

10 years, although some areas followed a fifteen-year sequence. On steep slopes, the burning was done during a time when surrounding areas were damp or green from a recent rain, or had been partially cleared by some earlier burning of individual plants. The Kumeyaay *Kuseyaay* (shaman specialist) in charge of burns also selected windless days with high humidity, and had the men and boys around any potential danger spots (Lee 1931). Immediately after the burn, the grain and seeds of various other plants that would eventually provide edible greens were broadcast over the slope. Some slopes were essentially "spot burned" as this or that chaparral plant needed renewal because it grew more rapidly than surrounding plants. If plant disease, dodder (*Cuscuta* sp.), or insect infestation started, infected areas were spot burned immediately, before the infestation could spread. Although some mistletoe was needed for a variety of purposes, too much could damage an infested tree and reduce food availability. Regular burning kept mistletoe from damaging oaks, mesquite, and pine trees as food sources.

As Lewis (1973 and this volume) has pointed out, the grain and other annuals sprout and grow the first several years. Gradually, as the chaparral increases in size, the grain (even though rebroadcast) ceases to sprout. After several more years, the annuals also cease resprouting as the chaparral gets larger. Like most arid land plants, the chaparral has roots that spread widely to consume all of the water falling in its area and the leaves exude oils and other substances which inhibit the growth of annuals. As this occurs, the amount of bare soil increases, thus exposing the surface to erosion. The number of years required for this sequence to occur varies with the species involved. Burn intervals therefore depended upon the plant communities concerned. For example, some small areas were left in sage and not burned for 25 to 30 years (unless there was a parasite infestation), because regular burns destroy sage.

In marshy areas, cattails and reeds were regularly burned to improve their qualities as sources of both food and materials for technical purposes (e.g., they supplied house thatching, boat reeds, and a cane stalk which was used for arrow shafts). They, along with basket grasses, were spot burned every three years; in addition, the root areas were dug around and heavy root clumps were divided--often for the purpose of establishing the plant elsewhere.

The desired plants in some locations were primarily fodder for animals; the vegetation eaten by deer, antelope, mountain sheep, rabbits and other meat sources was a part of the entire husbandry-burn regime. According to the plant specialists, Kumeyaay animal specialists kept watch on the food supply of deer, antelope, rabbit, and mountain sheep. When necessary, fodder areas were burned to refreshen the supply and maintain the animal food sources at peak production.

While this essay concentrates on plant production, the burning that occurred around each Kumeyaay village and its small scattered homesteads must be mentioned. These areas were "fireproofed" by a procedure that involved regularly clearing and sweeping the ground around each home and community center. No trash was allowed to accumulate near homes. All plants were kept away from the houses and meeting or religious centers, and any new plant growth was spot burned. Large chaparral bushes and other brush were kept well away from the homes; if any chaparral growth started nearby, it was spot burned after a rain.

The regular, frequent burning of each area was carried out according to a schedule that depended upon plant type and locality, as well as upon the occurrence of insects, parasites, or plant diseases. In addition, such factors as the humidity and the velocity and direction of the wind were also considered in scheduling a burn. If an area was burned regularly, the fuel that present was insufficient to support the kind of wildfire that damages trees.

WATER AND EROSION MANAGEMENT SYSTEMS

The ethnographic data collected from Kumeyaay elders included a description of a process in which rocks were aligned in parallel rows on alluvial fans along the desert mountain edge and in the mountain valleys east of the Laguna Crest. These rock ridges were also aligned across small drainage channels to slow the downward flow of rain water and to allow more to enter the ground. Elders described these alignments as having been built for the purpose of spreading the summer storm water and catching the fine silt carried by it; the areas behind the rock alignments were then used as planting locations. Such rock alignments had apparently been built on all steep slopes, including some near the ocean (before Spanish invaders restricted access to that area). This information is corroborated by Rivera y Moncada's 1776 account of his search for the leaders of the revolt against mission enslavement (Burrus 1967). After going north from San Diego, then inland above the San Dieguito River to somewhere near the San Pascual-Rancho Bernardo area, he saw a village below a steep slope. He attempted to round the slope and surprise the village, but carefully placed cactus and "thorny plants" prevented a surprise.

He then described the people fleeing along low rock walls or "trincheras," the Southwestern term used for low rock ridges which parallel a slope. Recently, Carrico (1987; personal communication 1989) has uncovered just such low, parallel rock walls traversing the slope in the region described by Rivera y Moncada, thereby lending archaeological support to both the ethnographic record and the historical account.

On the mesas, valley flats, and slopes, the grain and other food or medicinal annuals broadcast by the Kumeyaay covered the soil, protecting it from the erosional effects of rain and water runoff. The mesas and slopes had annuals interspersed throughout the chaparral. Then, as every drainage sloped into a valley, the rock alignments were placed to slow and spread the drainage of water as it moved into the valley. In the stream and river valleys, riparian plants were placed along the stream sides; some provided food, while many had medicinal properties, such as willow and sumacs. If a major storm made a new cut in the stream bank, the local villagers planted willow branches along the cut. To start the rapid return of plant cover, they also broadcast grain and other annuals. In some valleys, they placed grape cuttings near the stream as well. Upstream rock alignments were then checked and damage repaired.

Another erosion control and water management technique that was used may have been specific to Southern California. Many stream drainages in Southern California alternately widen out and then narrow again to a small rocky passage. At the head of the narrows, the Kumeyaay had learned to place boulders and brush to keep as much water as possible in the wider, upstream portion. After each storm, the proper *Kuseyaay* (shaman) would check and order the men of the band to repair any damage. Again, early written descriptions and maps of most valleys in San Diego County show small watery bogs at the lower ends of the valleys that graded into wet meadows. The valleys are also shown without the modern gullies. These descriptions (e.g., Crouch 1915; numerous topographic maps, 1856-1920) indicate that wet meadows existed in the lower valleys and knee-high grain was found in the slightly higher parts of the valley bottoms. Water ran on the surface in the narrow, rocky gorges. The boulder and brush work also maintained ground water, so that springs existed along the sides of each valley. Even in drought years, ground water was maintained close to the surface in most locations (San Diego Union 1870, San Diego Bulletin Feb. 19, 1870). These boulder-brush piled dams had to be regularly repaired after major storms, as did the rock alignments.

Some springs belonged to each band as a whole and were managed under the direction of the *Kwaaypaay* (band chief). The springs on "family lands" were managed by the family that owned them. All kept the springs cleaned out, and burned the ground around a spring yearly to keep chaparral away; only the broadcast grain was nearby. One food tree often was near enough to provide shade for the water during the heat of the day. This management kept transevaporation of plants to a minimum but shaded the spring and protected it from erosional silt. Along trails on the desert side of the mountains, where summer rains abounded, basins were gouged in rocks to catch rainwater to provide the runner or traveler with water.

GOVERNANCE AND LABOR REQUIREMENTS

The system just described required people knowledgeable about the management of planting, burning, and the placement of rock alignments and boulder dams, as well as sufficient human labor to do the work. In other words, it required the hierarchical system of specialists described by Boscana (1933) for the Luiseño-Juaneño and Fr. Sales (Rudkin 1956) for the Kumcyaay (also see Shipek 1992). Among the Kumeyaay, each *Kuseyaay* was responsible for the knowledge associated with one of the resources in the territory and for the way in which that resource was affected by the erratic weather. All worked in council, sharing specific information and discussing what needed to be done under each type of weather condition. The *Kuseyaay* council of each band kept the *Kwaaypaay* (band chief) informed of the condition of some resource or environmental feature in the band territory, and the people were then called together to do the work. In the national territory areas, the *Kuchut Kwataay* or tribal chief (Shipek 1982) and his council were responsible and organized the necessary work forces.

On the basis of mission birth and death rates, descriptive data, and later censuses, the Kumeyaay population is estimated to have been between 23,000 and 26,000 in 1769--about 6 people per square mile north of the border and probably slightly less south of it. Thus the necessary work force existed. However, the fact that this integrated system of management distributed labor evenly throughout the year suggests that the work could still have been carried out by the lower populations that existed at much earlier time periods.

OTHER EVIDENCE: EFFECTS OF MANAGEMENT CHANGES

The Spanish consistently commented on the "pastures" that once existed along the coast. In 1850, an American settler, Major Utt, remarked that this area held the finest grasslands (Kumeyaay grain fields) west of the Kansas plains and proceeded--along with other settlers--to place many hundreds of thousands of sheep in San Diego valleys, from the coast through the mountains (Crouch 1915; Board of Equalization records, San Diego County). The grain was eaten to the roots. The European immigrants, thinking the grain was natural, did not save seed for rebroadcasting, and it thus disappeared; many ground surfaces were left bare. Sheep and cattle were concentrated in the larger, wetter valleys (e.g., Pine Valley, Green Valley) during periods of drought; these areas then experienced major erosion in subsequent storms. After major storms, the rock alignments on the steep slopes and desert alluvial fans were not repaired and were gradually destroyed. The boulders and brush were not replaced in valley narrows, and erosional gullies destroyed the wet meadows. In some valleys, even European pasture grasses could no longer survive. Sage and creosote now predominate in locations once described as excellent pasture with knee-deep "grass."

Between 1900 and 1920, farmers began replacing cattlemen in some valleys. The farmer invariably plowed the wet meadow and "drained it" to provide himself with the best soil for his crops. One local farmer even advised the Mission Indian Agency that one reservation valley (Campo) could be improved by cutting and draining the meadow and then providing the local people with irrigation water by locating wells and using pumps (Bureau of Indian Affairs Records, Campo Agency). Unfortunately, breaking the surface of the wet meadows opened the extremely fine loam to erosion, which then destroyed the massive loam deposits, leaving only the underlying sand. Most valleys, instead of being characterized by the original wet meadows, abundant surface water, and numerous small springs described in early records, now have deep gullies, lack surface water, and have no small side springs at all.

TREE AND FOREST MANAGEMENT

The Kumeyaay never cut a living tree. Firewood was obtained from broken branches, dead trees, or from chaparral roots. Coppice stem growth (from plants whose roots send up new shoots when cut) was used for house beams. The Spanish and Americans, in contrast, cut innumerable pines and other trees for construction purposes. Most oak trees near the coast were destroyed for firewood and for tanning leather. Thousands of pines were cut in the mountains for railroad ties, mine timbers, and housing materials. As a result, wild (i.e., not planted) chaparral has replaced pine and oak in many locations.

Although the Forest Service has recently initiated a program of controlled burning, years of fire protection and control have allowed the development of a heavy undergrowth in many areas. This undergrowth, which includes poison oak and other undesirable plants, has replaced the former carpet of grain and annuals that once grew under the oak, pine, and other trees. In addition, the undergrowth is littered with dead leaves, pine needles, and broken branches that have accumulated over many years, and conditions now exist for the development of superheated fires capable of totally destroying mature trees.

CONCLUSION

The most damaging misconception that Europeans brought with them to California--as well as to the rest of the continent--was the belief that they were entering a "natural wilderness." In Southern California, the Spanish saw--but failed to recognize--a system of planting, harvesting, and managing the environment that was very different from that practiced in Europe; they therefore claimed that the native peoples only gathered what 'nature' produced. The replacement of the knowledgeable and effective Kumeyaay system of total environmental management by one that mistakenly incorporates the European concept of 'wilderness' has resulted in a loss of valuable water sources, massive erosion, insect and parasite infestations, destructive wildfires, and a severe depletion of plant and animal species.

IN RETROSPECT

Henry T. Lewis

This world...ever was, and is,
And shall be, ever-living Fire,
In measures being kindled
And in measures going out.
                    Heraclitus [c.540 - c.480 B.C.]

A former student, reflecting on how long ago it had been assigned as required reading in a seminar of mine, described *Patterns of Indian Burning in California* as "an historical piece." While far from being as historically early as the publications of Omer C. Stewart on Indian uses of fire to alter the environment (1951 etc.), it did represent a second attempt to generate anthropological interest in the topic of hunter-gatherer uses of habitat burning in North America.[1] As an "historical piece," the ecological interpretations are somewhat dated and more limited than would now be the case. At the same time, studies now being done go much further in placing the use of fire within the broader context of traditional ecological knowledge and practice--of which habitat burning is merely a part, albeit an extremely important part (e.g., see Anderson 1988, 1991a, 1991b, and other papers within this volume).

As a result of the republication of *Patterns* here (with only minor editorial corrections), I thought I should provide a retrospective on the ideas, events, and contexts which first led to my thinking about the topic and subsequently to researching and writing it up. As research, it represents one of those cases which, I suspect, occur rather more often than we like to admit in scholarly work, particularly our own: more the consequence of disparate circumstances than a neatly formulated, systematically and steadily worked-on research design. So far as bringing data and

---

[1] Meanwhile, along parallel lines, Rhys Jones (1969) had written an article on the uses of fire by Aborigines in Tasmania and, for an environment very similar to that of California, Sylvia Hallam (1975) published an important monograph on indigenous uses of fire in Western Australia.

ideas together on California Indian uses of fire is concerned, there were two fortuitous events involved going back, first, to when I was a graduate student at the University of California in Berkeley and, secondly, to an incident which occurred while I was a "seasonal ranger" during one of several summers that I worked for the National Park Service.

The first of these two contingencies occurred while I was taking a seminar in the fall of 1958, during my first year at Berkeley; the course was a required part of the graduate program that was somewhat grudgingly given by Robert F. Heizer on his special area of expertise, California Indians--his "revenge," as he described it, for having had to take the same seminar from A. L. Kroeber in the 1930s. In the process of reading a large number of monographs, I ran across several references which mentioned that Native Californians periodically set grassland, brush, and forest fires. In my view these pyrotechnics did not make a great deal of sense, particularly in light of the work that I was then doing in the Park Service, and especially that part which involved fighting forest fires.

The second happenstance occurred only a year and a half later, during the summer of 1960. In July of that year I was involved--along with approximately a thousand other individuals--in the essentially futile effort of trying to stop a large, extremely intense brush fire in Sequoia Park, a fire which was only extinguished when it ran out of fuel along the crest of a mountain ridge. Ignited near the bottom of a canyon, ten thousand acres of dense chaparral erupted in what was described as a "fire storm," in an area which had not been burned for 70 or more years. Except that no homes were destroyed or human lives seriously threatened, in its intensity it was much like the brush fire that occurred last year in the Oakland-Berkeley hills, or the other brush fires which regularly consume large areas of chaparral in central and southern California.

As a part of our ineffectual efforts to contain the conflagration, a firebreak was cut from two directions across a drainage. Very near to where the firelines were linked, we stumbled upon a long abandoned Indian campsite that was probably used by the Western Mono in the trans-Sierran trade of obsidian and salt. All indications were that it had been regularly used over a long period of time: it included a large, flat area of deeply incised bedrock mortars; two dozen or more large pestles, still upright in the mortar holes where they had been left; and an adjacent rock shelter with a virtual midden of obsidian flakes and broken tools. Almost completely overgrown by dense brush and a fairly large number of oaks, which were undoubtedly a source of acorns, the site was situated just a few yards from a ravine that, except for spring run-off, was apparently dry for most of the year.

At the time, given the fact that the "natural growth" in the burn area consisted of an impenetrable thicket of chaparral, I was puzzled by what would have made it a desirable campsite. In all respects--with the exception of the oak trees--it seemed an unlikely place for human habitation, even for brief periods of time. However, because the fire was within less than an hour of reaching and immediately crossing our thirty-foot wide fireline, and with instructions for us to get out as quickly as possible, I did not give the question of the site's unlikely location much further thought until a year later when I revisited the area to locate it for the Park Historian.

Twelve months after what had been described in the newspapers as the "total destruction" of brush and trees, a new and profuse growth of grasses, herbs, and sprouts of various chaparral species had emerged from the ashes. Most impressive was the number of deer observed browsing and grazing on the burn site, especially since none had been reported killed or even seen during the fire. At the same time--and during the same month as that of the previous summer--water was still running in the ravine, and the "unlikely place" for a campsite offered views up and down the drainage. It was at this point that I began asking myself serious questions about why Indians would have set fires in chaparral stands--and, conversely, why we did not. This led me to begin reading the considerable literature on the then relatively new subfield of fire ecology, especially those works concerned with California and similar Mediterranean-type regions. In the process, I came across the largely ignored works of Omer C. Stewart on the uses of fire by Native North Americans.

Following a hiatus of almost five years--a break which involved my doctoral studies in the Philippines--I began to seriously think about the contradiction between what Indians had done in setting fires and what environmental agencies were doing by suppressing them. This interest began to develop during my first teaching appointment at San Diego State College, the intellectual stimulus for considering the paradox coming from teaching courses and seminars in ecological anthropology.[2] With a

---

[2] It was also the case that the chairman of the department disapproved of my continued seasonal work with the National Park Service, and writing up the materials was my personal justification for the final three summers spent in Sequoia-Kings Canyon National Park while teaching at San Diego State College.

392

dissertation still to complete and courses to prepare for the first time, I had not given, nor could I afford to give, much research time and thought to questions about California Indian uses of fire. However, with the help of a research assistant, I was able to have a survey made of anthropological and historical documents, thus adding to the materials I had noted when doing my seminar paper eight years earlier.

On the basis of what was found, I began to organize the materials and consider the implications of what habitat burning would have meant to the adaptations of California Indians.[3]   To get beyond a simple compilation of examples about indigenous uses of fire, a context, or model, was required for making ecological sense of the observations and comments made by different observers, who were frequently talking about different kinds of habitats and describing different cultural-linguistic groups of Native Californians.   Few of the references amounted to more than a brief notation about why, where, when, and what kinds of habitats were involved; often, not even that much information was included. None were sufficiently detailed to allow the reconstruction of an overall technology of fire as used by particular groups.[4]   Over a number of months several perspectives for interpreting the information were considered and rejected, such as cataloguing "why" Indians burned, something that Stewart (1956) had earlier provided; reaching the simple and obvious conclusion that the better reported areas of California had the greater number of references to burning practices; or reaching the corollary idea that regions with larger populations and greater amounts of vegetation were reported as having been burned more frequently and intensely than, say, desert regions. The most interesting approach considered and briefly pursued was to look at the species of plants which ecologists had shown to follow in regular, sequential patterns in the years after a brush fire; these were then to be matched against the specific plants which native peoples collected from across a mosaic of periodically-burned chaparral stands at different stages

---

[3] Later, while teaching at the University of Hawaii (1968-1971), I was struck by the ecological parallels between California and Southwest Asia. As a result of considering the two areas, I proposed an hypothesis about the probable importance of fire for the origins of agriculture (Lewis 1972).

[4] However, this was subsequently and very successfully done by Timbrook, Johnson, and Earle (1982, and this volume) in their important review of Spanish sources on the Chumash of the Santa Barbara region.

of ecological succession. This was being considered when I came across a particular article that greatly helped to explain the largest number of references (which, as mentioned, were limited in what they provided). As described at some length in the text of *Patterns of Indian Burning in California*, the major breakthrough came when I discovered the collected works of Harold H. Biswell, and especially when I read his 1967 article on using fire to establish "wildland management."

Interpreting the data and writing it up continued intermittently during three years that I spent at the University of Hawaii (1968-71), where I was expected to focus my research and writing efforts on the Philippines--the result of which was the publication of what had essentially been my doctoral dissertation on rice farmers in northern Luzon (Lewis 1971)[5]. However, by the time I took up my current appointment at the University of Alberta in 1971, the first draft of *Patterns* was completed--after an earlier and shorter version had been turned down as a journal article--and subsequently submitted to and accepted for publication by Ballena Press as the first in their monograph series in anthropology. Even with its publication in 1973, I still viewed the work on hunter-gatherer uses of fire as simply the serendipitous consequence of the events just described, an interesting but only temporary diversion from my primary research concerns in Southeast Asia.

After coming to Alberta, I learned that there were still native peoples in the north of the province, and still further north in the Yukon and the Northwest Territories, who had used habitat fires until the late 1940s, when the increasingly effective enforcement of fire prevention laws made it difficult, even for people living in remote settlements, to continue traditional burning practices. During a study leave in 1975/76--the first part of which was spent in the Philippines--I began a second study of hunter-gatherer uses of fire, but with the major difference that I was able to interview the people who had both used and understood the technology and ecology of fire. Unlike the reconstruction of California Indian practices, which was merely based upon the occasionally recorded observations of outsiders, the amount and quality of knowledge available from consultants in northern Alberta was limited only by my ability to ask appropriate and meaningful questions. The interviews, which extended over three summers across parts of the aspen parkland and boreal forest regions

---

[5] While at the University of Hawaii I was further aided in collecting information by a second student, both of whom were credited in the Acknowledgements.

of northern Alberta, included questions, dialogues, and discussions with fifty-seven older people (Slavey, Beaver, Cree, Chipewyan, Metis, and three non-Native consultants), at least a third of whom were truly local experts on the ecology of fire.[6] The research resulted in several publications and one film (Lewis 1977, 1978a, 1978b, 1980, 1981, 1982b, 1990a). Again, comparisons formed an important part of the study, allowing me to test and verify information from different individuals, different cultural traditions, and different habitats and regions.

Continuing with an interest and emphasis on the importance of comparison, I accepted an invitation as visiting professor at the Australian National University in 1980 to consider Aboriginal uses of fire. During July and August of that year, I began a third study of hunter-gatherer uses of fire, which culminated in a four-month period of fieldwork in the Northern Territory between April and August of 1983. The research included comparisons of the burning practices currently used by Aborigines, cattle ranchers, and government agencies in parts of the monsoon savanna region of northern Australia (Lewis 1985, 1989a, 1989b, 1991b). Overall, the combined studies from California, Alberta, and northern Australia led to a consideration and development of an hypothesis about cross-cultural regularities in the ways that people in similar environments independently arrived at parallel solutions for alternately changing and maintaining local habitats (Lewis 1981, 1982a, 1991a; Lewis and Ferguson 1988).

Without the required seminar on California Indians at Berkeley and, alternatively, without having come across the "unlikely" Indian campsite in Sequoia, I probably would not have developed an interest in what has become a major preoccupation with the way in which humans have used and, in some areas, continue to use fire to facilitate human adaptations.[7] Yet, had I not been the one to work on California Indians, others would certainly have noted and undertaken research on the obvious contradiction between the complexity of indigenous environmental manage-

---

[6] Sadly, more than one-third of these individuals have since died. However, there still remains a considerable wealth of information on this and other forms of traditional ecological knowledge in the Canadian north.

[7] My current interests in the technology and ecology of fire concern the uses of post-harvest burning, or "stubble fires," by cereal farmers in southern Australia and in southern Italy for what these practices can further suggest about the role of fire in the origins of agriculture (Lewis 1972).

ment practices and the essential absence of such practices in societies like our own--just as research has been done in Australia and, years before that, was carried out in the prescient work of George M. Day (1952), the publications of Carl Sauer (1944, 1947, 1950, 1975) and Omer C. Stewart (1951, etc.), and Reynolds' (1959) work on Yosemite. In addition, several writers have subsequently carried out similar research on California and other West Coast areas (Anderson 1988, 1991a, 1991b; Anderson and Nabhan 1991; Boyd 1986; Norton 1979; Shipek 1989; and Timbrook et al. 1982).

At the same time, fire ecologists and advocates of prescribed burning have been gradually changing the official dogma that had propagated and maintained the argument for total fire exclusion and complete fire suppression as a distorted and dangerous form of "conservation." In fact, of course, it was not conservation, being the very opposite of indigenous practices that influenced environments long before the arrival of Europeans in the New World. Unfortunately, the widely-held popular view that fires, natural or man-made, are inherently destructive, and that fire is an intrusion into and not a desirable part of either natural or manipulated environments, still exists. This simplistic view of fire is being strongly reinforced today by some of the images being used to portray the destruction of tropical rainforest areas.

There is also an associated, extremely romanticized belief that "primitive people" live, or at least once lived, in some undefined condition of "harmony with nature," engaged in environmentally benign ways of exploiting resources which either could not or would not have allowed people to alter "what nature provides." However, among a growing number of ecologists, foresters, parks officials, and others there is the recognition that the "wilderness" found by Europeans--what Longfellow erroneously referred to as the "forest primeval"--was, in most parts of the continent and in varying degrees, a human artifact.

The argument referred to by Burcham (1959) and Clar (1959) in *Patterns*--claiming that Indian uses of fire were negligible because of a "lack of technological skills"--essentially represents the same ethnocentric view of hunting-gathering adaptations as "primitive" or "simple," but more with disdain than romantic admiration. It is also a view that directly equates technology with the variety and complexity of the tools that people use. In contrast to this very Western, materialistic view of technology, the anthropologist Robin Riddington has argued for a quite different approach to understanding how people relate to and act upon local environments:

396

> Perhaps because our own culture is obsessed with the production, exchange, and possession of artifacts, we inadvertently overlook the artifice behind technology in favour of the artifacts that it produces.... I suggest that technology should be seen as a system of knowledge rather than an inventory of objects.... The essence of hunting and gathering adaptive strategy is to retain and be able to act upon, information about the possible relationships between people and the natural environment. When realized, these lifegiving relationships are as much the artifacts of hunting and gathering technology as are the material objects that are instrumental in bringing them about [1982:471].

As the authors of the preceding papers have demonstrated, the technologies of hunting-gathering societies, when considered as *the knowledge that people use for practical purposes*, are complex and consist of much more than the relatively small assemblages of weapons, snares, nets, knives, and other devices and material objects that people use in the application of technological knowledge. With respect to the technology and ecology of fire, what I and others have written about Native California provides only the barest outlines of what was a very sophisticated understanding of the factors and relationships involved. With respect to the uses of prescribed burning, there was no "lack of technological skills" in the way in which hunter-gatherers in California and elsewhere influenced environmental systems.

I put forward a suggestion for consideration in *Patterns* concerning the significance of ecotones. With the exception of Peterson's (1977a, 1977b, 1978) study of hunter-gatherers in the northern Philippines, a discussion of the concept and its applicability to archaeology (Rhoades 1978), and an M.A. thesis by Reid (1987), relatively little research has been done on the importance of ecotones, or "edge areas," as significant factors in human adaptation and human evolution. Though ecotones are certainly exploited and maintained by means other than burning alone (Peterson 1977a, 1977b, 1978), prescribed uses of fire have been especially important--probably throughout most of human evolution--in creating and maintaining edge areas. However, as Reid has emphasized (1987), while the concept seems to have little utility in an analytical sense, the kinds of areas described as ecotones seem to have been recognized, managed, and utilized by all human societies.

So far the consideration and study of traditional resource management strategies has largely attracted the attention of people with research and academic interests similar to my own.[8] The usual responses that I have had from individuals in environmental agencies is that such knowledge, while interesting or even important as an historical precedent, is inappropriate in the context of modern concerns for the scientific management or conservation of parks and natural reserves. In a case involving two National Parks in northern Australia (Kakadu and Gurig), for example, one scholar has pointed out the central problems that government officials and environmental scientists seem to have in accepting traditional ecological knowledge as something of more than arcane interest:

> I believe that the desire to incorporate Aboriginal traditional knowledge is commendable and genuine, but that it will occur, in principle more readily in the interpretation than in the resource management area of the park operations.... I believe that Aboriginal knowledge will not be readily acceptable to Europeans (i.e., white Australians) with a scientific system of justifying knowledge [Weaver 1984:20].

Similarly, Robert Johannes, a marine biologists working with Micronesian fishermen in the western Pacific, has been even more critical of Western scientists for their unwillingness to accept traditional ecological knowledge and what the loss of that knowledge truly represents:

> Natural scientists have routinely overlooked the practical knowledge possessed by artisans.... It is one manifestation of the elitism and ethnocentrism that run deep in much of the Western scientific community. If unpublished notebooks containing the detailed observations of a long line of biologists and oceanographers were destroyed, we would be outraged. But when specialized knowledge won from the sea over centuries by formally unschooled but uniquely qualified observers--fishermen--is allowed to disappear as

---

[8] The International Union for Conservation of Nature and Natural Resources (IUCN) supports the study of traditional ecological knowledge, but it is very much ancillary to its main emphasis on scientific approaches to environmental concerns.

the westernization of their cultures proceeds, hardly anyone seems to care [Johannes 1981:ix].

In North America there are cases in which indigenous management practices are being gradually incorporated within parks and wilderness areas. In both Canada and the United States, provincial, state, and national park agencies have shown an increased interest in "traditional ecological knowledge," and (at least in northernmost regions) have begun to include local participation in the establishment, planning, and management of new parks and wilderness areas. However--except for parts of Alaska, the Yukon, the Northwest Territories, and northern British Columbia--Canada and the United States lag far behind Australia, where Aborigines now participate directly in the overall running of a considerable number of National Parks (Birckhead et al. 1992). Unfortunately, it will probably be some time before we see native North Americans involved in making major decisions about park planning, development, and operations, as is already the case in Australia. It is equally unlikely that we will see native people (as now regularly occurs in parts of Australia) carrying on the day-to-day subsistence activities of harvesting traditional foods, hunting and trapping animals, and regularly using prescribed burning within the boundaries of a national park--much less that such practices would be countenanced in the absence of official controls and supervision. It is even more difficult to imagine that Indians would be invited to provide a direct input into the operation of such established parks as Banff, Jasper, Yellowstone, or Yosemite, even though these areas were formerly managed by indigenous peoples.

To conclude my retrospective epilogue, three years ago I was asked to contribute a paper to a conference in southwestern Oregon. I explained to the symposium organizers that my original research on California had somewhat abruptly and artificially ended at the political boundaries of the state, and I had collected only a few references for their area of concern. I also mentioned that a comprehensive study had been carried out on the Willamette Valley of central Oregon by Robert M. Boyd (1986), though southwestern Oregon should have been included as a natural geographic extension and part of my earlier study.

In my presentation to the conference I summarized my earlier research on California, northern Alberta, and northern Australia, emphasizing the kind of work that should and could still be done using published and archival sources on indigenous uses of fire in southwestern Oregon. To my pleasant surprise, several Native American participants at the conference pointed out that there were still older people who knew about and understood the techniques and consequences of traditional burning practices; I refer briefly to some of that information in the published version of that paper (Lewis 1990b:82-83). The comments of one participant at the conference, while talking about her background in the South Umpqua River region, are worth repeating here because they add directly to what I wrote about California twenty years ago:

> When I was a very little girl, I remember asking (Uncle Bob), "When do you do the burning?" His reply was always, "When the time is right." He would often go out in the field, away from the house and sniff the air, also wet his finger and hold it up (although there was no wind that I could perceive), and say, "Not yet" or "its time." I never knew on what he based his reasoning. The fires were set annually, but I'm sure on a rotating basis. As for time of year, it would appear that some burning was done in the early Spring, although the bulk of it was in the Fall, perhaps after the first rain, for even in aboriginal times the annual fires were recognized as a way to balance the ecology. After Fall fires, there was a quick greening, providing food for the forest animals.

It is also the case that even within the formal boundaries of California my original survey of published sources was short of being fully comprehensive. In addition to the Spanish documents which were not considered, there are undoubtedly data available from other archival sources, particularly the fieldnotes of anthropologists who were working with native peoples in the first half of this century. And although I wrongly assumed that traditional knowledge of fire use no longer existed in California, both Kat Anderson (1988, 1991a, 1991b) and Florence Shipek (1989) have provided examples of how such understanding can still be found.

Following the original publication of *Patterns of Indian Burning in California*, one example of what had been missed in the search for references was brought to my attention. The overlooked publication was Kroeber and Gifford's (1949) *World Renewal: A Cult System of Native Northwest California*; the specific example refers to the Hupa. In scanning the titles of publications that I had assigned my student research assistant in San Diego, it had not seemed especially promising as a source of information about burning practices, given the topic involved. Because of that oversight, it is worth adding here for the traditional and yet very modern insights which it provides:

> ...*kixahansa*, the burners of the brush on the sacred mountain, Mt. Offield, and at Bacon Flat on Orleans Mountain. They have not functioned recently, because of the United States Forest Service prohibition against setting fires [Kroeber and Gifford 1949:8].

> The priest has to stand at the *yuxpit* (sacred sand pile) and look at the mountain all night. Formerly, on the night of his vigil, three men called *kixahansa* fired the brush on Mt. Offield so it would be clean. Now, because of the white man's regulations, the fire cannot be kindled; since the vigil comes at the dark of the moon, the priest has to gaze at the mountain in darkness. The men who fired the brush had to fast all day; they could not eat or drink until next morning. This annual burning was said not to cause forest fires, because it burnt only undergrowth.

> The extensive brush areas on Mt. Offield are due to this annual burning at the *pikiavish* (world renewal ceremony), Mary (Mary Ike, an informant) said; all the small fir trees were killed. She explained that the mountain is an immortal woman, whose "hair" has to be singed so there will not be many widows and widowers in the world. The mountain, however, is not a widow. The brush burning was an act of prophylactic magic ordained by the immortal who owned the Katimin sacred sweathouse. Now that the Indians no longer burn fires on Mt. Offield and no longer perform the Deerskin Dance, food is scarce and they are dying off, Mary said [Kroeber and Gifford 1949:21].

BIBLIOGRAPHY

Abbott, C.C.
  1879   Mortars and Pestles. Report of the United States Geographical
          Surveys West of the 100th Meridian, Vol. VII:70-92.
          Washington: United States Government Printing Office.

Aginsky, B.W.
  1943   Culture Element Distributions: XXIV, Central Sierra.
          Anthropological Records 8(4):393-468.

  1970   Pomo. Encyclopaedia Britannica 18:210.

Alcock, R.G.
  1941   Selection, Cutting, and Seasoning of Osage Orange Wood. The
          American Archer 4(2):5, 19.

Allen, E.
  1972   Pomo Basketmaking: A Supreme Art for the Weaver. Happy
          Camp: Naturegraph.

Anderson, E.
  1954   Plants, Man, and Life. London: A. Melrose.

Anderson, E.N., Jr.
  1978   A Revised, Annotated Bibliography of the Chumash and Their
          Predecessors. Socorro: Ballena Press.

Anderson, M.K.
  1988   Southern Sierra Miwok Plant Resource Use and Management
          of the Yosemite Region. M.A. thesis, University of California,
          Berkeley.

  1990   California Indian Horticulture. Fremontia 18(2):7-14.

  1991a   California Indian Horticulture: Management and Use of
          Redbud by the Southern Sierra Miwok. Journal of Ethno-
          biology 11(1):145-157.

1991b   Wild Plant Management: Cross-cultural Examples of the Small Farmers of Jaumave, Mexico, and the Southern Miwok of the Yosemite Region. Arid Lands Newsletter 31:18-23.

1991c   Plant Gathering as a Conservation Strategy: Learning from California's Earliest Resource Managers. *In* Natural Areas and Yosemite: Prospects for the Future, Proceedings of the Natural Areas Association Seventeenth Annual Meeting, J. Edelborck and S. Carpenter, eds., pp. 472-481.

1992   Indian Fire-based Management in the Sequoia Mixed Conifer Forests of the Central and Southern Sierra Nevada. Final Report to Yosemite Research Center, Yosemite National Park. Cooperative Agreement Order Number 8027-002.

n.d.   The Experimental Approach to Assessment of the Potential Ecological Effects of Horticultural Practices by Indigenous Peoples on California Wildlands. Ph.D. dissertation, Department of Forestry and Resource Management, University of California, Berkeley [1993].

Anderson, M.K., and G.P. Nabhan
1991   Gardeners in Eden. Wilderness Magazine 45:27-30.

Angel, M.
1881   History of Nevada with Illustrations and Biographical Sketches. Oakland: Thompson and West.

Anonymous
1896   Nut Culture in the United States; Embracing Native and Introduced Species. Washington: United States Department of Agriculture, Division of Pomology.

Appleton, R.A., Jr., and M. Kowta
1969   A Note on the Preconditions of Owens Valley Paiute Irrigation. Unpublished ms. on file at the Department of Anthropology, California State University, Chico.

Aschmann, H.
1959   The Evolution of a Wild Landscape and its Persistence in Southern California. Annals, Association of American Geographers 48(3):250-251.

1976   Man's Impact on the Southern California Flora. Symposium Proceedings: Plant Communities of Southern California, June Latting, ed., pp. 40-48. California Native Plant Society Special Publication No. 2.

Atkinson, C.E., J.H. Rose, and T.O. Duncan
1967   Salmon of the North Pacific Ocean. Prt IV, Spawning Populations of North Pacific Salmon in the United States. International North Pacific Fisheries Commission, Bulletin 23.

Axelrod, D.I.
1978   The Origin of Coastal Sage Vegetation, Alta and Baja California. American Journal of Botany 65:1117-1131.

Baker, R.
1992   The Clam "Gardens" of Tomales Bay. News from Native California 6(2):28-9.

Bancroft, H.H.
1883   The Native Races of the Pacific States. Vol. 1. San Francisco: A.L. Bancroft & Company.

1886   History of California, Vol. I, 1542-1800. San Francisco: The History Company.

Barbour, M., and J. Major, eds.
1977   Terrestial Vegetation of California. New York: John Wiley & Sons.

Barnett, H.G.
1937   Culture Element Distributions: VII, Oregon Coast. Anthropological Records 1:155-204.

1939   Culture Element Distributions: IX, Gulf of Georgia Salish. Anthropological Records 1(5).

404

Barrett, S.A.
1908   Pomo Indian Basketry. University of California Publications in American Archaeology and Ethnology 7:134-308.

1952   Material Aspects of Pomo Culture. Bulletin of the Public Museum of the city of Milwaukee 20(1-2):1-260.

Barrett, S.A., and E.W. Gifford
1933   Miwok Material Culture. Bulletin of the Public Museum of the City of Milwaukee 2(4):117-376.

Barrows, D.P.
1900   The Ethno-Botany of the Coahuilla Indians of Southern California. Chicago: University of Chicago Press.

Barth, F.
1956   Ecological Relationships of Ethnic Groups in Swat, North Pakistan. American Anthropologist 58:1079-1089.

1962   Nomadism in the Mountain and Plateau Areas of South West Asia. In The Problems of the Arid Zone: Proceedings of the Paris Symposium, pp. 341-355. Paris: UNESCO.

Basgall, M.
1987   Resource Intensification among Hunter-Gatherers: Acorn Economies in Prehistoric California. Research in Economic Anthropology 9:21-52.

Baumhoff, M.A.
1963   Ecological Determinants of Aboriginal California Populations. University of California Publications in American Archaeology and Ethnology 49(2):155-235.

Baxley, H.W.
1865   What I Saw on the West Coast of South and North America and at the Hawaiian Islands. New York: D. Appleton and Co.

Beals, R.L.
1933   Ethnology of the Nisenan. University of California Publications in American Archaeology and Ethnology 31(6):335-414.

Bean, L.J.
  1972   Mukat's People. Berkeley: University of California Press.

  1973   Social Organization in Native California. *In* 'Antap: California Indian Political and Economic Organization, L.J. Bean and T. King, eds., pp. 13-34. Ramona: Ballena Press.

Bean, L.J., and T. Blackburn
  1976   Native Californians: A Theoretical Retrospective. Ramona: Ballena Press.

Bean, L.J., and H.W. Lawton
  1973   Some Explanations for the Rise of Cultural Complexity in Native California with Comments on Proto-Agriculture and Agriculture. *In* Patterns of Indian Burning in California: Ecology and Ethnohistory, H. Lewis, pp. v-xlvii. Ramona: Ballena Press.

Bean, L.J., and W.M. Mason
  1962   Diaries & Accounts of the Romero Expedition in Arizona and California, 1823-1826. Palm Springs: Palm Springs Desert Museum.

Bean, L.J., and K. Saubel
  1972   Temalpakh (from the Earth): Cahuilla Indian Knowledge and Usage of Plants. Banning: Malki Museum Press.

Bean, W.
  1968   California: An Interpretive History. New York: McGraw-Hill.

Beckwith, E.G.
  1855   Report of Explorations for a Route for the Pacific Railroad, on the Line of the Forty-first Parallel of North Latitude [1854]. *In* Reports of Explorations and Surveys to Ascertain the Most Practical and Economical Route for a Railroad from the Mississippi River to the Pacific Ocean, Made Under the Secretary of War in 1853-54, Vol. II. 33d Congress, 2d Session, House Executive Document No. 91. Washington: A.O.P. Nicholson, Printer.

Beemer, E.
      1980   My Luiseño Neighbors. Ramona: Acoma Books.

Bell, M.M.
      1974   Chaparral Fuel Modification and Wildlife. *In* Symposium on
              Living with Chaparral, Proceedings, Murray Rosenthal, ed., pp.
              167-172. San Francisco: Sierra Club.

Benson, A.S.
      1982   The Noontide Sun: The Fieldnotes and Unpublished Manu-
              scripts of the Rev. Stephen Bowers. Master's thesis, California
              State University, Northridge.

Benson, L.
      1969   The Native Cacti of California. Stanford: Stanford University
              Press.

Berry, W.
      1981   Recollected Essays, 1965-1980. San Francisco: North Point
              Press.

Bettinger, R.L.
      1975   The Surface Archaeology of Owens Valley, California:
              Prehistoric Man-Land Relationships in the Great Basin. Un-
              published Ph.D. dissertation, University of California,
              Riverside.

      1976   The Development of Pinyon Exploitation in Central Eastern
              California, Journal of California Anthropology 3(1):81-95.

Bicknell, S.H.
      1992   Vegetation of Coastal California Sites Prior to European
              Settlement. Paper presented at the Eighth Annual California
              Indian Conference, Berkeley, California, October 16-18, 1992.

Birckhead, J., T. DeLacy, and L. Smith (eds.)
      1992   Aboriginal Involvement in Parks and Protected Areas.
              Canberra: Aboriginal Studies Press.

Biswell, H.H.
1959a Man and Fire in Ponderosa Pine in the Sierra Nevada of California. Sierra Club Bulletin 44(7):44-53.

1959b Prescribed Burning and Other Methods of Deer Range Improvement in Ponderosa Pine in California. Society of American Foresters Proceedings (San Francisco, California):102-105.

1961 Manipulation of Chamise Brush for Deer Range Improvement. California Fish and Game 47(2):125-144.

1963 Research in Wildland Fire Ecology in California. Tall Timbers Fire Ecology Conference Proceedings 2:63-98. Tallahassee.

1967 The Use of Fire in Wildland Management in California. *In* Natural Resources: Quality and Quantity, S.V. Ciriacy-Wantrup and J.J. Parsons, eds., pp. 71-86. Berkeley: University of California Press.

1968 Forest Fire in Perspective. Tall Timbers Fire Ecology Conference Proceedings 7:43-63. Tallahassee.

1989 Prescribed Burning in California Wildlands Vegetation Management. Berkeley: University of California Press.

Biswell, H.H., H. Buchanan, and R.R. Gibbons
1966 Ecology of the Vegetation of a Second-Growth Sequoia Forest. Ecology 47:630-633.

Biswell, H.H., and J.H. Gilman
1961 Brush Management in Relation to Fire and Other Environmental Factors on the Tehama Deer Winter Range. California Fish and Game 47(4):357-389.

Biswell, H.H., R.D. Taber, D.W. Hendrick, and A.M. Schultz
1952 Management of Chamise Brushlands for Game in the North Coast Region of California. California Fish and Game 38(4):453-484.

Blackburn, T.C.
    1975   December's Child: A Book of Chumash Oral Narratives.
            Berkeley: University of California Press.

Bolton, H.E., ed., tr.
    1911   Expedition to San Francisco Bay in 1770: Diary of Pedro
            Fages. Publications of the Academy of Pacific Coast History
            2(3):143-159.

    1926   Historical Memoirs of New California, by Francisco Palou.
            Berkeley: University of California Press.

    1927   Fray Juan Crespí: Missiionary Explorer on the Pacific Coast,
            1769-1774. Reprinted edition, 1971. New York: AMS Press.

    1930   Anza's California Expeditions. Vol. II. Berkeley: University of
            California Press.

    1967   Spanish Exploration in the Southwest, 1542-1706. New York:
            Barnes & Noble.

Boscana, Fr. G.
    1933   Chinigchinich. *In* Chinigchinich, a revised and annotated
            version of Alfred Robinson's translation of Father Geronimo
            Boscana's historical account of the beliefs, usages, customs and
            extravagancies of the Indians of this mission of San Juan
            Capistrano called the Acagchemen tribe, P.T. Hanna, ed. Santa
            Ana: Fine Arts Press.

Boyd, R.
    1986   Strategies of Indian Burning in the Willamette Valley.
            Canadian Journal of Anthropology 5:65-86.

Bright, W.L.
    1978   Karok. *In* Handbook of North American Indians, Volume 8:
            California, R. Heizer, ed., pp. 180-189. Washington, D.C.:
            Smithsonian Institution.

Brockett, L.P.
  1882   Our Western Empire or the New West Beyond the Mississippi.
          Philadelphia: Bradley, Garretson & Co.

Brown, A.K.
  n.d.   Unpublished Translation of Portions of Crespi's Journals. Ms.
          on file at Santa Barbara Mission Archive Library, Reference
          Files MS. 720.

  1965   The Various Journals of Juan Crespi. The Americas 21(4):375-
          398.

  1967   The Aboriginal Population of the Santa Barbara Channel.
          Berkeley: University of California Archaeological Survey
          Reports No. 69.

Bryant, E.
  1985   What I Saw in California. Lincoln: University of Nebraska
          Press.

Burcham, L.T.
  1957   California Range Land: An Historico-Ecological Study of the
          Range Resources of California. Sacramento: State of
          California, Department of Natural Resources, Division of
          Forestry.

  1959   Planned Burning as a Management Practice for California Wild
          Lands. Society of American Foresters Proceedings (San
          Francisco, California):180-185.

  1974   Fire and Chaparral Before European Settlement. In Sym-
          posium on Living with Chaparral, Murray Rosenthal, ed., pp.
          101-120. San Francisco: Sierra Club.

Burrus, E.J., S.J.
  1967   Diario del Commandante Fernándo Rivera y Moncada. Vol.I.
          Colección Chimalistae de Libros y Documentos Acerca de la
          Nueva España, Nos. 24, 25. Madrid: Ediciones José Porrúa
          Toranzas.

Byrne, R., J. Michaelson, and A. Soutar
    1977   Fossil Charcoal as a Measure of Wildfire Frequency in
            Southern California: A Preliminary Analysis. *In* Proceedings
            of the Symposium on the Environmental Consequences of Fire
            and Fuel Management in the Mediterranean Ecosystem, H.A.
            Mooney and C.E. Conrad, eds., pp. 361-367. USDA Forest
            Service General Technical Report WO-3. Washington: U.S.
            Department of Agriculture.

California Native Plant Society
    1988   California Native Plant Society's Inventory of Rare and
            Endangered Vascular Plants of California. California Native
            Plant Society Special Publication No. 1.

Callaway, D., J. Janetski, and O.C. Stewart
    1986   Ute. *In* Handbook of North American Indians, Vol. 11, Great
            Basin, W.L. d'Azevvedo, ed., pp. 336-367. Washington:
            Smithsonian Institution.

Carrico, R.
    1987   Archaeological Investigations at Westwood Valley, San Diego,
            California, Vol. 1. Prepared by Westec Services for R.B.
            McComic, San Diego.

Castetter, E.F., and W.H. Bell
    1951   Yuman Indian Agriculture: Primitive Subsistence on the Lower
            Colorado and Gila Rivers. Albuquerque: University of New
            Mexico Press.

Castro, D.
    n.d.   Spirit of the Nisenan [acrylic painting]. Spirit Places, Memorial
            Union Gallery, University of California, Davis, 1991.

Caughey, J.W. (ed.)
    1952   The Indians of Southern California in 1852. The B.D. Wilson
            Report and a Selection of Contemporary Comment. San
            Marino: Huntington Library.

Chalfant, W.A.
    1933   The Story of Inyo. Second edition. Bishop: Piñon Book Store.

Chamberlin, R.V.
1911   The Ethno-botany of the Gosiute Indians of Utah. American
        Anthropological Association Memoirs 11.

Chase, A.K.
1989   Domestication and Domiculture in Northern Australia: A
        Social Perspective. *In* Foraging and Farming: The Evolution
        of Plant Exploitation, D. Harris and G. Hillman, eds., pp. 42-
        54. London: Unwin Hyman.

Chestnut, V.K.
1902   Plants Used by the Indians of Mendocino County, California.
        Contributions from the U.S. National Herbarium 7(3):295-
        408.

Clar, C. R.
1959   California Government and Forestry from Spanish Days until
        the Creation of the Department of Natural Resources in 1927.
        Sacramento: California Division of Forestry.

Clark, G.
1904   The Indians of Yosemite. San Francisco: H.S. Crocker Co.

1927   A Yosemite Plea of 1907. Yosemite Nature Notes 6(2):12-
        15.

Clark, G.H.
1929   Sacramento-San Joaquin Salmon (*Oncorhynchus tschawytscha*)
        Fishery of California. California Department of Fish and
        Game, Fish Bulletin 17.

Cohen, M.N.
1977   The Food Crisis in Prehistory: Overpopulation and the Origins
        of Agriculture. New Haven: Yale University Press.

Cohen, M.P.
1984   The Pathless Way: John Muir and American Wilderness.
        Madison: University of Wisconsin Press.

412

Cook, S.F.
1941   The Mechanism and Extent of Dietary Adaptation among
        Certain Groups of California and Nevada Indians. Ibero-
        Americana: 18.

1960   Colonial Expeditions to the Interior of California: Central
        Valley, 1800-1826. Anthropological Records 16(6):239-292.

Coombs, G., and F. Plog
1974   Chumash Baptism: An Ecological Perspective. *In* 'Antap:
        California Indian Political and Economic Organization, L.J.
        Bean and T.F. King, eds., pp. 137-153. Ramona: Ballena Press.

Cooper, C.F.
1952   The Ecology of Fire. Scientific American 204(4):150-160.

Cooper, W.S.
1922   The Broad Sclerophyll Vegetation of California. Carnegie
        Institute of Washington Publications 319:1-124.

Costansó, M.
1910   The Narrative of the Portolá Expedition of 1769-1770. Edited
        by A. van Hemert-Engert and F. Teggart. Publications of the
        Academy of Pacific Coast History 1(4):3-69.

1911   The Portolá Expedition of 1769-1770: Diary of Miguel
        Costansó. Edited by F.J. Teggart. Publications of the Academy
        of Pacific Coast History 2(4):4-167.

Coues, E., ed.
1897   New Light on the Early History of the Greater Northwest:
        The Manuscript Journals of Alexander Henry, Fur Trader of
        the Northwest Company, and of David Thompson, Official
        Geographer and Explorer of the Same Company, 1799-1814.
        2 vols. New York: F.P. Harper.

Couture, M.
1978   Recent and Contemporary Foraging Practices of the Harney
        Valley Paiute. Master's thesis, Portland State University.

Couture, M.D., M.F. Ricks, and L. Housely
1986   Foraging Behavior of a Contemporary Northern Great Basin
        Population. Journal of California and Great Basin Anthro-
        pology 8:150-160.

Coville, F.V.
1892   The Panamint Indians of California. American Anthropologist
        (o.s.) 5:351-361.

Craig, S.
1967   The Basketry of the Ventureño Chumash. Los Angeles:
        University of California Archaeological Survey Annual Report,
        1966-1967:82-149.

Crouch, H.
1915   Reminiscences. Unpublished ms. on file in California Room,
        San Diego Public Library, San Diego.

Cuero, D.
1968   The Autobiography of Delfina Cuero as Told to Florence C.
        Shipek. Interpreter Rosalie Pinto Robertson. Los Angeles:
        Dawson's Book Shop. [Also see Shipek 1991.]

Cumberland, K.B.
1962   'Climatic Change' or Cultural Interference? New Zealand in
        Moahunter Times. In Land and Livelihood: Geographical
        Essays in Honour of George Jobberns, Murray McCaskill, ed.,
        pp. 88-142. Christchurch: New Zealand Geographical Society.

1965   Man's Role in Modifying Island Environments in the
        Southwest Pacific: With Special Reference to New Zealand.
        In Man's Place in the Island Ecosystem, F.R, Fosberg, ed.,
        pp.187-206. Honolulu: Bishop Museum Press.

Curtis, E.S.
1924   The North American Indian. Norwood: The Plimpton Press.

1926   The North American Indian, Vol. 15. Cambridge: The
        University Press.

414

Curtis, F.
  1959   Arroyo Sequit: Archaeological Investigations of a Late Coastal
          Site in Los Angeles County, California. Archaeological Survey
          Association of Southern California Paper No. 4.

Daubenmire, R.
  1968   Ecology of Fire in Grasslands. Advances in Ecological
          Research 5:209-266.

Davidson, F.A., and S.J. Hutchinson
  1938   The Geographical Distribution and Environmental Limitations
          of the Pacific Salmon (Genus *Oncorhynchus*). Bulletin of the
          U.S. Bureau of Fisheries 48:667-692.

Davis, J.T.
  1959   Further Notes on Clay Human Figurines in Western United
          States. University of California Archaeological Survey Reports
          No. 48, Paper 71. Berkeley.

  1966   Trade Routes and Economic Exchange Among the Indians of
          California. *In* Aboriginal California: Three Studies in Culture
          History. Berkeley: University of California Archaeological
          Research Facility.

Day, F.
  n.d.   Commentary on Whirlwind [oil painting]. Spirit Places,
          Memorial Union Gallery, University of California, Davis, 1991.

Day, G.M.
  1953   The Indian as an Ecological Factor in the Northeastern Forest.
          Ecology 34:329-346.

d'Azevedo, W.L., ed.
  1986   Handbook of North American Indians, Vol. 11, Great Basin.
          Washington: Smithsonian Institution.

Dibblee, T.W.
　1976　Geology of Santa Barbara County and Its Influence on Vegetation. *In* A Flora of the Santa Barbara Region, California, by Clifton F. Smith, pp. 7-13. Santa Barbara: Santa Barbara Museum of Natural History.

Dimbleby, G.W.
　1967　Plants and Archaeology. London: John Baker.

Dixon, R.B.
　1905　The Northern Maidu. American Museum of Natural History Bulletin 17(3):119-346.

　1907　The Shasta. American Museum of Natural History Bulletin 17(5):381-498.

　1908　Notes on the Achomawi and Atsugewi of Northern California. American Anthropologist 10(2):208-220.

Douglas, D.
　1833　Description of a New Species of the Genus Pinus. Linnaean Society of London Transactions 16:747-750.

　1959　Journal Kept by David Douglas During His Travels in North America, 1823-1827. New York: Antiquarian Press.

Downs, J.F.
　1966a　The Two Worlds of the Washo: An Indian Tribe of California and Nevada. New York: Holt, Rinehart and Winston.

　1966b　The Significance of Environmental Manipulation in Great Basin Cultural Development. *In* The Current Status of Anthropological Research in the Great Basin: 1964, W. d'Azevedo and others, eds., pp. 39-56. Reno: Desert Research Institute.

　1972　The Navajo. New York: Holt, Rinehart and Winston.

416

Downs, J.F., and R.B. Ekvall
1965   Animals and Social Types in the Exploitation of the Tibetan Plateau. *In* Man, Culture and Animals, A. Leeds and A. Vayda, eds., pp. 169-184. Washington: American Association for the Advancement of Science.

Driver, H.E.
1937   Culture Element Distributions: VI, Southern Sierra Nevada. Anthropological Records 1(2):53-154.

1939   Culture Element Distributions: X, Northwest California. Anthropological Records 1(6):297-433.

1961   The Indians of North America. Chicago: University of Chicago Press.

Driver, H.E., and W.C. Massey
1957   Comparative Studies of North American Indians. Transactions of the American Philosophical Society 46:163-456.

Drucker, P.
1937   The Tolowa and Their Southwest Oregon Kin. University of California Publications in American Archaeology and Ethnology 36(4):221-300.

1939   Culture Element Distributions: V, Southern California. Anthropological Records 1(1).

DuBois, C.A.
1931   Wintu Myths. University of California Publications in American Archaeology and Ethnology 28(5):281-403.

1932   Tolowa Notes. American Anthropologist 34:248-262.

1935   Wintu Ethnography. University of California Publications in American Archaeology and Ethnology 36(1):1-148.

Duncan, J.W., III
1964   Maidu Ethnobotany. M.A. thesis, San Francisco State University.

Eggan, F.
1966   The Cheyenne and Arapaho in the Perspective of the Plains: Ecology and Society. *In* The American Indian: Perspectives for the Study of Social Change, pp. 45-77. Chicago: Aldine.

Elias, T.S.
1980   The Complete Trees of North America: Field Guide and Natural History. New York: Van Nostrand Reinhold Co.

Englehardt, Z., O.F.M.
1920   The Missions and Missionaries of California, New Series: Local History: San Diego Mission. San Francisco: James H. Barry Co.

1930   The Missions and Missionaries of California, Vol. II. Upper California. Santa Barbara: Mission Santa Barbara (2nd. ed.).

Erikson, E.H.
1943   Observations on the Yurok: Childhood and World Image. University of California Publications in American Archaeology and Ethnology 35:257-301.

Evans, Col. A.S.
1873   Á la California: Sketches of Life in the Golden State. San Francisco: A.L. Bancroft & Co.

Evermann, B.W., and H.W. Clark
1931   A Distributional List of the Species of Freshwater Fishes Known to Occur in California. California Department of Fish and Game, Fish Bulletin 35.

Ewers, J.C.
1955   The Horse in Blackfoot Indian Culture. Bureau of American Ethnology Bulletins 159.

Ewers, J.C., ed.
1959   Adventures of Zenas Leonard, Fur Trader. Norman: University of Oklahoma Press.

Farris, G.J.
1980   A Reassessment of the Nutritional Value of Pinus monophylla. Journal of California and Great Basin Anthropology 2(1):132-136.

1982a   Aboriginal Use of Pine Nuts in California: An Ethnological, Nutritional, and Archaeological Investigation into the Uses of the Seeds of Pinus lambertiana Doug. and Pinus sabiniana Doug. by the Indians of Northern California. Unpublished Ph.D. dissertation, University of California, Davis.

1982b   Pine Nuts as an Aboriginal Food Source in California and Nevada: Some Contrasts. Journal of Ethnobiology 2(2):114-122.

1983   California Pignolia: Seeds of *Pinus sabiniana*. Economic Botany 37(2):201-206.

Faye, P-L.
1923   Notes on the Southern Maidu. University of California Publications in American Archaeology and Ethnology 20(3):35-53.

Felton, E.K.
1965   California's Many Climates. Palo Alto: Pacific Books.

Fernández, G., O.F.M.
1800   Questions Sent by the Governor of California, Don Diego de Borica, to the Commandantes, and the Replies of the Fathers of Mission Purísima. Translation by Maynard Geiger, O.F.M. Ms. on file at the Santa Barbara Museum Archive Library.

Ferris, W.A.
1940   Life in the Rocky Mountains: A Diary of Wanderings on the Sources of the Rivers Missouri, Columbia, and Colorado, from February, 1830, to November, 1835, P.C. Phillips, ed. Denver: Old West Publishing Co.

419

Fields, V.M.
1985   The Hover Collection of Karuk Baskets. Eureka: Clarke Memorial Museum.

Fisher, A.D.
1968   The Algonquian Plains? Anthropologica 10:219-234.

Flannery, K.V.
1973   The Origins of Agriculture. In Annual Review of Anthropology, B.J. Siegel, A.R. Beals, and S.A. Tyler, eds., Vol. 2, pp. 271-310. Palo Alto.

Forbes, J.
1963   Indian Horticulture West and Northwest of the Colorado River. Journal of the West 2:1-14.

Ford, H.C.
1887   Notes on Excavations Made in Indian Burial Places in Carpinteria. Report of the Proceedings of the Santa Barbara Society of Natural History, pp. 11-19.

Foster, G.M.
1944   A Summary of Yuki Culture. Anthropological Records 5(3):155-244.

Fowler, C.S.
1986   Subsistence. In Handbook of North American Indians, Volume 11: Great Basin, W.L. d'Azevado, ed., pp. 64-97. Washington, D.C.: Smithsonian Institution.

Fowler, C.S., and S. Liljeblad
1986   Northern Paiute. In Handbook of North American Indians, Vol. 11, Great Basin, W.L. d'Azevedo, ed., pp. 435-465. Washington: Smithsonian Institution.

Fowler, C.S., and J.F. Matley
1979   Material Culture of the Numa: The John Wesley Powell Collection, 1867-1880. Smithsonian Contributions to Anthropology No. 26.

Fowler, C.S., and N.P. Walter
    1985   Harvesting Pandora Moth Larvae with the Owens Valley
           Paiute. Journal of California and Great Basin Anthropology
           7:155-165.

Fritz, E.
    1931   The Role of Fire in the Redwood Region. Journal of Forestry
           29:939-950.

Fry, D.H.
    1973   Anadromous Fishes of California. Sacramento: California
           Department of Fish and Game.

Gamble, L.H.
    1983   The Organization of Artifacts, Features and Activities at Pitas
           Point: A Coastal Chumash Village. Journal of California and
           Great Basin Anthropology 5(1,2):103-129.

Gayton, A.H.
    1946   Culture-Environment Integration: External References in
           Yokuts Life. Southwestern Journal of Anthropology 2:252-
           268.

    1948   Yokuts and Western Mono Ethnography. Anthropological
           Records 10(1/2).

Geertz, C.
    1963   Agricultural Involution: The Processes of Ecological Change
           in Indonesia. Berkeley: University of California Press.

Geiger, M. (ed.)
    1970   Letters of Luis Jayme, O.F.M. San Diego, October 17, 1772.
           Los Angeles: Dawson's Book Shop.

Gendar, J.
    1991-2 Report on Panel Discussions and Workshops in California
           Indian Basketweavers Gathering Special Supplement. News
           from Native California 6(1):15, 16, 18, 20, 22, 24, 26, 28, 32,
           34, 36.

Gibbs, G.
  1853   Journal of the Expedition of Colonel Redick M'Kee...1851. *In* Henry R. Schoolcraft, Historical and Statistical Information Respecting the History, Condition, and Prospects of the Indian Tribes of the United States, III:99-177. Philadelphia.

Gifford, E.W.
  1931   The Kamia of Imperial Valley. Bureau of American Ethnology Bulletins 97:1-94.

  1939   California Balanophagy. *In* The California Indians, A Source Book, R.F. Heizer and M.A. Whipple, eds., pp. 301-305. Berkeley: University of California Press.

Gifford, E.W., and S. Klimek
  1939   Culture Element Distributions: II, Yana. University of California Publications in American Archaeology and Ethnology 37(2):71-100.

Gifford, E.W., and A.L. Kroeber
  1939   Culture Element Distributions: IV, Pomo. University of California Publications in American Archaeology and Ethnology 37(4):117-254.

Goddard, P.E.
  1903-04 Life and Culture of the Hupa. University of California Publications in American Archaeology and Ethnology 1(1):1-88.

  1904   Hupa Texts. University of California Publications in American Archaeology and Ethnology 1(2):89-368.

Goldschmidt, W.R.
  1951   Nomlaki Ethnography. University of California Publications in American Archaeology and Ethnology 42(4):303-443.

Gould, R.A.
  1980   Living Archaeology. Cambridge: Cambridge University Press.

422

Gove, P.B.
1971   Webster's Third New International Dictionary of the English Language Unabridged. Springfield: G. & C. Merriam.

Great Basin Films
1979   The Earth is Our Home (film). Ogden.

Griffin, J.R.
1976   Regeneration in *Quercus lobata* Savannas, Santa Lucia Mountains, California. American Midland Naturalist 95(2):422-435.

1977   Oak Woodland. *In* Terrestial Vegetation of California, M.G. Barbour and J. Major, eds., pp. 383-413. New York: John Wiley & Sons.

1980   Animal Damage to Valley Oak Acorns and Seedlings, Carmel Valley, California. *In* Proceedings of the Symposium on the Ecology, Management, and Utilization of California Oaks, T. Plumb, tech. coord., pp. 242-245. USDA Forest Service General Technical Report PSW-44. Washington: U.S. Department of Agriculture.

Grinnell, G.B.
1923   The Cheyenne Indians: Their History and Ways of Life. 2 vols. New Haven: Yale University Press.

Guinn, J.M.
1917   Some Early History of Owens River Valley. Historical Society of Southern California Annual Publications 10:42-46.

Gunther, E.
1926   An Analysis of the First Salmon Ceremony. American Anthropologist 28:605-617.

1928   A Further Analysis of the First Salmon Ceremony. University of Washington Publications in Anthropology 2:129-173.

Hallam, S.J.
    1975   Fire and Hearth. Canberra: Australian Institute of Aboriginal Studies.

Hanes, T.L.
    1971   Succession After Fire in the Chaparral of Southern California. Ecological Monographs 41:27-52.

    1977   California Chaparral. *In* Terrestial Vegetation of California, M.G. Barbour and J. Major, eds., pp.417-469. New York: John Wiley & Sons.

Hardy, O.
    1929   Agricultural Changes in California, 1860-1900. Proceedings of the Pacific Coast Branch of the American Historical Association, 1929, pp. 216-230.

Harlan, J.R.
    1975   Crops and Man. Madison: American Society of Agronomy, Crop Science Society of America.

Harrington, J.P.
    n.d.   Unpublished fieldnotes on file at the National Anthropological Archives, Smithsonian Institution.

    1932   Tobacco Among the Karuk Indians of California. Bureau of American Ethnology Bulletins 94:1-284.

    1934   A New Original Version of Boscana's Historical Account of the San Juan Capistrano Indians of Southern California. Washington: Smithsonian Institution.

    1942   Culture Element Distributions: XIX, Central California Coast. Anthropological Records 7:1-46.

Harris, D.R.
    1975   Review of Patterns of Indian Burning in California: Ecology and Ethnohistory, by Henry T. Lewis. American Anthropologist 77:685-686.

1989   An Evolutionary Continuum of People-Plant Interaction. *In* Foraging and Farming: The Evolution of Plant Exploitation, D. Harris and G. Hillman, eds, pp. 11-26. London: Unwin Hyman.

Harris, D.R. and G.C. Hillman (eds.)
1989   Foraging and Farming: The Evolution of Plant Exploitation. London: Unwin Hyman.

Hartesveldt, R.J.
1964   Fire Ecology of the Giant Sequoia: Controlled Fires May Be One Solution to Survival of the Species. Natural History Magazine 73:12-19.

Hartesveldt, R.J., and H.T. Harvey
1967   The Fire Ecology of Sequoia Regeneration. Tall Timbers Fire Ecology Conference Proceedings 7:65-77. Tallahassee.

Hattori, E.M.
1975   Northern Paiutes on the Comstock: Archaeology and Ethnohistory of an American Indian Population in Virginia City, Nevada. Nevada State Museum Occasional Papers No. 2.

Haury, E.W.
1976   The Hohokam, Desert Farmers & Craftsmen: Excavations at Snaketown, 1964-1965. Tucson: University of Arizona Press.

Havard, V.
1895   Food Plants of the North American Indians. Torrey Botanical Club Bulletin 22:98-123.

Hayes, B.
1929   Pioneer Notes from the Diaries of Judge Benjamin Hayes. Los Angeles: Privately Printed.

Heady, H.F.
1972   Burning and the Grasslands in California. Unpublished paper presented at the Annual Meeting of the Tall Timbers Fire Ecology Conference.

1977   Vallcy Grassland. *In* Tcrrcstial Vcgctation of California, M.G. Barbour and J. Major, eds., pp. 491-514. New York: John Wiley & Sons.

Hedges, K.
1973   Hakataya Figurines from Southern California. Pacific Coast Archaeological Society Quarterly 9:1-40.

Heffner, K.
1984   Following the Smoke: Contemporary Plant Procurcmcnt by the Indians of Northwcst California. Eurcka: Six Rivcrs National Forcst.

Hcintzclman, S.P.
1857   Rcport of July 15, 1853. Thirty-fourth Congrcss, 3rd Scssion, Housc Exccutivc Documcnt No. 76, pp. 34-58.

Heizer, R.F.
1950   Kutsavi, a Grcat Basin Indian Food. Kroebcr Anthropological Socicty Papcrs 2:35-41.

1955   California Indian Linguistic Rccords: Thc Mission Indian Vocabularies of H.W. Henshaw. Anthropological Rccords 15(2):85-202.

1958   Prehistoric Central California: A Problcm in Historical Developmental Classification. University of California Archaeological Survey Reports 41:19-26.

Heizer, R.F., and R.K. Beardslcy
1943   Fired Clay Human Figurines in Central and Northern California. American Antiquity 9(2):199-207.

Heizer, R.F., and A.B. Elsasser
1980   Thc Natural World of thc California Indians. California Natural History Guides No. 46. Berkeley: University of California Press.

Heizer, R.F., and D.M. Pendergast
  1955   Additional Data on Fired Clay Human Figurines from California. American Antiquity 21(2):181-185.

Heizer, R.F., and M.A. Whipple
  1971   The California Indians: A Source Book. Berkeley: University of California Press.

Helbaek, H.
  1960   The Paleoethnobotany of the Near East and Europe. *In* Prehistoric Investigations in Iraqi Kurdistan, R. Braidwood and B. Howe, eds. Chicago: University of Chicago Press.

Henry, D.
  1985   Preagricultural Sedentism: The Natufian Example. *In* Prehistoric Hunter-Gatherers: the Emergence of Cultural Complexity, T.D. Price and J.A. Brown, eds., pp. 365-384. New York: Academic Press.

Heusser, L.
  1978   Pollen in the Santa Barbara Basin, California: A 12,000-Year Record. Bulletin of the Geological Society of America 89:673-678.

Hewes, G.W.
  1942   Economic and Geographical Relationships of Aboriginal Fishing in Northern California. California Fish and Game 28:103-110.

  1947   Aboriginal Use of Fishing Resources in Northwestern North America. Unpublished Ph.D. dissertation. University of California, Berkeley.

Hickerson, H.
  1965   The Virginia Deer and Inter-tribal Buffer Zones in the Upper Mississippi Valley. *In* Man, Culture and Animals, A. Leeds and A. Vayda, eds., pp. 43-65. Washington: American Association for the Advancement of Science.

Hicks, R.
    1985   Culturally Altered Trees: A Data Source. Northwest Anthropological Research Notes 19(1):100-118.

Hill, J.H., and R. Nolasquez
    1973   Mulu'wetam: The First People. Cupeño Oral History and Legends. Banning: Malki Museum Press.

Hitchcock, A.S.
    1971   Manual of the Grasses of the United States. 2 volumes. New York: Dover Publications.

Ho, P-T.
    1975   The Cradle of the East. An Inquiry into the Indigenous Origins of Techniques and Ideas of Neolithic and Early Historic China, 5000-1000 B.C. Chicago: The Chinese University of Hong Kong/University of Chicago Press.

Hoadley, R.B.
    1980   Understanding Wood: A Craftsman's Guide to Wood Technology. Newtown: Taunton Press.

Holm, B.
    1982   On Making Horn Bows. *In* Native American Bows, by T.M. Hamilton, Appendix I. Missouri Archaeological Society Special Publication No. 5.

Holt, C.
    1946   Shasta Ethnography. Anthropological Records 3(4):299-349.

Hooper, L.
    1920   The Cahuilla Indians. University of California Publications in American Archaeology and Ethnology 16(6).

Horne, S.P.
    1981   The Inland Chumash: Ethnography, Ethnohistory and Archaeology. Ph.D. dissertation, University of California, Santa Barbara.

428

Horton, J.S., and C.J. Kraebel
  1955   Development of Vegetation After Fire in the Chamise
          Chaparral of Southern California. Ecology 36:244-262.

Howay, F.W.
  1940   The Journal of Captain James Colnett Aboard the Argonaut
          from April 26, 1769 to Nov. 3, 1791. Toronto: The Champlain
          Society.

Hudson, J.W.
  1893   Pomo Basket Makers. Overland Monthly 21(126):561-578.

Hudson, T., and T. Blackburn
  1982   The Material Culture of the Chumash Interaction Sphere. Vol.
          I: Food Procurement and Transportation. Los Altos: Ballena
          Press/Santa Barbara Museum of Natural History.

  1983   The Material Culture of the Chumash Interaction Sphere. Vol.
          II: Food Procurement and Transportation. Los Altos: Ballena
          Press/Santa Barbara Museum of Natural History.

  1985   The Material Culture of the Chumash Interaction Sphere. Vol.
          III: Clothing, Ornamentation, and Grooming. Menlo Park:
          Ballena Press/Santa Barbara Museum of Natural History.

  1986   The Material Culture of the Chumash Interaction Sphere. Vol.
          IV: Ceremonial Paraphernalia, Games, and Amusements.
          Menlo Park: Ballena Press/Santa Barbara Museum of Natural
          History.

  1987   The Material Culture of the Chumash Interaction Sphere. Vol.
          V: Manufacturing Processes, Metrology, and Trade. Menlo
          Park: Ballena Press/Santa Barbara Museum of Natural
          History.

Hudson, T., T. Blackburn, R. Curletti, and J. Timbrook, eds.
  1977   The Eye of the Flute: Chumash Traditional History and Ritual
          as Told by Fernando Librado *Kitsepawit* to John P. Har-
          rington. Santa Barbara: Santa Barbara Museum of Natural
          History.

Hudson, T., J. Timbrook, and M. Rempe
1978   Tomol: Chumash Watercraft as Described in the Ethnographic Notes of John P. Harrington. Socorro: Ballena Press/Santa Barbara Museum of Natural History.

Hudson, T., and E. Underhay
1978   Crystal in the Sky: An Intellectual Odyssey Involving Chumash Astronomy, Cosmology, and Rock Art. Socorro: Ballena Press/Santa Barbara Museum of Natural History.

Humphrey, R.R.
1962   Fire as a Factor in Range Ecology. New York: Ronal Press.

Hunter, J.E.
1988   Prescribed Burning for Cultural Resources. Fire Management Notes 49(2).

Jack, Klamath River
1916   Letter of May 27, 1916 to Fish and Game Commission. California Fish and Game 2(4):194-195.

James, G.W.
1903   Indian Basketry. New York: Henry Malkan.

Jennings, J.D.
1956   The American Southwest: A Problem in Cultural Isolation. Society for American Archaeology Memoirs 11:59-128.

Jennings, J.D., and E. Norbeck
1955   Great Basin Prehistory: A Review. American Antiquity 21:1-11.

Jensen, A.
1976   Lovelock Dune Corn Cob: A Preliminary Report. Nevada Archaeological Survey Reporter, pp. 13-17, Nevada Archaeological Survey, University of Nevada, Reno.

Jepson, W.L.
1921   The Fire-type Forest of the Sierra Nevada. The Intercollegiate Forestry Club Annual 1:7-10.

1922   Revision of the California Species of the Genus Arcto-staphylos. Madrona 1:79-96.

1923   The Trees of California. Second edition. Berkeley: Sather Gate Book Shop.

1930   The Role of Fire in Relation to the Differentiation of Species in the Chaparral. International Botanical Congress Proceedings 5:114-116.

Johannes, R.E.
1981   Words of the Lagoon: Fishing and Marine Lore in the Palau District of Micronesia. Berkeley: University of California Press.

Johannessen, S. and C. Hastorf
1990   A History of Fuel Management (A.D. 500 to the Present) in the Mantaro Valley, Peru. Journal of Ethnobiology 10(1):61-90.

Johnston, B.E.
1962   California's Gabrielino Indians. Los Angeles: Southwest Museum.

Johnston, V.R.
1970a   The Ecology of Fire. Audubon 72:76-81, 85, 88, 90, 92, 99, 100, 102, 104, 106, 108, 110, 112, 114, 116-119.

1970b   Sierra Nevada. Boston: Houghton Mifflin Co.

Jones, R.
1969   Firestick Farming. Australian Natural History 16:224-228.

Jordan, D.S.
1896   The Fishes of North and Middle America. United States National Museum, Bulletin 47(1).

Kearney, M.
1974   Introductory. Journal of California Anthropology 1:4-5.

Keeley, J.E. and S.C. Keeley
  1988   Chaparral. *In* North American Terrestial Vegetation, M. Barbour and W. Billings, eds., pp. 165-207. Cambridge: Cambridge University Press.

Keeley, S.C., J.E. Keeley, S.M. Hutchinson, and A.W. Johnson
  1981   Postfire Succession of Herbaceous Flora in Southern California Chaparral. Ecology 61(6):1608-1621.

Kelly, I.T.
  1932   Ethnography of the Surprise Valley Paiute. University of California Publications in American Archaeology and Ethnology 31(2).

  1964   Southern Paiute Ethnography. University of Utah Anthropological Papers No. 69.

  1991   Interviews with Tom Smith and María Copa: Isabel Kelly's Ethnographic Notes on the Coast Miwok Indians of Marin and Southern Sonoma Counties, California. Mapom Occasional Papers 6. San Rafael.

Kern, E.M.
  1876   Journal of Mr. Edward M. Kern on an Exploration of Mary's or Humboldt River, Carson Lake, and Owens River and Lake in 1845. *In* Report of Explorations Across the Great Basin of Territory of Utah for a Direct Wagon-route from Camp Floyd to Genoa, in Carson Valley, in 1859, by Captain J.H. Simpson, pp. 475-486. Washington: U.S. Government Printing Office.

Kilgore, B.M.
  1970   Restoring Fire to the Sequoias. National Parks Magazine 44:16-22.

  1972   Fire's Role in a Sequoia Forest. Naturalist 23:26-37.

Killinger, G.B., and W.E. Stokes
  1951   Chufas in Florida. University of Florida Agriculture Experiment Station Bulletins 419:5-16. Gainsville.

432

King, C.D.
  1973 The Explanation of Differences and Similarities Among Beads
        Used in Prehistoric and Early Historic California. *In* 'Antap:
        California Indian Political and Economic Organization, L.J.
        Bean and T. King, eds., pp. 77-92. Ramona: Ballena Press.

King, C.D., J. Triem, J. Parsons, N. Anikouchine, B. Texier, L. Cummings,
and M. Alexander
  1991 Oak Park Zone 3 Phase II Archaeological Resource Assess-
        ment: Two Processing and Camping Sites in Southeastern
        Ventura County. Ms. on file at the U.C.L.A. Archaeological
        Information Center and Ventura County Resource Manage-
        ment Agency.

King, L.B.
  1969 The Medea Creek Cemetery (4-LAn-243): An Investigation of
        Social Organization from Mortuary Practices. Los Angeles:
        University of California Archaeological Survey Annual Report
        1968-1969:23-68.

Kniffen, F.B.
  1928 Achomawi Geography. University of California Publications
        in American Archaeology and Ethnology 23(5):297-332.

  1939 Pomo Geography. University of California Publications in
        American Archaeology and Ethnology 36(6):353-400.

Knight, R.
  1965 The Re-examination of Hunting, Trapping, and Territoriality
        Among the Algonkian Indians. *In* Man, Culture and Animals,
        A. Leeds and A. Vayda, eds., pp. 27-42. Washington:
        American Association for the Advancement of Science.

Komarek, E.V., Sr.
  1967 The Nature of Lightning Fires. Tall Timbers Fire Ecology
        Conference Proceedings 7:5-41. Tallahassee.

Komarek, R.
  1963 Fire and the Changing Wildfire Habitat. Tall Timbers Fire
        Ecology Conference Proceedings 2:35-43. Tallahassee.

Kotok, E.I.
  1934   Fire, a Major Ecological Factor in the Pine Region of California. Pacific Science Congress Proceedings (Canada) 5:4017-4022. Toronto: University of Toronto Press.

Kowta, M.
  1965   A Note on the Origins of Paiute Irrigation. Unpublished ms. on file at the Department of Anthropology, California State University, Chico.

Koyama, S., and D.H. Thomas
  1981   Affluent Foragers: Pacific Coasts East and West. Senri Ethnological Studies 9. Osaka.

Kroeber, A.L.
  1908a   Ethnology of the Gros Ventre. American Museum of Natural History Anthropological Papers 1(4).

  1908b   Ethnography of the Cahuilla Indians. University of California Publications in American Archaeology and Ethnology 8:29-68.

  1925   Handbook of the Indians of California. Bureau of American Ethnology Bulletins 78. Washington: Smithsonian Institution.

  1932a   The Patwin and Their Neighbors. University of California Publication in American Archaeology and Ethnology 29(4):253-423.

  1932b   Yuki Myths. Anthropos 27:905-940.

  1939   Cultural and Natural Areas of Native North America. University of California Publications in American Archaeology and Ethnology 38.

  1941   Culture Element Distributions: XV, Salt, Dogs, Tobacco. Anthropological Records 6:1-20.

  1952   [See Kroeber 1925]

434

Kroeber, A.L., and S.A. Barrett
  1960   Fishing Among the Indians of Northwestern California. Anthropological Records 22:1-156.

Kroeber, A.L., and E.W. Gifford
  1949   World Renewal: A Cult System of Native Northwest California. Anthropological Records 13:1-154.
Kroeber, T.
  1961   Ishi in Two Worlds. Berkeley: University of California Press.

Kroeber, T., and R. Heizer
  1968   Almost Ancestors: The First Californians. San Francisco: Sierra Club.

Kunkel, P.
  1962   Yokuts and Pomo Political Institutions: A Comparative Analysis. Unpublished Ph.D. dissertation, University of California, Los Angeles.

Lanner, R.M.
  1981   The Piñon Pine: A Natural and Cultural History. Reno: University of Nevada Press.

La Pérouse, J.F.G. de
  1968   A Voyage Round the World Performed in the Years 1785, 1786, 1787, and 1788 by the Boussole and Astrolabe. Vol. I. New York: Da Capo Press.

Latta, F.F.
  1977   Handbook of Yokuts Indians. Second edition. Santa Cruz: Bear State Books.

Laubin, R., and G. Laubin
  1980   American Indian Archery. Norman: University of Oklahoma Press.

Lawton, H.W.
  1968   The Dying God of the Cahuilla: Ethnohistoric Evidence of a
          Colorado River-derived Agricultural Complex in Southern
          California. Graduate Seminar Paper in English 275A, The Oral
          Epic, University of California, Riverside.

  1974   Agricultural Motifs in Southern California Indian Mythology.
          Journal of California Anthropology 1:55-79.

Lawton, H.W., and L.J. Bean
  1968   A Preliminary Reconstruction of Aboriginal Agricultural
          Technology Among the Cahuilla. The Indian Historian 1(5):18-
          24, 29.

Leach, H.R., and J.L. Hiehle
  1957   Food Habits of the Tehama Deer Herd. California Fish and
          Game 43(3):161-178.

LeConte, J.L.
  1855   Account of Some Volcanic Springs in the Desert of the
          Colorado, in Southern California. American Journal of Science
          and Arts 19:1-6.

Lee, M.H.
  1931   The Indians and I. San Diego: Thomas Givens Dawson.

  1937   Indians of the Oaks. Boston: Ginn & Co.

Lee, R.B., and I. Devore, eds.
  1968   Man the Hunter. Chicago: Aldine.

Leeds, A.
  1965   Reindeer Herding and Chukchi Social Institutions. *In* Man,
          Culture and Animals, A. Leeds and A. Vayda, eds., pp. 87-
          128. Washington: American Association for the Advancement
          of Science.

Leopold, A.S.
  1950   Deer in Relation to Plant Succession. North American Wildlife
          Conference Transactions 15:571-580.

Leopold, A.S., S.A. Cain, C.M. Cottam, I.N. Gabrielson, and T.L. Kimball
    1963   Wildlife Management in the National Parks. Report of Advisory Board on Wildlife Management to Secretary of the Interior Udall. 23 pp. mimeo.

Lesant, M.
    1822   Recherches Sur Las Composition Chinique Des Tubercules Du Souchet Comestible. Journal of Pharmacology, Ser. 2, Ann. 8, pp. 497-513.

Levy, J.E.
    1961   Ecology of the South Plains: The Ecohistory of the Kiowa, Comanche, Cheyenne, and Arapaho, 1830-1870. American Ethnological Society Proceedings:18-25. Seattle: University of Washington Press.

Lewis, H.T.
    1971   Ilocano Rice Farmers: A Comparison of Two Phillippine Barrios. Honolulu: University of Hawaii Press.

    1972   The Role of Fire in the Domestication of Plants and Animals in Southwest Asia: A Hypothesis. Man 7:195-222.

    1973   Patterns of Indian Burning in California: Ecology and Ethnohistory. Ramona: Ballena Press.

    1977   Maskuta: The Ecology of Indian Fires in Northern Alberta. Western Canadian Journal of Anthropology 7:15-52.

    1978   Fires of Spring (film). Edmonton: University of Alberta Motion Picture Services.

    1980   Indian Fires of Spring. Natural History 89:76-83.

    1981   Hunter-Gatherers and Problems for Fire History. *In* Proceedings of the Fire History Workshop, pp. 115-119. General Technical Report RM-81, Rocky Mt. Forest and Range Experiment Station, U.S. Forest Service.

1982a   A Time for Burning: Traditional Indian Uses of Fire in the
        Western Canadian Boreal Forest. Edmonton: Boreal Institute
        for Northern Studies, University of Alberta.

1982b   Fire Technology and Resource Management in Aboriginal
        North America and Australia. *In* N. Williams and E. Hunn,
        eds., Resource Managers: North American and Australian
        Hunter-Gatherers, pp. 45-67. Boulder: Westview Press.

1985   Why Indians Burned: Specific versus General Reasons. *In* J.
        Lotan, B. Gilgore, W. Fischer, and R. Mutch, eds., Symposium
        and Workshop on Wilderness Fire Proceedings, pp. 75-86.
        Missoula: Intermountain Forest and Range Experiment Station,
        Forest Service, U.S. Department of Agriculture.

1989a   Ecological and Technical Knowledge of Fire: Aborigines vs.
        Park Rangers in Northern Australia. American Anthropologist
        91:940-961.

1989b   Non-Agricultural Management of Plants and Animals:
        Alternative Burning Strategies in Norther Australia. *In* R.
        Hudson, K. Drew, and L. Baskin, eds., Wildlife Production
        Systems: Economic Utilization of Ungulates, pp. 54-74.
        Cambridge: Cambridge University Press.

1990a   Traditional Ecological Knowledge of Fire in Northern Alberta:
        Something Old, Something New, Something Different. *In* R.
        Ironside and P. McCormack, eds., Proceedings of the Fort
        Chipewyan and Fort Vermillion Bicentennial Conference, pp.
        222-227. Edmonton: Boreal Institute for Northern Studies,
        University of Alberta.

1990b   Reconstructing Patterns of Indian Burning in Southwestern
        Oregon. *In* N. Hannon and R. Olmo, eds., Living With the
        Land: The Indians of Southwestern Oregon, pp. 80-94.
        Medford: Southern Oregon Historical Society.

438

1991   Technological Complexity, Ecological Diversity, and Fire Regimes in Northern Australia: Hunter-Gatherer, Cowboy, Ranger. *In* A. Rambo and K. Gillogly, eds., Profiles in Cultural Evolution, pp. 261-288. Ann Arbor: Museum of Anthropology, University of Michigan.

1992   The Technology and Ecology of Nature's Custodians: Anthropological Perspectives on Aborigines and National Parks. *In* J. Birckhead, T. DeLacy, and L. Smith, eds., Aboriginal Involvement in Parks and Protected Areas, pp. 1-13. Canberra: Aboriginal Studies Press.

Lewis, H.T., and T.M. Ferguson
1988   Yards, Corridors, and Mosaics: How to Burn a Boreal Forest. Human Ecology 16:57-77.

Los Angeles Star (newspaper)
1858   The Owen's Lake Expedition--Gold Rumors from Mono Lake. The Los Angeles Star, August 21, 1858, p. 2.

1859   Expedition to Owen's Lake. The Los Angeles Star, August 27, 1859, p. 2.

Loud, L.L.
1918   Ethnogeography and Archaeology of the Wiyot Territory. University of California Publications in American Archaeology and Ethnology 14(3):221-423.

Lowie, R.H.
1909   The Northern Shoshoni. American Museum of Natural History Anthropological Papers 2(2).

1924   Notes on Shoshonean Ethnography. American Museum of Natural History Anthropological Papers 20(3).

Luomala, K.
n.d.   Unpublished ms. on Diegueño Indians.

Margaleff, R.
 1968   Perspectives in Ecological Theory. Chicago: University of
        Chicago Press.

Margolin, M.
 1981   The Way We Lived: California Indian Reminiscences, Stories
        and Songs. Berkeley: Heyday Books.

Mason, H.L.
 1957   A Flora of the Marshes of California. Berkeley: University of
        California Press.

Mason, O.T.
 1894   North American Bows, Arrows, and Quivers. Smithsonian
        Institution Annual Report for 1893:631-679.

 1900   The Hudson Collection of Basketry. American Anthropologist
        2:346-353.

 1904   Aboriginal American Basketry: Studies in a Textile Art
        Without Machinery. Washington: Report of the U.S. National
        Museum for 1902.

Maximilian, A.P. (Prince of Wied-Neuwied)
 1904-7 Travels in the Interior of North America. [Originial English
        edition London, 1843.] *In* Early Western Travels, 1748-1846,
        a Series of Annotated Reprints of Some of the Best and
        Rarest Contemporary Volumes of Travel, Descriptive of the
        Aborigines and Social and Economic Conditions in the Middle
        and Far West, During the Period of Early American
        Settlement, R.G. Thwaites, ed., vols. 22-25. Cleveland: A.H.
        Clark Co.

Mayo, N.
 1941   Agricultural Statistics of Florida. Florida Agricultural Statistical
        Report 1941, p.97.

McCarthy, H.
 n.d.   Unpublished fieldnotes, Southcentral Sierra Nevada, 1984-
        1992.

McDonald, P.
   1978   Silviaculture--Ecology of Three Native California Hardwoods
           on High Sites in North Central California. Unpublished Ph.D.
           dissertation, Oregon State University.

McMillin, J.H.
   1956   The Aboriginal Human Ecology of the Mountain Meadows
           Area in Southwestern Lassen County, California. M.A. thesis,
           Sacramento State College.

Meighan, C.W.
   1959   California Cultures and the Concept of an Archaic Stage.
           American Antiquity 24:289-305.

Merriam, C.H.
   n.d.   California Journal, 1898-1935. Ms. on file at Department of
           Anthropology, University of California, Davis.

   1955   Studies of California Indians. Berkeley: University of
           California Press.

Merrill, R.E.
   1923   Plants Used in Basketry by the California Indians. University
           of California Publications in American Archaeology and
           Ethnology 20:215-242.

Miller, H.A.
   1963   Use of Fire in Wildlife Management. Tall Timbers Fire
           Ecology Conference Proceedings 2:19-30. Tallahassee.

Minnich, R.A.
   1983   Fire Mosaics in Southern California and Northern Baja
           California. Science 219:1287-1294.

Mirschitzka, S.
   1992   Usage and Management of Marine Resources on the
           Northwest Coast. European Review of Native American
           Studies 6(1):9-16.

Mooney, H.A.
    1977a Southern Coastal Scrub. *In* Terrestial Vegetation of California, M.G. Barbour and J. Major, eds., pp. 471-489. New York: John Wiley & Sons.

    1977b The Carbon Cycle in Mediterranean-Climate Evergreen Scrub Communities. *In* Proceedings of the Symposium on the Environmental Consequences of Fire and Fuel Management in Mediterranean Ecosystems, H. Mooney and C. Conrad, eds., pp. Washington: U.S. Department of Agriculture.

Mooney, H.A., and C.E. Conrad, eds.
    1977 Proceedings of the Symposium on the Environmental Consequences of Fire and Fuel Management in Mediterranean Ecosystems. USDA Forest Service General Technical Report WO-3. Washington: U.S. Department of Agriculture.

Muir, J.
    1894 The Mountains of California. Garden City: Doubleday.

Muller, C.H.
    1966 The Role of Chemical Inhibition (Allelopathy) in Vegetational Composition. Torrey Botanical Club Bulletins 93(4):332-351.

    1969 Allelopathy as a Factor in Ecological Process. Vegetatio 18:348-357.

Muller, C.H., R.B. Hanawal, and J.K. McPherson
    1968 Allelopathic Control of Herb Growth in the Fire Cycle of California Chaparral. Torrey Botanical Club Bulletins 95(3):225-231.

Muller, W.H., and C.H. Muller
    1964 Volatile Growth Inhibitors Produced by Salvia Ieucophylla: Effect on Seedling Growth and Respiration. Torrey Botanical Club Bulletins 91(4):415-422.

Munz, P.A.
    1959 A California Flora. Berkeley: University of California Press.

442

1965   [See Munz 1959]

1968   [See Munz 1959]

Munz, P.A., and D.A. Keck
1949   California Plant Communities. El Aliso 2:87-105.

Murphy, E.V.
1959   Indian Uses of Native Plants. Fort Bragg: Mendocino County
        Historical Society.

Murphy, R.F., and Y. Murphy
1960   Shoshone-Bannock Subsistence and Society. Anthropological
        Records 16(7):293-338.

Nabhan, G.
1985   Gathering the Desert. Tucson: University of Arizona Press.

Nabhan, G., et al.
1991   Conservation and Use of Rare Plants by Traditional Cultures
        of the U.S./Mexico Borderlands. In Biodiversity: Culture,
        Conservation, and Ecodevelopment, M.L. Oldfield and J.B.
        Alcorn, eds., pp. 127-146. Boulder: Westview Press.

Nash, R.
1982   Wilderness and the American Mind. New Haven: Yale
        University Press. (3rd. ed.)

Netolitzky, F.
1911   Nahrungs- und Heilmittel der Urägypter [Food and Medication
        of the Ancient Egyptians]. Die Umschau 46:953-956.

1912   Hirse und Cyperus aus dem Prahistorischen Ägypten [Millet
        and Cyperus from Prehistoric Egypt]. Beihefte zum Botan-
        ishcen Centralblatt 29:1-11.

Newman, S.C.
1974   Indian Basket Weaving. Flagstaff: Northland Press.

Nichols, R.F., and D.G. Smith
1965   Evidence of Prehistoric Cultivation of Douglas-fir Trees at Mesa Verde. *In* Contributions of the Wetherill Mesa Archaeological Project, D. Osborne, assemb., pp. 57-64. Society for American Archaeology Memoirs No. 19.

Nomland, G.A.
1935   Sinkyone Notes. University of California Publications in American Archaeology and Ethnology 36:149-178.

Norton, H.
1979   The Association between Anthropogenic Prairies and Important Food Plants in Western Washington. Northwest Anthropological Research Notes 13:175-200.

O'Connell, J.F.
1974   Review of Patterns of Indian Burning in California: Ecology and Ethnohistory, by Henry T. Lewis. Journal of California Anthropology 1(1):118-120.

Odum, E.P.
1969   The Strategy of Ecosystem Development. Science 164:262-270.

1971   Fundamentals of Ecology. Third edition. Philadelphia: W.B. Saunders Co.

Oliver, S.C.
1962   Ecology and Cultural Continuity as Contributing Factors in the Social Organization of the Plains Indians. University of California Publications in American Archaeology and Ethnology 48(1):1-90.

O'Neale, L.M.
1932   Yurok-Karok Basket Weavers. University of California Publications in American Archaeology and Ethnology 32(1):1-184.

Ord, E.O.C.
  1850   Lt. E.O.C. Ord's First Report to General Riley. Executive
          Document No. 47, Thirty-first Congress, Senate, First Session,
          pp. 119-127.

Orr, P.C.
  1968   Prehistory of Santa Rosa Island. Santa Barbara: Santa Barbara
          Museum of Natural History.

Ortiz, B.
  1988a   On Tradition and the State's Gathering Policy. News from
          Native California 2(2):24-25.

  1988b   Baskets of Dreams. News from Native California 2(4):28-29.

  1991   It Will Live Forever: Traditional Yosemite Indian Acorn
          Preparation. Berkeley: Heyday Press.

  1991-2 Elsie Allen and Susan Billy in California Indian Basketry
          Today: A Special Report on the 1991 California Indian
          Basketweavers Gathering. News from Native California
          6(1):16-17.

Parmenter, J.
  1977   Effects of Fire on Pathogens. *In* Proceedings of the Sym-
          posium on the Environmental Consequences of Fire and Fuel
          Management in Mediterranean Ecosystems, H. Mooney and
          C.E. Conrad, eds. USDA Forest Service General Technical
          Report WO-3. Washington: Department of Agriculture.

Patch, R.
  1951   Irrigation in East Central California. American Antiquity
          17:50-52.

Patencio, F.
  1943   Stories and Legends of the Palm Springs Indians. Los Angeles:
          Times-Mirror Co.

Peri, D.
  1985   Pomoan Plant Resource Management. Ridge Review 4(4).

Peri, D.W., and S.M. Patterson
    1978   An Ethnographic and Ethnohistoric Survey and an Assessment of Native American Interests in the SUNEDCO Geothermal Leasehold, Mendocino County, California. A report prepared for Ecoview Environmental Consultants, Napa, California. (Ms. on file at the Ethnographic Laboratory, Sonoma State University.)

    1979   Ethnobotanical Resources of the Warm Springs Dam-Lake Sonoma Project Area, Sonoma County, California. San Francisco: U.S. Army Corps of Engineers.

Peri, D.W., S.M. Patterson, and S.L. McMurray
    1985   The Makahmo Pomo: An Ethnographic Survey of the Cloverdale (Makahmo) Pomo. San Francisco: U.S. Army Corps of Engineers.

Peterson, J.T.
    1977a   Ecotones and Exchange in Northern Luzon. *In* K. Hutterer, ed., Economic Exchange and Social Interaction in Southeast Asia: Perspectives from Prehistory, History and Ethnography, pp. 55-71. Ann Arbor: University of Michigan.

    1977b   The Merits of Margins. *In* N. Wood, ed., Cultural-Ecological Perspectives on Southeast Asia, pp. 63-73. Athens: Center for International Studies, Ohio University.

    1978   The Ecology of Social Boundaries: Agta Foragers of the Phillippines. Urbana: University of Illinois.

Piddocke, S.
    1965   The Potlatch System of the Southern Kwakiutl: A New Perspective. Southwestern Journal of Anthropology 21:244-264.

Piper, C.
    1924   Forage Plants and Their Culture. Revised edition. New York: Macmillan.

Plumb, T.
1980   Response of Oaks to Fire. *In* Proceedings of the Symposium on the Ecology, Management, and Utilization of California Oaks, T. Plumb, tech. coord., pp. 202-215. USDA Forest Service General Technical Report PSW-44. Washington: U.S. Department of Agriculture.

Plumb, T., and A. Gomez
1983   Five Southern California Oaks: Identification and Postfire Management. USDA Forest Service General Technical Report PSW-71. Washington: U.S. Department of Agriculture.

Plumb, T., and P. McDonald
1981   Oak Management in California. Pacific Southwest Forest and Range Experiment Station, General Technical Report PSW-54.

Pope, S.T.
1918   Yahi Archery. University of California Publications in American Archaeology and Ethnology 13(3).

1925   Hunting with the Bow and Arrow. New York: G.P. Putnam's Sons.

Potts, M.
1977   The Northern Maidu. Happy Camp: Naturegraph Publishers.

Pourade, R.F.
1960   The History of San Diego: The Explorers, Vol. I. San Diego: Union-Tribune Publishing Co.

Powell, J.W.
1875   Exploration of the Colorado River of the West and Its Tributaries, Explored in 1869, 1870, 1871, and 1872, Under the Direction of the Secretary of the Smithsonian Institution. Washington: Government Printing Office.

Powers, S.
1872   The Northern California Indians (The Euroc and Cahroc). Overland Monthly 8:425-435, 539.

1874   The Northern California Indians: XI, Various Tribes (Acho-
        mawi, Yana, Sierra Maidu). Overland Monthly 12:412-424.

1877   Tribes of California. U.S. Geographical and Geological Survey
        of the Rocky Mountain Region, Contributions to North
        American Ethnology 3.

Priestley, H.I.
    1937   A Historical, Political, and Natural Description of California
            by Pedro Fages, Soldier of Spain. Berkeley: University of
            California Press.

Purdy, C.
    n.d.   Pomo Indian Baskets and Their Makers. Reprinted by the
            Mendocino County Historical Society, Ukiah.

Pyne, S.
    1982   Fire in America: A Cultural History of Wildland and Rural
            Fire. Princeton: Princeton University Press.

Rappaport, R.A.
    1971   The Flow of Energy in an Agricultural Society. Scientific
            American 224:116-122, 127-132.

Ray, V.F.
    1942   Culture Element Distributions: XXII, Plateau. Anthropological
            Records 8(2).

Record, S.J., and R.W. Hess
    1943   Timbers of the New World. New Haven: Yale University
            Press.

Reid, D.K.
    1987   Fire and Habitat Modification: An Anthropological Inquiry
            into the Use of Fire by Indigenous Peoples. M.A. thesis,
            University of Alberta.

448

Reynolds, R.D.
   1959   The Effect upon the Forest of Natural Fire and Aboriginal
           Burning in the Sierra Nevada. M.A. thesis, University of Cali-
           fornia, Berkeley.

Rhoades, R.
   1974   The Ecotone Concept in Anthropology and Ecology. Papers
           in Anthropology 15:23-36.

Riddell, F.
   1966   Comments on Ecology and Culture Change. *In* The Current
           Status of Anthropological Research in the Great Basin: 1964,
           W.L. d'Azevedo, W.A. Davis, D.D. Fowler, and W. Scuttles,
           eds. Reno: Desert Research Institute.

Riddington, R.
   1982   Technology, World View, and Adaptive Strategy in a Northern
           Hunting Society. Canadian Review of Sociology and Anthro-
           pology 19:469-481.

Rivers, B.J.
   1980   Interview Notes Obtained from Ramsey Blake, Dixie Valley
           Aporige, Fall River Mills, California. Ms.

Roberts, H.H.
   1932   The First Salmon Ceremony of the Karok Indians. American
           Anthropologist 34:426-440.

   1980   Concow Maidu Myths of Round Valley--1926. Association for
           Northern California Records and Research, Occasional
           Publication 5. Edited by Dorothy J. Hill.

Roberts, R.K.
   1932   Conservation as Formerly Practices by the Indians in the
           Klamath River Region. California Department of Fish and
           Game, Fish Bulletin 18:283-290.

Rostland, E.
   1952   Freshwater Fish and Fishing in Native North America.
           University of California Publications in Geography 9.

449

Rudkin, C., trans. and ed.
1956 Observations on California, 1772-1790, by Father Luis Sales, O.P. Los Angeles: Dawson's Book Shop.

Rundel, P.W.
1971 Community Structure and Stability in Giant Sequoia Groves of the Sierra Nevada, California. American Midlands Naturalist 85:478-492.

Rutter, C.
1908 The Fishes of the Sacramento-San Joaquin Basin, with a Study of Their Distribution and Variation. United States Bureau of Fisheries, Bulletin 27:103-152.

Sampson, A.W.
1944 Plant Succession on Burned Chaparral Lands in Northern California. University of California Agricultural Experiment Station Bulletin 685:1-144. Berkeley.

Sanchez, Fr. José Bernardo
n.d. Diario de la Caminata que hizo El P. Perfecto Payeras en union del P. Sanchez por la Sierra desde San Diego hasta San Gabriel. Archivo de la Misión de Sta. Barbara. Tome IV, 1806-1821:209-229. Ms. on file at Bancroft Library, University of California, Berkeley.

Sapir, E.
1910a Kaibab Paiute Notes. Ms. on file at the American Philosophical Society Library, Philadelphia.

1910b Yana Texts. University of California Publications in American Archaeology and Ethnology 9(1):1-235.

Sauer, C.O.
1936 American Agricultural Origins. In Essays in American Anthropology, R.H. Lowie, ed. Berkeley: University of California Press.

1944 A Geographical Sketch of Early Man in America. Geographical Review 34:529-537.

1947   Early Relations of Man to Plants. Geographical Review 37:1-25.

1950   Grassland Climax, Fire, and Man. Journal of Range Management 3:16-20.

1952   Agricultural Origins and Dispersals. New York: American Geographical Society.

1975   Man's Dominance by Use of Fire. *In* B. Perkins, ed., Geoscience and Man, Vol. 10. Grasslands Ecology: A Symposium, pp. 15-26. Baton Rouge: Louisiana State University Press.

Sauer, J.
1977   Fire History, Environmental Patterns, and Species Patterns in the Santa Monica Mountains Chaparral. *In* Proceedings of the Symposium on the Environmental Consequences of Fire and Fuel Management in Mediterranean Ecosystems, H.A. Mooney and C.E. Conrad, eds., pp. 383-386. Washington: United States Forest Service General Technical Report WO-3.

Schenk, S.M., and E.W. Gifford
1952   Karok Ethnobotany. Anthropological Records 13(6):377-392.

Schlesinger, W.H., J.T. Gray, D.S. Gill, and B.E. Mahall
1982   *Ceanothus megacarpus* Chaparral: A Synthesis of Ecosystem Processes During Development and Annual Growth. Botanical Review 48(1):72-117.

Schlick, M.D.
1984   Cedar Bark Baskets. American Indian Basketry and Other Native Arts 4(3):26-29.

Schmeider, O.
1927   The Pampa: A Natural or Culturall Induced Grass-land? University of California Publications in Geography 2(8):255-270.

Schweinfurth, G.
　1884　Further Discoveries in the Flora of Ancient Egypt. Nature
　　　　29:312-313.

Secoy, F.R.
　1953　Changing Military Patterns on the Great Plains. American
　　　　Ethnological Society Monographs 21.

Shapalov, L., and A.C. Taft
　1954　The Life Histories of the Steelhead Rainbow Trout (*Salmo
　　　　gairdnerii gairdnerii*) and Silver Salmon (*Oncorhynchus kisutch*)
　　　　with Special Reference to Waddell Creek, California, and
　　　　Recommendations Regarding Their Management. California
　　　　Department of Fish and Game, Fish Bulletin 98.

Shepard, P.
　1967　Editor's Foreword. *In* The Subversive Science: Essays Toward
　　　　an Ecology of Man, P. Shepard and D. McKinley, eds., pp. 1-
　　　　10. Boston: Houghton Mifflin Co.

Shimkin, D.B., and R.M. Reid
　1970　Socio-cultural Persistence Among Shoshoneans of the Carson
　　　　River Basin (Nevada). *In* Languages and Cultures of Western
　　　　North America, E.H. Swanson, Jr., ed.

Shipek, F.C.
　1971　Prepared Direct Testimony of Florence C. Shipek, Anthropolo-
　　　　gist. Exhibit B-50. Federal Power Commission Project No. 176,
　　　　San Diego County, California.

　1977　A Strategy for Change: The Luiseño of Southern California.
　　　　Ph.D. dissertation, University of Hawaii. Honolulu.

　1982　Kumeyaay Socio-Political Structure. Journal of California and
　　　　Great Basin Anthropology 4(2):296-303.

　1989　An Example of Intensive Plant Husbandry: The Kumeyaay of
　　　　Southern California. *In* D. Harris and G. Hillman, eds.,
　　　　Foraging and Farming: The Evolution of Plant Exploitation,
　　　　pp. 159-170. London: Unwin Hyman.

452

1991   Delfina Cuero. Menlo Park: Ballena Press.

1992   The Shaman: Priest, Doctor, Scientist. *In* L. J. Bean, ed., California Indian Shamanism, pp. 89-96. Menlo Park: Ballena Press.

Show, S.B., and E.I. Kotok
1924   The Role of Fire in the California Pine Forests. United States Department of Agriculture Bulletin No. 1294, pp. 1-80. Washington.

Simpson, L.B., ed., tr.
1938   California in 1792: The Expedition of José Longinos Martínez. San Marino: Huntington Library.

1961   Journal of José Longinos Martínez: Notes and Observations of the Naturalist of the Botanical Expedition in Old and New California and the South Coast, 1791-1792. San Francisco: John Howell Books.

Smith, C.F.
1956   Botanizing on the Burn. Santa Barbara Museum of Natural History Quarterly 31(3):33-39.

1976   A Flora of the Santa Barbara Region, California. Santa Barbara: Santa Barbara Museum of Natural History.

Smith, D.E., and F. J. Teggart, eds.
1909   Diary of Gaspar de Portolá During the California Expedition of 1769-1770. Publications of the Academy of Pacific Coast History 1(3):31-89.

Smith, J.R.
1929   Tree Crops: A Permanent Agriculture. New York: Brace and Co.

Smithsonian Institution
1983   Tule Technology [film]. Washington: Smithsonian Institution, Office of Folklife Programs.

Snyder, J.O.
    1908   The Fishes of the Coastal Streams of Oregon and Northern California. United States Bureau of Fisheries, Bulletin 27:153-189.

    1931   Salmon of the Klamath River, California. California Department of Fish and Game, Fish Bulletin 34.

Sparkman, P.S.
    1908   The Culture of the Luiseño Indians. University of California Publications in American Archaeology and Ethnology 8:187-234.

Spier, L.
    1923   Southern Diegueño Customs. University of California Publications in American Archaeology and Ethnology 20:297-358.

Spinden, H.J.
    1917   The Origin and Distribution of Agriculture in America. International Congress of Americanists Proceedings 19:269-276.

Spott, R., and A.L. Kroeber
    1942   Yurok Narratives. University of California Publications in American Archaeology and Ethnology 35:143-265.

Standiford, R., tech. coord.
    1991   Proceedings of the Symposium on Oak Woodlands and Hardwood Rangeland Management, October 31-November 2, 1990, Davis, California. USDA Forest Service General Technical Report PSW-126. Washington: U.S. Department of Agriculture.

Steward, J.H.
    1930   Irrigation without Agriculture. Michigan Academy of Sciences, Arts, and Letters Papers 12:149-156.

1933   Ethnography of the Owens Valley Paiute. University of California Publications in American Archaeology and Ethnology 33(3).

1934   Two Paiute Autobiographies. University of California Publications in American Archaeology and Ethnology 33(5).

1938   Basin-Plateau Aboriginal Sociopolitical Groups. Bureau of American Ethnology Bulletins 120. Washington.

1941   Culture Element Distribtions: XIII, Nevada Shoshone. Anthropological Records 4(3).

1943   Culture Element Distributions: XXIII, Northern and Gosiute Shoshoni. Anthropological Records 8(3).

1970   The Foundations of Basin-Plateau Shoshonean Society. *In* Languages and Cultures of Western North America, E.H. Swanson, ed., pp. 113-151. Pocatello: Idaho State University Press.

Steward, J.H., and E. Wheeler-Voegelin
1974   The Northern Paiute Indians. *In* American Indian Ethnohistory: California and Great Basin Indians (Paiute Indians III), D.A. Horr, ed., pp. 9-328 (repaginated). New York: Garland Publishing.

Stewart, H.
1984   Culturally Modified Trees. The Midden 16(5):7-9.

Stewart, O.C.
1941   Culture Element Distributions: XIV, Northern Paiute. Anthropological Records 4(3).

1942   Culture Element Distributions: XVIII, Ute-Southern Paiute. Anthropological Records 6(4).

1943   Notes on Pomo Ethnogeography. University of California Publications in American Archaeology and Ethnology 40(2):29-62.

1951   Burning and Natural Vegetation in the United States. Geographical Review 41(2):317-320.

1954   The Forgotten Side of Ethnogeography. *In* R. Spencer, ed., Method and Perspective in Anthropology, pp. 221-248. Minneapolis: University of Minnesota Press.

1955a   Forest Fires with a Purpose. Southwestern Lore 20:42-46.

1955b   Why Were the Prairies Treeless? Southwestern Lore 20:59-64.

1955c   Forest and Grass Burning in the Mountain West. Southwestern Lore 21:5-9.

1956   Fire as the First Great Force Applied by Man. *In* Man's Role in Changing the Face of the Earth, W.L. Thomas, ed., pp. 115-330.

1963   Barriers to Understanding the Influence of Use of Fire by Aborigines on Vegetation. Tall Timbers Fire Ecology Conference Proceedings 2:117-126. Tallahassee.

Stickney, F.S., D.F. Barnes, and P. Simpson
1950   Date Palm Insects in the United States. United States Department of Agriculture Circular 846.

Stone, L.
1873   On the Sacramento Salmon (Report on Operations at the U.S. Salmon Hatchery Station on the McCloud River in 1872). Reports of the Commissioner of the United States Commission on Fish and Fisheries, pp. 168-215.

Storer, T.I.
1932   Factors Influencing Wild Life in California, Past and Present. Ecology 13:315-327.

Storer, T.I., and R.L. Usinger
1963   Sierra Nevada Natural History: An Illustrated Handbook. Berkeley: University of California Press.

Strong, W.D.
    1929   Aboriginal Society in Southern California. University of
            California Publications in American Archaeology and
            Ethnology 26:1-329.

Sturtevant, E.L.
    1919   Sturtevant's Notes on Edible Plants. Edited by U.P. Hedrick.
            Albany: J.B. Lyon Company.

Sullivan, A.
    1974   Remote Imagery Studies in Hidden Valley, Nevada. Journal
            of California Anthropology 1:114-117.

Suttles, W.
    1968   Coping with Abundance: Subsistence on the Northwest Coast.
            In Man the Hunter, R.B. Lee and I. Devore, eds., pp. 56-
            68. Chicago: Aldine.

Sweeney, J.R.
    1956   Responses of Vegetation to Fire: A Study of the Herbaceous
            Vegetation Following Chaparral Fires. University of California
            Publications in Botany 28:143-250.

    1968   Ecology of Some "Fire-type" Vegetations in Northern
            California. Proceedings of the Tall Timbers Fire Ecology
            Conference 7:111-125. Tallahassee: Tall Timbers Research
            Station.

Sweet, L.E.
    1965a   Camel Pastoralism in North Arabia and the Minimal Camping
            Unit. In Man, Culture and Animals, A. Leeds and A. Vayda,
            eds., pp. 129-152. Washington: American Association for the
            Advancement of Science.

    1965b   Camel Raiding of North Arabian Bedouin: A Mechanism of
            Ecological Adaptation. American Anthropologist 67:1132-1150.

Sweet, M.
    1962   Common Edible and Useful Plants of the West. Healdsburg:
            Naturegraph Co.

Swetnam, T.W.
   1984   Peeled Ponderosa Pine Trees; A Record of Inner Bark Utilization by Native Americans. Journal of Ethnobiology 4:177-190.

Swezey, S.
   1975   The Energetics of Subsistence-Assurance Ritual in Native California. Contributions of the University of California Archaeological Research Facility 23:1-46.

Taylor, A.S.
   1861   The Indianology of California (Third Series). California Farmer and Journal of Useful Sciences, November 8, 1861, p. 58.

   1862   The Indianology of California (Third Series). California Farmer and Journal of Useful Sciences, March 28, 1862.

Taylor, N., ed.
   1961   Taylor's Encyclopedia of Gardening, Horticulture, and Landscape Design. Boston: Houghton Mifflin Co.

Teaford, M.
   1930   Statement on Mono/Chukchansi burning in Madera County. Reported in Madera County School Histories, Vol. I. On file at Madera County Library, Oakhurst.

Teit, J.A.
   1928   The Salishan Tribes of the Western Plateaus, F. Boas, ed., pp. 23-396. Bureau of American Ethnology, Forty-fifth Annual Report.

Telewski, F.W., and M.J. Jaffe
   1986   Thigmomorphogenesis: Field and Laboratory Studies of *Abies fraseri* in Response to Wind or Mechanical Perturbation. Physiologia Plantarum 66:211-218.

Theodoratus, D.J., D.W.Peri, C.M. Blount, and S.M. Patterson
　　1975　　An Ethnographic Survey of the Mahilkaune (Dry Creek)
　　　　　　Pomo, Contract No. DACW07-75-C-0022 of the U.S. Army
　　　　　　Corps of Engineers, San Francisco District.

Thompson, L.
　　1916　　To the American Indian. Eureka: Cummins Press.

Tibesar, A., ed.
　　1955　　Writings of Junípero Serra. Vol. I. Washington: Academy of
　　　　　　American Franciscan History.

Timbrook, J.
　　1982　　Use of Wild Cherry Pits as Food by the California Indians.
　　　　　　Journal of Ethnobiology 2(2):162-176.

Timbrook, J., J.R. Johnson, and D.D. Earle
　　1982　　Vegetation Burning by the Chumash. Journal of California and
　　　　　　Great Basin Anthropology 4(2):163-186.

Train, P., J.R. Henrichs, and W.A. Archer
　　1974　　Contributions toward a Flora of Nevada No. 45: Medicinal
　　　　　　Uses of Plants by Indian Tribes of Nevada. In American
　　　　　　Indian Ethnohistory, Paiute Indians IV, D.A. Horr, ed., pp. 53-
　　　　　　257. New York: Garland Publishing.

Treganza, A.E.
　　1947　　Possibilites of an Aboriginal Practice of Agriculture Among
　　　　　　the Southern Diegueño. American Antiquity 12:169-173.

　　1956　　Horticulture with Irrigation Among the Great Basin Paiute:
　　　　　　An Example of Stimulus Diffusion and Cultural Survival.
　　　　　　Papers of the Third Great Basin Archeological Convention.
　　　　　　University of Utah Anthropological Papers 26:82-94.

Treide, D.
　　1965　　Die Organisierung des indianischen Lachsfangs im Westlichen
　　　　　　Nordamerika. Veroffentlichungen des Museums für Völker-
　　　　　　kunde zu Leipzig, Heft 14. Berlin: Akademie-Verlag.

True, D.L.
  1957   Fired Clay Figurines from San Diego County, California. American Antiquity 22:296-301.

Turney-High, H.H.
  1941   Ethnography of the Kutenai. American Anthropological Association Memoir No. 56.

Ucko, P.
  1989   Foreword. *In* Foraging and Farming: The Evolution of Plant Exploitation, D. Harris and G. Hillman, eds., pp. ix-xviii. London: Unwin Hyman.

Underhill, R.M.
  1965   Red Man's Religion: Beliefs and Practices of the Indians North of Mexico. Chicago: University of Chicago Press.

Van Cleve, R.
  1945   A Preliminary Report on the Fishery Resources of California in Relation to the Central Valley Project. California Fish and Game 31:35-52.

Vayda, A.P.
  1961   Expansion and Warfare Among Swidden Cultivators. American Anthropologist 63:346-358.

Vankat, J.L.
  1970   Vegetation Change in Sequoia National Park, California. Unpublished Ph.D. dissertation, University of California, Davis.

Veatch, J.A.
  1858   Notes of a Visit to the "Mud Volcanoes" in the Colorado Desert in the Month of July, 1857. American Journal of Science and Arts 26:288-295.

Voegelin, E.W.
  1938   Tübatulabal Ethnography. Anthropological Records 2(1):1-90.

  1942   Culture Element Distributions: XX, Northeastern California. Anthropological Records 7(2):47-251.

460

Vogl, R.J.
    1968   Fire Adaptations of Some Southern California Plants.
            Proceedings of the Tall Timbers Fire Ecology Conference
            7:79-109. Tallahassee: Tall Timbers Research Station.

Wallace, W.J.
    1957   The Clay Figurine from Death Valley National Monument,
            California. Masterkey 31(4):131-134.

    1978   Southern Valley Yokuts. In Handbook of North American
            Indians, Vol. 8, California, R.F. Heizer, ed., pp. 448-461.
            Washington: Smithsonian Institution.

Washington, F.B.
    1976   Customs of the Indians of Western Tehama County. In A
            Collection of Ethnographical Articles on the California Indians,
            R.F. Heizer, ed. Ramona: Ballena Press.

Wassen [sic], W.
    1862   The Owens River Indian War. The Delta (newspaper), Visalia,
            May 8, 1862, p. 2.

Wasson, W.
    1862   [Communication]. In Document 47, Report of [James W. Nye}
            Relative to Difficulties with the Indians of Owens River. In
            Report of the Commissioner of Indian Affairs for 1862. In
            Report of the Secretary of Interior for 1862. House Executive
            Document 1, Part 2, pp. 368-371. Thirty-seventh Congress,
            Third Session, Dec, 1, 1862-Mar. 3, 1863. Washington: U.S.
            Government Printing Office. (U.S. Serials Set 1157).

Waterman, T.T., and A.L. Kroeber
    1938   The Kepel Fish Dam. University of California Publication in
            American Archaeology and Ethnology 35:49-80.

Watson, D.S.
    1934   West Wind: The Life of Joseph Reddeford Walker, Knight of
            the Golden Horseshoe. Los Angeles: Privately printed for
            Percy H. Booth by Johnck and Seeger, Printers.

Weatherwax, P.
  1954   Indian Corn in Old America. New York: Macmillan Company.

Weaver, S.M.
  1984   Progress Report: The Role of Aboriginals in the Management
          of Cobourg and Kakadu National Parks, Northern Territory,
          Australia. (Unpublished ms.)

Wells, P.V.
  1962   Vegetation in Relation to Geological Substratum and Fire in
          the San Luis Obispo Quadrangle, California. Ecological Mono-
          graphs 32(1):79-103.

Wessells, H.W.
  1853   Journal of H.W. Wessells in Command of Military Escort of
          R. McKee, 1851. United States House of Representatives, 34th
          Congress, 3rd Session, Executive Documents, 1853. Document
          76, Serial 906, pp. 59-68.

Wheat, M.
  1967   Survival Arts of the Primitive Paiutes. Reno: University of
          Nevada Press.

White, T.
  1954   Scarred Trees in Western Montana. Montana State University
          Anthropology and Sociology Papers No. 17.

Wilke, P.J.
  1978   Late Prehistoric Human Ecology at Lake Cahuilla, Coachella
          Valley, California. University of California Archaeological
          Research Facility Contributions 38.

  1988   Archery Bows of Horn, Antler, and Bone in Interior Western
          United States: Historic and Ethnographic Records. Ms.
          submitted for publication.

Wilke, P.J., ed.
  1976   Background to Prehistory of the Yuha Desert Region.
          Ramona: Ballena Press.

Wilke, P.J., R. Bettinger, T.F. King, and J.F. O'Connell
  1972   Harvest Selection and Domestication in Seed Plants. Antiquity
          46:203-209.

Wilke, P.J., and D. Fain
  1972   An Archaeological Cucurbit from Coachella Valley, California.
          Archaeological Research Unit, Department of Anthropology,
          University of California, Riverside. 3 pp. (Mimeo.)

Wilke, P.J., T.F. King, and S. Hammond
  1975   Aboriginal Occupation at Tahquitz Canyon: Ethnohistory and
          Archaeology. *In* The Cahuilla Indians of the Colorado Desert:
          Ethnohistory and Prehistory, pp. 45-73. Ramona: Ballena
          Press.

Wilke, P.J., and H.W. Lawton
  1975   Early Observations on the Cultural Geography of Coachella
          Valley. *In* The Cahuilla Indians of the Colorado Desert:
          Ethnohistory and Prehistory, pp. 9-43. Ramona: Ballena Press.

Willey, G.R., and P. Phillips
  1955   Method and Theory in American Archaeology II: Historical-
          Developmental Interpretation. American Anthropologist 57:723-
          819.

Williams, N., and E.S. Hunn, eds.
  1982   Resource Managers: North American and Australian Hunter-
          Gatherers. Boulder: Westview Press.

Willoughby, Nona
  1963   Division of Labor among the Indians of California. University
          of California Archaeological Survey Reports 60:7-79.

Winter, J.
  1974   Aboriginal Agriculture in the Southwest and Great Basin.
          Ph.D. dissertation, University of Utah.

Wirtz, W.O., II
    1974   Chaparral Wildlife and Fire Ecology. *In* Symposium on Living with Chaparral, Murray Rosenthal, ed., pp. 7-18. San Francisco: Sierra Club.

Wittfogel, K.A.
    1957   Oriental Despotism: A Comparative Study of Total Power. New Haven: Yale University Press.

Woodbury, R.B.
    1961   A Reappraisal of Hohokam Irrigation. American Anthropologist 63:550-560.

Wolf, Carl
    1945   California Wild Tree Crops. Anaheim: Rancho Santa Ana Botanic Garden.

Wyeth, N.J.
    1851   Indian Tribes of the South Pass of the Rocky Mountains; the Salt Lake Basin; the Valley of the Great Saaptin, or Lewis' Rivers, and the Pacific Coasts of Oregon. *In* Historical and Statistical Information Respecting the History, Condition, and Prospects of the Indian Tribes of the United States: Collected and Prepared Under the Direction of the Bureau of Indian Affairs per Act of Congress of March 3rd, 1847, by Henry R. Schoolcraft, Part 1, pp. 204-228. Philadelphia: Lippincott, Grambo & Co.

Yarrow, H.C.
    1879   Report Upon the Operations of a Special Party for Making Ethnological Researches in the Vicinity of Santa Barbara, California. *In* Report of the United State Geographical Surveys West of the 100th Meridian, Vol. VII:32-47. Washington: United States Government Printing Office.

Yen, D.E.
    1989   The Domestication of Environment. *In* Foraging and Farming: The Evolution of Plant Exploitation, D. Harris and G. Hillman, eds., pp. 55-75. London: Unwin Hyman.

Ziegler, A.C.
    1968   Quasi-Agriculture in North-Central California and its Effect on Aboriginal Social Structure. Kroeber Anthropological Society Papers 38:52-67.

Zigmond, M.L.
    1981   Kawaiisu Ethnobotany. Salt Lake City: University of Utah Press.

Zohary, D.
    1969   The Progenitors of Wheat and Barley in Relation to Domestication and Agricultural Dispersal in the Old World. *In* The Domestication and Exploitation of Plants and Animals, P.J. Ucko and G.W. Dimbleby, eds. Chicago: University of Chicago Press.

INDEX

466

470

herding 46
Hermizonia ramosissima 136
Hesperocnide 141
Heterotheca 141
hickory 274
Hohokam 336, 372
Homogi 169
Hoopa 97, 104, 314
Hopland 179-180
Hordeum 119, 138, 141
  californicum 138
horticultural complex 340, 370-372
horticulture 159, 340, 365, 372
huckhau 169
huckleberry 87, 89
Hunan 336
hunting 16-19, 27-28, 37-39, 41, 43, 46-
  47, 49, 52, 54, 56, 62, 69, 72, 82, 90, 91,
  95-96, 98, 100, 104, 108-109, 112, 117,
  120, 127-128, 134-135, 147-148, 154,
  218, 232, 243, 274, 322, 330, 332-333,
  365, 376, 395-396, 398
  and gathering 16-18, 27-28, 37, 43, 47,
    52, 54, 56, 69, 96, 100, 108, 112, 134,
    332, 365, 376, 396
Hupa 44, 96-98, 169, 173, 197, 198, 219,
  308, 311-312, 314, 316, 323, 399
Hydrophyllaceae 142
Hypochoeris 141
Idaho 29, 248
insect 19, 106, 162, 165, 202, 382-384,
  388
Iridaceae 143
irrigation 19, 32-34, 45, 214, 326, 329-
  330, 332-333, 336, 338-342, 344, 346-
  348, 351, 353-360, 364, 366-377, 387
Ishi 244
islay 136, 239
Italy 368, 394
Jacumba 34, 36
Jasper 398
jays 217, 219
Juglans nigra 231
Juncaceae 141

Juncus 141
juniper 241, 243-247, 249, 251-257, 267,
  271, 274-275, 277
  bows 267, 275, 277
  heartwood 245
  staves 275
Juniperus 241, 243-247, 271
  californica utahensis 247
  monosperma 245
  occidentalis 244
  osteoperma 241, 244
  scopulorum 245, 271
  utahensis 245
Kakadu 397
Kalispel 242
kamashuk 44
Kamia 34-35, 42, 331
Kammatwa 319
Karok 44, 55, 87, 89, 91, 96-98, 103, 154,
  163, 234, 308, 311-312, 318-320, 323
Karuk 166, 173, 197-198, 204, 209, 211,
  221, 224
Katimin 320, 400
Kato 98, 308, 322-323
Kawaiisu 244, 274
Kaweah brodiaea 171
Kechayi 321
Kepel 314, 316, 318
khutash 136-137
Kiliwa 35
Kings Canyon National Park 110, 391
Kitanemuk 41, 135
Klamath 96, 114, 208, 221, 302-305, 308,
  311-312, 314, 316, 318-320, 322-324, 326
Klikitat 242
knocking 218-220, 225, 227, 234
kous 29
Kumeyaay 21, 35, 379-388
Kuseyaay 383, 385-386
Kutenai 242
Labiatae 142
larkspur 124
larvae 202, 374-376
Lasthenia 141

472

474